Fanny Elssler

ALSO BY IVOR GUEST

NAPOLEON III IN ENGLAND
THE BALLET OF THE SECOND EMPIRE, 1847–58
THE BALLET OF THE SECOND EMPIRE, 1858–70
THE ROMANTIC BALLET IN ENGLAND
FANNY CERRITO
VICTORIAN BALLET-GIRL
ADELINE GENÉE
THE ALHAMBRA BALLET
THE DANCER'S HERITAGE
LA FILLE MAL GARDÉE (editor)
THE EMPIRE BALLET
A GALLERY OF ROMANTIC BALLET
THE ROMANTIC BALLET IN PARIS
DANDIES AND DANCERS

Fanny Elssler in *The Swiss Milkmaid*. Miniature by Albert Theer from a painting by Carl Agricola, *c.* 1831.

Coll. Mr John H. Russell.

IVOR GUEST

Fanny Elssler

WESLEYAN UNIVERSITY PRESS
Middletown, Connecticut

SBN 8195 4022 6

LIBRARY OF CONGRESS CATALOG CARD NUMBER: 74–105507
FIRST AMERICAN EDITION 1970

PRINTED IN GREAT BRITAIN

Contents

Contents

Illustrations

This study of her favourite ballerina
is dedicated, with affection,
to the memory of
LILLIAN MOORE
in gratitude for her inspiring example
as a dance historian and her generous
and unfailing help and guidance

Introduction

Today, more than a century after she danced her last step on the stage, a compelling magic still attaches to the name of Fanny Elssler. To her fellow Viennese above all she remains a popular heroine, almost a folk figure, to whom a seemingly endless stream of articles is devoted in magazines and newspapers, many embellished and embroidered beyond the bounds of fact as is the fate of all legends. Her memory is kept alive, too, by novels and novelettes, dramas, operettas, films, even ballets, which recount in more or less fanciful terms incidents from the life of one of the greatest ballerinas of her day.*

For the serious student of her career, Austria offers many attractions for a sentimental pilgrimage. Relics of her life abound. In the Theatre Collection of the Austrian National Library there is preserved, in an almost perfect state, the pink satin costume, decorated with black lace and silver braid, in which she danced her famous *Cachucha*. It is perhaps the last of many such costumes she wore for this dance, which was as celebrated in her day as Pavlova's *Dying Swan* was to become in the next century. Presented to the Vienna Opera by her son-in-law, Victor von Webenau, it was kept in the ballet-master's office until the retirement of Josef Hassreiter. Scores of letters written by and to her, including many from her elderly lover, Friedrich von Gentz, lie neatly in folders in Vienna's Stadtbibliothek. Further south, in the quiet

* The biographies of Fanny Elssler will be found in the bibliography at the end of this book. Among the novels are Irma Höfer's *Fanny Elssler*, Julius von Ludassy's *Der tanzende Stern*, Eugen Dernburg's *Fanny Elssler* and Bernard Grun's *Fanny Beloved*. There have been several ballets based on her life: *Fanny Elssler*, with choreography by Garbagnati, produced at the Teatro y Circo de Madrid on June 20th, 1873; *Fanny Elssler*, with choreography by Margarethe Wallmann and music by Nador, produced at the Vienna State Opera on October 6th, 1934, with Gusti Pichler as Elssler; and *Fanny Elssler*, with choreography by Norman McDowell, produced for television in April 1962 with Olga Ferri as Elssler and Rosella Hightower as Taglioni. In 1934 an operetta, *Fanny Elssler*, with music by Johann Strauss II arranged by Grun and Stalla and libretto by Hans Adler, was produced in Berlin. Lillian Harvey played Fanny Elssler in a film produced in 1937. In 1943 a play about Fanny Elssler and Gentz, *Hofopernballett* by George von Terramare, was produced in La Paz, Bolivia, with Erna Terrel as the ballerina.

country town of Eisenstadt, in the province of Burgenland, is a fascinating cache of personalia, displayed in a room in the Haydn Museum.
Here can be seen many little personal belongings, letters, caricatures,
statuettes and prints, to say nothing of those most evocative relics—her
ballet shoes, stamped with the name of Janssen of Paris who also made
Taglioni's shoes, much lighter than dancer's shoes are today, unblocked
and patiently darned above the toe to give strength. And one should not
overlook the private collections, of which by far the most important is
the Dance Archive of Derra de Moroda in Salzburg. Here are more
shoes, castanets which one notices are unusually small, and a profusion
of prints and drawings. Here too one can hold in one's hand a beautifully
engraved admission ticket to her benefit performance in Havana, close
one's eyes and imagine the rustle of silk dresses and the tuning up of the
orchestra. . . .

The telling of Fanny Elssler's life story, however, is more than a
sentimental journey into the past, for her career has a relevance to
dancers and followers of the ballet today. From her period, coloured
with the ideas of Romanticism, we have inherited a lasting legacy, not
only in the few ballets of that time which have survived, but also in the
dance style as it was then taught and practised, and few dancers have
left their mark on the tradition of ballet more indelibly than Fanny
Elssler. She represented, as every student of the dance will know, one of
the two contrasting aspects of Romantic ballet. She was a rival of the
great Taglioni, but such was the divergence between their styles that
they shared supremacy in a dual firmament. The poet Théophile
Gautier, who was a declared partisan of Fanny Elssler, spoke of her as a
pagan ballerina in contrast to the Christian ballerina who was Taglioni,
and this often-quoted comparison gives us an illuminating insight into
the art of these two great dancers.

Taglioni was a spirit of the mist, floating through moonlit forest
glades in a soft cloud of white muslin. She produced a transcending
poetic vision through her genius as a dancer, and in particular, her
gentle, flowing style which, without exaggeration, created a wholly new
school of dancing. Thus she emerged as the ideal interpreter of the
spirit-creature whose love for a mortal was to provide the theme for so
many ballets of the time: a manifestation of that quest for the infinite
and the unattainable which so obsessed the imagination of Romantic
poets.

Fanny Elssler, on the other hand, was made of different stuff. No
pallid, willowy Sylphide, she presented the dance in its earthly form,
turning the heads of the public with her bold, voluptuous *Cachucha* and
other character dances, and enhancing her performances with a dramatic

power such as no dancer had possessed before. While Taglioni suggested man's spiritual yearnings, Elssler conveyed the passions and desires of this world and all the animation and colour of real life. Both ballerinas were supreme in their own styles, but in one respect Fanny Elssler was superior. Taglioni maintained her supremacy and did not progress, while Elssler added, with experience, deeper and deeper tones to her dramatic genius.

Her rendering of *Giselle*, with its emphasis laid on the tragedy of the heroine's madness in the first act, set the standard for the performance of this role much more strongly than that of Carlotta Grisi who created it. This was admitted even in her day. "*Giselle*," wrote the music critic Chorley, "was a charming ballet even before Mlle Fanny Elssler came, who turned the romantic and gently melancholy story into a piece of tragic pathos, as powerful as was ever exhibited by mime." It is incredible that the books on the history of *Giselle* hardly mention the name of Elssler, who, as contemporary evidence indicates, was the greatest interpreter of the role in her day.

Fanny Elssler's other characterisations, such as Esmeralda and Catarina, have not survived, but undoubtedly there still remains a vestige of her Lise in *La Fille mal gardée* in the mime scene in the second act which Karsavina remembered and restored for the Royal Ballet. Descriptions of this scene as it was given by her in Russia are sufficiently precise to indicate that it has probably been handed down with little alteration.

The famous *Cachucha* retired with Fanny Elssler. The memory of her performance must have daunted other dancers from performing it after her retirement, but it was to survive through the efforts of a German dancing master who taught for more than fifty years in Odessa. Friedrich Albert Zorn published the fruits of his experience in 1887 in a book which was a manual not only of technique but also of his system of dance notation, and to illustrate how the movements of the upper body could be notated, he chose, to our good fortune, the *Cachucha*. His notation of this famous dance remained unread for generations until, at my suggestion, my wife Ann Hutchinson deciphered it and staged it for the Royal Ballet's educational group, "Ballet for All", in 1967.* The result was revealing, for the dance, while being a stylisation in the sense that it was created specially for stage performance, was largely composed of steps and movements in the authentic Spanish classical idiom. And it bore out contemporary descriptions and showed the scope for the bewitching interpretation with which Fanny Elssler gave it. The score

* In June 1969 the Viennese ballerina Christl Zimmerl danced this *Cachucha* at the Vienna State Opera.

of this dance as produced for the Royal Ballet has been recorded in Labanotation with full details of timing and style which were not included in the less sophisticated Zorn notation and therefore had to be deduced from secondary sources.

All this is now woven into the fabric of ballet's tradition, but this is not Fanny Elssler's only claim to posterity. She was the first leading ballerina to visit America, and her travels in the Eastern States and Cuba brought her triumphs which have surely never been surpassed. Her wanderings took her farther afield than any other dancer until Pavlova in the following century. Most of the great cities of Europe, from Vienna, Paris, London and Milan to St Petersburg and Moscow, acclaimed her genius before, with a singular firmness of purpose, she retired at the age of forty-one to live out a peaceful retirement in her beloved Vienna.

This is the career which is chronicled in these pages, and here I should like to acknowledge all the help which has been so generously forthcoming from individuals, libraries and museums in both the Old World and the New. First of all I must mention my dear friend, Miss Lillian Moore, who as always placed the fruits of her knowledge at my disposal and, to my great sorrow, did not survive to read the text. The late Frau Bertha Niederle and Herr Anton Preissegger jun. have been assiduous in conducting research for me in Vienna. To Madame Derra de Moroda I owe the privilege of seeing her great collection and the pleasure of two happy days spent in her library. Professor Riki Raab, herself the author of a biography of Elssler, kindly allowed me to see her notes and gave me permission to include as an appendix the genealogical tree of the Elssler family which she has so painstakingly compiled. The chapters on Elssler's American tour would have been greatly poorer without the assistance of many American friends. I was spared an immense amount of labour by the most generous gesture of Mr Allison Delarue, who placed at my disposal his manuscript on the life of Henry Wikoff and five voluminous notebooks of source material. Miss Helen Willard at the Theatre Collection of the Harvard College Library was indefatigable in answering my many queries, and I have also to thank Miss Susan Parsons of the Library of the Boston Athenaeum. Mr Edwin Binney, 3rd, made available to me a collection of letters which he had purchased, and also helped with other details. To Miss Genevieve Oswald of the Dance Collection of the New York Public Library I owe a further debt. My thanks are due, too, to Mrs H. Gregory Gulick for permission to quote from letters from Wikoff to Clarkson, to Professor Samuel Eliot Morison for sending me an extract from his forthcoming biography of Harrison Gray Otis, to Mr Gervase Butler for supplying me with a copy of Elssler's power of attorney in favour of August

Belmont, and to Mrs Allston Dana for drawing my attention to material about Longfellow. Dr Enrique H. Miyares gave me some amusing details about Pancho Martí; and Miss Elfrida Mahler helped me with research in Cuba. My thanks are also due to Mr John H. Russell for allowing me to reproduce the lovely miniature of Elssler in *The Swiss Milkmaid*, and to Mr Norman Crider for letting me use, once again, the Lepaulle painting of Elssler which he discovered in Paris. For answering questions relating to Elssler's career in Paris I am indebted to M. André Ménetrat of the Paris Opéra Library and to Mlle Marie-Françoise Christout. Signora Vittoria Ottolenghi and Professor Ulisse Prota-Giurleo have given generously of their time to supply me with details of Elssler's career in Italy. Last, but far from least, I owe a deep debt to many Russian friends. Mr Yuri Bakhrushin allowed me to use his unpublished monograph on Fanny Elssler in Russia, and Mr Yuri Slonimsky kindly sent me information about Fanny Elssler's engagement in Russia, compiled from the files of the Direction of the Imperial Theatres preserved in the Central State Historical Archives in Leningrad. I am also indebted to Miss Natalia Roslavleva and Miss Vera Krasovskaya for patiently answering questions and generally enabling me to relate Elssler's visits to Russia in fuller detail than has been done before. For assistance in translation I have to thank Mr J. Stewart Barker, Miss Maria Calderon, Miss Irina Kirillova and Miss Maria Szentpal, and for staunch work at the typewriter, coping with my drafts, Miss Naomi Stamelmann and Miss Philippa Heale. Finally, I have to thank my wife and Mr G. B. L. Wilson for reading through the typescript and making numerous useful suggestions for its improvement.

My thanks are due to the following libraries, archives and museums for providing me with facilities for research and answering queries: the Theatersammlung and the Bildarchiv of the Öst. Nationalbibliothek, the Historische Museum der Stadt Wien, the Stadtbibliothek, and the Landesarchiv für Niederösterreich, Vienna; the Landesmuseum and the Haydn Museum, Eisenstadt; the British Museum and the Victoria and Albert Museum, London; Cambridge University Library; the Central Library, Bristol; the Bibliothèque de l'Opéra, the Archives Nationales and the Bibliothèque de l'Arsenal, Paris; the Museo Teatrale alla Scala, Milan; the Theatermuseum Clara Ziegler-Stiftung, Munich; the Kestner-Museum, Hanover; the New York Public Library (Dance Collection and other divisions) and the Hispanic Society of America, New York; the National Archives, Washington; the Boston Public Library and the Library of the Boston Athenaeum, Boston; the Theatre Collection of the Harvard College Library, the Trustees of the Ralph

Waldo Emerson Memorial Association, Houghton Library, and the Trustees of the Longfellow House, Cambridge, Mass.; the Enoch Pratt Free Library, Baltimore; the Princeton University Library; the Virginia State Library; the Free Library of Philadelphia; the Leningrad State Theatre Library; the Bakhrushin Theatre Museum, Moscow; and the Biblioteca Nacional Jose Martí, Havana.

Finally, a word about the nomenclature of ballets adopted in different countries. I felt it would be confusing and unnecessarily pedantic to give different names for the same ballet, and so I have arbitrarily adopted the name by which in my opinion the work is most commonly known. Readers may like to know that Auber's opera *La Muette de Portici* was called *Der Stumme von Portici* in Berlin and Vienna; that his opera *Le Dieu et la Bayadère* was *Der Gott und die Bajadere* in Berlin and Hamburg and *Brama und die Bajadere* in Vienna; that *La Fille mal gardée* was *Das schlechtbewachte Mädchen* in Vienna and Berlin; that *Die Fee und der Ritter* became *La Fée et le Chevalier* in London and *The Prince and the Fairy* in New York; that *The Swiss Milkmaid* was variously known as *La Laitière suisse* and *Das Schweizer Milchmädchen*, and was given as *Nathalie* at the Paris Opéra; that *La Somnambule* was presented as *Therese, die Nachtwändlerin* in Berlin; and that *Le Délire d'un peintre* became *Des Malers Traumbild* in German-speaking cities. In Cuba, of course, Fanny's repertory was billed in Spanish, and in Russia the titles of the ballets were given in Russian as well as French.

Gumpendorf, Fanny Elssler's birthplace. Painting by Adelsheim, 1790.

Historische Museum der Stadt Wien.

The Kärntnertortheater, Vienna, *c.* 1830.

Fanny Elssler as a child
dancer. Watercolour by
Johann Stefan Decker.

Historische Museum der Stadt Wien.

Fanny Elssler. Watercolour
by Carl Agricola, 1830. (Formerly
the property of Elisabeth
Schumann, destroyed during
World War II.)

I

The Rise of an Infant Prodigy

IN THE EARLY YEARS OF THE NINETEENTH CENTURY the Viennese suburb of Gumpendorf lay separated from the city by a belt of well-cared-for parkland known as the Glacis. Looking out across the trees its inhabitants had a fine view of the rooftops of Vienna and the tall tapering spire of St Stephen's Cathedral rising above the sturdy walls of the fortifications. It was to this unpretentious little town, shortly after 1800, that there came Johann Florian Elssler, who moved with his family into the house numbered 42.* His reason for settling in Gumpendorf was less the charm of the place itself than the desire to be near his master, the composer Josef Haydn, who on his retirement had taken a modest house near the Palace of Schönbrunn.

Johann Florian represented the second generation of his family to have worked for Haydn. The Elsslers came originally from Silesia, but in the middle of the eighteenth century Josef Elssler, Johann Florian's father, had entered the service of Prince Esterhazy in Eisenstadt and been attached, as music copyist and valet, to Haydn, the Prince's Kapellmeister. The composer became very fond of his servant and became godfather to his children. After Josef Elssler's death, his sons Josef and Johann Florian took over the copying work, but it was the latter who eventually succeeded his father as valet and amenuensis to the ageing composer. He proved himself indispensable, accompanying his master on his travels, fussing over him when he was tired, playing cards with him, and catering to his every need. After Haydn's retirement he controlled his household with a solicitude that brought the composer much comfort in his declining years. Indeed his affection for his master at times bordered on the ecstatic. One day when he was about his duties, he was seen to stop before Haydn's portrait and incense it with a perfuming pan, like a priest before the altar.

He was at hand when the serenity of Haydn's home was brutally shattered by war. In 1809, when Napoleon's armies invaded Austria, a

---

* The site is now occupied by No. 15 Hofmühlgasse. In those days the houses were numbered consecutively without reference to the streets. This was even so in Vienna itself, where the house numbers reached a figure beyond 1,000!

battery of French guns took up position close to the house to bombard the capital. Several bombs exploded near by as Haydn was getting up. The old man never recovered from the shock. He was seized with a violent fit of trembling and was unable to walk unaided from that day on. Cared for by his devoted servants, he grew gradually weaker. In Johann Florian's own words, he allowed himself to be tended "so readily and peacefully that we were amazed . . . and when we asked him how he was, he kept answering, 'Cheer up, children, I am all right.'" Slowly his strength ebbed away and on the last day of May 1809 he died with Johann Elssler at his side and a French sentry standing guard outside the house.

The passing of the great composer ended an era in the life of Johann Florian Elssler, who was to live on his memories for the rest of his days. Haydn had left a legacy of 6,000 gulden to his "faithful and upright servant Johann Elssler". It was a much needed bequest, for life became increasingly difficult after the composer's death, and to make ends meet, Johann Florian was driven to sell some of his master's manuscripts which had come into his possession.

There were already four children when Haydn died. Johann Florian's wife Theresia was a seamstress, whose father, Johann Prinster, earned his living making plaster figurines and played the fiddle in his spare time. Johann Florian married his *"schöne Roserl"* in Eisenstadt on January 23rd, 1800, and in August of that year was presented with his first-born who was called Johann: in later life this boy was to enter the Franciscan monastery of Maria Lanzendorf as Brother Pacificus. All the younger children who reached maturity were to follow musical or artistic careers. Joseph, the second son, was to become a professional tenor and chorus-master at the Berlin Opera House. Anna, who was called Netty, was to join the Vienna Court Opera as a mime, and Therese, who was born on April 5th, 1808, and baptised Theresia after her mother, was to make an even more successful career as a dancer. Haydn, who had stood as godfather to the sons (his housekeeper, Anna Kremnitzer, was godmother to the girls), would have been proud of the achievements of Johann Florian's offspring, but he never saw the youngest child who was to make the name of Elssler ring round the whole civilised world. This was the girl who was born on June 23rd, 1810, and though baptised Franziska, was always to be called by the diminutive of Fanny.

The child would have been too young to remember the historic winter of 1812, when the tide of war turned and Napoleon's armies were checked in the vastness of Russia and rolled back into Europe. Nor could she have appreciated the excitement of war-weary Vienna when the allied armies crossed the French frontiers and converged on Paris, and diplomats began to turn their minds to making the peace. With Napoleon exiled, sovereigns and statesmen gathered in Vienna to reshape the continent in the aftermath of the great series of wars which had set Europe ablaze after the French Revolution.

Vienna during the days and nights of the Congress was a gay city, where pleasure, romance and above all music provided distractions which were almost too much for the statesmen. *"Congrès ne marche pas,"* observed the Prince de Ligne, *"il danse."* Balls, banquets, receptions, music festivals, processions, firework displays, gala performances followed one another in a feverish round. Music played an important part in these amusements, for Vienna was a city which prided itself on its musical activities, and even more, on the musical geniuses working within its walls. Beethoven was still active in 1815, Franz Schubert was publishing his first *lieder*, the music of Haydn and Mozart was frequently heard. At the Kärntnertortheater, which lay just inside the walls of the city by the gate where the road to Carinthia emerged, Beethoven's *Fidelio*, in its final version, was one of the latest novelties, and the ballet had been strenthened by the engagement of two celebrities from Paris, the ballet-master Jean Aumer and Emilie Bigottini, the leading ballerina of the Opéra, famous for her sensitive interpretations.

As Fanny grew up she quickly became conscious of the wealth of musical activity in Vienna. In her home music was the most frequent subject of conversation. Johann Florian instilled a great reverence for Haydn in his children, and often must have sat at the piano and played pieces by his beloved master, which can hardly have failed to set the children dancing. The Elsslers had no connection with the Opera House, but one of their neighbours happened to be a dancer there and would regale the children with tales of the make-believe world behind the curtain. After a show of reluctance, Johann Florian agreed to take his younger daughters to a performance. For Fanny the experience was overwhelming. The splendours of the stage seemed so wonderful that she imagined it must be Heaven itself.

With so many mouths to be fed, life was not easy for the Elsslers. Indeed the family's fortunes were so low that it was essential for the children to begin earning their living as soon as possible, and one by one the three girls became dancers. The family had moved from Gumpendorf and settled in the Brauhaus in the district of Margareten, where Frau Elssler augmented the meagre family income as a laundress. But this barely relieved the poverty to which they were reduced, and they only survived these difficult years through the generosity of their neighbours, the Gauls. These good people came to their rescue on

many occasions, and turned a deaf ear when their own relatives remonstrated that they were in fact supporting two families. Frau Gaul
gave the Elssler girls her daughters' cast-off dresses and shoes, and when
Therese and Fanny began going to the ballet school and had nothing to
wear for their classes, she had new clothes made for them. The story
was even handed down in the Gaul family that Frau Gaul sometimes
took away her daughters' new shoes to give them to the two little
dancers, leaving her own children to go about in their slippers. The bond
which linked the two families lasted for several generations. Frau Gaul's
son Franz was to design the commemorative medal which was struck
when Fanny returned to Vienna after her visit to America, and one of
the earliest works of her grandson Gustav was a picture of Fanny
dancing the *Cracovienne*, painted when he was six.

At this time there were only two ballet schools for children in Vienna,
one at the Theater in der Josefstadt, and the other, Horschelt's school
at the Theater an der Wien. The former was a long way from the
Brauhaus, so it is probable that Therese and Fanny made their way to
the Theater an der Wien for their classes. Indeed legend has it that
Fanny gained her first stage experience there as a member of Horschelt's
Kinderballett. Friedrich Horschelt, a ballet-master from Cologne, had
assembled a company of child dancers, whose well-drilled performances
were an important feature of the Viennese theatre from 1815 to 1821.
Among them were several children who were later to become well-
known: Therese Heberle and Angioletta Mayer, the three daughters of
the tragedienne Sophie Schröder, of whom Wilhelmina was to grow up
to be a famous prima donna, and a good-looking boy called Anton
Stuhlmüller. But while these talented children were applauded on the
stage, voices were being raised in protest at their exploitation, for they
were not only poorly paid but exposed to more serious dangers. A
paper of the time wrote obliquely: "When you consider the surroundings of these children behind the scenes in the theatre, you cannot help
but fear for their susceptibilities; the ripest fruit first falls. People are
saying some quite extraordinary things about these popular little
artists." Prince Alois Kaunitz-Rittberg, a notorious sensualist, was
the centre of a scandal involving a number of the girls. His penchant for
young girls was so well-known that needy, unprincipled mothers would
stand with their daughters on the staircase of his palace for the prince to
make his choice. Fortunately for him, the investigation was suppressed
by higher authority and at the request of the Emperor the company was
disbanded.

In later life Fanny denied having been a member of the Horschelt
Kinderballett, but the tradition has persisted. It was even rife when

she was at the height of her career. In 1844 the paper, *Der Wanderer*, printed a sentimental story telling how Fanny discovered in the *corps de ballet* of the Scala, Milan, the daughter of her one-time dresser when she was a member of the Horschelt company. Little more than twenty years had passed since it had been disbanded, and many theatregoers would have still had vivid recollections of its performances and its members. One can only conjecture why Fanny did not then deny the story. If it was true, she must have realised that a denial which many would know to be false could only damage her; if it was untrue, she might have considered it too harmless to require comment.*

The story opened with a quarrel between two of the child dancers, Angioletta Mayer and Fanny Elssler, over the possession of a bouquet. "Horschelt, the unforgettable ballet-master of this little artistic world, a true father of his pupils, sees the beautiful girls of his *corps de ballet* with their faces contorted and their make-up ruined by tears. 'For Heaven's sake, what do you look like? Mama, make these girls up again as quickly as possible, or I shall have a fit.' Frau Horschelt, the ballet-master's mother, makes up the two children in a trice, for the curtain is about to rise . . . This interlude took place in a dressing-room of the Theater an der Wien . . .

"The dressing of the children and their quick changes were entrusted partly to the children's mothers and partly to experienced dressers. One of the best of the latter was Frau Christl, a widow of twenty-five or twenty-six who had taken Fanny under her special protection, and to whom Fanny was particularly devoted. All the sweets she received every evening were given to her dear Christl. She never gave away flowers, however, and even withered blooms were carefully packed away in little boxes.

"Among the children of the ballet Fanny was not one of the most striking in appearance, although her soulful eyes already exerted their magic power. Angioletta Mayer was the prettiest of all. Fanny was never envious, and the greater the applause one of her colleagues obtained, the happier she became. She also clapped them with her little hands and covered them with kisses when they came back into the wings. She helped pick up flowers and bouquets as if they had been presented to her; she merely begged for a tiny rose or carnation, which she then pressed to her heart, and she was as happy as a queen."

* Emil Pirchan states in his biography that Fanny's name appears in documents concerning the investigation, but I have been unable to confirm this despite an exhaustive search in the archives of Vienna. A list of children engaged by Horschelt up to 1816 does not contain the name of Elssler. (Archiv des Ministeriums des Inneren und der Justiz, Faszikel 87, Th. IV M6.)

The story continued with Christl breaking the news that she was leaving to be married and giving Fanny a little cornelian cross which had been blessed. Many years later Fanny noticed a dancer at the Scala, Milan, wearing an identical cross, and in this way discovered the daughter of her dear Christl.

Even if she had been a member of the Kinderballett, it could only have been for a very short time and she must have left some years before the scandal at the Kaunitz Palace. Therese and Fanny joined their eldest sister Anna at the Kärntnertortheater, the Vienna Court Opera, early in 1818, and came under the care of Aumer. Horschelt, with all his talent for training children, was only a provincial in comparison with Aumer, who was a ballet-master in the mainstream of French tradition. Aumer's experience had not been confined to the Paris Opéra, although he had danced there with success and produced a ballet there. Having studied under Dauberval, choreographer of *La Fille mal gardée*, and staged his first ballets in the freer atmosphere of the Théâtre de la Porte-Saint-Martin in Paris, he brought to his teaching a certain warmth that was lacking in the classical French school as practised at the Opéra, where technical virtuosity was cultivated with an obsessive regard for form and correctness to the detriment of expression. From Aumer Fanny acquired a polish to the technique she was already beginning to master and in addition a style that had its roots in the traditions of French ballet.

Fanny's name first appeared on a playbill of the Kärntnertortheater on April 20th, 1818, when at the age of seven she played the part of Hymen in Aumer's ballet, *Die Hochzeit der Thetis und des Peleus*. Before long she was proficient enough to take her place in the *corps de ballet*, and she was almost certainly on the stage on the historic evening of June 10th, 1822, when a young ballerina, six years older than herself, called Marie Taglioni, made her first public appearance in a "new anacreontic *divertissement*" by her father: the bill for the second performance two days later listed "Elssler the younger" among the bacchantes. Fanny soon began to make an impression, and an English visitor, Count Gronow, recalled in his memoirs that it was "in 1822 that I saw this beautiful person for the first time. She was originally one of the *figurantes* at the Opera in Vienna, and was at this time about fourteen years of age [*sic*], and of delicate and graceful proportions. Her hair was auburn, her eyes blue and large, and her face wore an expression of great tenderness."

At the time of Fanny's emergence as a member of the ballet company, the director of the Kärntnertortheater was Domenico Barbaja. For astuteness and business flair this colourful and original character had few equals. He had risen in life from the humblest beginnings. As a youth he had worked as a waiter in a café, but soon bettered himself by inventing a method of mixing cream with coffee or chocolate and giving his name to the concoction, *caffé* or *cioccolatta barbaiata*. Then, after making a fortune by speculating in army supplies and managing the gambling casino of Naples, he entered the world of the theatre. In 1809 he was appointed director of the Royal Theatres in Naples, a post which he was to hold with only brief intervals for more than thirty years, until a few months before his death. A born impresario, he had a special gift for discovering nascent talent, and when he arrived in Vienna it was not long before he noticed the promising young dancer in the *corps de ballet*, whose progress he encouraged as, with growing experience, she developed a rare combination of technical proficiency and personal charm.

In her first years at the Vienna Opera, Fanny was to dance in ballets by three important choreographers—Filippo Taglioni, Louis Henry and Armand Vestris—and to have the opportunity of observing at close quarters the style and technique of Amalia Brugnoli and Elise Vaque-Moulin, who were both early exponents of *pointe* work, which at that time was very much of a novelty. By 1823 her name was appearing regularly on the playbills. On January 12th, as "Elssler the younger", she was listed in the cast of Filippo Taglioni's *Lodoiska*; on February 26th she danced in a *pas de deux* in Henry's *Arsene*; on March 6th she and her sister were Graces in Henry's *Paris*; and on May 12th she appeared in Henry's *Ismaan's Grab*.

The growing impression she was making on the public was to be reflected in the succession of parts which she took over in Armand Vestris's *The Fairy and the Knight*, which was produced for Brugnoli's début on the last day of 1823. This four-act faery ballet was to remain in the repertory for a number of years. It was inspired by an earlier ballet by Didelot, *Zelis*, in which Armand Vestris had danced in London in 1812, but the choreography was new and so was the score, an arrangement of Rossini, Pacini and Romani. The plot described the attempts of the infatuated fairy to seduce the knight and the intervention of Cupid who in the concluding moments turns the fairy into stone. Little did Fanny imagine, at the time of its first performance, that one day she would be dancing Brugnoli's role of the fairy Viviane, but as the weeks went by she took over a succession of parts of increasing importance. At one of the early performances, on January 29th, 1824, she succeeded her sister as the Rosemaiden's lover; on February 3rd she played the part of Rosine, the Fairy's confidante, "with due dignity and grace"; and when Théodore Rozier, Aumer's daughter, fell ill later in the month she replaced her in the role of Iseult, the knight's fiancée, "with great success".

For a young dancer not yet fourteen this was encouraging progress. Already she was emerging from the anonymous ranks of the *corps de ballet*, and during the next year she was cast in small parts in several new productions: Louise in Armand Vestris's Spanish ballet *Eleonore* (February 20th, 1824), Beda in his *Bluebeard* (March 13th, 1824), a page in Aumer's *Les Pages du duc de Vendôme* (November 30th, 1824). Her name also appeared in the cast lists of Vestris's *Psyche* (May 29th, 1824), *Aline* (October 11th, 1824) and *Alexander in Indien* (March 23rd, 1825), and Louis Henry's *Amenie* (January 12th, 1825) and *Undine* (March 6th, 1825).

In the summer of 1825 Barbaja decided to show the young dancer to Naples. A visit to Italy, he foresaw, would give her valuable experience, and in addition her presence would add a welcome flavour of youth to the strong company he was assembling for the forthcoming season at the Teatro San Carlo. Nor is it impossible, in the light of what was to follow, that there had been a special request for her presence. At that time the Kingdom of Naples was very much under the influence of Austria and indeed was still occupied by Austrian troops, and the King's brother, Leopold, Prince of Salerno, was the husband of an Austrian Archduchess and a frequent visitor to Vienna.

Barbaja had also engaged Anna and Therese, and together the three sisters travelled to Italy with their mother as chaperone. The following eighteen months were to broaden and enrich Fanny's experience enormously. Presumably she studied under one or more of the three celebrated teachers then working in Naples—Pietro Hus, Salvatore Taglioni and Paolo Samengo—and by dancing in the shadow of Brugnoli and Vaque-Moulin, she persevered in her endeavours to emulate the feats they were performing on the *pointes*. But the most valuable experience which Naples had to offer for her artistic development was the introduction to the work of the great Italian choreographers, Salvatore Viganò and Gaetano Gioja. Viganò had originated a new school of choreography by combining the art of ballet construction which he had learnt at first hand from Dauberval with the expressive pantomime that was an age-old feature of the Italian theatre. He fashioned his ballets with a close link between gesture and rhythm, and subordinated everything to the dramatic implications of the narrative. He had been dead for several years when Fanny arrived in Naples, but his ballets were still remembered and revived, and they must have opened the younger dancer's eyes to the possibilities of presenting drama through the dance.

Viganò's mantle had now fallen on the shoulders of his disciple,

Gaetano Gioja, who conceived his ballets as huge dramatic canvases much in the spirit of his master. One of his greatest works was *Cesare in Egitto*, originally produced in Milan in 1807, and it was in this that Therese and Fanny first danced before the Neapolitan public at the San Carlo on July 6th, 1825. Viganò had himself acknowledged that this grand heroic ballet was superior to any of his own works, and with Samengo and Brugnoli playing Caesar and Cleopatra, it created an unforgettable impression on the public and no doubt on Fanny too. Working under Gioja was to prove an inspiring but short-lived experience for the young ballerina. On October 4th she played the part of Rosalia in his *Fedeltà e Trionfo*. This was to be followed by a revival of *Acbar Gran Mogul*, but the rehearsals were abruptly cut short when the choreographer collapsed. The dancers were never to see him again. He died the following spring, and it was Salvatore Taglioni who completed the production, in which Therese and Fanny were featured in the dances.

At about the same time Fanny played a minor role in Salvatore Taglioni's *Alcibiade*, and on July 6th, 1826, she appeared in his *L'Ira d'Achille*. There was always something new being prepared. On August 19th Viganò's *Didone* was revived, with Brugnoli and Samengo as Dido and Aeneas, and Fanny and Therese appearing in a *pas de huit* to variations on a theme by Rossini, and on October 4th, another Viganò revival was presented, *Giovanna d'Arco*, with Marietta Ronzi-Vestris as Joan of Arc and Fanny being again applauded in a *pas de huit*. All three sisters took part in the next novelty, Louis Henry's *Selico*. The last work in which Fanny appeared in Naples was Samengo's *Pemile*, presented on New Year's Day, 1827.

As well as captivating the Neapolitan public with her youthful but already voluptuous charms, Fanny had aroused the desire of the King's brother, the Prince of Salerno, who ruthlessly seduced her. In later years she confided in Harriet Grote that this elderly libertine had forced her mother to sell her to him, and that she had yielded because he was too powerful and unscrupulous to be made an enemy. Certainly her heart was not seriously affected. Count Prokesch described Leopold as "Fanny's first purchaser, who had her body without touching her soul". The affair between the prince and the dancer was no secret in the salons of Naples, and to put an end to the scandal Leopold was hurriedly transferred to the Papal Guard of Honour in Rome. Meanwhile Fanny returned quietly to Vienna where, on June 4th, 1827, she gave birth to a baby boy. This untoward sequel to her Italian visit was the source of great embarrassment, and for the sake of her career little Franz Robert was spirited away to Eisenstadt, where he was to be cared for and brought up by her relations.

II

The Last Love of Friedrich von Gentz

THE PROGRESS WHICH FANNY HAD MADE as an artist during her absence in Italy must have been immediately recognised when she reappeared at the Kärntnertortheater in September 1827. Her technique had acquired added strength and assurance, and contact with the histrionic style of the great Italian choreographers had sown the seeds of a dramatic gift which she was to develop throughout her career. Small parts now began coming her way, and in November she created the secondary role of Giulietta in Paolo Samengo's *Ottavio Pinelli*.

All was not smooth sailing, however, for in the spring of 1828 her progress suffered a temporary setback when Barbaja resigned as Director of the Vienna Opera and the theatre remained closed for the rest of the year while a new lessee was being sought. Happily the appointment of his successor augured well both for the ballet and for her. Through his association with Barbaja, the new Director, Count Robert von Gallenberg, had acquired not only a useful knowledge of the theatre but also a certain reputation as a ballet composer. Fanny had danced to his music, and her performances had made a favourable impression. Soon he was on intimate terms with the two sisters, and he and Therese probably became lovers: on September 29th, 1829, Therese gave birth to a child who was significantly named Robertine, with Fanny and himself standing as its godparents. Meanwhile Fanny herself was benefiting from this close relationship with the new Director, who was giving her the opportunities she needed to prove herself as a ballerina.

She was selected to play the title-role in Astolfi's new ballet, *Mathilde, Herzogin von Spoleto*, on the evening the opera house was reopened, January 6th, 1829. A certain tendency towards exaggerated gestures in her miming would disappear with experience, but her fresh charm and strong technique were enough to earn her the leading part of Cleopatra in Astolfi's *Cäsar in Egypten* on April 9th. A month later she took over the leading role of Amalie in *Ottavio Pinelli*. This was a real test, since it had been created only a few months before by Brugnoli, but Fanny "overcame the hazards of the part in the most remarkable way, overshadowing everyone else". Before the summer was over she was given another creation, the heroine Ambrosia in Astolfi's *St Clair*. It was a rewarding, critical year, at the end of which Gallenberg saw his faith in her justified and she found herself, at the age of nineteen, fêted and acclaimed in her native city. "To say that Fanny Elssler is making progress as an artist with each role," commented *Der Sammler* in December, "would be quite superfluous."

This was the stage she had reached when she played for the first time the leading role of the fairy Viviane in *The Fairy and the Knight* on November 25th, 1829. Again she had to contend with memories of Brugnoli, and again she triumphed. Brugnoli was specially renowned for her proficiency in *pointe* work, and Fanny was applauded to the echo for the "bravura and finish" with which "she executed the most brilliant *pas* of her predecessor". About the only blemish in her performance was a certain lack of temperament in her miming. Summing up, the critic of the *Bäuerles Theaterzeitung* concluded: "Fanny Elssler has long been known as a remarkable artist, for her diligence alone has lately produced such surprising results that very few of her contemporaries can compare with her." Her admirers were growing in number with every appearance, and it was on this evening that Friedrich von Gentz, the most renowned political writer of his day and the friend and adviser of the Chancellor, Prince Metternich, became aware of her existence. His diary entry for that day gave no indication of the overwhelming passion that was shortly to consume him. He merely wrote that "the extremely charming ballet . . . was made particularly beautiful by Fanny Elssler and Pauline Hasenhut."

Some days later, on December 5th, he was again in the theatre, watching her as Emma in a revival of Horschelt's *Der Berggeist*. The bravura of her dancing was again remarked by the press, and Gentz went home "truly charmed".

Indeed he was already more than charmed. At the end of December he braved the fierce cold to see her again, after sending her four beautiful camellias by the obliging Gallenberg. The first introduction was effected little more than a week later, on January 4th, 1830, at one of Countess Gallenberg's musical soirées. Gentz was a little disappointed. "In close proximity," he confided to his diary, "she gives the impression of an ordinary but pretty woman of the bourgeoisie, so that all the theatrical magic was lost." The old man's ardour was only momentarily damped, however, and he continued his regular visits to the theatre. He was taken by Gallenberg to Fanny's dressing-room, he sent her gifts on the occasion of her benefit, and he greedily received "the very encouraging glance" and "the friendly look" which she seemed to bestow on him

from the stage. At the end of February he met Fanny socially once
again, at Gallenberg's. "Fanny was delightful," he wrote afterwards,
"and pleased me better than I had expected outside the theatre. But she
remains a closed book to me, she is like a beautiful statue. Does she
possess a soul? That I do not yet know."

So, persistently but patiently, Gentz entered the life of Fanny Elssler.
In years he was more than three times her age, but he pursued her with a
vigour that surprised even him and with an experience of the art of
seduction which he had gained in countless adventures. Until now there
had been little romance or stability in his private life. Unsuccessful in
marriage, he had early sought distraction from the mounting pressure of
literary work in gambling, carousing and satisfying his lust for women
even in the most sordid brothels, vices which consumed all the money
he could earn and more. Such vagaries had not interfered with the
progress of his career. His writings against Napoleon had won the
esteem of all who were engaged in the struggle against French domina-
tion. He was made an Imperial Counsellor, and after the war Metternich appointed him secretary to the Congress of Vienna and a number
of other European conferences.

Worn out by work and excesses, and gripped by arthritis, Gentz
grew old before his time. A friend who saw him in 1823, when he was
not yet sixty, described him as an unsteady, stooping figure with a
reddish wig and dark spectacles. Not long after this he began taking the
waters at Gastein, and to his incredulous delight the cure brought
about a quite miraculous regeneration. He wrote to his friend, Rahel
von Varnhagen that he had "such a lively feeling of well-being as I
scarcely knew in my best years . . . Not only did my mind regain its
youthful freshness and my heart a quite unusual degree of exhilaration,
but even my outward appearance has been rejuvenated and all my
bodily strength has been regained". To the joy of his friends he began
to be seen again in society, which he had shunned for many years, and
it was while he was experiencing this new vigour that he met the last
and the greatest of his many loves, Fanny Elssler.

Gentz was somewhat reticent about the manner in which he made her
acquaintance, writing guardedly to his sister of "a most extraordinary
train of events which I cannot recount to you here". His diary, however,
makes it clear that Gallenberg not only arranged the introduction, but
afforded Gentz opportunities of meeting Fanny until, by the spring of
1830, the relationship had developed into a friendship. Whether this
was a disinterested gesture on Gallenberg's part, or whether Gentz,
with his powerful connections, had been able to perform some service
to the Director, who was encountering financial difficulties in his

enterprise, is a matter for conjecture. Certainly Gentz laid siege to Fanny's heart with all the means open to him. He showed her every attention, sent her artificial flowers on her name-day (explaining that fresh flowers were too melancholy a symbol of fragility) and persuaded his young friend, Anton Prokesch, to write verses which he could send to her.

By April he was visiting Fanny regularly at her home, bringing her little gifts when she was unwell, spending hours with her in discussion, and ingratiating himself not only with her, but also with her family. At the same time he followed her career assiduously, seldom letting a performance pass which he did not see. The season's novelty was Auber's opera, *La Muette de Portici*, in which Fanny appeared in a *pas de deux* with a distinguished partner from Paris, Albert, dancing "with terrific bravura and remarkable assurance". Gentz never tired of seeing this, but he took a very different view of Albert's ballet, *Der Zauberring*, which was produced on April 29th with Fanny as Adeline. "Fanny did not shine much," he recorded disapprovingly. "It was as if I had never loved Fanny, and as if the things I loved best were repelling me."

Meanwhile Gallenberg was engaged in a losing struggle to keep the finances of his enterprise under control. He had assumed the post of Director in the mistaken belief that his experience of the theatre would make up for his lack of financial backing, but even before the opera house had reopened under his management he was in difficulties, and his generous policy of enriching the repertory of opera and ballet swelled the deficit. By May 1830 it was clear that only a miracle could avert a catastrophe. The rot had even penetrated the company. "In the evening," recorded Gentz in his diary on May 8th, "the dear old ballet, *The Fairy and the Knight*, danced by an assortment of *danseuses* on account of the defection of two male dancers." A few days later Countess Gallenberg sought his advice before her audience with the Emperor the following day, but the situation was irretrievable and on the evening of the 16th a ruined and disillusioned Gallenberg left for Hungary.

With the coming of summer Fanny found herself deeply involved emotionally in this new friendship. She responded to Gentz's devotion with increasing warmth, discovering him as not merely a suitor but a mentor as well. Having started her theatrical career so young, her general education had been necessarily limited. She was, however, naturally intelligent, and she eagerly absorbed the knowledge and wisdom which he was able to teach her. Of all the influences which went to make up her character, the intellectual education she received from Gentz was probably the most formative.

Though they saw one another regularly, they exchanged letters, as lovers do, in the long hours of separation. Early in May Gentz was still addressing her by the polite *Sie*, but by June 3rd he was using the intimate form of *Du*. "I never knew such bliss on earth," he told her. "How can I thank you for this, my Fanny. 'My!' In this single syllable more than heaven lies, and you have written it and your eyes have strengthened it." Now he was seeing her every day. He escorted her to the artist Agricola, who was painting her portrait; he accompanied her to the theatre; when she fell ill, he sent his own doctor to attend her; he invited her to his estate at Weinhaus, just outside Vienna; and in everything he was her devoted cavalier. They became wholly absorbed in one another. In a note of July 3rd, Fanny wrote. "I will keep the kisses until this evening, but then I shall kiss you so as to drink in your soul."

Gentz was almost bewildered by the suddenness of this passion. "Her beauty alone cannot explain the fire she has kindled in me," he confessed to the Countess Fuchs. "There must be another mystery above that. Supernatural things are coming to pass." In August the news of the revolution in Paris came as a great personal shock to a man who had devoted his life to the maintenance of the existing order, but the mention of Fanny's name was enough to restore his serenity. He was at peace. A friend who had observed him during a performance of the ballet remarked how still and silent he was and assumed from this that his relationship with Fanny was untroubled. "Such calm," he commented, "presupposes harmony and security." When he heard these words, Gentz murmured: "He is not altogether wrong."

At the end of July Gentz was obliged to accompany Prince Metternich to Königswart. The prospect of a few days' absence from his beloved appalled him. "Without doubt," he wrote to her, "the pain I suffered when I left you will follow me at every step, but your tender and noble words will forever remain deep in my heart." Next morning, as he was waiting for the post-horses, he wrote again. "All my thoughts are with you, dear Fanny. Why must I leave Vienna? Why cannot I look into your eyes once more?" In Königswart he waited anxiously for the courier. He treasured her letters, for he knew that it was an effort for her to write, and he took advantage of every free moment to tell her of his doings. He was naïvely encouraged whenever his friends showed indulgence towards his relationship with her, and he told Fanny of his pleasure when the conversation at supper touched upon it "in such a charming way and with so much delicacy that I had no cause whatever to complain". Fanny sent him some pressed flowers she had picked, accompanied by some verses, and another day, to show that she was not neglecting her studies in his absence, she began her letter with a few phrases in French: "*Bon jour cher Gentz, tu es bien etonner, que*

je t'ecriez en français, n'est-ce-pas? Tu voir comme je suive tes conseilles . . .
Adieu, dear Gentz, I kiss you in German fashion and remain your
German Fanny."

Fanny was as sad as Gentz during this enforced separation, and on a
picnic outing at Die Brühl, near Mödling, she could not wait to return
home to find his letter. "I was continually thinking of you, so I could
not enjoy myself very much," she told him in the letter she wrote that
evening. "When I think, 'If only Gentz were with me, but unfortunately it cannot be so,' then I lose all desire to enjoy myself. If only I
could believe that you were longing for me, which I am assured of
when I read your letters, that you are really fond of me, that you are so
kind, though Fate treats you so unkindly; but courage, my dear Gentz,
God still exists, the two of us are still alive, and so long as that is so we
must not despair. Happy days will return and will make up for the
many empty, unhappy ones. Just have courage, my dear Gentz. I
cannot hide from you that it grieves me not a little that in every one of
your letters you suggest that they tire me or that I must puzzle over
them. Do you really think I cannot read them, or do you think perhaps
that they cause me difficulty? Oh no, you are wrong, my dear friend.
The sadder they are, the more they prove to me how kind you are to me,
and these two are very sad. You really are so kind, and that pleases me
constantly. I am truly very fond of you, since from your letters I can
derive courage, for I can appreciate that as you have already given me
so much, how much must I not give you."

It was after his return to Vienna that their love reached its culmina-
tion and Fanny gave herself to him. On the evening of September 8th,
he wrote in his diary in red ink: "This evening, which ended at half
past 11, can only be described in rose-coloured characters. The happiness
which was granted to me today I shall never forget." Four days later he
was almost brutally explicit: "To Fanny's where I passed a heavenly
evening. I spent an hour and a half in bed with her."

He had reached the peak of happiness. "In a short time I won her
love," he confided to his sister a few days later. "I found in her what I
had never expected, a simple, noble, undemanding person, free from all
coquetry to an unbelievable degree, who took the greatest pride and
found the greatest happiness of her life in her relationship with me . . .
I owe to this girl a sum of happiness over the past six months which at
my age I should never have thought it possible to attain . . . And the
most remarkable thing of all is that I have been able to enjoy this
liaison to its fullest extent without causing the least interruption to my
work and without upsetting the noble company whom, for political
reasons, I have not abandoned, and by whom I am still held in high

regard, and without causing my friends in any way to express opinions or issue warnings."

Throughout this summer Fanny had been dancing with increasing success. After Gallenberg's departure the theatre was managed by a provisional board of directors until Louis Duport, a former dancer, was awarded the concession. These changes did not impede Fanny's progress. One critic reported that her ovations were as tumultuous as Paganini's. Vienna could no longer hope to keep such a star to itself, and a contract was negotiated for Fanny and Therese to give a number of guest performances in Berlin in October and November 1830. The *Bäuerles Theaterzeitung* bade her farewell with a glowing appreciation. "Because her every movement is born of a natural grace, her talent develops freely and spontaneously. She can portray the most diverse characters, but best of all the simple, mischievous ones, for she has an inner sympathy with the Italian character. We have indeed never known her to fail, never seen her make a false step. Fire and precision are at the heart of her portrayals. We see her depart from her native city, convinced that the fame which she has won here and takes with her, she will bring back twofold."

The lovers were now faced with another long separation. The morning before her departure Fanny lay on her bed drenched in tears for fully quarter of an hour before she could eat her breakfast, and when they met again that evening there were more tears, mingled with a thousand kisses. On the morning of September 18th Fanny left for Berlin, feeling nervous and apprehensive at what lay before her.

Gentz had done his best to see that she found friends in Berlin. To Rahel von Varnhagen, whose salon he had frequented in his younger days, he explained his passion for Fanny with such frankness that he would never have dared send the letter had it not been committed to the safe hands of an Austrian courier. To his delight Rahel replied with sympathy and understanding, and lost no opportunity in making Fanny's acquaintance and visiting the theatre to see her dance.

The sisters were introduced to the Berlin public in two popular French ballets produced by Antoine Titus. Their first appearance was on September 30th in *La Somnambule*, and a week later, on October 8th, Fanny enjoyed a splendid triumph in *The Swiss Milkmaid*, which was based on a ballet by Filippo Taglioni. The role of the milkmaid gave her the opportunity of displaying her acting ability, particularly in the scene where the heroine, thinking she is alone, expresses her love before the hero's statue, only to find, to her confusion, that the young man has taken the statue's place.

Still spellbound by Fanny's appearance as the Swiss milkmaid, Rahel

Leopold, Prince of Salerno.

Öst. Nationalbibliothek, Bildarchiv.

The Duke of Reichstadt.

Öst. Nationalbibliothek, Bildarchiv.

Anton Stuhlmüller. Lithograph by
Bormann.

Öst. Nationalbibliothek, Bildarchiv.

Count d'Orsay.

Coll. Mr Allison Delarue.

Gentz's house at Weinhaus. Watercolour by Karl Leiden.

Friedrich von Gentz. Engraving by
C. F. Merckel from a drawing by
Johann Christian Schoeller.

Count von Gallenberg.

Öst. Nationalbibliothek, Bildarchiv.

Historische Museum der Stadt Wien.

wrote to Gentz on October 9th: "The dear girl flashed for the first time into the company of strangers at my house like a young hare, with long, smiling, trusting, flattering glances. I had her sit near me, and she pressed closely, like a child in the womb, so that we could speak softly together. I was unable to do so, however, and so was she. Finally I asked her, 'Have you heard from Vienna?' 'Indeed, often,' she said, released at last from her silence, and with a sparkling and friendly smile she asked, 'Are you writing too?' 'Yes, indeed, tomorrow perhaps, or even today.' Was this to be all, just small talk? I asked her to give you my regards. Was there ever greater diplomacy? To come to the point, neither of us said anything much, but we got on well together. We promised to see each other again. The pretty sister is something of a hindrance to me, however, though merely because I cannot cope with both of them. In a week's time they are free of performances and rehearsals, and so I am almost making myself ill with preparations. [Fanny] pleased me greatly, and her bearing is charming and comes from within, but she kept her white gloves on and was dressed up to the chin, so that I could see nothing of her neck and hands, nor could I judge the shape of her head because she had crowned it with a beautiful beehive decorated with flowers.

"But yesterday—have you seen her Milkmaid?—the complete Venus rose from the waves. She was applauded like some great singer, step by step, nothing was missed by the public, and the way she thanked them with yet another dance! What intelligence, what patience, what forethought and finesse! You see, nothing has escaped me and I am still observant. I am specially glad that she pleased me, so that I can praise her to you with all my heart. How unpleasant it would be not to be able to agree with you, and that I could not have done had I not added my applause. She was dressed like an angel, like grace itself. Her gaiety and heavenly childishness, her gratitude to her fellow dancers and friends in the ballet — it was really the height of her art! She never oversteps her capabilities: what a wise Italian rule! Furthermore, she comes from a school which I like, and not the absurd, soulless, horizontal-bar school which I detest and which bores me stiff, the new French school . . . Fanny saw me and my friends, and thanked us with fleeting glances for our loud applause and bravos. And the way she thanked both the King and the public from the stage, all the time retaining the friendly pleasure of a child, completely unspoilt! . . . She conquered completely and shared her joy, and she was recalled again and again. The elder sister was also greatly applauded, and quite rightly too, the dear creature. She is a goddess of victory, an amazon, a Minerva, a muse, a child of kings, or whatever noble character you like to think of. Yesterday, thanks to her costume and headdress, she looked like a biblical princess, though no painter could ever depict such a Pharaoh's daughter, and she managed to enhance her memorable presence by her dancing and swell the already tumultuous applause. Her height goes well with her costume, which she knows how to dominate and turn into a thing of grace. She was completely victorious."

Meanwhile, back in Vienna, poor Gentz was pining. He visited the Elsslers' home in Krugerstraat, and sat with Fanny's cousin Hermine on "the dear red sofa". "In Fanny's absence," he wrote in his diary on November 13th, "it is not easy to find a pleasant occupation or pastime in which to indulge." He fretted when her letters did not arrive, and he became anxious when he learnt of her success, fearing that she might be tempted to prolong her stay in Berlin. When he was told how she was besieged by admirers, he was so upset that Fanny had to reassure him. "I beg you, dear friend," she wrote, "not to worry unnecessarily. Do not be alarmed by the tattle of certain people, believe no one but our friend Prokesch. He alone tells the truth, he knows people and he knows me too." Prokesch was one of Gentz's closest friends, but one thing which the old man would not do even for him was to let him read Fanny's letters. "I am exceedingly sorry," he said, "but I cannot show you Fanny's letters, for they are not well written, and in this respect I have an indomitable, if absurd, purism."

A six-week visit to Pressburg, where Metternich remarried, came as a welcome diversion, for all this brooding and anxiety were having a damaging effect on Gentz's health. It was a consolation to him that Metternich and other friends spoke freely of his affair with Fanny. "It is almost unbelievable," he wrote to Prokesch's fiancée, Irene Kiese-wetter, "that society should excuse my relationship with Fanny and speak of it with interest and benevolence, a relationship which would have become a scandal among the Jews, and madness for the Pagans." He was torn between his desire to be with her and his concern for her career. "I have good grounds to believe," he wrote to Rahel on October 18th, "that Fanny will not readily listen to any proposition which will keep her from me for any length of time. If you understood our relationship better, and knew of certain circumstances which I cannot commit to paper, you would not regard this conviction of mine as a mere idle dream. Nevertheless, the proposition could be of such a nature that I myself would feel obliged in conscience to advise her to accept it. But whether this be so or not, the mere suggestion of this danger so shocked and frightened me that it cruelly disturbed the delicious impression which all your other words had on me, and I spent a dreadful night, since I had read your letter between one and two in the morning on returning from a *soirée dansante* . . . At the moment she has a two-month engagement in Berlin and has solemnly promised to be back in Vienna in the first days of December, if not sooner, since I shall certainly be back there by the end of this month. I have, however, recently asked her not to remain in Berlin any later than November 15th, and this for very good reasons which I cannot write either to her or to you. You will be doing me a service which I shall never forget if you will support my request. As you so rightly guess, I can scarcely endure the torment of her absence any longer. While she was here, which was in itself one of the wonders of my existence, all my duties seemed light, even the most unpleasant ones (and today almost all are unpleasant), and I have not been in the least remiss in my public behaviour. Now I am overcome with depression. Please tell her all this if you have the chance to speak to her about our relationship. Tell her also, and this is completely true, that even my health is suffering."

Rahel's letters helped to keep his vision of Fanny bright. On November 18th she described a homely scene. "She is now making with her own hands, for her sister and herself, headdresses of cords and ribbons like those of a fairy, and as graceful as if they came from Paris, and with such a flair as is only found in the most individual of characters. Also she does her own hair."

Gentz had also wanted his sister Lisette to meet Fanny while she was in Berlin, and to her too he laid bare his heart, proclaiming proudly: "*I* have conquered her, which is the highest of all arts, even if the least understood, without having offered her *anything at all* except my heart, whose worth she recognised; a victory which, at my age, must be classed with those which can only be expected in fiction." She would, he went on, find the dancer "simple, unassuming, and not in the least coquettish, indeed rather timid and shy. She is usually quiet and withdrawn with people whom she does not know well . . . I beg you, among other things, not to overlook Fanny's hands, and to say to her that I told you to pay particular attention to them."

Gentz was gratified to learn that Fanny had been warmly received by his sister, to whom he confided the anxieties which were pressing on his mind in her absence. "The triumph which the two sisters, and especially Fanny, have had in Berlin," he wrote, "brings me joy on the one hand and anxiety on the other. Not that the thought has occurred to me that anyone would ever succeed in detaining her in Berlin. I for my part was *too* sure of this, and when the witty Varnhagen wrote to me, 'You have nothing to fear, *the child will not stay without you*,' these words gave me special pleasure because I realised that others had appreciated this and shared my opinion of her. It annoyed me, however, that the acclaim which she won led to exaggerated and unseemly demonstrations, that she was forced to exert herself to the point of damaging her health, that she was put into one ballet after another, and that difficulties were placed in the way of her return to Vienna when it need not have been delayed. In addition I was very sorry to note from your almost daily letters that as well as the actual performances in Berlin and Potsdam, she had a number of long and wearying rehearsals which prevented her from visiting you, which she so much longed to do."

Fanny had been drawing full houses in Berlin whenever she appeared, and the resident ballerina, Angelica Saint-Romain, had to accept a temporary eclipse. On October 29th, when Fanny played the part of Arsene in *Die neue Amazone*, a handful of Saint-Romain's supporters made a public protest. A few hisses were heard when Fanny made her first entrance, but were quickly drowned by the applause. A little later, after Saint-Romain had danced in a *pas de deux*, her partisans began to shout for their favourite, only to be turned upon by the rest of the public and forced to leave the theatre. The two sisters ended their series of performances peaceably by producing *Ottavio Pinelli*. Their last appearance was to have taken place on November 30th, but they were prevailed upon to appear once more, on December 7th, when Fanny played the part of Rosette in Dalayrac's opera, *Deux Mots*.

After the performance their admirers serenaded them beneath the windows of their brother Joseph's house, where they were staying. The next day they began their journey back to Vienna. They went by way of Prague, and travelled in great haste, covering some four hundred miles in only six days. Gentz, though he could hardly wait to see his Fanny again, thought she was foolish to make such a precipitate and fatiguing journey, but was agreeably surprised to find her suffering from no ill effects when he called on her within a few hours of her arrival in Vienna. Her pleasure in being home again was increased by the discovery that Gentz had had her room redecorated while she was away. That evening the old man went happily to sleep. "Dream of Fanny," he recorded in his diary, "who torments me beyond all reason."

Fanny's reappearance at the Kärntnertortheater was some days away, so Gentz was rewarded by a succession of five intimate evenings with her. "Without rhyme or reason," he reflected after the first of these, "we tell ourselves what we mean to one another, and the link between us is forged anew." He listened to her account of her Berlin triumphs, and like young lovers they spent a whole evening "sorting out and reading the unbelievably large mass of letters we had written to one another during our separation".

The strain of this separation, added to his anxiety about the state of

Europe, the feeling that his role was played out and the fruits of his life's work were being lost, and increasing money worries, had been weighing heavily on Gentz, but Fanny's return momentarily restored his cheerfulness. "I find her exactly as I had left her in every respect," he told his sister, "and especially in her feelings and devotion to me. A girl of her position, who prefers to remain quietly in my company after three months of homage and acclaim, is indeed a rare creature, and never have I realised more strongly what a treasure she is than since her return. She alone knows how to sweeten the saddest days of my life (for the present days are so in every respect) . . . Only with her do I enjoy my existence and rejoice again in the strength of my youth, which had left me after such a long, busy and stormy career, and which she alone was able to restore."

Gentz was as devoted as ever, and in the early days of January he sent her some hot-house flowers from Weinhaus with a note: "I hope they will bloom all the longer to please your dear eyes. I wish I were in their place and need never leave your room, for that is the only place where I am content." The basis of their relationship, however, was shifting, for instead of the spry diplomat in the full flush of pride at his conquest, Fanny found an ageing man who was becoming increasingly dependent upon her. The lover had become a doting uncle, and the hours of tenderness and passion were replaced by "study evenings". "From the goblet of love," wrote Gentz in his diary on January 30th, 1831, "*surgit amari aliquid quod in ipsis floribus angit* (there comes a bitterness which torments even among the flowers themselves). From me, and from me alone, stems this bitter conclusion. She, the beloved, deserves boundless thanks and praise. An angel could not do more for me."

If outwardly, to Fanny at least, Gentz may have seemed at peace, he was inwardly being consumed by a great melancholy. Small things upset him. A friend told him of a remark of the Emperor about his liaison with Fanny, "which," he tried to make out, "makes no impression upon me since I expect nothing of the Emperor and care little about his opinions". Some days later another friend told him "with the best of intentions how some silly fool (the famous Prince Taffiakia) was proclaiming himself to be Fanny's suitor. This ridiculous piece of news affected me far more than it should have done". That evening he went to Fanny "and recovered as far as I could from the disasters of the day", but the next day he was "so exhausted in mind and body that even this charming girl's caresses could not rouse me".

Rahel received his confidences in a letter of January 21st. "My relations with Fanny," he told her, "and her incomparable behaviour towards me are now the only bright spots in my existence. However, not

even this tender and happy liaison can secure me lasting peace. There
are hours when, even in her presence, I undergo the sad experience
described in such striking terms by one of our greatest poets of antiquity . . . You certainly know Lucretius:

medio de fonte leporum
Surgit amari aliquid, quod in ipsis floribus angit.

When one reaches this point, one has reason to complain. But I hide
the secrets of my chagrin from Fanny as much as I can. The more she
retains her serenity and her freedom of spirit, the more am I sure of
finding in her the palliatives and the relaxation without which I would
soon succumb." The following day he wrote to Rahel again, telling her
he was "teaching Fanny French and German, as though she were a
much loved child. This is the only occupation which has retained any
charm for me, and only by doing this can I forget the cares of old age
and death. I regard her as a gift from Heaven, as a spring bloom flowering amid ice fields and graves".

On February 4th Fanny repeated her triumph in *The Swiss Milkmaid*
at the Kärntnertortheater, performing "the soubrette role . . . with
complete mastery". A few days later she wrote about this success to her
sister-in-law in Berlin, revealing a fluency that said much for the education she was receiving from Gentz. "You will be very angry, my dear
Minna," she began, "that I have not written to you for so long, yet you
know that I mean well. If only I could find more time! There are so
many things to do, and it is not always possible to do what one most
likes to do. I have been earning a lot of money, which is not a bad thing,
is it? My income has been very good, better than I had expected, for one
cannot expect to make much out of an old ballet. The best thing of all
was that I had a great success in the role of the Milkmaid. It was something new for the public to see me in a comic part. They are used to
seeing me always in serious roles, so it pleased them all the more. If you
want to read my notices, you have only to go to Deichmann, who has
our theatre newspaper. I advise you, however, to take plenty of Eau de
Cologne with you, for I shall be able to smell it as far as Vienna when he
is talking to you . . . We are working with both hands and feet to get
rid of Herr Duport, because he never gives the public anything new,
but I feel that, if this succeeds, it will be difficult to find a better Director.
What are our admirers doing? How do they like the ballet? I am very
anxious to know whether Marie Taglioni is coming, and what sort of
success she will have."

Minna replied promptly, and a few weeks later Fanny wrote again,
enclosing a letter for Gentz's sister. "What you wrote to me about the

theatre I found really amusing. It would be remarkable if Marie Taglioni did not come back to Berlin this time. I wish most heartily she would, for she is already awaited so eagerly, and also because it would be so important for our stay there. I will explain this more clearly to you later, dear Minna. My good Minna, I hope that you will be kind and hand the enclosed letter to the Fräulein, that is, if you can, dear Minna. For a long time now—that is, at least since I came back—Gentz has been unwell. (This reminds me of the story of Katy and her father, who caught fever and her mother succumbed.) Gentz is not seriously ill, you can assure his sister of that, but he does not feel at all well. But they need not be worried about this, you can assure them."

In March 1831 Amalia Brugnoli and her husband, Paolo Samengo, paid a short visit to Vienna, and for a time Fanny had to take second place. A new ballet, set in the period of the Crusades, *Das befreyte Jerusalem*, with music by Gallenberg, was produced by Samengo for Brugnoli's first appearance on March 17th. Fanny was in no way thrown into the shade, and in April, when Brugnoli played her old role of Ismele in *Bluebeard*, in which Fanny had succeeded her, the *Bäuerles Theaterzeitung* left its readers in no doubt as to which of the two dancers its critic preferred. Fanny, he wrote, "can stand alongside any other artist, including her illustrious predecessor, Mlle Brugnoli-Samengo, with an easy conscience".

Shortly after Brugnoli's departure, when Fanny took over the part of Armida in *Das befreyte Jerusalem*, this critic returned to the theme. "Your critic must admit," he began, "that he finds himself embarrassed by Mlle Elssler's exceptional talent, since he never succeeds in assessing her performances sufficiently highly. She treats this newest role so completely differently that once again one finds it hard to give her sufficient praise. Her dancing . . . left nothing to be desired, and her acting too, particularly in the final passionate scenes, was most genuine and charming. Even a despairing Armida should not destroy her grace by over-violent movements, and it is greatly to Mlle Fanny Elssler's credit that she found the means to remain true to life in the moments of greatest grief and at the same time to retain her nobility. If Tasso had seen this Armida, his imagination would have been fired by her genuineness, which was so great that Rinaldo had to be dragged away forcibly by his friends, and indeed it seemed quite unnecessary for the chief of the invading army to have recourse to a love potion before following her."

Samengo remained in Vienna long enough to produce a new ballet specially for Fanny. This was *Theodosia*, which had a score by Gallenberg and was first presented on June 11th, 1831. If proof of Fanny's superiority over Brugnoli were needed, she now supplied it. In the scene where Theodosia's two children were taken from her, her acting reached the height of tragedy. Now she was going from one triumph to another. In July the *Bäuerles Theaterzeitung* declared that she was dancing in *Blue-beard* better than either Brugnoli or she had danced before. "Her double pirouettes on *pointe*, her unusual strength and stamina, her charm, lightness and precision were all individual parts of an integrated whole."

During these busy and triumphant months Fanny did not neglect her old chevalier. Seldom a day passed when they did not see one another. Sometimes he would take breakfast with her, and many evenings they passed together in intimate conversation or reading. If the day was fine, he would drive her to Weinhaus, or accompany her to the Prater, or stroll with her on the Bastei to watch the firework displays. When she moved to a new apartment that summer, he helped her choose the decorations. Despite their difference in age and his now uncertain health, they were still very close. "I flatter myself," Fanny wrote to Prokesch, who was then in Rome, "that you will soon write either to my friend or to me; you know that he and I are as one heart." At the end of July she rented a small house in Baden to be near him, a short holiday that was curtailed when she was recalled to Vienna for the rehearsals of Louis Henry's new ballet, *Orpheus and Eurydice*. This was produced for the sisters' benefit on September 10th.

Another separation was now threatening to disturb the peace of the lovers, for Fanny and her sister had signed a contract to dance in Berlin during the winter. "Even now my heart bleeds at the thought of this parting," Gentz wrote to Rahel, "and I really do not know how I shall bear it this time." Torn between his need for her companionship and his awareness of the demands of her career, he realised that Fanny's art must come first. "If I could prevent her going to Berlin by offering her money," he told his sister, "I would shrink from nothing to obtain this end, even though it brought about my ruin. But other considerations restrain me. Fanny has made wonderful progress in her art. Today she is the first dancer in Europe (and not only in my prejudiced eyes), she has a long and brilliant career before her, and I am not so selfish as to want to stand in the way of a twenty-year-old girl who will long outlive me. Even had I half a million and could make this over to her tomorrow, marry her the next day and remove her from the theatre, my principles— not sensitivity to public opinion, nor ridicule—would hold me back. The theatre is her vocation. Nature—that is, God—has given it to her, and blessed her with the richest gifts, so is it right for me to interfere, even if the happiness of my remaining days depend on it? No! She will, and must, bewitch Berlin, and later, as I see it, Paris and London. I am content with what she can give me, without jeopardising her future. What this philosophy costs my heart, nobody knows but I and Fanny herself, who will leave me with a heavy heart because she appreciates my feelings no less than my principles."

Gentz was genuinely disturbed about the danger of cholera, but the epidemic that was sweeping Europe abated before Fanny was due to leave Vienna. As her departure drew near he became specially attentive, and on his evening visits to Fanny's apartment he was often accompanied by his young friend, Anton Prokesch. "We had a room there called 'Portici,'" recalled Prokesch, "reserved for our communal readings and our work, pleasantly furnished and full of flowers, the most delightful place imaginable. Between ten and eleven o'clock Fanny brought us coffee, and with full confidence in one another we read or talked among ourselves." Their discussions ranged over many subjects, from religion and immortality to more trivial matters, and they read works by Goethe, Schiller, Börne and other writers.

Fanny's departure on November 14th was a wrench which Gentz found difficult to bear. The old man looked to Prokesch to stave off the awful melancholy that assailed him, and the two of them spent many an evening at "Portici" trying to recapture the happy hours of the past. While Gentz was counting the days until his beloved's return, Prokesch kept up his spirits by his cheerful presence or, if he could not be with the old man, by writing to him. "With every day, my dearest friend," he wrote on January 3rd, 1832, "the time when you will see your beloved Fanny draws nearer. Do you realise that today we are at the 50th day? Therefore there are only 40 more to go . . . In certain circumstances it is indeed true that there is no last time, but for our comfort there is a last time, a last day, for Fanny in Berlin. I would defend this fact to the death, although I do not doubt that the entire youth of Berlin would gladly do me battle. If I do not see you at midday, I will see you tonight in 'Portici.'" Alongside the name "Portici" Gentz wrote the following note, intended for Fanny's eyes: "This is Prokesch's name for the house in the Kärntnerstrasse, which I prefer to call 'Elysium.'"

It was during her three months' absence that Gentz wrote the following note in his diary. "I often think I might be happier, more at peace perhaps, if I loved her less, but can you hold back the waters from flooding your house and vineyards in their preordained course or the consuming fire from destroying your home? Work and repose, pleasure and suffering, only have a meaning for me through her, and freedom itself would be a burden to me if I had to dream away my days far from her, for I am in chains even if they are chains of roses. That blissful roguishness, that enchanting smile, from which one drinks and drinks until one is completely bewitched, and all without any artifice or striving for effect, not a breath of coquetry in it! But if it were artifice, the magical smile would not come from the soul, it would simply be one more proof that women are fearful creatures. One should never, even under the most painful circumstances, believe in the impossible, for it can always happen. When a great sorrow darkens everything around us, and the last ray of hope and peace, which only Heaven can send, fades away, no one should believe that the everlasting stars have been extinguished. They are still shining above the clouds, and every sorrow is but a cloud. It disperses and disappears. Why in this world should there ever be a last time? Why should everything tragic and painful depend on this? The only way to find salvation and comfort is by an effort of will to turn the last into the first and make a new beginning."

Meanwhile in Berlin the sisters were rekindling the previous year's enthusiams in *Ottavio Pinelli*, *The Swiss Milkmaid* and *Die neue Amazone*. Fanny was particularly admired as the milkmaid. "Every inch of her is roguish, charming grace," wrote the Berlin correspondent of the *Bäuerles Theaterzeitung*. "All her movements are tender and soft. What suppleness and charm! Her steps are like forget-me-nots, borne aloft by zephyrs and floating down to earth again. And what a mime! Our pretty Viennese is a Cicero of mime, a Demosthenes. Her inimitable expressiveness and her mute eloquence say more than the loudest orator. And how simple she was as the milkmaid . . . Her dancing was throughout both naïve and witty."

In these three ballets Fanny was only repeating earlier successes, but on December 20th, 1831, she appeared for the first time in her career as the dumb girl Fenella in Auber's opera, *La Muette de Portici*. This tragic opera traced the story of Masaniello, who led the people of Naples in a revolt against their oppressors, only to be killed by his own followers. The heroine, Masaniello's sister Fenella, whose seduction by the duke's son fills the hero with revenge, was conceived for a mime and was recognised as a touchstone of a dancer's dramatic ability. It was a difficult undertaking for a young artist, and the *Berliner Zeitung* had reservations about Fanny's interpretation. "We cannot entirely agree with the reading of the role by this talented mime," its critic wrote, "yet she played it true to life and in certain scenes very beautifully. For example, the way she fell asleep was very touching, and so was her parting from her brother before he plunged into battle, her fear for her lover's life, and many other passages. What in our opinion she did not achieve was the progressive development of the character, which can only reach its full effect if it conveys a fearful and searing pain. Mlle Elssler was often monotonous and at times even merry, and frequently introduced minor passions like contrariness and curiosity, when she should have created a greater effect through anger and indignation, which would have added to the spirit of the character. All quick and lively movements of the body must be avoided if the character is really to emerge as a tragic one."

The interest of the public was kept up by frequent changes of programme. For their benefit on January 11th, 1832, the sisters produced *The Fairy and the Knight*, and on the 22nd Fanny appeared in another opera by Auber, *Le Dieu et la Bayadère*, playing the mime role of Zoloe which had been recently created in Paris by Marie Taglioni. Of her performance in this work, Zelter wrote glowingly to Goethe that it was "such a complete success that I really found great delight in the music. It seems more Indian than anything we have had before, in its spirit, its novelty, its lightness, its flow, and our guest, Mlle Elssler (the Bayadere), did not merely dance but acted with such complete conviction as I have not seen since Viganò. The whole house was delighted. The girl's face was the focal point for a thousand eyes, its features a spectrum of an extraordinary range of expression. Charm, modesty, even merriment and roguery mingled together as if borne on the gentle air. All this was particularly noticeable today when another pretty dancer—one of our best—had to vie with her in winning the favour of the God, who wished to test their love through jealousy, and since Fanny's movements were always softer and tenderer she quite unconsciously gained the victory. There is something to be said for exchanging the outmoded Parisian style of jumping with straddled legs for the soft, sinuous movements of a young body, which delights the eye without offence".

Shortly after this, on February 1st, Fanny appeared for the first time in her career in Dauberval's comedy ballet, *La Fille mal gardée*, which she produced in collaboration with Anton Stuhlmüller, who played opposite her as Colas. It was another triumph for her. "Fanny has shown us," wrote the Berlin *Figaro*, "that there is a humorous and a tragic kind of dance. Not only her face but her feet have a mimetic expressiveness. When her mouth laughs, her whole body laughs. If her mouth weeps, her feet too trace tragic movements. This time she was merriment itself, and earned stormy applause for her carefully thought out interpretation."

Fanny Elssler and Anton Stuhlmüller had much in common, for they were both Viennese, they were of an age, and both were making rapid progress in their careers. Stuhlmüller, a pupil of Horschelt, partnered Fanny in a number of *pas de deux* and was becoming more popular with every appearance. Fanny was naturally attracted to this good-looking, virile young man, and the progress of their friendship was observed and reported back to Vienna, where it reached the ears of Metternich. One day Metternich drew Prokesch aside and told him that Fanny was deceiving their friend Gentz, and Prokesch had to tell the Chancellor how harmful it would be, even if the report were true, to inform Gentz, who was entirely dependent on Fanny and would never recover if he lost her.

Fanny gave her last appearance in Berlin on February 22nd, and lost no time in returning to Vienna, bringing with her presents of jewellery she had received from the King of Prussia, who had attended many of her performances. Gentz was delighted to have her back, and found her the same simple and unspoilt girl who had left him three months before. But, whether or not he sensed that her heart was no longer exclusively his, he soon began to realise that things had changed. "The first day I was happy," he told Count Münch, "but I felt at once that my feelings for her had lessened. On the second day it was more so, and on the third day they were dead. The good child does everything she can. She does her best to cheer me up, but all is in vain. Here," he said, pointing to his heart, "her picture has faded."

Gentz's last illness began very soon after Fanny's return. "I am not suffering from any specific painful or dangerous illness," he told his sister. "Since the middle of March a high degree of weakness and discomfort, together with a complete aversion to food and an unnatural tendency to sleep, has so weakened my physical condition that I have lost all spirit and will. The evil is not to be located in this or that organ. It is my nervous system as a whole which is affected, without any doctor being able to diagnose the reason for this particular change, nor I myself being able to give it credence. I feel like someone emerging from a long and serious illness. I can reproach myself for no excess or physical or mental over-exertion, and my general lassitude is a mystery to me. For several weeks I have not left my room. The weather was so uninviting, the countryside so lacking in charm owing to the long drought, and my disinclination to make any movement so great that I could not once bring myself to take even a short walk. Yesterday, however, I went to Weinhaus for the first time and allowed a warm sun to shine on me there for two or three hours. They are trying many fortifying medicines, and I eagerly await the result. During the whole of this sad time Fanny has been my only support, daily my true companion (as far as her duties allowed), and has been the light of my life in many a dark hour. Her character has developed in the most noble manner and my feeling for her is no longer merely a spiritual love but also a grateful adoration."

Gentz's illness had not interrupted her performances at the Kärntnertortheater, where she enjoyed many triumphs that summer, the greatest of which were in the Auber operas, *La Muette de Portici* and

Le Dieu et la Bayadère. Her performance as Fenella was hailed by the Viennese as a superb example of dramatic skill. "The understanding and exactitude with which she played Fenella surpassed all expectations," wrote the *Bäuerles Theaterzeitung.* "Her great anxiety at her first entrance, when she has just come from the prison, pursued by the guards, the pure piety of her bearing during the wedding prayers, and her sudden fear when she recognises her lover's voice were all splendidly portrayed by Mlle Fanny Elssler. Her finest moment, however, was her expression and noble bearing when she repulsed the guards who were trying to recapture her. In the second act the scene with her brother was played with telling truth. It is praiseworthy that in the third act she sat in a row with the other girls in the market scene, not joking with them, but preserving an expression of bewilderment and pain on her noble features. Even the way in which she twice stood up and anxiously looked around for her brother indicated clearly and distinctly her understanding of the character and her deep insight into the spirit of the role. The highspot of her performance was in the fourth act, during Elvira's aria, when she passed gradually from indignation to submission and finally to bitter tears. Loud applause rewarded this intelligent artist who throughout the entire performance and particularly in this effective scene proved herself to be a complete actress. In the fifth act her expression of belief in her brother's madness and her last moments were equally effective. By this portrayal Mlle Fanny Elssler has woven one of the finest roses into the richly blossoming garland of her fame as an artist, and your critic must admit that he has seen nothing like her acting since he saw Mlle Bigottini as Nina."

Gentz was never to see this wonderful performance, for which she had been preparing when her little room was given the name of "Portici" by Prokesch the previous winter. He had now lost his will to live and was refusing to take the medicines which his physicians prescribed. The end came, somewhat unexpectedly, in the morning of June 9th, 1932. Prokesch was away from Vienna, and it fell to Metternich to break the news. "The real reason for his death," he told him, "was a complete exhaustion of his strength, the fuel was used up, and it is to this that the increasing irritability of his nervous system during the last eighteen months may be attributed. Everything which brought him tranquillity had vanished, and at the same time his own sensitivity was increasing . . . Gentz was a man who disassociated himself from any kind of romanticism, yet for some five or six years a kind of romantic feeling awoke in him and it developed to a high degree from his acquaintance with F. Romantic love in an old man soon exhausts his spirit, and the end is not long delayed."

Fanny was genuinely heartbroken, and her sister had to assume the task of writing to Lisette Gentz in Berlin. All Fanny could bring herself to write was a short, pathetic postscript: "Oh God, how I wish I could write a few comforting words to my dearly beloved friends and *sisters*, but my soul is *too* full of sadness. May God give you and me the strength to bear it." When Prokesch returned to Vienna some weeks later, Fanny threw herself into his arms weeping and told him of their old friend's last hours. And when he saw her on the stage in September, he had to record in his diary: "Even she has aged." Fanny's last service to Gentz, who had died in debt, was to place a simple tablet over his grave. She was to treasure his memory all her life, and when, in her old age, some-one mentioned his name, her voice faltered as she murmured, "Ah yes, such a good old gentleman."

A chapter in her life had closed, for no one would ever take Gentz's place as her mentor. Her friend, Betty Paoli, summed up the benefits which Fanny derived from this friendship. "Fanny was not what one might call intellectual," she wrote, "that is to say, she had no witty ideas, made no startling remarks, and never allowed herself to pass rash judgment on people and things. On the other hand, she possessed real natural intelligence, and she was extraordinarily tactful. Gentz took it upon himself to further Fanny's intellectual leanings and to fill the many gaps in her knowledge. She had the advantage of having had one of the most brilliant stylists to teach her German grammar . . .

"Gentz was not able to blind Fanny with a display of riches. What was it then that chained Fanny to him in spite of this, what sort of affection was it? . . . That she should have loved him, loved him in the way Gentz said, is absolutely incredible, but on the other hand it is certain that without feelings of warm and deep sympathy she would never have entered into a more intimate relationship with him. In my opinion gratitude was the main reason for this feeling. Fanny's heart was capable of giving this absolute unselfish devotion its full worth. Until then she had only been admired, fêted and desired, homage had been paid to her talent and her beauty—but who had ever considered or cared about her value as a human being? Whose idea was it to further her intellectual development? Although Fanny was too young at that time and, because of her defective education, too undeveloped to realise the strength of Gentz's intellect, she could dimly perceive it and respect it. Her associa-tion with him opened up vistas of which she had never dreamed, and she absorbed his teachings eagerly. Thus it may be explained how Fanny found satisfaction in an apparently incompatible union. We must not overlook the fact that hers was not a passionate nature. Perhaps it would be truer to say that the passion which is inseparable from any true artistic talent expressed itself solely in Fanny's art. In life her temperament found expression best in an even, quiet cheerfulness. Nobody could have been less emotional than she, who was positively afraid of anything violent or stormy. Not only her physical life, but also her soul, was ruled by the law of measured beauty. I can see in this characteristic a definite reason why in this affair, which would have soon become distasteful to other women of her age, and more so of her profession, she found lasting pleasure. Even when she was old, she used to recall the days she had spent with Gentz, and until her death she held the tenderest memories of her dear friend."

Her English friend, Harriet Grote, was one of the privileged few who received her confidences about her relationship with Gentz. "*Depuis que j'ai connu Gentz,*" Fanny told her, "*je n'ai jamais pu supporter un homme bête.*"

"Did you love him?" Mrs Grote asked her.

"Not exactly," Fanny replied. "He fascinated me by his manner of talking, by his delicate attentions, and by his adoration of me: besides he was so influential in Vienna that I felt it a great compliment that he should be at my feet. I often felt, however, the restraint which his monopoly of my person and the vigilance with which he looked after my actions imposed upon me. I worked hard at the Opera; rehearsals and practices in the daytime, and three times a week performances in the ballet on the stage; these with domestic duties, meals and needlework for my own clothes, left me but slender leisure, and I used to envy my Opera companions when they got a chance holiday and went out junketing to parties in the environs on a Sunday with other young folk, whilst I was debarred from all such enjoyments. On the days when I was at leisure, Gentz used to take me in his carriage to Weinhaus, a suburban villa belonging to him, about a quarter of an hour's drive from Vienna, and there we used to stay all the afternoon, dining there, and in summer walking in the garden, until 10 o'clock, when he would bring me home again. We were usually alone, but sometimes Gentz would invite a friend or two to dine with us. Baron Prokesch not infrequently came to Weinhaus. My mother was extremely desirous that I should continue under Gentz's protection, for she thought that so long as I was in his hands no risk was to be apprehended to my professional career being interrupted by my having children, for the earnings of my sister and myself were the chief support of my family. Gentz gave me few presents, but paid the current expenses of my father's and mother's house-keeping over and above what Therese and I earned by our dancing. Gentz would go to shops and buy expensive gowns and other articles on credit, and he then gave them to ladies of rank whom he wished to propitiate. The house at Weinhaus was elegant, and he kept a good establishment and a good table. He himself ate moderately and drank but little. He told me again and again that when he died, the house and everything in it should be mine, but on his death everything was seized by his creditors and I got not even a legacy, for he was heavily in debt."

Scene from *The Swiss Milkmaid*. Engraving by Zinke from a drawing by
Johann Christian Schoeller.

Öst. Nationalbibliothek, Theatersammlung.

Scene from *Theodosia*, with Fanny Elssler. Engraving by Zinke from a drawing
by Johann Christian Schoeller.

Fanny Elssler in *La Muette de
Portici*. Engraving by Andreas
Geiger from a drawing by
J. C. Schoeller.

Bibl. de l'Opéra, Paris.

Fanny Elssler in *L'Ile des pirates*.
Oil painting by G. Lepaulle.

Coll. Mr Norman Crider.

III

London Interlude

THE PASSING OF OLD GENTZ, which was Fanny's first touch with
death, left a deep wound which only a few weeks later, at the end of
July 1832, was cruelly reopened when her mother too passed away, after
ailing for several months. To lessen her double grief, Fanny absorbed
herself in her career, and it was to be in the theatre, in the attentive
presence of Anton Stuhlmüller, that she found the consolation she
needed. Stuhlmüller was dancing in Vienna as guest artist, shining by
Fanny's side with bold displays of virtuosity. When the two sisters
went to Berlin in the autumn, he accompanied them and shared their
success, and it was there that his friendship with Fanny developed into a
brief, passionate love affair. Their idyll continued into the spring, when
they visited Weimar together, but their paths were then to part and their
romance withered and died.

New fields were now awaiting Fanny and Therese. The fame they had
won in Vienna and Berlin had come to the notice of Pierre Laporte,
manager of the King's Theatre in London, who offered them an engagement for the summer opera season. It was an exciting proposal, for
London was then an important stepping stone in a dancer's career, only
one rung removed from the uppermost place on the ladder of fame—
Paris. Unlike most European opera houses, the King's Theatre was a
privately run enterprise, which received no subsidy from State or Court
but relied for its support on subscriptions from the aristocracy and high
society. In the prospectus sent out to the subscribers for the 1833 season,
the names of Fanny and her sister appeared in distinguished company:
Marie Taglioni headed the ballerinas, Pauline Leroux and Angelica
Saint-Romain were also expected, and the great *danseur noble*, Albert, led
the male dancers.

A spectacular new ballet, *Faust*, with choreography by Deshayes and
music, of "great merit", by a then unknown composer called Adolphe
Adam, had opened the season some weeks before the sisters arrived in
London. It was in this work that they made their debut on March
9th. During rehearsals their height had presented Deshayes with a
problem, which he had solved by rearranging the *corps de ballet* so that

the taller dancers were placed nearest them. Even then, according to one report, "the *débutantes* appeared like inhabitants of a higher sphere, and the pygmies who surrounded them seemed to belong to some Lilliputian land". But their trim figures and Fanny's beauty commanded admiration, although the press was at first somewhat reserved. *The Times* called them "both dancers of considerable merit. They want something of the lightness and agility of the best specimens of the French school, but possess strength and grace in a conspicuous degree, with a style in some respects quite original. Therese, who is uncommonly tall, adopts a manner of which grandeur is the chief characteristic, while her sister inclines more to the simple and expressive style. Both were most favourably received, and Fanny, who danced a *pas de deux* with Albert, was encored in one portion of it. She would be more successful if her appeals to the audience for applause were not quite so frequent." The *Morning Post*, noting Fanny's agility and neat execution, thought that in some respects she resembled Brugnoli.

Early in April Taglioni disembarked at Dover. She was curious to see the two sisters, and had even referred to them, some weeks before, in a letter to her friend, the Marquis de Maisonfort. "There are two dancers from Germany who must by now have arrived, the demoiselles Elssler," she told him. "They say the younger one is very pretty and dances very well. It seems that if I can get the better of this talent, I have no other rival to fear. I believe they are coming to Paris. The elder of these two ladies produces the ballets herself."

Taglioni arrived in London to find that Fanny had not only aroused admiration by her dancing, but had turned the heads of many of the male supporters of the ballet. One of the most assiduous of her new admirers was the social butterfly, Count Alfred d'Orsay, a man of doubtful masculinity who nevertheless had a great fascination for women. Fanny was flattered by the presence of such an elegant and amusing cavalier, and the warmth of their friendship quickly became the talk of the town.

"Alas! it is too true!" bewailed a gossip-writer in the *Age*, "the pretty German *danseuse* did *not* trip on 'the light fantastic toe' with her usual grace and sprightliness on Saturday se'ennight, and the diurnal critics of the Monday were, in stating the melancholy circumstance, 'for the nonce', correct. The languor of the fair Fanny Elssler, though unaccountable to the audience, was a matter of no mystery, however, to my friend Lord S. He, poor fellow! knew the *cause too well*—and that one of the greatest errors he, as a good-natured man, ever committed, was introducing the handsome 'French Count' *after the Ballet*, on *Tuesday* the 26 ult., to Fanny. He little imagined that the impression made by the

Count on the charming *danseuse* would have been so powerful as to prevent either her *heart* or her *heels* being at ease ever since. *On dit*, that some of our fashionable *belles* are quite *piqué* at the pretty German's success."

The flamboyant figure of Count d'Orsay had distracted the gossip-mongers from noticing the beginning of Fanny's friendship with the Marquis de La Valette. For the moment it amounted to no more than a casual acquaintance. The Marquis gave a dinner party for Taglioni, and the two sisters, escorted by d'Orsay, were among the guests. In their moments of leisure there was never any shortage of obliging friends, ready to squire them on outings in and around London. Their visit coincided with the racing season, and not having to dance on the evening of Derby Day, they were taken to watch the classic race at Epsom. The sun was shining and the crowd so great that the refreshment booths ran out of provisions, but by a happy chance Fanny and Therese met Taglioni, who invited them to share her picnic lunch.

For two young dancers still at the threshold of fame it was a stimulating experience to participate in a season in the presence of so many great figures of the musical and operatic worlds. Many of the most celebrated singers of the day—Pasta, Sontag, Malibran, Giulia and Giuditta Grisi, Rubini, Tamburini—had signed engagements with Laporte, Bellini was conducting his own operas, Rossini and Paganini were both in town, and now Marie Taglioni had arrived to lead the ballet. It was many years since Fanny had last crossed the path of Taglioni, who in the meantime had become the most famous ballerina in Europe. Her creation of *La Sylphide* at the Paris Opéra just a year before had sealed the triumph of Romanticism in ballet, and was setting a fashion on the ballet stage for white-clad spirits who exerted a fatal fascination over the minds of mortal men. An influenza epidemic, which decimated the company of the King's Theatre, postponed the occasion when Taglioni and Fanny Elssler were seen in the same ballet, but at last, on April 27th, the confrontation took place in *Flore et Zéphyr*.

There was no question at this stage of rivalry between the two ballerinas. *The Times* considered Fanny and her sister to be "immeasurably inferior to Taglioni", but acknowledged that they were "exceedingly skilful". The *Morning Herald*, however, was more perceptive, noting at this early date the contrast between the styles of Taglioni and the Elsslers. "Grace," wrote its critic, "still floats upon [Taglioni's] movements like a raiment, and from her boldest efforts she descends upon the ground with that feathered lightness as if all the gnomes and sylphs that once did homage to Belinda supported her limbs with myriads of invisible wings. She, however, like the general *corps de ballet*, has, since we last saw her, studied to emulate the wonders of Brugnoli's toe, and, without emulating Fanny Elssler in the marvellous style, she performed some very neat movements in it. She has become more addicted to the pirouette than formerly, and whirls in the full angle of 94° [*sic*] with a boldness which, be it confessed, has not been the characteristic of *the* Taglioni. The Elsslers danced on this occasion with great spirit, and Fanny was admirable in her minute *pas*. The style of both sisters is, however, of the earth; and, as for Therese, she would have been a choice Prima Donna for Bacchus in his festivals, or for Poussin when he painted them."

After holding the centre of the stage in Vienna and Berlin, it may have been a chastening experience for Fanny to take second place to Taglioni in ballets from the latter's repertory and to appear only in the *divertissement* in the curiosity of the season, Cortesi's heavily dramatic Italian ballet, *Ines de Castro*. But her talent was recognised, and on July 9th she had the satisfaction of accompanying Taglioni in a *Menuet de la Cour* and *Gavotte*.

Two days later the two ballerinas danced together again. Under the terms of their engagement, Fanny and Therese were entitled to a benefit performance, and advertisements duly appeared in the press announcing that this would take place on July 11th and that applications for tickets might be made to the sisters at their lodgings at No. 9 Haymarket. Taglioni, though on the point of leaving for Dublin, agreed to dance a *pas de deux* with Fanny, and Therese added novelty to the programme by staging the first London production of *The Fairy and the Knight*. That some of the older habitués recognised it as Didelot's *Zelis* in a new guise did not blind the public to the merits of the choreography, particularly in the "exceedingly complicated and beautiful" evolutions of the *corps de ballet*. *The Times*, which had tended to be condescending about the two sisters, now began to change its tone. "These two ladies," wrote its critic, "have since their first appearance advanced themselves very considerably in the estimation of the admirers of superior dancing in this country; and although they are not (as who is?) comparable to Taglioni, yet their elegance and agility are sufficient to justify the praises they have received here, and to render them an important acquisition to any *corps de ballet* in Europe."

This benefit had brought Fanny and Therese a welcome windfall of some £800, which they needed to see them through the coming winter. For an immediate engagement was out of the question. As a result of her passionate affair with Stuhlmüller, Fanny found herself pregnant. The Viennese papers reported that she travelled north to Edinburgh, but she was back in London a few weeks later and it was there, on October 26th, that she gave birth to a baby girl. The utmost discretion had to be observed in the interests of Fanny's career. Her sister was in the secret, and so was Jean-Baptiste Nadaud who led the orchestra for the ballet at the King's Theatre, and on November 19th these two accompanied Fanny and the baby to the Catholic chapel in Spanish Place. Father Reardon had no idea of the identity of the mother, and baptised the child with the names Theresa Anne Catherine Jane, as the daughter of "Frances Dubois and her husband Anthony"—for whose absence an acceptable explanation was offered—with Therese, also masquerading under the name of Dubois, and Nadaud as the godparents.

IV

Fanny and the Napoleonic Legend

FANNY SPENT THAT WINTER QUIETLY, far from the public gaze and very much absorbed in caring for her baby daughter. But the pressing demands for her services could not be resisted for long, and early in 1834 she set out with her sister for Berlin, where she was eagerly awaited by a legion of admirers, not least among them being the elderly King of Prussia himself, Friedrich Wilhelm III. "She brings back my youth to me," he had been heard to say. And it was rumoured that he had commanded the Director of the Berlin Opera to offer her a permanent engagement on any terms which she might propose, and that she had even been offered, and had refused, a generous life pension if she would sign an eight-year contract. Fanny's visit to Berlin early in 1834 was, then, a short one. She appeared in only one new work, a light ballet called *Die Maskerade*, which she and Therese staged themselves. But if the visit was uneventful, it provided Fanny with the opportunity she needed to regain her strength for the task that lay before her, her second London season.

She had hardly begun to unpack her luggage at her London lodgings at No. 138 Regent Street when Count d'Orsay turned up to welcome her back with exaggerated ecstasy. He was to meet with an unexpected rebuff, for Fanny made it quite clear that she had no intention of appearing too closely linked with the rather disreputable swain of Lady Blessington. The cooling off between the young ballerina and her "cast off dear 'duck'" was quickly observed by the gossip-writers, and there was much wagging of tongues as people wondered how it came about. One paper, the *Satirist*, reported a rumour that d'Orsay had tired of his mistress:

> In the hours of love, dear Count, last year
> My charms were held by you most *dear*.
> True, quoth the Count: but passion will not keep;
> This year, for change, I hold thee just as *cheap*.

Fanny certainly seemed free from care in her performances, which began on April 15th. *The Times* noted a new development in her style, which it described as "exceedingly graceful and piquant", and more specifically the *Morning Herald* observed that she had acquired "a pirouette on tip-toe". As for Therese, she had gained in lightness and now gave "her Patagonian bounds with less danger than formerly to the trap-doors".

Among the male dancers whom Laporte had engaged that season, one in particular stood out—Jules Perrot, an ugly young man who was to figure importantly in Fanny's future career. After an apprenticeship spent in the popular theatres on the Paris boulevards, he had joined the Opéra and become the partner of Taglioni. Taglioni, who did not often praise her partners, said he danced like a dream, for what he lacked in physical appearance he more than made up in vigour and technical precision. Perrot danced with Fanny for the first time on May 10th, 1834, in Therese's new ballet, *Armide*. It was a modest work with only a vestige of plot about the ensnaring of Rinaldo by the enchantress Armida and his subsequent rescue. The heart of the work consisted of two *pas de deux*, one for the two sisters and the other for Fanny and Perrot. No two styles could have contrasted more strongly than those of Fanny's two partners. Therese "imitated . . . the steps and motions of a masculine performer with much expression, yet not with much fidelity", while Perrot bounded about the stage with the elasticity of a rubber ball. As Therese had no doubt intended, it was Fanny's evening. The critic of *The Times* was so impressed by "a most elaborate and exceedingly clever specimen of her short, rapid, and *staccato* style of dancing" that he called her "one of the most fascinating dancers on the stage".

He was not alone in this opinion. Fanny's reputation was growing rapidly, and many people guessed the motive which brought the lumbering figure of Dr Louis Véron, Director of the Paris Opéra, to London. His attention had been drawn to Fanny Elssler some three years before, when his friend, Alphonse Royer, had written to him from Vienna. Fanny's reputation was then still modest—as also was her salary, for Royer remembered how she and her sister trudged home in the snow after the performance with baskets under their arms. Véron was then too concerned with reconstituting the ballet company under Taglioni to be interested in new talent. Now, however, the time was ripe to launch another ballerina, and he had arrived in London with the object of luring Fanny Elssler to Paris.

"There" in London, wrote the doctor in his memoirs, "I saw Mlle Elssler, of whom I had already heard much. I was particularly taken with her charming and lively features, which were full of expression, and by her talent as a dancer, which was somewhat individual. Therese

. . . had less in her favour; she was taller than her sister. Fanny very much wanted to come to Paris, and received me warmly. In London these two artists were only receiving a modest salary, and the theatre was not being very regular in its payments. Therese, however, was apprehensive about their appearing in Paris, and she resisted until the last minute my proposals for engaging herself and her sister whom she dominated. I offered them . . . 40,000 francs a year. In order to achieve my aim, I sought to give them a good impression of the administration of the Paris Opéra. I invited them to dinner at Clarendon's Hotel in the best company. The dinner did great credit to the chef, and at the dessert course a silver salver was brought in laden with nearly 200,000 francs worth of jewels and diamonds. The salver was circulated with the fruit, and the Mlles Elssler, who were pressed to take their choice, would only accept two of the most modest pieces, valued at 6,000 to 8,000 francs . . . The Elsslers' contract could only be signed on the day of my departure, after a clause had been inserted at Therese's insistance to the effect that the three-year engagement could be terminated by either party at the end of the first fifteen months."

Véron was one of those personalities who seem larger than life, and so, sometimes, were his stories. Fanny and Therese were not offered anything like 40,000 francs a year. Their contract, in fact, bound them to the Opéra for a term of three years, determinable as Véron related, but at a salary of 8,000 francs a year, plus bonuses of 125 francs for each appearance.

While the two sisters were completing their engagement in London, Véron returned to Paris to prepare the ground for their debut. His methods were to have startling results. Fully aware of the power of the press, he derived much publicity through a daily theatrical paper, the *Courrier des Théâtres*, which, as well as publishing details of performances, contained columns of well-informed backstage news and gossip. Its proprietor, Charles Maurice, was a venal, malicious creature who augmented his honestly earned income by taking money from authors and artists in exchange for favourable publicity. Véron made good use of Maurice's services, and the engagement of Fanny and her sister was skilfully publicised in advance. The famous dinner party at Clarendon's Hotel was reported at the end of May, and a few days later, on June 2nd, the curiosity of Paris was aroused by the hint of a romantic love affair.

"Something which has no bearing on the question, but which will nevertheless do her much good, will add to the anticipated success of the Paris debut of one of the Mlles Elssler," reported Maurice. "When this artist was appearing on the Vienna stage, people were curious to know whether she interested a prince who was very dear to the French nation and who died in the flower of youth to the sorrow of our age. Whether this rumour is well-founded or not, it is certainly one that will stimulate interest and curiosity in Mlle Elssler. Whether it is seen only as an excuse for poignant memories, as a thought associated with so many cruelly disappointed hopes, or as an occasion . . . to express feelings which people who have not renounced their principles have for the illustrious dead, the opportunity will be seized to see and applaud her, and ponder."

No Frenchman could have failed to identify this prince as the Duke of Reichstadt, Napoleon's son and heir, who since his death two years before had become a martyr in the growing Napoleonic legend. Taken to Vienna as a child when Napoleon's empire fell in ruins, he had been brought up in the gilded prison of Schönbrunn Palace, where every effort had been made under Metternich's direction to transform the one-time King of Rome into an Austrian prince. A new title, the Duke of Reichstadt, was created for him, and when the boy was allowed to emerge into Viennese society, he was dressed in the white uniform of the Austrian army. But the efforts to efface the memory of his father failed, and in his lonely isolation he conceived a fervent cult for the Emperor and ceaselessly and hopelessly dreamed of being restored to the Imperial throne and vindicating his father's ideals. If his death— from consumption, a malady which gave a romantic interest to his memory—put an end to these hopes, it only served to strengthen the Napoleonic legend in France, which now had its martyr in the pale and slender golden-haired prince whose portrait hung on many humble walls throughout the country.

The story of Fanny's supposed love for this romantic hero was for a time allowed to pass without confirmation or contradiction, and in Véron's eyes must have seemed a heaven-sent publicity item as the day of her debut approached. The legend quickly took root, and the critic, Jules Janin, elaborated on the theme in the influential *Journal des Débats*. "Not long ago, in Vienna," he began with typical prolixity, "in the great park shaded with old trees that surrounds the royal palace, there glided one evening, beneath the arched window of the young Duke of Reichstadt, who was listening for the distant sound of her footsteps, Fanny Elssler . . . Fanny Elssler is now no longer in Germany, for there is nothing left for her there. Alas, she could dance there no longer after the shining eyes had closed which had gazed lovingly upon her. The young prince's box is now empty, and he visits the theatre no more to find the German Fanny on the stage and visitors from France in the auditorium, greeting simultaneously with the same look his two loves, Fanny and France. Now this last leaf of imperial

laurel has dropped from the paternal crown, Fanny has nothing more
to do in Vienna."

This was exaggerated fancy, but despite denials and explanations the
legend, once started, was to prove too good to die, and throughout the
rest of her life Fanny had to combat a popularly held belief that she
had been the King of Rome's evil genius. An example of this appeared
in a biography of the Duke of Reichstadt in 1853, which presented her
as "the siren who enraptured this most inflammable adolescent, the
Armida who managed for a time to enslave this latter-day Rinaldo in
the delights of her fairy palace". More than twenty years later the story
was still circulating, having been elaborated and twisted to show her in
an unfavourable light. In 1876 an American paper described how she
had been employed to dispel the prince's depression and inform her
masters of everything he told her. She was supposed to have mas-
queraded as a peasant girl and to have appeared by design, tending the
flowers in a secluded part of the gardens at Schönbrunn where he used
to take his walk. He duly fell in love with her and they became lovers,
but the liaison was broken off when he recognised her on the stage.
In true novelette fashion the story closed with the tragic young prince
never recovering from the shock of his deception.

Such a legend had an obvious appeal for writers of fiction. The
elder Dumas was the first to make use of it, in his novel, *Les Mohicans
de Paris*. His readers had no difficulty in identifying the model for the
character of Rosenha Engel, a Viennese ballerina who at Metternich's
instigation is introduced into the palace to seduce the Duke of Reichstadt and turn his thoughts away from his political ambitions, but who
falls in love with him and helps to rescue him and restore him to the
Imperial throne. Years later Edmond Rostand introduced Fanny under
her own name in his verse drama, *L'Aiglon*, which he wrote for Sarah
Bernhardt. And there have been other, lesser works of fiction which
have incorporated this romantic tale, and no doubt the list is not yet
closed.

Mysteries, of course, have a special fascination, and there will
always be people ready to advance fanciful theories even in the face of
the most convincing explanations. So it was with the legend of Fanny
Elssler and the King of Rome. However, none of the supposed testimony in support of it bears careful scrutiny. Frau Gaul was understood
to have claimed that she had visited Fanny in her apartment in Vienna
and been requested more than once to leave by the back door because
the Duke of Reichstadt was expected. She never admitted to seeing
the Duke arrive, and the explanation which Prokesch, who was one of
Reichstadt's closest friends, offered in his memoirs gave the lie to this.

"What had given rise to this gossip," he wrote, "was that the Duke's messenger had sometimes been seen entering the house where Fanny Elssler lived. But the messenger came there because Herr von Gentz and I had a room at the dancer's house which we used as a working and reading room, and this servant, certain of usually finding me there, brought me short notes from the Duke or came to ask me to call on him." Another example of wishful testimony related that when Fanny was questioned on the subject in a Viennese salon many years later, she drew aside with tears in her eyes, and what was obviously her reaction to an unpardonable impertinence was construed as distress at the recollection of a lost lover.

How the legend arose in the first place is at least understandable. The Duke of Reichstadt first appeared in society towards the end of January 1831, and the period from then until his death less than eighteen months later coincided with Fanny's early triumphs at the Kärntnertortheater. Alphonse Royer recalled that in those days "the prince freely attended her performances in the right-hand proscenium box". It seemed that he worshipped her from afar, and the critic of *Le Constitutionnel* may not have been inventing when he wrote that the Duke could not watch Fanny in a pathetic role without showing his emotion, "for the Duke of Reichstadt was mad about the dance—witness the pretty waltz whose motifs he dictated to one of his favourite musicians". The seeds of the legend may have been sown when the gossip-mongers caught whispers of the unsuccessful attempt which was certainly made to entangle the prince in an affair with Therese Peche of the Burgtheater. Popular rumour, which so easily and so often distorts the truth, seems to have confused this scandal with the Duke's perfectly innocent admiration for the dancer.

Persuaded perhaps by Véron to let Paris believe the story for the sake of publicity, Fanny made no public comment on these rumours, but in private she consistently denied that she had ever been the lover of the Duke of Reichstadt. She freely satisfied Véron's curiosity by assuring him with all sincerity and frankness that the passion of Napoleon's son for her was only "a made up tale", and she said the same to her friend, Mme de Mirbel, the miniaturist.

To Mrs Grote she was even more explicit, and the memoir which her English friend made of this conversation gave the final lie to the legend. "Gentz," she wrote, "was terrified at any indication of Fanny's preference for anyone else. In particular he was desperately jealous of the young Duke of Reichstadt . . . whose admiration for the charming *danseuse* was publicly known, and to no one more unmistakably than to Fanny herself. Never was His Royal Highness known to miss a ballet wherein she appeared, and his earnest gaze was always directed to her movements during the evening. Fanny used to peep through the slit in the drop curtain before the performance began, and would exclaim, '*Ah! voilà mon petit Prince! toujours à son poste!*' He was constantly to be seen walking on the fortifications near to which the Elssler family lived in the hope of seeing Fanny as she went to the theatre . . . I have more than once questioned Fanny on this point, and her replies convinced me that she had been effectively prevented from encouraging the passion of her Royal admirer. Her mother exercised a watchful control over her daughters, never leaving them unattended when out of the house, and when in it, little danger was to be apprehended. They occupied a flat some three stories up with a single door of entry so that no one could come in unobserved."

"So you never really had the curiosity to make the Prince's acquaintance," Mrs Grote once asked Fanny.

"I beg your pardon," Fanny replied, "I should have liked to do so, but I was so closely guarded that it was difficult. My mother trembled as to what might befall her, if the higher powers suspected that the Duke had formed an acquaintance with me, and accordingly I dared not so much as look out of the window. I might perhaps have liked to have a Napoleon for my lover, but—" here she hesitated and lowered her voice—"it would have been the death of Gentz. I knew that. I could not bear to cause his death. He was after a manner too dear to me."

V

Paris, the Ultimate Goal

ALTHOUGH RAILWAY CONSTRUCTION WAS BEGINNING, there
were still no lines laid in the summer of 1834 to speed the traveller from
London on his way to Paris. Even by the quickest route, through
Brighton and Dieppe, the journey could not be done in less than fifty-
four hours, and in summertime many people who were unafraid of sea-
sickness preferred to take the steam packet from Tower Stairs and
enjoy the panorama of shipping and the leafy countryside as the ship
made its way down the Thames to the open sea. The most tedious part
of the journey was the carriage drive to Paris, some thirty hours on the
road with regular stops every five miles or so to change horses.

In this manner, one day in July, Fanny arrived in the Paris of King
Louis-Philippe, a bustling metropolis of nearly three-quarters of a
million souls, a city of graceful churches and imposing public buildings,
of bridges, narrow streets and pleasant gardens, of shops and cafés,
theatres and dance halls. Everywhere there were reminders of the
crowded history of France, of its long line of kings, and more recently,
still within the memory of the middle-aged, of the Revolution and the
nightmare of the Terror and the martial glories of Napoleon which had
followed. If Fanny had entered Paris by the Barrière de l'Etoile, her
eyes would have rested on the gigantic triumphal arch begun many
years before to celebrate Napoleon's victory over Russia and, in 1834,
still unfinished. She may then have driven down the Avenue de Neuilly,
through the Champs Elysées to the Place de la Concorde, where a bare
pedestal of white marble stood to receive a monument to Louis XVI
who had been guillotined on the spot.

Fanny's thoughts would have been concentrated on her forthcoming
debut at the Opéra, which she found to be a pleasing but not particularly
imposing theatre in the Rue Le Peletier, leading off the fashionable
Boulevard des Italiens. Dr Véron gave the two sisters a warm welcome,
and in their first weeks in the French capital they learnt much about this
remarkable character. For the man who controlled the operatic and
balletic destinies of France Véron was remarkably young in years,
younger in fact than his coarse, ugly exterior suggested. But his youth

was compensated by indomitable self-assurance and a flamboyant personality which enabled him to direct the Opéra with an authority displayed by few of his predecessors, however experienced and distinguished. During his thirty-six years he had tried his hand at several professions. Beginning life as a doctor, he had launched a successful patent medicine for curing sore throats, and shortly before taking over the Opéra had turned his activities to journalism, founding the *Revue de Paris*. He was very much a man of his time, a self-made man, who saw his role less as a leader of culture than as a purveyor of entertainment in the new bourgeois society emerging from the 1830 Revolution.

He had shaped his policy accordingly, and in 1834 Fanny and Therese arrived in Paris to find the Opéra basking in a period of rare prosperity. Financial success and artistic triumph were going hand in hand under Véron's touch. Meyerbeer and Auber were at the peak of their creative powers in the field of opera, while the ballet had never been more glorious than in the early 1830s with Taglioni at its head. When Véron had taken over, profiting from a freedom which no previous director had enjoyed, a fresh breeze had blown through the dusty corridors of the Opéra, bringing with it the revivifying ideas of a new artistic philosophy, Romanticism.

By promoting Taglioni to the position of star ballerina, Véron had only confirmed an already acknowledged supremacy, for her style was so astoundingly novel that she had stamped her influence on French ballet from the very day of her debut at the Opéra in 1827. Her father, Filippo Taglioni, was her mentor, not only giving her private classes, but producing the ballets in which she appeared. The most famous of these, created two years before Fanny's arrival in Paris, was *La Sylphide*, which had given Taglioni her greatest role. Fanny never concealed her admiration of Taglioni. Describing her some years later to Henry Wikoff, she recalled how, "graceful as a swan, she glided across the scene, leaving in her wake much wonder and delight. No one comprehended her perfection more fully, no one enjoyed it more heartily than I did".

Some of the lesser dancers of the Paris Opéra must have also impressed the young newcomer from Vienna. Lise Noblet was a correct technician of the old French school, Pauline Leroux was beginning to make her mark with her unusual gift for expression, and Véron was personally encouraging the rising star of the beautiful Pauline Duvernay. Jules Perrot was the principal male dancer, and when Fanny arrived a talented French-trained dancer from Copenhagen, August Bournonville, was completing a series of guest appearances.

On his return to Paris, Véron at once began to plan for the launching of his new ballerina. A new ballet, *La Tempête*, was already in preparation, and his first thought was to give Fanny the leading role which had in fact already been learnt by Duvernay. Then, not wishing to disappoint Duvernay, and moved perhaps by her tears, he decided that the scenario should be rewritten to include another ballerina role.

In the last few weeks of rehearsals the obliging Charles Maurice slipped tantalising reports into the columns of his paper. "Until now," he informed his readers on August 19th, "Mlle Elssler (Fanny) has only marked her steps at rehearsals, without giving any idea of her style of dancing . . . But at last this dancer has thrown aside her reserve and given way to her inspiration so that those watching could judge the nature of her talent. According to them, Fanny Elssler's talent consists of great vivacity, astonishing strength, precision coming out of apparent disorder, rich *pointes*, an abundance of well-beaten *entrechats*, much suppleness, legs which rise easily above the level of the hips, and eyes and head movements which are particularly enticing. Add to that a pretty face, ravishing shoulders, fine arms, perfect legs and feet, and you can easily forecast a mad success."

A few weeks later, on September 3rd, Maurice had more to say. "The more the dancers of the Opéra see Mlle Fanny Elssler dancing at rehearsals, the greater their hopes of a great success. What confirms this idea is that according to the experts, Mlle Fanny's dancing has a character all its own which distinguishes it from that of all her new companions."

And on September 6th: "Mlle Fanny Elssler's success with her new companions is such that this dancer may well found a school, following the example of her who taught them to 'taglionise.' Already the movements, variations and *enchaînements* of the pretty German girl are being imitated in rehearsal by several of these dancers who are determined to 'elsslerise' before a month is out."

When Fanny arrived in Paris she thought she had reached the pinnacle of her art. She had conquered every known difficulty, and invented many new ones. But the experience of watching Taglioni destroyed these illusions and filled her with alarm. It came as a shock to realise how much higher was the standard of dancing in Paris, and she quailed before the ordeal that faced her, realising the consequences that failure would bring.

Fortunately the old God of the dance, Auguste Vestris, a wrinkled satyr of a man who had been the darling of Parisian audiences before the Revolution, befriended her and offered to prepare her for her debut. In his studio Fanny toiled like a slave, spurred, even frightened, to almost superhuman efforts by the excitement that her forthcoming appearance was causing among the public. Soon, to her encouragement, she realised she was making enormous progress. "It was not so much in elementary studies that I gained from Vestris," she explained, "but rather in style and tone. He sought to give me grace and expression; in short, *his* finish to my poses and carriage."

The entire staff of the Opéra, from Véron, who was personally supervising the production, down to the least important stage hand, seemed to be living for *La Tempête* alone. Nearly 70,000 francs were being expended on the sets, properties and costumes, and some novel lighting effects were being devised for the grotto scene at the end of the second act. The night before the first performance Véron, Duponchel, who was in charge of the scenic department, and three of the stage designers had to rush round Paris in a desperate attempt to obtain some special gas burners which had not been delivered. Meanwhile, Maurice was busily playing his part in the publicity campaign, which culminated with a report on the eve of the first night that all the boxes had been booked for the first six performances. Then, as a final precaution, and on Véron's advice, Fanny came to an arrangement with Auguste, the leader of the claque.

Consequently the audience that filled the Opéra on the evening of September 15th, 1834, was more curious to see Véron's new ballerina than the ballet. Indeed *La Tempête* turned out to be a banal piece, far removed from Shakespeare's comedy on which it was vaguely based. The scenario had been written by the tenor, Adolphe Nourrit, the author of *La Sylphide*, but this time inspiration had eluded him.

Fanny did not appear at all in the first act, in which Oberon uses his magic powers to wreck Fernando's ship off the Island of Spirits. There Fernando falls in love with Léa, and is allowed to remain on condition that he proves the purity of his love. The audience showed little enthusiasm, and behind the scenes Fanny sensed that things were going badly. Always nervous before a performance, she clung anxiously to Therese, praying that all would be well.

She was feeling nervous enough when the time came for her to go into the wings, but her apprehension was increased by the sight of the stage hand giving the signal for the orchestra to strike up with his left foot instead of the right. When she remonstrated that he had flouted a theatrical superstition, it was too late, for the music had already begun for the second act. "Never mind, Mlle Fanny," he said cheerfully, "next time I will tap with my right foot." Little did he then know that the bad luck was to strike at him. At the next performance he gave the signal with so much force that he broke a bone in his foot.

Before Fanny's appearance in the second act there was a short scene in which Léa and Fernando are brought to a secluded part of the island

Fanny Elssler dancing the
Cachucha in *Le Diable
boiteux*, with Barrez
(Asmodeus) and Mazilier
(Cleophas) looking down
from the rooftop.
Engraving by Timms from
a drawing by Jules
Collignon.

Furore! Fanny Elssler dancing
the Cachucha. Lithograph by
Franz Seitz.

Fanny Elssler in her Cachucha costume. Lithograph by Lafosse from a drawing by Achille Deveria and Barre.

Museo alla Scala, Milan.

Fanny Elssler's Cachucha costume.

Öst. Nationalbibliothek, Theatersammlung.

to spend the night together. Léa hangs a gauze curtain between them, but Caliban, who is jealous of Fernando, conjures up the daughters of night to send the lovers to sleep and transport them to the enchanted realm of the fairy Alcine. It was at this point that Fanny first appeared to the audience, reclining on a couch completely covered with a veil. Awakened by Caliban, Fernando sees her and goes to remove the veil. The atmosphere in the theatre became charged with excitement. "The house was silent, and almost breathless with expectation," Fanny wrote afterwards. "My veil was thrown back, and instantly every opera-glass was levelled at my devoted [*sic*] head. I shrunk under the intensity of the gaze, so fixed and piercing; I fancied I was burning under the ardent stare directed so steadily upon me. As glass after glass was withdrawn, the pent-up feelings of the house found relief in loud murmurs of satisfaction, as I was told, being too anxious to determine the point for myself."

The fairy Alcine exerts all her allurements to charm Fernando. She tells him that an evil spirit has assumed Léa's form to seduce him, and that she has come to save him. Blushingly she confesses her love, then hides her face in her hands. Offering to share her kingdom with him, she gives him a talisman as proof of her sincerity. Fernando is about to yield when he remembers his love for Léa, and he uses the talisman to break her spell. The fairy's palace disappears, and in an apotheosis he is reunited with Léa in the grotto of the ondines.

The ovations at the end left no doubt of Fanny's personal triumph. "My dancing," she wrote, "gave equal pleasure [to that aroused by her appearance], and as the ballet went on, I rose in public estimation, till at the close I was called for, and received the heartiest tokens of admiration and goodwill, more than I either deserved or expected; yes, far more."

The public's reaction was confirmed when Fanny read the reviews in the papers. First to appear was Charles Maurice's tribute. "There was not half a second's uncertainty over Fanny Elssler's first appearance yesterday," he wrote. "At the very sight of this pretty woman elegantly reclining on a sofa, surrounded by fantastic objects, the audience felt a benevolence which was soon shown to be justly deserved. When she rose Mlle Fanny had the whole house at her feet. Seeing this ravishing person dart forward and the charms of her shoulders, arms and beautifully shaped legs unfold, seeing the sparkle of her eyes with their irresistibly provocative appeal, the whole audience broke into applause. Their pleasure turned to enthusiasm as Mlle Fanny danced in a style peculiar to herself . . . It is only by seeing her that an exact idea can be formed of her, for no description could be adequate. The erudite call her style a *danse tacquetée*, which signifies that it consists chiefly of little steps, rapid, precise, sharp, biting the boards, and always as vigorous and delicate as they are graceful and brilliant. *Pointes* play an important part in her dancing, commanding attention and admiration; she circles the stage with no apparent fatigue and without losing any of her incredible aplomb or gentle charm. There could be no more striking contrast with the justly appreciated talent of Mlle Taglioni, whose dancing is all *ballonnée.*"

During the following week Maurice's praise was echoed by the critics of the daily newspapers. Castil-Blaze in *Le Constitutionnel* noted the "delicate perfection" of her style and, in particular, "a trill of *battements*, such as Paganini might play on his violin". *Le Moniteur* was impressed by her dramatic qualities. "Her acting—true to life, animated and expressive—reveals everything which is passing through her mind. She has no mannerisms and not the slightest affectation; her talent is distinguished by sincereity, freshness, youth, and a welcome intelligence: that is how I would describe Mlle Elssler the actress . . . As a dancer, nothing could be more delightful. Her perfection has no rough edges, her grace is always controlled by technique. She performs the greatest difficulties without any effort." Finally Jules Janin added his tribute in the *Journal des Débats*. "She dances," he wrote, "but her steps are so delicate, her technique so correct, her two little feet so agile that one wonders whether she is dancing at all or whether she is immobile. Fanny Elssler does not dance, she acts. She is beautiful, tall, shapely. One might take her for a duchess in the good old days of duchesses."

Marie Taglioni was most curious to see her, and was seen in a box at more than one of her early appearances at the Opéra. "The day before yesterday," wrote Maurice, "we saw with our own eyes Mlle Taglioni applauding Mlle Elssler's dancing with several of her fingers. This is great praise." Taglioni, however, had reservations. "Since my return to Paris," she wrote to a friend, "I have spent a long time exercising my legs, a thing which I consider important since I have to maintain a reputation which people have been pleased to throw into the shade a little in order to work up that of Mlle Fanny Elssler, who made her debut on the 15th of last month in a scene interpolated in the new ballet, *La Tempête*. The ballet is pitiful, and it will need all the splendour of the sets and all M. Véron's power over the presss to keep it going for a time. Mlle Elssler gave much pleasure. We recognised a certain perfection of timing with which she makes the rapid movements which characterise her style of dancing. Hers, however, is a style which deprives the body of grace. I do not think that her success will be a financial one. I find that M. Véron has forced it a little, this success, and I would go so far as to say that he has wanted to impose it on the public."

Véron's plan was to stimulate interest by encouraging a rivalry between the two ballerinas. Just a week after Fanny's debut Taglioni reappeared in *La Sylphide*, and for the rest of the year the two dancers more or less alternated in the programmes. The wisdom of Véron's strategy was proved by the box office receipts, which seldom fell below 6,000 francs a night and sometimes approached 9,000 francs.

The appearance of a rival may have shaken Taglioni, but it did not dislodge her from her supremacy. Fanny had enjoyed an undeniable triumph, but she had only been seen in a makeshift role hurriedly inserted in a very mediocre ballet, and her success was partly due to her physical charms. Even though a militant admirer of Taglioni chalked the phrase "La Sylphide or death" on the wall of the Opéra, the division of the public into Taglionists and Elsslerists did not represent a serious threat to Taglioni. "The public did not for a minute think of sacrificing the wings of the Sylphide for the *pointes* of Alcine," concluded Charles de Boigne, a young *abonné* with a passion for the ballet. "Out of the throne of the dance which Taglioni occupied on her own, two thrones were made: one a little higher for the Sylphide, and the second a little lower for Alcine." Nevertheless it was a highly satisfactory beginning, and thanks to the clever publicity organised by Véron, Fanny found herself a celebrity. Her lightness inspired a pun which went the round of Paris, "*Est-ce une femme ou est-ce l'air?*" and the Grands Magasins du Temple du Goût put on sale a material called "Elsslérine", which was described as "a transparent material with a light lining for ball and evening gowns, made by a new process".

Charles de Boigne had thought it a mistake to launch Fanny without the support of her sister. Véron, however, had decided that Therese should appear in the double role of choreographer and her sister's partner, and the preparation of her *pas de deux* had to take second place to the new ballet. Consequently her own debut was delayed until October 1st, when this *pas de deux* was inserted in Auber's opera, *Gustave*. Therese had feared that her height—she was 5 feet 6 inches, which was excessively tall for a dancer in those days—would tell against her, but although it earned her the epithet of "*la majestueuse*", this was not bestowed on her unkindly. She appeared on this occasion *en travesti*, for which her height was in fact an asset, and Jules Janin described her as "a tall and beautiful creature with an admirably shaped leg, who will become the best male dancer at the Opéra, not excepting Perrot, over whom Therese has the advantage of a very delicate figure and lovely features. As a *danseuse* Mlle Therese is a little tall, particularly when compared to her sister who is so tiny . . . Without thought for herself, Therese has generously given Fanny the most beautiful poses and the liveliest pieces of music, she shows off her sister as much as she can, and dances herself only to give her time to recover her breath . . . The pit . . . rapturously applauded them both, particularly at the conclusion of the *pas*, when the two of them link arms back to back, a very novel and lively effect."

Some weeks later, on November 12th, the sisters added a character dance to their repertory, a *pas styrien*, which gave a foretaste of the type of dance which Fanny was later to perform so triumphantly. In this *pas de deux*, which was also the invention of Therese, new facets of Fanny's style were brought out. "Turning," commented Maurice, "is nothing to a dancer, and generally is not a movement which is pleasing to the audience. But you should see how Fanny Elssler does it in the *pas styrien*. It is like nothing we have seen before; here we have elegant rapidity, imperturbable aplomb, a carefree spinning which electrifies the public. At other moments Mlle Fanny cleverly breaks away from the ordinary mechanics of these sort of *pas* by tricks of the body and a tasteful play of the features which add drama and interest to the action. To justify such remarks in a simple *pas*, in which many other dancers would pass unnoticed, demands the gifts of a mime and a remarkable dancer combined. Mlle Therese Elssler makes a fine looking Styrian man, but if the eyes are persuaded that she is a man, the heart does not want to believe it."

Louis Véron was no less delighted by the success of his *protégée* than he was taken with her charms. Hoping for an easy conquest, he lavished his attentions on Fanny, but she possessed the advantage of having a vigilant chaperone in her sister. If his intentions were thwarted, he showed no ill feelings, and when Louis Henry produced *Chao-King* at the Théâtre Nautique in October, he booked boxes for Taglioni and Duvernay, and appeared himself in the most conspicuous box of all sitting between the two sisters.

Meanwhile the alternation of Taglioni and Elssler evenings at the Opéra continued throughout the winter. "After the rain comes fine weather," wrote Maurice. "After Mlle Taglioni we have Mlle Elssler . . . and Mlle Taglioni succeeds Mlle Elssler. There is eternal spring, the sun without clouds, the oasis without the desert." To the prints which were now appearing there was added, in the spring, a novel if ephemeral souvenir for Fanny's admirers to buy. The confectioner Coutar fashioned her likeness in sugar candy, and hundreds of copies of this tasty statuette were sold.

Véron had had a motive in taking the two sisters to the first night of *Chao-King*. A plan was already forming in his mind to engage the choreographer, Louis Henry, to produce a new ballet at the Opéra in which Fanny would have the principal role. By the spring of 1835 all arrangements had been made and rehearsals of the new work were well under way. *L'Ile des pirates*, as it was called, was almost ready when Paris was shocked by an attempt to assassinate the King. On July 28th, the fifth anniversary of the 1830 Revolution was celebrated by a review of the army and National Guard in the streets of Paris. As Louis-Philippe was riding down the Boulevard du Temple, attended by three of his sons and an imposing staff, an infernal machine discharged a hail of bullets into the procession, narrowly missing the King but killing more than a dozen soldiers and spectators, including the veteran Marshal Mortier, and wounding many more. The perpetrators of this incident were quickly arrested, and a few days later the victims were given a state funeral at the Invalides.

The first night of *L'Ile des pirates* was to take place on August 12th, just a week after the funeral. The theatres were doing badly in the days following the attempt, and rumours of a Bonapartist plot might have made Fanny fear for her popularity, lest her supposed association with the Duke of Reichstadt should provoke some sort of demonstration in the theatre. The two sisters were filled with anxiety as the first night approached, and on the day before they sent a note to Charles Maurice. "We beg you, dear Sir," they implored him, "to be kind enough to protect us as you have done until now. You are so good, you make artists so happy with your benevolence. You will always find the two sisters your very devoted friends, Therese and Fanny Elssler."

Happily these fears proved groundless, and if the ballet itself roused little interest, Fanny made a very definite impression with her interpretation of the leading role. The plot was ordinary enough. The heroine Mathilde and some of her friends are captured by pirates. Mathilde's lover Ottavio follows them and joins the pirate band, and the ballet ended with a noisy battle in which the pirates are vanquished and Mathilde and Ottavio reunited. Not even Fanny's personal fascination could save the ballet from oblivion, and it was to be remembered only by the velvet toque of her costume, which set a fashion.

Her disappointment over the new ballet was soon forgotten in fresh triumphs. In October she was granted leave of absence and went to Berlin for a short engagement. Waiting for her there were her brother Joseph and his wife Minna, and a whole army of admirers who had been pining for her for nearly two years. She stirred their enthusiasm in several favourite ballets, and astonished them all by the progress she had made. "Just as it was said of Raphael," wrote one of the Berlin critics, "that he would have been a great painter even if he had had no hands, so might it be said of her that, without feet, she would have still been a great dancer, for she seems to dance not only with her feet but with her soul. As the Milkmaid, her feet laugh; as Ismaela [in *Bluebeard*], they weep." Anton Stuhlmüller was engaged at the same time, so it was quite like old times. Many tears were shed when the time came in January to say farewell. Nine days later Fanny and her sister were back in Paris, tired and exhausted after their long jolting journey over the icy roads.

VI

The Cachucha

SHORTLY AFTER THE PRODUCTION OF *L'Ile des pirates* Dr Véron retired from the management of the Opéra to enjoy the sizeable fortune he had accumulated in the four years of his enterprise. His successor was Henri Duponchel, a man of a very different stamp. Where Véron had been rough and flamboyant, running the Opéra with the firm control of a businessman, Duponchel was polished, scrupulous and serious, but lacking the commercial flair of his predecessor.

One of the new Director's first actions was to review the existing contracts, and this led to an embarrassing situation with Fanny and her sister. Duponchel considered that their salaries were excessive, and yet he was reluctant to terminate their engagement, as he had power to do. Véron, who with his fortune made was in generous mood, advised Duponchel to try and negotiate a reduction in their salary, at the same time promising the two sisters that he would make good personally any reduction they might agree to. When Duponchel reported the success of his mission, Véron could not forbear revealing that he had paid the two dancers 15,000 francs out of his own pocket so that they should suffer no loss during the eighteen months—from November 1st, 1835 to May 31st, 1837—which their contract had left to run. Such was the version Véron related in his memoirs. Duponchel never published his side of the story, but perhaps Véron found himself under a liability which he could not pass on to his successor. Whatever the truth, Fanny was certainly grateful to Véron for smoothing out the difficulty, and hearing that he was looking for a cook, passed over to him her own servant, Sophie, a cantankerous Norman peasant who was to rule the doctor's bachelor household for many years to come.

This reduction in the sisters' establishment came at a moment when economies were necessary, for they had suffered heavily through the collapse of the Falconnet banking house in Naples. It was through this bank that Fanny received her annuity of 3,000 ducats from the Prince of Salerno, and Therese the income from a settlement made by François Falconnet, whose mistress she had been for a few months. This calamity gained them much sympathy. "People at the Opéra," wrote a collector of backstage gossip, "are very upset over this mishap because the German girls, although they are a little haughty, are humane and charitable to the poor and specially to their countryfolk."

The early months of 1836 were uneventful. All the energies of the Opéra were concentrated on the production of Meyerbeer's new opera, *Les Huguenots*, and apart from a new *pas de deux* the sisters danced nothing new until, on April 18th, Fanny appeared for the first time in a role of Taglioni's. The ballet of *Nathalie* was none other than *The Swiss Milkmaid* under a different name. Fanny's success was never in doubt. Her acting was praised by Maurice, who suggested that the Opéra should make more use of this side of her talent, and she shone as a dancer in another new *pas de deux*, a *valaisienne* which Therese had arranged.

In the spring the sisters received a visit from their cousin Hermine. Hermine Elssler, who was also a dancer, was on her way to London to appear at the King's Theatre, and by passing through Paris she hoped not only to see her relations but to arrange a debut at the Opéra. She stayed with Fanny and Therese for some weeks, and Charles Maurice obligingly inserted a paragraph in his paper stating that her debut was imminent, but to her disappointment nothing transpired.

Hermine had travelled to Paris in interesting company. At the Custom House in Munich she had met the dramatist, Franz Grillparzer, who was also bound for Paris. Being prone to depression he was glad to have a travelling companion, particularly a pretty young woman. When they parted, Hermine invited him to visit her at her cousins' home, but his call was not a success. He found her less pretty than he remembered, and was revolted by the presence of an elderly General who was paying court to her. Although there were a number of distinguished people there, including the composer Auber, the lugubrious Grillparzer decided not to stay.

The playwright, who was a great admirer of Taglioni, was still in a surly mood when he went to the Opéra to see Fanny and Therese in *La Tempête*. "Therese," he wrote in his diary, "a dancing Strasbourg Cathedral or Tower of St. Stephen, pleased me just as little here as in Vienna, although she does remarkable things and has as much grace as circumstances allow. Fanny, who is far prettier although she too has some of the angles of Gothic script, seems to have made great progress in her dancing. So far as her acting is concerned, I found the contrary to be the case, if I compare her with what she was in *The Fairy and the Knight*. It is the same chewing over of the same sweet, with kissing and bowing and curtsying in every form . . . Also Fanny lacks that ethereal, airy touch which alone makes dancing pleasurable for me. She is a body full of desires that dances, rather than a soul with passion. In all other respects she has a multitude of qualities. Her feet have more strength than elasticity. Her arms and hands are often truly graceful. Her upper torso lacks suppleness. The whole effect tends towards hardness. Perhaps nothing is more revealing of the decline of the fine art of dancing than the enormous success of my compatriots, a success in which I nevertheless rejoice for their sake."

Fanny was at that time in the throes of rehearsing the new ballet, *Le Diable boiteux*, which a month later, on June 1st, 1836, was to provide her with her greatest Parisian success, the role of Florinda, the *Cachucha* dancer.

Based on the novel by Le Sage, the ballet's scenario was packed with local colour, fantasy and interesting situations, and gave the designers and the choreographer, Jean Coralli, full scope to evoke the splendour of eighteenth-century Spain. The limping devil of the title is Asmodeus, who offers his services to Cleophas, a penniless student, in gratitude for releasing him from a bottle in which he has been imprisoned. With a wave of his magic crutch he materialises the three ladies whom Cleophas has met at a masked ball—the wealthy Dorotea, the dancer Florinda, and the poor working girl Paquita—and bestows riches on the student. The second act is taken up with Cleophas's pursuit of the temperamental Florinda. At rehearsal she complains that her *pas de deux* gives too much prominence to her partner, and during the performance she pretends to sprain her ankle. Cleophas takes his chance to pay court to her in her dressing-room, but is interrupted by the ballet-master and another admirer. The little devil convinces him finally of her fickleness by taking him on to the rooftops, from where he looks down into her salon as she dances a sensual *Cachucha* before a host of adoring admirers. Turning his attention to Dorotea, Cleophas is challenged to a duel by a young officer and, frustrated again, loses his entire fortune at the gaming table. In the final scene Asmodeus reveals that the officer is Florinda in disguise. Generously she gives a purse of gold to Paquita, with whom Cleophas is united.

Fanny Elssler's dramatic talent had already been appreciated in Paris, but this was the first time that the Opéra had given her a role which really brought it into play. Now at last she could be properly judged, as in scene after scene she added to the character of Florinda. Her display of temperament at finding the *pas de deux* not to her liking, her cunning in pretending to sprain her ankle, her fickle treatment of Cleophas, her assumption of male disguise, and her generosity to Paquita—all these contributed to a lively and well developed characterisation.

Equally this role gave her splendid opportunities as a dancer. No one understood her style better than Therese, and it was she who arranged the *pas de deux* which was one of the highlights of the ballet, a dance full of "effective moments, bold thrusting movements and graceful poses". But it was the *Cachucha* which raised the enthusiasm of the public to its highest pitch. This was arranged by Fanny herself and was based on an authentic model. Spanish dancing had become popular in Paris when four celebrated dancers from Madrid—Dolores Serral, Manuela Dubinon, Francisco Font and Mariano Camprubí—arrived, only a few months before Fanny's debut at the Opéra, to take part in the carnival balls and regular performances. They danced in the classical Spanish style, which had been developed towards the end of the previous century and introduced elements from ballet technique such as *entrechats* and *pistolets*, and their repertory included *boleros*, *seguidillas manchegas*, the *corraleras sevillanas*, the *fandango*, the *zapateado* . . . and the *cachucha*. Fanny must have seen them dance on several occasions, both in Paris and in London, and since no other Spanish dancers of note were appearing in either capital at the time, they must have provided her with the inspiration for her *Cachucha*. Very probably, too, she studied the elements of classical Spanish dancing under one or other of them, and learnt some of the dances of their country.

Fanny Elssler's *Cachucha*, while danced to the melody of the Spanish dance of that name, was not a mere copy of it but an original stylisation based on elements of Spanish classical technique. It required a performance which only a dancer of her interpretative gifts could give, for it began on a restrained, almost playful note and worked up to a voluptuous climax. "This dance," wrote Bournonville in a tantalisingly brief description, "begins with a graceful advance, and then a few steps back. She performed the first part as though inviting the audience to share a little joke, but in the second part her whole face lit up with a passionate glow which radiated a halo of joy. This moment never lost its effect, and from then on the whole dance became a game in which she drove the public crazy with delight." It was to become her most famous dance, and she was to perform it to the very end of her career. It at once set the seal on her reputation as the representative of the colourful, earthy aspect of ballet, in contrast to the spiritual aspect personified by Taglioni, and in all parts of the house on the night she first danced it people were saying that she was as great in her own way as Taglioni in hers.

It was in this ballet that she first roused the admiration of Théophile Gautier. A self-professed Romantic, he had already earned a reputation as one of the leading writers of the new school, his first novel, *Mademoi-*

selle de Maupin, having created a great stir in the literary world the year before. Passionately fond of the theatre, Gautier found a special pleasure in the dance, and when he became the theatre critic of the newspaper, *La Presse*, in 1837, he was to direct his rich gifts of verbal imagery towards describing the dancers and ballets he saw. That he admired Taglioni went without saying, but it was Fanny Elssler who stirred his susceptible masculine heart. "*Le Diable boiteux*," he wrote, "was the ballet *par excellence* for Fanny Elssler, that German girl who has transformed herself into a Spaniard; Fanny Elssler, the *cachucha* incarnate, the *cachucha* of Dolores raised to the state of a classical model; Fanny Elssler, the most spirited, precise and intelligent dancer who ever skimmed the boards with the tip of her steely toe."

His pen lingered lovingly over a description of her charms in this ballet. "Fanny Elssler is tall, well formed and well shaped. Her legs are fashioned like those of Diana the Huntress, their strength in no way depriving them of grace. Her head, small like that of an antique statue, sits with pure and noble lines on satiny shoulders which need no rice powder to give them their white complexion. Her eyes have a most poignant expression of mischievous voluptuousness, which is heightened by the half-ironical smile playing on the corners of her finely curved lips. Finally, these features, as regular as if they were made of marble, lend themselves to expressing every emotion, from the most tragic grief to the craziest comedy. Very soft, silky, glossy brown hair, usually parted in *bandeaux*, frames her brows, which are as suited to bear the goddess's gold circlet as the courtesan's coronet of flowers. Although she is a woman in the full acceptance of the term, the slender elegance of her figure allows her to wear male attire with great success. Just now she was the prettiest girl, and here she is the most charming lad in the world. She is Hermaphrodite, able to separate at will the two beauties which are blended in her."

Of all the moments in this ballet which he treasured in his memory none was more vivid and precious than her *Cachucha*. "She comes forward," he wrote, "in a basquine skirt of pink satin trimmed with wide flounces of black lace; her skirt, weighted at the hem, fits tightly on the hips; her wasp-like figure is boldly arched back, making the diamond brooch on her bodice sparkle; her leg, smooth as marble, gleams through the fine mesh of her silk stocking; and her small foot, now still, only awaits the signal from the orchestra to burst into action. How charming she is, with her high comb, the rose at her ear, the fire in her eyes and her sparkling smile. At the tips of her rosy fingers the ebony castanets are aquiver. Now she springs forward and the resonant clatter of her castanets breaks out; she seems to shake down clusters of rhythm with her hands.* How she twists! How she bends! What fire! What voluptuousness! What ardour! Her swooning arms flutter about her drooping head, her body curves back, her white shoulders almost brush the floor. What a charming moment! Would you not say that in that hand, as it skims over the dazzling barrier of the footlights, she is gathering up all the desires and all the enthusiasm of the audience? We have seen Rosita Diaz, Lola, and the finest dancers of Madrid, Seville, Cadiz and Granada; we have seen the *gitanas* in Albaicín, but nothing approaches that *Cachucha* as danced by Elssler."

Not only Gautier but all Paris was speaking of this voluptuous new dance. Nothing like it had been seen on the Opéra stage before. According to Charles de Boigne the main body of the public needed several performances to recover from the initial shock, but the influential occupants of the *loges infernales*, the boxes bordering on the front of the stage, and the stalls took to it at once. "The contortions, the movements of the hips, the provocative gestures, the arms which seem to seek and embrace an absent lover, the mouth crying out for a kiss, the thrilling, quivering, twisting body, the captivating music, the castanets, the strange costume, the shortened skirt, the low-cut, half-open bodice, and above all Elssler's sensual grace, lascivious abandon and plastic beauty" appealed most directly to those who were sitting closest to the stage. The sensuality of her movements was irresistible. On June 12th she had to repeat the dance, an unprecedented event which was soon to become commonplace.

In August Fanny danced the *Cachucha* by royal command at the Grand Trianon, before Louis-Philippe and Ferdinand II of Naples. Court protocol put a damper on the applause, but a few days afterwards Fanny received a tangible mark of royal approval in the form of a porcelain luncheon service.

Three days later she and Therese left Paris on the first stage of their journey to Bordeaux, travelling with much luggage in a berlin drawn by four posthorses. They were to give a series of performances at the Grand Théâtre, the most splendid theatre in the French provinces which claimed a strong tradition of ballet. Dauberval had produced his most famous works there, including the still popular *La Fille mal gardée*, which had been chosen as one of the ballets in which Fanny was to dance. Judging from their repertory, the two sisters worked very hard. After opening in *Nathalie*, they were seen in *Le Carnaval de Venise, La Somnambule, Cendrillon, Jean de Paris, La Sylphide, Le Dieu et la Bayadère, Robert le Diable*, as well as in interpolated *pas* in other operas.

* Several pairs of Fanny Elssler's castanets exist. They are all unusually small, almost of child's size, having a diameter of concavity of 3.5 or 4 cm.

The *Cachucha* shocked some people at first, but it soon conquered Bordeaux as it had triumphed in Paris. At the end of their visit the director of the theatre, Solomé, gave an open-air fête in their honour at the village of La Forête, with illuminations, fireworks, conjuring and a specially composed cantata, and when they returned to the Hôtel de Rouen in Bordeaux they found many artists and lovers of the dance waiting to serenade them. Their success in Bordeaux led them to extend their engagement there, forgetting that they had promised to dance in Marseilles before returning to Paris. This oversight was to cost them 2,500 francs in damages.

As the sisters set off on their return journey to Paris a sudden cold spell gripped the countryside. Being anxious to get back to the warmth of their apartment, they urged the coachman to drive with all speed. But as they were approaching Orleans in the early hours of October 24th, the rear axle of their carriage broke. The nearest house was some miles away, and imprudently they got out and, shivering with cold for they had not brought many warm clothes, trudged along the muddy road to seek help. As soon as the carriage was repaired they continued their journey. On arriving in Paris Fanny tried at first to conceal that she had caught a chill, but Therese saw she was ill and put her to bed. The doctor came and bled her, but the next day she was worse. He then called in two colleagues, and leeches were applied. This treatment seemed to have little effect, and by the evening of that day Fanny's condition had become desperate. For several days she hovered between life and death, and Paris lay in dread that it might lose one of its greatest dancers so soon after the sudden death of the singer, Maria Malibran. Happily the crisis passed, and from the eleventh day of her illness Fanny slowly began to recover. Paris breathed a sigh of relief. "Just one more victim which death will not claim," wrote the *Revue de Paris*. "After Malibran, Fanny Elssler: that would have been too cruel."

Not until the end of December was Fanny well enough to leave her apartment in the Rue Laffitte. If she had wondered whether the public's interest in her had in any way lessened, she was soon to be reassured. In reporting her illness in great detail, the press had been responding to the anxiety and affection of the public. While she was recovering a beautiful, lifelike statuette by Jean-Baptiste Barre, depicting her in a pose from the *Cachucha*, was offered for sale. It struck a strong chord in the imagination of other artists, for Achille Deveria and others based lithographs on it and it was to inspire a host of souvenirs. Another indication that the *Cachucha* was far from forgotten was provided when it figured prominently in the decorations of the new dance hall, the Salle Musard.

Paris was indeed so proud of Fanny's *Cachucha* that when Serral, Dubinon, Font and Camprubí performed the "authentic" *Cachucha*, critics rose to defend her version. Fanny's "poor little *Cachucha*," wrote Maurice, "which has done no harm to anyone . . . now seems to be the object of a strange and tardy plot . . . Is it not strange that in an age of impudence, cynicism and licence people find fault with a dance which really has none of the qualities so valued by our theatre-goers, and which the dancer performs with a reserve that everyone recognises? To prove the truth of this, you only have to see the authentic *Cachucha* performed by the Spanish dancers . . . For the Opéra's modifications, and those which Fanny with her excellent taste has added, are plain to see."

VII

Gautier's Pagan Ballerina

FEW PEOPLE HAD ANY SUSPICION of the heartbreaking ordeal which Fanny had to endure before returning to the stage. Her illness had left her so weak that she even had to learn to walk again. Not until January could she think of taking class. Old Vestris then welcomed her into the privacy of his studio, and with great determination and devotion set to work strengthening her weakened muscles and restoring her technique. To begin with, she could not perform some of the simplest steps. Day after day she struggled desperately to recover what she had lost. Her teacher was constantly soothing and encouraging her, at times weeping with her when it seemed that no progress was being made. For several weeks the two of them strove alone in the studio, until at last their efforts were rewarded. One day, as if by magic, Fanny felt her strength return, and with a cry of delight she began to dance as though suddenly released, and continued until she collapsed exhausted on the floor. The victory was won.

The outside world little suspected how close she had come to an enforced retirement. The first time she visited the Opéra after her illness, she was overwhelmed by the concern and affection of the dancers when she promised them she would soon be dancing again. Not long afterwards came the news that her formidable rival, Marie Taglioni, was to leave the Opéra in the spring. The prize of absolute supremacy was almost in her grasp, and it became doubly important to establish herself at her very first appearance.

All the toil and tears of her long struggle were to bring their reward, for the public went wild with enthusiasm when she made her return in *Le Diable boiteux* on April 3rd, 1837. The volume and warmth of the applause which greeted her first entrance took her visibly aback, but this was nothing compared with the thunderous ovation after the *Cachucha*. Bouquets were still falling at her feet when she began her encore, and at the end, when some of the dancers picked up a crown of flowers and placed it on her head, she could not restrain her tears. Her only sadness that evening was that old Vestris could not be present at her triumph. He had suffered a slight stroke a few days before, the price

perhaps for the exertions he had so selflessly expended to restore Fanny
to her art.

Some time before her illness Fanny had arranged to dance in London
during the summer of 1837, but Laporte released her from the contract
to enable her to spend a few quiet weeks with her family in Vienna. Once
there, however, it was not easy to resist demands to give a few performances at the Kärntnertortheater, and on July 27th Fanny played there,
for the first time, the title role in *Nina*. The heroine of this sentimental
ballet endured many vicissitudes before the happy ending, including an
attack of madness that was brought on by the fear of a broken romance.
It was a part specially suited to a dancer with dramatic ability, and Fanny
gave a masterly performance "I am not exaggerating," wrote the critic
of *Bäuerles Theaterzeitung*, "when I describe her acting as gripping and
deeply moving, or when I say that her depiction of oncoming madness
was truly horrifying and really touched the hearts of the spectators . . .
Noverre wrote in his *Letters on Dancing* that 'beauty is of much less
importance to the features than intelligence,' and the truth of this
observation was brought home to me by Fanny Elssler's Nina. Her
features can express every shade of pain and joy. The slightest movement
is reflected there, just as the most violent sensation and all the changing
emotions from the ecstasy of love to deepest despair, and all is so
realistic and natural that every moment is a truly artistic creation . . .
While Fanny's portrayal of the onset of madness made such a shattering
impression, her melancholy and her distress at the loss of her lover were
no less true to life. Her silent brooding was so masterly and her gradual
awakening from grief on recognising her lover so heart-rending that her
final salvation came as a real relief, and it is understandable that the
public regarded the quieter moments of her performance as the high-
spots of the evening."

But the greatest sensation of these appearances was created by the
Cachucha, which was new to the Viennese. On the first two evenings she
danced it, it was wildly encored, but from the third evening onwards the
audiences clamoured so much that she had to perform it a third time.
"In eight performances," recorded Heinrich Adami, "Fanny danced the
Cachucha twenty-two times, yet who can boast that he knows this dance
completely or can say that the twenty-second performance was not just
as interesting as the first. That this should be so is the finest victory of
natural grace over art, just as a rose, though seen a thousand times, is
still a rose and the queen of flowers. I have been present at many a
stormy evening in the theatre, but I have never witnessed such general
and unrestrained excitement as at the last appearance, and particularly
after the *Cachucha* had been performed a third time. Without having

Therese Elssler. Lithograph by Jentzen, 1831.

Öst. Nationalbibliothek, Bildarchiv.

Fanny Elssler. Lithograph by Grevedon, 1835.

Bibl. de l'Opéra, Paris.

Fanny Elssler in *Le Brigand de Terracina*. Lithograph by Weld Taylor.

British Museum.

Fanny Elssler in *La Volière*. Lithograph by M. Gauci from a drawing by J. Deffett Francis.

Victoria and Albert Museum.

counted I would wager that on that evening alone [the two sisters] were called back at least twenty times."

The *Cachucha* became the rage of Vienna. Quick to respond to public demand, Johann Strauss the elder produced a *Cachucha Galop* which, according to a note on the original score, was "composed . . . an hour before the opening of the ball, copied by the copyist, performed without rehearsal, won great applause and was repeated three times". Another of the city's waltz kings, Josef Lanner, used the melody for his waltz, *Amors-Flügel*. It was included in a music festival in the Water Glacis, and at the Theater an der Wien the jovial comedian, Wenzel Scholz, his fat body bulging out of a costume just like Fanny's, brought the house down with a parody of the dance. After Fanny had left Vienna, her place was taken by a younger ballerina, Fanny Cerrito, who was persuaded, perhaps against her better judgment, to include this exciting new dance in her repertory. Such boldness aroused violent feelings. "There are men once contented and carefree," it was reported, "who have had sleepless nights . . . because someone has dared to dance the *Cachucha* after Fanny Elssler. The very thought of it caused them more worry than burdened Hannibal when he crossed the Alps, or Alexander the Great when he defeated the Persians. Not for many a day will the arguments die down."

This great triumph in Vienna had done much to restore Fanny's morale, and she returned to Paris not only refreshed by the change of scene, but confident she could accept the challenge which Taglioni's departure from the Opéra presented. How successfully she acquitted herself she was soon to judge from a poetic analysis of her style which appeared in *La Presse* above the signature, G.G. These initials concealed the collaboration of Théophile Gautier and Gérard de Nerval, but those familiar with the works of these two young writers could not fail to recognise the brilliant verbal imagery of Gautier.

"The dancing of Fanny Elssler," they wrote, "could not be further removed from the academic conceptions; it has a character all its own which sets her apart from other ballerinas. Hers is not the aerial, virginal grace of Taglioni, it is something much more human which appeals more sharply to the senses. Mlle Taglioni is a Christian dancer, if one can use such an expression about an art which is proscribed by Catholicism. She floats like a spirit in the midst of a transparent mist of white muslin with which she loves to surround herself, she resembles a happy spirit who scarcely bends the petals of celestial flowers with the tips of her pink feet. Fanny Elssler is a completely pagan dancer. She reminds one of the muse Terpsichore with her tambourine and her dress slit to reveal her thigh and caught up with clasps of gold. When she fearlessly bends back, throwing her voluptuous arms behind her, one has a vision—one of those beautiful figures from Herculaneum or Pompeii that stand out in white relief against a black background, accompanying their dance with sonorous *crotala*. Virgil's line, *'Crispum sub crotalo docta movere latus,'* involuntarily springs to mind. The Syrian slave girl whom he so loved to see dancing beneath the pale trellis of the little inn must have had much in common with Fanny Elssler.

"Undoubtedly spiritualism is something to be respected, but in the dance some concessions can well be made to materialism. Dancing after all has no other object than to show beautiful bodies in graceful poses and develop lines which are pleasing to the eye. It is silent rhythm, music to be seen. Dancing is ill suited to expressing metaphysical ideas; it expresses only the passions—love, desire with all its coquetries, the aggressive male and the gently resisting woman. These are the subjects of all primitive dances.

"Fanny Elssler has understood this truth perfectly. She has dared more than any other dancer of the Opéra. She was the first to bring to those modest boards the bold *Cachucha* without sacrificing anything of its native flavour. She dances with her whole body, from the top of her head to the tips of her toes. Also, she is a true and a beautiful ballerina, while the others are nothing more than pairs of legs struggling under static bodies."

With this eulogy ringing in her ears, Fanny presented two new characterisations to the Parisian public. On September 15th she played Lise in *La Fille mal gardée* for the first time at the Opéra, and just ten days later she took over the role of the dumb girl Fenella in *La Muette de Portici*. Each of these roles revealed the dramatic side of her talent in a different way, Lise being the heroine of a charming, rustic love story and Fenella the pathetic victim of tragedy.

Fanny's interpretation of Lise was sensationally original. She gave it with "a profound, unknown, almost disquieting sense" which so haunted Théophile Gautier's memory that when he was reviewing another dancer's performance in it sixteen years later, he could not help recalling, with a surfeit of erudite classical allusions, how wonderful she was. She danced it, he remembered, "with the friendliest artlessness and the most divine rusticity. She seemed like some Napaea who has been forced to seek refuge in a farm to escape the pursuing Oegipan, and with her marble hands is churning the milk of the heifer Io, of the eternally pink udders. From time to time she deigned to let fall from her beautiful sculptured lips the smile of a goddess who does not wish to preserve her incognito with discreet worshippers. Then, when some fellow from the vulgar village pantomime appears, she beats her butter with a significant affectation of activity. Everyone understands this mute message which says, in charming gestures, 'For you I am the white nymph of antiquity, the Terpsichore with the silver buskins, the young Greek bacchante whose pink foot blushes at the touch of the snows of Taygetus. For them I am only Lise, the affable girl in short skirts who spins yarn and churns butter. But beneath my brown cloth sleeves, look at my arms of marble—they are those which the Venus of Milo has lost.'

"It was thus that the great pagan ballerina played this role, filling us, in spite of the subject's apparent frivolity, with a mysterious terror, like a sort of sacred apprehension of which we did not then comprehend the cause, which was later revealed to us by Heinrich Heine's superb article, 'The Gods in Exile.' If Jupiter has become a seller of rabbit skins on a small island in the North Sea, if Bacchus wears a friar's habit, if Mercury is devoting himself to the export trade as a broker of souls, then Venus, after planting that fool of a knight Tannhäuser there, must have been dancing at the Opéra under the form and name of Fanny Elssler, a wholly appropriate occupation for a fallen divinity of ancient Olympus. It was this vague sense of foreboding which made us shiver with voluptuous apprehension at this pleasantly absurd ballet which the goddess perfumed with the scent of ambrosia and illumined with a mythological phosphorescence. Behind the roguish features of Lise we sensed the sacred mother of gods and men."

If her rendering of the mime role of Fenella was not so surprisingly original, it was impressed with a profound and powerful realism which made the restrained acting usually seen in ballets seem genteel and ineffectual by comparison. Hector Berlioz hailed her as the greatest mime since Bigottini. "There could not have been a finer rendering," he wrote, "with more natural gestures, or more implicit with simplicity, grace and warmth, of the poor girl's anguish at seeing her seducer lead her rival to the altar and her powerlessness to prevent it. And when, repulsed a second time by the guards who bar her entry into the church, Fenella sat on the ground and dissolved into tears, just as a Fenella of real life would have done, the whole audience burst into applause at this revelation of a talent of the first order. Such expressiveness in features, movement and pose is hard to maintain for long, yet Mlle Elssler kept it up to the end. Without excessive gestures and by her timing to the rhythm of the music, in the Italian manner, she often displayed wit and always the truest sensitivity."

Impressive though they turned out to be, these two new interpretations were intended as no more than stopgaps to keep the public content while a new ballet was being prepared. When she was still recovering

from her illness, Duponchel had shown her the scenario of this pro-
jected work, which was based on a play by Scribe, and soon afterwards
she had the opportunity of listening to the music by Alexandre Montfort.
Shortly after her return in the spring she and Therese had begun to
rehearse the scenes in which they appeared, and by the time they
returned to Paris after their visit to Vienna the choreographer, Jean
Coralli, had completed the work.

Fanny's role in *La Chatte métamorphosée en femme* was that of a
Chinese princess, Kié-li, who pretends she is a cat in human shape in
order to win the love of a young man whose affections are entirely
lavished on his pet cat. The Chinese setting enabled Duponchel to
indulge his fancy regardless of expense in devising a spectacular production. It was reported that he had imported some costumes from
Canton to serve as models for the designer, and Fanny must have been
delighted when she first saw the cat costume, a ravishing confection of
feathers.

Unfortunately the imagination devoted to the production was not
matched in the scenario, which the critics roundly condemned for its
triviality when they saw the first performance on October 16th, 1837.
What praise their reviews contained was mainly reserved for Fanny.
"Mlle Elssler," wrote Jules Janin, "is so pretty and lively, she has such
grace and such suppleness, her small movements are so pretty, she
plays the paw in the white velvet glove so well, she presses mischievous-
ness and coquetry so far that more than once one forgets the absurdity
of the plot and ineffectiveness of the dances." Charles Maurice also paid
tribute to her interpretation. "The suppleness, the elegant softness, the
velvet lightness, the witty vivacity, the dramatic expression, always
tasteful and charming, which Mlle Fanny reveals charmed and captivated
the audience to the point where they thought they were seeing a play,
when in fact there was only a ravishing actress before them."

Ever since she was a child Fanny had had a horror of cats, but when
she began studying her role in this ballet she decided to bring up a little
white kitten to observe its movements. It required a considerable effort
of will to overcome her antipathy when she touched the animal, but the
needs of the artist were stronger than the fears of the woman. The
value of these observations was proved in the scene when she had to
play with a ball of wool and lap a bowl of milk. At the first performance
Fanny had an unnerving experience during this scene. The princess,
disguised as a cat, has just wrought havoc in the young man's room, and
he places a bowl of milk on a table in order to catch her. Warily, Fanny
approached the table and put her hand in the bowl. At that moment
Joseph Mazilier, who was playing the student, leapt at her and knocked

the table. The bowl overturned and the milk spilled on Fanny's back as she crouched beneath the table. Being hot from exhaustion, she began to shiver. She became fearful of catching a chill and risking a recurrence of her illness of the previous winter, but she gave no indication of her apprehension as she played the rest of the scene with all her sprightly vivacity.

Fanny was now at the peak of her career, and Paris, ever curious about the love life of its celebrities, was puzzled to find the sisters not fitting into the accepted pattern. They seemed to be leading exemplary lives, doing much entertaining and revealing all the signs of good breeding which were the hallmarks of a society hostess. Acquaintances who looked for evidence of a favourite were disappointed. No one took very seriously the constant attendance of Scheitzer, an old Viennese friend whom Fanny consulted about her financial affairs, and the rumour that he paid her 10,000 francs a month for this favour was disbelieved when it was known that Fanny had several times refused propositions made by another banker. Seekers of scandal were driven to wonder whether any of the servants were favoured—the athletic manservant who appeared to be devoted to Fanny, or the tall ex-dancer, Ropiquet, who played the violin when Therese was composing her choreography.

The Parisians found it difficult to accept that the voluptuous passion which Fanny put into her *Cachucha* was not reflected in her private life. But hers was not a very passionate nature, and indeed there was a certain ambivalence in her nature which Gautier perceived. During the summer of 1837 he had several opportunities of studying her in his newly assumed role of dramatic critic, and he obviously derived much pleasure from the commission to contribute an article about her to the Gallery of Beautiful Actresses, which was being published by *Le Figaro*. It appeared in the issue of October 19th, just a few days after the première of *La Chatte métamorphosée en femme*.

"Fanny Elssler," he described, "is tall, supple and well formed; her wrists are slim and her ankles delicate; her legs, which are purely and elegantly shaped, are the strong slender legs of Diana, the virgin huntress; her kneecaps are neat and well defined, and the whole knee beyond reproach; her legs are very different from those of the ordinary dancer, whose body seems to have shrunk into her stockings and settled there; here are not the calves of a parish beadle or a knave of clubs which excite the admiration of the old men of the orchestra stalls and set them polishing the lenses of their opera-glasses, but two beautiful legs from an antique statue worthy of being cast and lovingly studied . . .

"Another point to praise: Mlle Elssler has rounded and well shaped arms which do not reveal the bone of the elbow and have nothing of the miserable shape of her companions' arms, whose frightful thinness makes them look like lobster claws dabbed with wet-white. Her bosom is full, a rare thing in the world of *entrechats* where the twin hills and the snowy mountains of which students and minor poets sing appear totally unknown. Nor can one see moving on her back those two bony triangles which are like the roots of torn off wings.

"As for the shape of her head, we admit that it does not appear as graceful as it is reputed to be. Mlle Elssler has superb hair which frames her temples, lustrous and glossy like the wings of a bird, but its dark shade appears a little too Mediterranean for the Germanic set of her features—it is not the right hair for the head or the body. This peculiarity is disturbing and upsets the harmony of the whole. Her very dark eyes, their pupils like two little stars of jet set in a crystal sky, do not match her nose which, like her forehead, is quite German.

"Mlle Elssler has been called a 'Spaniard of the North,' which was intended as a compliment. It is, however, a defect. Her smile, the whiteness of her skin, the set of her features, and her calm brow are German, while her hair, her tiny feet, her pretty delicate hands and the rather bold arch of her back are Spanish. Two natures and two temperaments clash within her; her beauty would have been greater had one of these types predominated. She is pretty, but she lacks race; she wavers between Spain and Germany. And this same indecision is to be seen in her sexual characteristics: her hips are rather undeveloped, her breasts are no fuller than those of a hermaphrodite of antiquity. Just as she is a charming woman, so might she be the most charming boy in the world.

"We will close this portrait with a few words of advice. Mlle Elssler should smile more openly and more often. Her smile is sometimes restrained, and she shows her gums too often. In certain bending positions, the lines of her features are badly presented, the eyebrows become tapered, her mouth turns up at the corners, her nose becomes pointed giving her an unpleasant sly expression. Also, Mlle Elssler should not wear her hair so high on her head; dressed lower, her hair would break the too rigid line between her shoulders and the nape of her neck. We also counsel her to paint her pretty fingernails a paler pink: this is an unnecessary vanity."

Gautier's admiration for Fanny grew each time he saw her, and he had many opportunities to do so that winter, for with Taglioni in St Petersburg, she had no rival to share her sceptre at the Opéra. Her *Cachucha* was still enough of a sensation to be parodied as the *Caoutchouctcha* by Odry at the Variétés and performed on horseback by a Miss

Kennebel at the new circus on the Champs Elysées. Already the poet was revising his appreciation of her beauty of the previous autumn, and early in the summer of 1838 another article on Fanny Elssler appeared above his signature.

"Fanny Elssler," he wrote, "holds the golden sceptre of beauty in her white hands. She has only to appear to inspire a thrill of passion in the audience which is more flattering than all the applause in the world, for it is addressed to the woman, not the performer, and one always feels more proud of the beauty given by God than of the talent which is self-developed.

"One can say without hesitation that Fanny Elssler is the most beautiful woman of all those now on the stage. Others may have certain points of greater perfection—larger eyes, or a more expansive smile—but none is so completely pretty as Fanny Elssler. Her charm lies in the perfect harmony between her head and her body; she has the right hands for her arms, the right feet for her legs, shoulders which are the very shoulders that go with her bust. In a word, she is *ensemble*. Forgive us for using this picturesque slang word, but nothing in her is beautiful at the expense of anything else. Seeing her, one does not exclaim, as one does of some women, 'What beautiful eyes!' or 'What beautiful arms!' but 'What a desirable and charming creature!' For because everything about her is elegant, attractive and well proportioned, no single part commands one's attention, and one's eyes caress the full length of her smooth and rounded form, which might belong to some divine piece of marble from the age of Pericles. That is the secret of the extreme pleasure one feels in looking at Fanny Elssler, the Ionian dancer whom Alcibiades invited to his suppers in the costume of the Graces, with loosened belt, a crown of myrtle and linden on the table, and golden *crotala* chattering at the end of her tapering hands.

"Fanny Elssler has often been compared with Diana the huntress. This comparison is not just. Diana, huntress though she be, had something of a crabbed old spinster about her; the boredom of everlasting virginity gives to her profile, so noble and pure in other respects, a touch of coldness and severity. Although evil-tongued mythologists claim that she had fifty children by her lover Endymion, the snowy marble out of which she is carved gives her the appearance of a virgin '*alpestre e cruda*,' as Petrarch would say. Such a suggestion is nowhere to be found in the features of Mlle Elssler. Besides, the great anger which Diana showed against Acteon for surprising her when bathing shows that she must have had some defect to conceal, a flat chest or a knobbly knee, for a really beautiful woman surprised in the nude does not show such ferocious modesty. Mlle Elssler would have no need to change anyone into a stag. The legs of Diana are delicate, spare, a little long, as is appropriate for the legs of rustic divinity made for striding through the woods and putting deer to flight. Those of Mlle Elssler have a fuller shape, though they are no less firm, and their strength is accompanied by a voluptuous roundness which the huntress lacks.

"If Mlle Elssler resembles anyone rather than herself, it must be the son of Hermes and Aphrodite, the Hermaphroditus of antiquity, that ravishing chimera of Greek art.

"Her admirably shaped arms are less rounded than those of the average woman, but plumper than those of a girl. Their supple and expressive lines suggest the form of a marvellously beautiful young man with a touch of effeminacy like the Indian Bacchus, Antinous or the statue of the Apolline. The same similarity extends to the rest of her beauty, which is made still more attractive and piquant by this delicious ambiguity. Her movements are impressed with this double character. Through the amorous languor, the feminine loveliness and all the gentle charms of the ballerina, one senses the agility, the bursting speed and the steely muscles of a young athlete. So Mlle Elssler pleases everyone, even those ladies who cannot bear the sight of a ballerina."

This unusual beauty was of the kind that inspires artists, and the descriptive praise of Gautier was complemented by tributes in other media. The younger Dantan interrupted his series of grotesque caricature figures to make a fine bust of her, and her friend Mme de Mirbel painted a miniature of great delicacy which was exhibited in the 1838 Salon. Unfortunately the artist had injudiciously had the portrait mounted in the same frame as a miniature of the Duc d'Orléans, the heir to the throne. The juxtaposition of the prince and the ballerina created an absurd scandal, which resulted in the two miniatures being withdrawn from the exhibition. The incident did no harm to Fanny, for it was the Court which appeared ridiculous in the eyes of the public.

That summer, on May 5th, Fanny and Therese were given a benefit performance at the Opéra which left them richer by more than 18,000 francs. Many celebrated artists gave their services, including Mlle Mars who, in spite of her years, played Suzanne in *Le Mariage de Figaro*, and Fanny and Therese appeared in some *tableaux vivants* and a new ballet. The *tableaux vivants*, based on well-known paintings, were a novelty, but though they were said to be very popular in Germany, they failed to impress the Paris public. Fanny appeared in Gérard's *Corinne au cap du Misène*, and Therese, her hair flowing, featured in Horace Vernet's *Judith et Holopherne*.

Therese's new ballet, *La Volière,* which brought the lengthy programme to a close in the early hours of the morning was hardly more successful. The scenario was dismissed as absurd, although it did have a certain relevance to Therese's anxiety for the future of their professional relationship, which the appearance in Fanny's life of a lover was now endangering. Its author was Eugène Scribe, but he had decided to remain anonymous, perhaps as a protest at the alterations which had been made to it. "If the strangely fashioned and ill constructed things that authors bring you for acceptance were put on the stage, with all their imperfections on their head," Fanny commented, "many a name's bright renown would be damned by failure the most complete and mortifying. Indeed, there is hardly an instance where the ballet produced bears even a family resemblance to the one presented." It was reported that the original manuscript of *La Volière*, which was bought by a collector for 2,000 francs, contained a number of marginal notes in Fanny's handwriting.

In the ballet Therese Elssler played the part of Thereza, who, deceived long before by her lover, is bringing up her younger sister Zoe in a remote corner of San Domingo in total ignorance of the existence of the male sex. A young man inevitably appears, and Zoe, who has to be told that he is a bird, entices him into a cage. When he escapes, she is warned that he is dangerous and must be killed as soon as he is caught. Finally, after a number of simple adventures, love triumphs and Zoe and the young man are united.

The ballet was dropped after four performances, but Fanny's performance was remembered. In a creole costume which suited her to perfection, she played the part of Zoe "with a childlike grace, an artless agility, and a quite adorable sense of mischief". In the *pas de deux* which Therese arranged for them both, one moment in particular remained in Gautier's memory, "when the two sisters run, hand in hand, from the back of the stage, thrusting their legs forward in unison, which surpasses anything that can be imagined for its effect, correctness and precision. You would think that one is the other's shadow, and that each is advancing with a mirror by her side which follows and reflects her every movement".

Early in June the sisters crossed the Channel to dance in London after an absence of four years. It was a season of special brilliance. Not only had Laporte concluded an imposing list of engagements, with Taglioni and the Elsslers heading the ballerinas, but everyone was in town and in festive mood with the coronation of Queen Victoria only a few weeks away. After watching Taglioni perform in a poor ballet called *Miranda*, Fanny made her first appearance a few days later, on June 19th, dancing a new *pas de deux* with Therese and featuring in Deshayes' ballet, *Le Brigand de Terracina*. This ballet version of Auber's

opera, *Fra Diavolo*, had been a successful novelty of the previous season,
when Duvernay had created the role of Zerlina. One of the most striking
moments in the ballet was a *pas seul* in which the heroine, in her nightdress, dances before a mirror, and a lithograph of Fanny in this scene,
drawn on stone by Weld Taylor, was published later in the summer.
In this and other scenes she had little difficulty in establishing her
superiority over her predecessor. "While Elssler is present," wrote the
Morning Post, "we can have no occasion to lament the absence of
Duvernay. The dance before the looking-glass was particularly charming. She introduced a playfulness and abandon which had an excellent
effect. The pathetic scene was equally well played, and her unwilling
pas in the robbers' den was admirably managed. The *Morning Herald*
was particularly interested in her technique, reporting that she had
"decidedly improved, and [had] attained a strength and precision far
beyond any other dancer on the stage. Her moving through the most
complicated steps on the point of her pretty feet is a wonderful effect.
It is, however, more the result of strength than gracefulness of action,
and it will be admired for its difficulty and not for its elegance." Later
in the month, on June 26th, her *Cachucha* was acclaimed as "the masterpiece of *Cachucas* [sic] . . . essentially different to all other, and yet far
more beautiful; as the original it stands alone". Duvernay's rendering,
which London had seen the year before, was quite eclipsed.

The lodgings which the sisters had taken that season, at No. 120
Pall Mall, were conveniently close to the theatre and not far from the
processional route which Queen Victoria took when she drove to her
Coronation on June 28th. There was to have been a performance at the
opera house that evening, but it had to be postponed because carriages
were not permitted to circulate in the Haymarket. The announcement
that the Queen would attend the next performance created an exceptional
demand for seats, and many people managed to gain admission to the
pit before the public was allowed in. Some opera-goers who had paid
their money were unable to find a place, and those who could were so
tightly packed that about a hundred of them, including several ladies,
made their way into the stalls and were handed up on to the stage. There,
in the wings, they remained during the whole performance, to the
annoyance not only of the rest of the audience, but even more, of the
performers, who found their entrances and exits obstructed. Ironically,
those who had come to see the Queen were disappointed, for she left
without entering her box because of the confusion.

Fanny never liked the King's Theatre, and this experience only added
to her distaste. She considered it "the vilest of all stages. Never was
there anything so ill contrived, inconvenient and mean; it runs half way

across the pit, as if it had escaped the hands of the carpenter, and gone off on a voyage of discovery for itself, so that a portion of the audience is behind the artists. And then the want of room in the scenes is lamentable, and, at the same time, ludicrous. One goes through such bumping, jerking, and jamming, as almost to dislocate limbs, let alone the tearing and disordering of dresses, and of all things else. They have a custom here of letting in a swarm of subscribers, who inundate and occupy the only vacant corners that may exist, so that getting on the stage is often more arduous than to perform when there. I often find myself in the predicament of an unlucky fish in a glass vase, swimming round and in vain, and find escape nowhere. The dressing-rooms are bad—in short, behind the curtain all is unworthy this favourite resort of the *beau monde*, and the most opulent of European cities".

Fanny's opinion of the house itself was no more favourable. Compared with "the sunny and elegant aspect" of the Paris Opéra, it was "a cheerless expanse", with its tiers of boxes, hung with dusky red curtains, rising high above the stage, resembling so many pigeon holes. The public that filled this auditorium seemed no less strange. The aristocracy, Fanny observed, were haughty in their bearing, but more splendidly dressed and bejewelled than any other audience she had experienced. There was, however, a lack of naturalness about them. It was as though they were self-conscious at being observed by all and sundry in the pit. "Of the hundreds who fill the benches of the Italian Opera," wrote Fanny, "how few there are who devote themselves to the artists or the scene. How much more of their attention is directed to the stars and ribands of the greater actors who fill the boxes about them."

Whatever she felt about the theatre, Fanny liked England and the English. Sometimes, when time permitted, she would drive out of London and explore some of the countryside. On one of these outings she had difficulty in finding a room when night fell. At last the landlady of one hotel took pity on her and persuaded another guest to share her room. Shortly after this lady had retired, she heard the sound of soft singing and peeped through the curtains of her bed. To her astonishment she saw her companion, clad only in a shift, performing a fantastic dance before the mirror. At that moment Fanny turned and saw the frightened face peering at her.

"Don't come near me, for God's sake!" cried the lady in alarm.

"Why, what is the matter, what do you think I am?"

"I don't know! A lunatic? A sleepwalker?"

"You are mistaken," laughed Fanny. "I am Fanny Elssler."

Reassured, the lady begged Fanny to continue, and sat up in bed admiring what must have been the strangest performance ever given of the *Cachucha*—danced in a shift by the flickering flame of a night light.

Soon after this Fanny and Therese returned to Paris. On the boat which carried them across the Channel they were joined for breakfast by an English journalist who, obviously unaccustomed to dancers' appetites, was surprised to observe them consuming a respectable quantity of beef-steaks, washed down by a pint of sherry.

VIII

La Valette

THERESE WAS GROWING INCREASINGLY disturbed that summer to see her sister succumbing to the influence of a young diplomat of great charm and experience in the art of seduction. So too was a devoted friend with whom Fanny exchanged an intimate correspondence. "I do not know and have never seen the sieur . . .," he wrote, "but he is well-known in this country. I am told that the title by which you describe him is a poetic licence on his part, unless, like the Marquis de Carabas, he has been ennobled by his cat. People say he is the son of an employee at a post station. Such a lineage is nothing to be ashamed of . . . but what is wrong is to pass oneself off as something one is not. However, this individual is apparently richly endowed with audacity, loquacity and a talent for intrigue, and has hitched himself to one star after another as far as the Foreign Office. I hope, dear Alma, you will leave him there, or at least receive him with reserve and prudence."

With an ease and rapidity that dismayed many of Fanny's admirers whose advances had met with no success, Félix, Marquis de La Valette, progressed from being her business adviser to the coveted place of her lover. Few men understood dancers better than he. Pauline Guichard had borne him a child before he had moved on to the fresher charms of her namesake, Pauline Duvernay. This second affair was short-lived, for Duvernay accepted the offer of a wealthy Englishman, and he returned to Paris, unbowed and unabashed, to seek consolation in the arms of the soprano, Rosina Stoltz—and to aim his sights at the greatest prize the Opéra had to offer, the heart of Fanny Elssler.

The origins of this attractive rich young man, who had gained many friends through the careless abandon with which he scattered his money, were, as Fanny's correspondent had rightly pointed out, obscure. His father was a shadowy figure whose only claim to be remembered was that he was the lover of the actress, Mlle Duchesnois. Félix was born in Senlis, in northern France, in 1806, and after his father's death was brought up by the actress in Paris. In his early twenties he held a minor post in the office of the Prime Minister, the Comte de Martignac. Then for some years he drifted rather aimlessly from one occupation to another, seemingly to have no particular ambition. For a while he worked in a stockbroker's office, and made a somewhat fleeting appearance as a bank clerk at Laffitte's. Thanks to his fortune, he was able to make some powerful and useful friends. Dr Véron facilitated his introduction to the world of the ballet, while the interest he acquired in the *Journal des Débats* brought him into contact with the power behind the press. By the 1830s he had emerged into the social limelight as a personable young man with an enviable fortune and a dubious title. That purveyor of scandal, Horace de Viel-Castel, called him "a La Valette of the street corner", and scornfully remarked that he was as much a marquis as his porter.

No one, however, could deny his ability. His shrewdness and cunning were qualities which admirably befitted him for the diplomatic service, in which he was to pursue a long and distinguished career, rising to fill posts of the highest eminence. During the Second Empire he was to become successively ambassador in London and Constantinople, Minister of the Interior, and briefly Foreign Minister, and at long last Napoleon III, in recognition of his services to France, would confirm his title of Marquis. When he died in 1881, his youthful conquests among the dancers of the ballet were not entirely forgotten. Recalling his love for "the arts, hunting, horses, carriages, indeed all the elegant things in life", *Le Figaro* was to comment that "evil tongues gleefully counted the successes in love which he had enjoyed in his youth, forgetting that the finest compliment one can pay to a man is to say he was much loved by women".

La Valette made the most of the power which his liaison with Fanny Elssler brought him. Given the slightest chance, he would intervene as her champion, demanding rights which she in her natural modesty would not have thought of claiming, and consolidating her supremacy with such ferocious persistence that the exasperated Duponchel finally sought to be rid of him and begged his partner, Aguado, to arrange a diplomatic posting for the young man. A sadder consequence of the appearance of La Valette in Fanny's life was the rift with Therese. When La Valette was accepted as Fanny's protector, he found himself received into their joint household, where his *parvenu*'s sense of the social proprieties was offended by the presence of Therese's lover, the one-time dancer Ropiquet. He refused to allow this lowly individual to occupy the same standing in the household as himself. "Take him as a valet, if you wish," he told Therese. "Let him serve us at table and serve you in bed, my dear sister-in-law. Your sister and I will make it our duty to treat him as a friend, but do not ask us to treat him as a brother-in-law—that would be scandalous!"

With feelings of love and pride at stake there was no room for compromise. La Valette could not conceivably accept Ropiquet as his social equal, and Ropiquet and his sister, whose influence over Therese was complete, persuaded her that the only solution was to leave the family household. The two sisters parted with some bitterness, and for a while they were not on speaking terms, although they continued to dance together. As a result of this rift Fanny lost a number of friends who considered that she should have shown more consideration for her sister's feelings.

Despite this unfortunate development in her private life, Fanny's supremacy on the stage seemed unassailable. The interest which was aroused by the debut of a young Danish ballerina, Lucile Grahn, caused her little concern. She was still the idol of Paris; a new rose was named after her, and she was the object of countless other flattering tributes. But she had lost her wise counsellor. Therese had known exactly what Fanny could and should undertake, and had she been at her sister's elbow when Duponchel suggested that she should take over some of Taglioni's roles, Fanny might well have replied with a wise and firm refusal. Alarmed at the depletion of the ballet repertory after the failure of the last three new productions, Duponchel was desperately searching for a success. Fanny well knew that no ballets suited Taglioni's ethereal quality better than *La Sylphide* and *La Fille du Danube*, yet, encouraged no doubt by La Valette, she yielded to the entreaties of the Director. As was to be expected, the champions of Taglioni were aghast at what they considered presumptuous sacrilege, while even many of her own admirers must have doubted the wisdom of this hazardous enterprise.

"You would have smiled out of pity from the height of your cloud to learn that a simple mortal has dared to separate your name from that of the Sylphide," wrote Sophie Gay, the novelist, to Marie Taglioni after attending the first night of the revival of *La Sylphide* with Fanny Elssler on September 21st, 1838. But if the partisans were unimpressed, several of the more influential critics welcomed the return of such an excellent ballet to the repertory.

Despite an unnerving moment at the beginning, when she struck her foot violently in her rapid ascent up the chimney, Fanny gave a performance which was far from being an imitation of Taglioni's. If she was a more earthbound Sylphide, she was also a more dramatic one, creating an impression by her interpretation rather than by the poetry of movement which was the secret of Taglioni's rendering. Her sister, who had not entirely forsaken her, had again contributed to her success by arranging, to music by Casimir Gide, a *pas de deux* which the two of them danced in perfect harmony.

Gautier had been in London during the summer, and had been present when Taglioni made her reappearance there wearing a profusion of diamonds and emeralds which she had brought back from her triumphant season in Russia. To the Romantic poet such a show of worldly riches seemed to sully the pure poetic genius of the ballerina, and he had not recovered from his disillusionment when, in his review of Fanny's Sylphide, he endeavoured to analyse the contrasting styles of the two dancers.

"Mlle Taglioni, worn out after her interminable travels, is no longer what she was," he began brutally. "She has lost much of her lightness and elevation. When she makes her entrance, she is still that white mist bathed in transparent muslin, that ethereal, chaste vision, that divine delight which we know so well, but after a few bars signs of fatigue appear, she becomes short of breath, perspiration dapples her brow, her muscles grow tense with strain, her arms and bust become flushed. What a few moments before was a real Sylphide is now merely a dancer—the greatest dancer in the world, if you wish, but no more than that. The princes and kings of the North, in their imprudent and merciless admiration, have so applauded her, so bemused her with compliments, buried her under such a shower of flowers and diamonds that they have weighted down those intangible feet which, like those of the amazon Camilla, do not bend the blades of grass she walks upon. They have laden her with so much gold and precious stones that Marie-full-of-grace is unable to resume her flight and can do no more than timidly skim the ground like a bird whose wings have been drenched.

"Today Fanny Elssler is in the full force of her talent; she can only vary her perfection and cannot go further, because beyond the very good is the too good, which is nearer to the bad than one thinks. She is a man's dancer, just as Taglioni was a woman's dancer: she has elegance, beauty, a bold and petulant vigour, extravagant daring, a sparkling smile, and above all an air of Spanish vivacity tempered by a German simplicity which makes her a very charming and adorable creature. When Fanny is dancing, you think a thousand happy thoughts, your imagination strays into palaces of white marble flooded with sunlight and standing out against a deep blue sky, like the friezes of the Parthenon; you imagine yourself leaning on the balustrade of a terrace, with roses above your head, a cup of Syracuse wine in your hand, a white greyhound at your feet, and beside you a beautiful woman in a dress of flesh-coloured velvet, with feathers in her hair; you hear the chatter of tambourines and the silvery tinkle of bells.

"Mlle Taglioni made you think of cool and shaded valleys, whence a white vision suddenly darts forth from the bark of an oak tree before

Fanny Elssler. Miniature by
Ferdinand Waldmüller.

Haydn Museum, Eisenstadt.

Fanny Elssler. Oil painting by
Emile Champmartin, 1839.

Coll. the late Mlle. Carlotta Zambelli.

Fanny Elssler dancing the Cracovienne. Watercolour by C. G.

Coll. the late Miss Lillian Moore.

Fanny Elssler dancing the Tarantella in *La Tarentule*. Lithograph by J. Bouvier.

Victoria and Albert Museum.

the gaze of a surprised and blushing shepherd; she might have been taken for one of those Scottish fairies of whom Walter Scott speaks, who roam in the moonlight by a mysterious fountain, with a necklace of dewdrops and a thread of gold around her waist.

"If I may express it thus, Mlle Taglioni is a Christian dancer and Mlle Elssler is a pagan dancer. The daughters of Miletus, the beautiful Ionians, who were so celebrated in antiquity, must have danced like her.

"So Mlle Elssler, while Mlle Taglioni's roles are not suited to her temperament, can replace her in anything without risk or peril, for she is sufficiently versatile and talented to adapt herself and assume the particular guise of the character. Friday's test showed that Mlle Elssler did not overestimate her ability in undertaking the repertory of her formidable rival . . .

"Mlle Elssler's costume was ravishingly fresh. Her dress might have been cut from dragonfly wings, and her slippers made of satiny lily petals. A crown of convolvulus, of an ideal pink, encircles her brown hair, and behind her white shoulders two little wings of peacock's feathers quiver and shimmer, wings that are superfluous with such feet.

"The new Sylphide was fervently applauded. She displayed infinite delicacy, grace and lightness in her performance. She appeared and vanished like an impalpable vision . . . In the *pas* with her sister she excelled herself; nothing more graceful can be imagined. Her miming, when she is caught by her lover in the folds of the enchanted scarf, expresses sorrow and forgiveness, the sense of fall and irreparable error with rare poetic feeling, and her last long look at her wings as they lie on the earth is a moment of great tragic beauty."

This article caused great annoyance to the supporters of Taglioni, and some of the more militant of them decided to launch a counter-attack when *La Fille du Danube* was revived on October 22nd. They created such an uproar in the theatre that it was difficult to appraise Fanny's performance. A burst of whistling greeted her first entrance, but this was quickly drowned by applause. Her first *pas* showed at once that she was to give an interpretation quite different from Taglioni's. In this dance the heroine pretends to dance badly so as to divert the unwelcome attentions of the Baron. Taglioni had suggested this awkwardness only very superficially and had soon forgotten the demands of the plot, but Fanny acted the whole time, appearing to struggle with her natural desire to dance and every now and then having to be reminded by her sweetheart of the need to keep up the pretence. At the end of this dance whistling was again heard through the cheering.

During the interval the chief of the *claque*, Auguste, called his men together and ordered them to deal severely with any outburst in the next act. At the first sound of whistling, the whole pit seemed to rise to their feet and a pitched battle broke out as the *claqueurs* mercilessly pummelled anyone they suspected of belonging to the small anti-Elssler faction. Many innocent spectators were victims of their excessive zeal. One man who peaceably turned away from the stage in order to read his scenario was beaten up, and so was an innocent neighbour who came to his aid. Many of the occupants of the boxes and amphitheatre, enraged at the hostile reception, shouted encouragement to the *claqueurs* and applauded them as they manhandled the demonstrators from the theatre. Gautier thought it was glorious that Fanny should excite such violent feelings, but she was deeply upset by the fracas and danced most of the ballet in tears.

By now Gautier was in no doubt as to which of the ballerinas he preferred. "To our taste," he admitted in his review, "Mlle Elssler is as good as Mlle Taglioni. First of all she has the immense advantage of being more beautiful and younger. Her pure and noble profile, the elegant shape of her head, and the delicate line of her neck give her the air of an antique cameo of incredible charm. Eyes sparkling with mischief and delight and a smile which is simple and humorous light up and give life to her happy features. Add to these precious gifts her full, rounded arms, a rare quality in a dancer, her supple figure well set on the hips, legs of Diana the huntress which, were they not as mobile, lively and restless as the wings of a bird, might have been sculpted out of Pentelicus marble by some Greek artist of the age of Phidias, and to crown everything, her allurement and her physical charms—*veneres cupidinesque*, as the ancients called those inborn and inexplicable qualities.

"As a ballerina, Mlle Elssler has strength and precision, clear gestures and vigorous *pointes*, a petulant boldness which shows itself in the very Spanish arching of her body, and a happy and serene facility in everything she does, which make her dancing one of the sweetest sights in the world. She also has what Mlle Taglioni did not have, a profound feeling for drama. She dances as well as, and acts better than, her rival."

Fanny's remarkable dramatic talent was now being recognised, and it was perhaps with a view to giving her a role that would take the measure of this gift that Duponchel chose the playwright, Saint-Georges, to write the scenario for her next ballet. It was a happy decision, for *La Gipsy* turned out to be a work of unusual originality. After seeing the general rehearsal, Gautier gave a warning that his readers might find the action "a little cruel for ballet", but promised that Fanny attained such sublime heights in her miming that she would take her place among the greatest tragediennes. This was an exciting claim, which was obviously intended to suggest a comparison with Rachel, the young actress who had recently been shattering the complacency of the Comédie-Française with her burning portrayals of the classical tragedies.

There was no disappointment when the curtain rose on the first performance of *La Gipsy* on January 28th, 1839. Through the collaboration of a new scenarist and a new choreographer, Fanny was given her greatest success since *Le Diable boiteux* and the run of failures which had dogged Duponchel's management was broken. Saint-Georges had not only produced a plot filled with dramatic interest, but had dared to give the ballet a tragic ending, while Joseph Mazilier had responded to the challenge of the scenario by arranging a production that told the story clearly and with great attention to background detail. Musically, the work was inevitably uneven, since each act was written by a different composer. The second act, which contained much of the dramatic action, was the most interesting, being the first work for the Opéra by a young musician, Ambroise Thomas, who was to become one of the great operatic composers of the century. The first and third acts were respectively performed to music by François Benoist and Count Marliani.

Fanny did not appear at all in the first act, in which the heroine Sarah, the daughter of Lord Campbell, is rescued as a child from a wild animal by Stenio, a fugitive Roundhead who has joined a band of gypsies, and is shortly afterwards kidnapped by another gypsy, Trousse-Diable.

Twelve years have passed between this and the second act, which was set in an Edinburgh street by moonlight, with the gypsy tent pitched at one side. Urged on by Trousse-Diable, the gypsies rob a young man as he comes out of a tavern, but their queen, Mab, makes them restore what they have stolen. It was at this moment that Fanny made her first entrance as the grown-up Sarah. Hearing the uproar, the girl emerges from the tent. Stenio runs to her side and takes her in his arms. Mab, who is in love with him too, threatens Sarah for daring to be her rival, but is forced to marry them when Stenio chooses Sarah as his bride. Mab's authority is challenged by Trousse-Diable, who urges the gypsies to refuse to go to the fair. The situation is saved by Sarah, who comes out of the tent, tambourine in hand, to find the gypsies sullenly refusing to move, and soon, by the infectious gaiety of her dancing, has them all on their feet, following her merrily to the fair. This was a brilliant scene which made a great impression on the English critic, H. F. Chorley. "The folk lay couched in fifties," he described, "huddled together in their wild and picturesque clothes as only the French stagemanagers know how to group forms and colours. How she moved hither and thither, quick and bright as a torch, lighting up one sullen heap of tinder after another, gradually animating the scene with motion, till at last the excited rout of vagabonds trooped after her with the wild vivacity of a chorus of Bacchanals, made a picture of many pictures, the brightness and spirit of which stand almost alone in the gallery of similar ones."

The scene then changed to the market place, where the great fair is in progress. The set, described Gautier, was "very beautiful, full of open space, sunshine and light, with a bridge with massive arches revealing bluish crevices of great depth, and the town rising in uneven crystallisations like some enormous madrepore; in short, a view which, according to people who have visited the place, is extremely realistic". The gypsies come darting among the people who throng the fair, and after a while the crowd parts, making room for Fanny and her sister, as Sarah and Mab, to dance a *pas de deux*. This was "one of those delightful dances," wrote Gautier, "in which one is reminded of the beating of dove's wings by the way the two sisters gently flutter and quiver in their white muslin cloud". Then, after a brief pause, Fanny reappeared in another costume to dance a wonderful mazurka, the *Cracovienne*, which Mazilier had designed as a pendant to the famous *Cachucha*. "It was the most coquettish, roguish costume imaginable," went on the enchanted Gautier. "Fanny's trim figure was encased in a white tunic, sparkling with three rows of buttons and galloons of silver braid, which enhanced the bright colours of her blue silk skirt and scarlet boots with their metal heels and tiny golden spurs. Two long plaits tied with red ribbon escaped from a black military cap, which was decorated with a cockade and a white feather." "Was it a woman, a youth, or a sprite?" asked Jules Janin in his review. "No one could tell, for she danced at the same time like a coquettish young woman, like a youth in love, and like a sprite on a fine May morning. In this dance she displayed all her playful graces, her gentle frolicsome smile, and her taking gestures." "It is impossible to describe this dance," added Gautier. "It has a rhythmical precision mingled with a charming abandon, a tense and bounding nimbleness that surpasses one's imagination; and the metallic chatter of her spurs, which are a kind of castanets worn on the heels, accentuates every step and gives the dance a quality of joyous vivacity which is quite irresistible."

Congratulating Sarah on her success, Mab maliciously gives her a miniature, knowing that it will be recognised as the one article which was not returned to the young man after he was robbed. To Mab's delight Sarah is arrested, and in the next scene is brought for trial before Lord Campbell. In a struggle she uncovers the scar on her arm which she received when attacked by the wild animal, and Lord Campbell recognises her as his long-lost daughter. The act closed with a reconciliation. "Sarah is crazy with happiness," described Gautier. "Indeed, the transition is abrupt: from a gypsy to a great lady, from gaol to a drawing room, from the shadows into the light! What a striking change of fortune! What an unexpected recognition, worthy of the romanesque drama! Mlle Elssler, throughout this act, rose to the most sublime heights of tragedy. Noble pride in innocence, energy, tears, grief, love, intoxicating joy—she runs through the whole gamut of human emotions. Only Miss Smithson or Mme Dorval could have attained such transports of pathos, such forceful miming."*

In the third act a ball is to be given to celebrate Sarah's return. Overcome with sadness, Sarah is recalling the carefree days of gypsy life when Stenio climbs through the window. Hearing her father and his guests approach, she conceals him. This was the cue for what Chorley remembered as another highlight of Fanny's performance, "the scene of the minuet danced by the heroine to gain time, and to distract attention from her lover in concealment hard by, whose life was perilled. Lord Byron, when speaking of his own dramas, has subtly dwelt on the power of suppressed passion. Few things have been more fearful than the cold and measured grace of Mlle Fanny Elssler in this juncture, than the manner in which every step was watched, every gesture allowed its right time, so that neither flurry nor faltering might be detected, than the set smile, the vigilant ear, the quivering lip controlling itself. It is in moments like these that Genius rises above talent".

This scene was suddenly interrupted by the appearance of Mab, who gives away Stenio's hiding place. Sarah explains to her shocked father that he is her husband, and at last convinces him that he is not a gypsy but a nobleman in misfortune. During this scene Mab reappears, accompanied by one of the gypsies. A shot rings out and Stenio falls dying. Mad with rage and despair, Sarah rushes at Mab and stabs her, before swooning in her father's arms.

Duponchel was grateful to Fanny for giving him such a success, and watched over her with an almost fatherly concern. When he observed the nervous strain which she endured each time she changed into her *Cracovienne* dress, a costume change that had to be completed during a

* These two actresses had a special appeal for Gautier. Henrietta Smithson was the English Shakespearean actress who created a great impression on the young Romantics when she visited Paris with Charles Kemble's company in 1827; she later married Berlioz. Marie Dorval was the star of many Romantic dramas, and after many years playing in the boulevard theatres was engaged at the Théâtre Français, where in 1835 she created the part of Kitty Bell in de Vigny's *Chatterton*.

short bridging passage of music, he ordered that the ballet should be changed to give her more time.

Meanwhile, relying on her now as his only star ballerina, he had lost no time in starting preparations for a new ballet. This too was designed to exploit her talent as an actress, but in contrast to the drama of *La Gipsy*, the plot of *La Tarentule* was light and amusing. At the end of March Fanny injured herself through falling downstairs and was absent from the stage for a few weeks. To avoid postponing the new work until the autumn, Duponchel purchased a month of her holiday, and *La Tarentule* was presented on June 24th, 1839. There was just time for three performances before she left Paris for London at the end of the month.

To a slight musical accompaniment by Casimir Gide, Scribe's scenario was translated into action by Jean Coralli, the choreographer of *Le Diable boiteux*. Dawn is breaking over an Italian village when the curtain rises, and the hero Luidgi is beginning to serenade his sweetheart Lauretta, when a gang of bandits appears. Luidgi and his friends rescue the lady Clorinde from their clutches, and she rewards him generously before leaving to accept hospitality in a nearby convent. After this Dr Omeopatico, a quack with a thousand cures, makes an imposing entrance. Recently widowed and looking round for a young wife, he is attracted by Lauretta, but she spurns him and explains she is engaged to Luidgi. The village then celebrates Lauretta's engagement, and she dances a sparkling tarantella. Gautier described her costume in loving detail. "A green bodice decorated with silver encloses her supple figure, a very short white gauze skirt reveals her charming legs, worthy of a Greek sculptor, a crown of flowers rests on her brown hair, and castanets chatter at the tips of her fingers . . . The grace, lightness and precision which Lauretta puts into this dance is beyond imagination. It is a thing at once ethereal and forceful, modest and intoxicating, that cannot be described. Sprightliness and passion are blended with rare felicity, the girl's reserve always tempering the very southern fire of this dance." The gaiety of the scene is suddenly shattered as Lauretta comes forward, pale and frightened, to announce that Luidgi has been bitten by a poisonous tarantula. "Mlle Elssler's miming in this scene rose to the very height of sublime tragedy," Gautier continued. "With terrifying truth she portrayed the progress of the malady and the increasing convulsions of the sick man's dancing; the most precise description in speech could not have been clearer than her gestures." Luidgi then enters performing "spasmodic *cabrioles*", finally collapsing exhausted. Omeopatico looks on unfeelingly, and only brings out his cure when Lauretta desperately promises to marry him.

The second act opens in Lauretta's bedroom. While the heartbroken Luidgi goes to seek help from Clorinde, Lauretta has somehow to resist the Doctor's advances on their wedding night. This was a scene which Fanny performed with a wonderful sense of comedy. Left alone with the old man, Lauretta tricks him into leaving the room and locks the door, but he makes his way back through the window. She then eludes him for a time by hiding behind the dressing table, and finally has the idea of pretending that she too has been bitten by a tarantula. She begins with "the prettiest *cabrioles* in the world", which become quicker and quicker. After she has broken the phial of medicine he has offered her, Omeopatico tries to seize her as she leaps and spins about the room with ever-increasing rapidity, administering kicks which, as Gautier noted with amusement, "would not have been disavowed by Deburau, the greatest man in the world for kicks in the behind".* When Lauretta's friends come in, she tells them to pretend she is dead. Omeopatico takes to his heels, pursued by the young men of the village.

The scene changes to the mountainside, near the convent where Clorinde has taken refuge. Lauretta's funeral procession appears. Luidgi, returning from the convent, recognises Lauretta on the bier, but she opens her eyes and motions him to join in the pretence. Omeopatico arrives to recognise Clorinde as his wife whom he had all too prematurely believed killed by bandits. Lauretta then comes to life and is reunited with Luidgi, and the doctor and his wife drive away out of their lives.

Any fears that the public might have been shocked at such a light work being produced on the stage of the Opéra were unrealised. The scene of the funeral procession—"a sort of burlesque parody of *Romeo and Juliet*", as one critic called it—had indeed caused a little concern during rehearsals, but Auguste, the leader of the *claque*, had finally reassured Duponchel by telling him: "Never fear, I shall take the death gaily."

Exhilarated by two triumphant creations in the past six months, and acclaimed on all sides as a dancer-actress with a remarkably wide range from light comedy to tragedy, Fanny left Paris for London with Therese, unaware of the disenchantment in store for her on her return only a few weeks later.

---

* Jean-Gaspard Deburau was the great mime of his day. His pantomimes were among the most popular entertainments of the Paris boulevards, and were memorable for his pathetic rendering of the character of Pierrot.

IX

Preparations for the American Tour

ON HER ARRIVAL IN LONDON in the summer of 1839 Fanny faced
another confrontation with Taglioni. For the past month Taglioni had
been gathering triumphs at the King's Theatre in her father's ballet,
La Gitana, which had been created for her during her visit to St Petersburg the previous winter. An insinuating suggestion had been made
that Fanny's recent success, *La Gipsy*, was no more than a copy of this,
but this was untrue. Both ballets were original, and it was purely a
coincidence that the heroine of each was a girl stolen in childhood by
gypsies. What was deliberate, however, was the inclusion in *La Gitana* of
a Spanish character dance, in which Taglioni attempted to challenge
Fanny on the latter's own ground.

For Fanny it was not a propitious moment to appear at the King's
Theatre when Taglioni's success in *La Gitana* was so fresh. She and her
sister made their first appearance of the season on July 11th in a *pas de
deux*, and hurriedly staged *La Gipsy*, which was included in the
programme just two weeks later. It was performed eight times before
the season closed, but in spite of its spectacular scenery by Grieve
and Fanny's "fine melodramatic acting", it did not achieve its full
effect.

Fanny had no complaint about the manner in which the English
critics reviewed her performances. Indeed their impartiality and in-
corruptibility was a refreshing change from the intrigue and self-
interest with which the theatrical press in Paris was riddled. In London
the critics were not found backstage, and there was no unwritten
obligation to reward them for their favour; on the contrary, the offer
of a banknote—acceptable, even expected, by some critics in Paris—
would be considered an insult.

When she returned to Paris after what had appeared, on the evidence
of her reception by the London public, to be a successful season, Fanny
was appalled to find everyone talking about an abject failure. It was not
difficult to trace the source of these tales. A certain French critic, J.
Chaudes-Aigues, had been sending articles from London proclaiming
the complete victory of Taglioni. Falsely reporting that Fanny had

danced in the same ballet as Taglioni, he had declared that everyone considered that the comparison was bound to be fatal to the younger dancer. "What an imprudence on the part of Fanny Elssler!" he exclaimed. "Worse than an imprudence, it was childishness. Unfortunately there comes a time in life, even to a pretty woman—and Mlle Elssler has learnt this—when one can no longer be childish."

Such unfair, even dishonest, reporting was not only wounding to Fanny's pride but also, as was no doubt intended, damaging to her reputation. Though Fanny made no reply or protest, her friends seethed with indignation, and Théophile Gautier raised the subject when he wrote and asked her to send details of her next London season. "You remember," he told her, "how the newspapers, full of letters written from London, mistreated you. It would be good to remedy this little setback, which had no real foundation at all but which made some impression on people who are always ready to accept the judgment of others."

Somehow Fanny had lost the goodwill of a section of the Paris press which, though notoriously venal, was none the less powerful. To her chagrin she found herself assailed in a venomous campaign that was continued into the following year by Charles Maurice, who not long before had been one of her warmest champions. With malicious delight, he now reported how she had reappeared at the Opéra after her return from London, "still quite crippled from her recent fall in London at the feet of Mlle Taglioni. So conscious was she of this that she sought consolation from a swarm of *claqueurs*, whose cure was totally ineffective". Maurice reported that the house was quite empty, and emptier still two days later. Although it was August, there was some truth in this statement. Receipts for the rest of the year were disappointingly low, sometimes dropping to little more than 2,000 francs and only once rising above 4,000 francs, when a performance of *La Gipsy* at the end of September drew nearly 6,000 francs. Another source of disappointment was that Lucile Grahn, who had now been permanently engaged, was drawing almost as many spectators as she.

Fanny felt the unfairness of this hostile campaign most keenly. "Ah, these men of the press!" she declared, "the terror of their craft; doubtless they are meant to secure some good end, else why do they live and prosper? The enlightened friends of art, and foes to all oppressive authority, I hear them styled, when I have sometimes murmured at their usurpation; but how impossible it is to hold power without abusing it, and how cruelly do these enemies of absolute control tyrannise over us poor artists! A thoughtless word, an absent look, an idle jest may seal our luckless doom. Should their high displeasure be incurred, what would be left us but the loss of position and bright renown—all we have and all we hope for—and thus are we bowed down in abject submission."

It was significant that these malicious attacks were being made by that very section of the press which was used by theatre managers to advertise their attractions. So devious were the intrigues behind the campaign that no one knew for certain what motives activated it. Had Fanny, or her advisers, caused offence by lack of expected generosity? Was it part of a campaign to extol Lucile Grahn at her expense? Whatever its inspiration, it had the effect of weakening the ties that bound her to Paris and impelling her towards a new adventure more exciting in prospect than any other experience in her career.

The extraordinary proposition that she should visit America had first been made to her by Seguin, the London theatrical agent, in the summer of 1838. Later that same year she and her sister had been offered a six months' engagement at the Park Theatre, New York. Though Seguin had urged acceptance, the very thought of dancing in such a remote corner of the globe seemed preposterous and the matter was dropped. In any event, Fanny was contractually bound to the Opéra until the summer of 1841, and in the summer of 1839 she signed another engagement with Duponchel extending her commitment by a further four years on the same terms.

Thousands of miles away in New York, the management of the Park Theatre was not prepared to accept Fanny's refusal as final. The dominant partner, Stephen Price, saw in her engagement the means of retrieving the fortunes of the house which had been shattered by the economic panic of 1837 and by competition from Wallack's National Theatre. To a man of Price's experience and connections, it seemed a very feasible project. He had been associated with the Park Theatre for some thirty years, and was as much at home in London as in his native New York; for a time he had been lessee of Drury Lane, he was a member of the Garrick Club, and he and his young wife kept a fine establishment in Russell Square. For him, therefore, Paris was within comparatively easy reach, and he resolved to make a personal approach to the dancer. Not knowing her personally, nor anyone close to her, he decided to seek the assistance of an American friend.

Henry Wikoff was a wealthy young man of twenty-seven who had spent several years travelling in Europe, satisfying a passionate curiosity in the affairs of the world by observing and, where possible, gaining the acquaintance of great men and women of his time. The stage held a special fascination for him, and he had already shown a natural talent as an impresario by arranging the London debut of Edwin Forrest, the

American tragedian, whom he had wisely counselled on the choice of play for the occasion.

Price found his young friend quietly reading in his study, unaware of the new chapter in his life which was about to open. He came to the point at once. Explaining that he was on the verge of bankruptcy, he outlined his plan to engage Fanny Elssler to dance at the Park Theatre for forty nights. "I will give her half the house, less the expenses," he declared. "This ought to put $30,000 in my pocket, which will tide me over my difficulties. Will you aid me?"

Wikoff restrained his excitement and tried to take a realistic view. "Fanny Elssler," he pointed out, "would be as likely to embark for the moon as go to America. Besides, the Director of the Opéra would oppose it desperately. Moreover, I don't know her."

Price would not be put off, and when the door had closed behind him Wikoff had been persuaded to secure him an interview with the dancer. This was not a difficult undertaking, for it happened that he was acquainted with the Marquis de La Valette. As he expected, the Marquis was to be found at the exclusive Jockey Club. Wikoff must have half expected a rebuff, but surprisingly La Valette fell in with the idea at once and invited Wikoff to bring Price to meet Fanny at her apartment at No. 39 Rue Laffitte the very next afternoon.

The two Americans were punctual, but the dancer and her protector were already waiting for them. They soon got down to business. While Fanny sat listening serenely, she was observing the visitors with keen curiosity. They were the first Americans she had met at close quarters. It was Price who interested her the more. He was "an oldish man, stout, and cross-looking, stiff in movement, slow of speech, with a very sharp eye", but she noted in his favour that his manners were gentlemanly and that he seemed frank and businesslike.

Price was pleased with the results of this first interview. "A mighty simple, unpretending sort of a body," he observed to Wikoff as they walked back through the streets of Paris. "I expected something very different."

Wikoff's initial reluctance to become involved with Price's managerial problems was already wearing thin. This was due, as he admitted to himself, not so much to pity for Price in his misfortune as to the charms of Fanny herself. "I was struck by her quiet lady-like appearance," he recalled. "She was above medium height, and divinely formed, as I had often seen her on the stage. Her features were well shaped, and the eyes, of dark grey, wonderfully soft and gentle. Her head was beautifully shaped, the countenance singularly sweet and winning. Every movement was the incarnation of grace. What puzzled me was that so meek and placid a creature should have made such a *furore* in Europe, on and off the stage. One would have supposed, from her retiring air and modest deportment, that she had been reared in a convent, or had budded in some 'cool sequestered vale,' far away from the haunts of men and the purlieus of the opera-house. Could she be as innocent and confiding as she looked? Had the admiration of suitors, the enthusiasm of multitudes, the homage of princes, fallen unnoticed on the ground? Could she have walked, or rather danced, over so many hot ploughshares without scorching her tiny feet? Was it possible to live in the malarious atmosphere in which she had been bred, and preserve purity of mind, goodness of heart, and sincerity of character? It seemed to me wellnigh incredible."

When Price had to return to London with nothing settled, Wikoff readily agreed to look after his interests and do what he could to persuade Fanny to sign the desired contract. The task was made infinitely more agreeable when La Valette encouraged him to see Fanny as often as he wished to remove her apprehensions at embarking on what she regarded as a very perilous adventure. However, it was still very doubtful whether the project could be realised, for, as La Valette explained, Fanny was entitled to only three months' holiday in the year, which would not be time enough, and it seemed unlikely that Duponchel would release her for longer because of the effect that her absence would have on the box office.

La Valette must have been surprised by the ease with which he persuaded Duponchel to extend Fanny's leave of absence. It was settled that Fanny should be released from her duties at the Opéra from March 1st to August 15th, 1840, and a contract was drawn up under which she was to arrive in New York early in April and dance at the Park Theatre on thirty-six evenings until the end of June; the receipts were to be divided equally between Price and herself after a deduction of $150, and on her benefit nights the receipts were to be shared without any deduction.

On October 8th the Marquis and Wikoff took the contract to Fanny's apartment. At the sight of the fateful document, she was overwhelmed with apprehensions. She would have dearly liked to forget the whole business, but she could not let down her two friends at this late stage. So, with great trepidation, she took the pen and signed her name at the foot of the page. Wikoff then added his signature as Price's agent, and La Valette signed as witness.

It was only then that La Valette revealed his motive in supporting the American project. His explanation, however, that he had been ordered to join a diplomatic mission to Persia may have been only half the story, for rumour had it that he had been forced to apply to the

Prime Minister for a salaried post after running through his fortune and being no longer able to borrow. "When I am gone," he said to Wikoff, "there will be no one here to give advice to Fanny, and she will be at the mercy of a silly mischievous crowd, who will torment her life out. She expresses the utmost confidence in your straightforwardness and good feeling, and begs that you will allow her to consult you when occasion demands . . . More than that, I would like to ask you to look after her welfare in Paris up to the time of her departure. She needs a friend to guide her, and it would make me comfortable to think I had provided her one who could be trusted." He only regretted that Wikoff could not go to New York with her, "for how she is to get on there without speaking the language, and utterly ignorant of business, I cannot imagine".

Just a week later Fanny accompanied the Marquis as far as the first post on his journey. Duponchel breathed a sigh of relief at seeing this nuisance depart, and at once tongues began to wag with conjectures of who would replace the Marquis in Fanny's affections. It was rumoured that she had tender feelings for Lucien Petipa, with whom she rehearsed *La Tarentule* not only at her apartment but also in her dressing-room, and there was a story that she had had to defend herself against the advances of the artist, Emile Champmartin, whose portrait of her had been exhibited in the 1839 Salon.

All this was idle gossip, for Fanny remained scrupulously loyal to La Valette. If she was developing another close friendship, it was not with a suitor but with a remarkable English lady whom she had first met when dancing in London in 1838. Harriet Grote had entered Fanny's life with an introduction from Gentz's friend, Rahel von Varnhagen, and the two women, so dissimilar in temperament and social background, found themselves immediately attracted to one another. Mrs Grote was a formidable character who quite overshadowed her brilliant but retiring husband, George Grote, who was preoccupied with his parliamentary duties and his study of ancient Greek history. While they both delighted in intellectual company, there was a side to Mrs Grote's character that her husband did not so fully share. She was a bohemian; she felt an affinity with artists, whom she liked to patronise, and to the amusement of her contemporaries, who were not accustomed to such individuality in women, she was eccentric. "Now I know the meaning of the word 'Grotesque'," her friend Sydney Smith had quipped one evening at a party, when she made an entrance wearing a striking pink turban. And it was again he who, when asked his opinion of the Grotes, replied: "I like them, I like them, I like him, he is so ladylike; and I like her, she is such a perfect gentleman."

Fanny became fascinated by this strange Englishwoman. Mrs Grote's intellectual superiority, the ease with which she conversed with statesmen and scholars, her boldness of thought and expression, were characteristics that seemed almost out of place in a woman. So too was her decisiveness. "She never crosses the room," Fanny observed, "without her mind being made up to do it." Fanny at first found Mrs Grote rather intimidating, but she was soon captivated by the warmth of her personality, her kindness, sympathy and tolerance. Further, her knowledge of music and her artistic gifts were qualities which the ballerina specially appreciated, no less indeed than her almost masculine skill in driving a four-in-hand. Soon the two women were enjoying one another's company as though they had known each other all their lives. "With me," Fanny wrote, "she is as playful, simple and unsophisticated as a child."

Harriet Grote exerted all her charm to gain Fanny's friendship. Quixotically, she dreamed of being able, as she put it, "to aid her to acquire a competency that she may quit the opera house, whose associations are uncongenial to her", but for the present she offered more practical assistance to further the success of her forthcoming visit to America.

"I write to you," she addressed her friend, Mrs Jameson, in London, "to beg . . . that you will lend me your assistance to carry out my views of being serviceable to our *Pet*, F.E., whose welfare I have steadily at heart, and not less so since I have had further opportunities of conversing with and observing her . . . I am getting a little 'endways' in Fanny's good graces, and flatter myself she is becoming more disposed to unfold herself to me, but you cannot think how reserved I found her at first, and how ticklish a game I have found it to push our conversation further than the neutral topics on which people, not on intimate terms, commonly discourse. However, I consider myself now 'en bon train', but as my stay here [in Paris] will be only a short one, (say till the 18 or 20 Decr.) I want you to aid me in forming a sort of plan (which I may lay before her also) for her to be made more happy and comfortable in America during the visit she has covenanted to pay them there in the spring. I shall strain all my little 'canvass' to reach this object, and shall, for her, incur, or at least consent to incur, personal obligations to such of my American acquaintances as will hold out the hand of sympathy and good feeling to this gifted member of a debased profession, on her arrival at New York . . . Now will you ask Fanny Butler and C. Sedgwick to take notice of her? Or are there any others you think you could influence favourably? . . . If you come to Paris before I go, (which I devoutly desire) we can devise better, together, our means than asunder, wherefore I pray you to try 'to wind up your ends' and trot off to the Tower to embark your dear self for the port of Boulogne. We have only seen F *dance* twice since we came. She never appears *more* than once a week, and seems to be in the highest possible favour at the 'Academie'! Last night, (I resume since yesterday this letter) we saw her in the 'Tarentule.' I never admired her more, soit pantomime, soit dance [*sic*]. Farthermore I *laughed* to excess, as did my two female companions . . . whom I took with me. As for Mr G he was so absorbed in his divinity that he could not laugh, but his attention was rivetted to her during every scene.

"He pays her the most charming compliments, some of them *extravagant*, which *she receives* with an entire calmness and indifference of manner, as tho' she were so used to incense that it made no sort of impression upon her! He says he does not care for that, as he only utters them to 'let off' the current of his own admiration, and not to ingratiate himself with her, which *I* believe to a certain degree."

Meanwhile, discharging the pleasant task given him by La Valette, Wikoff was paying regular visits to Fanny's apartment, often in answer to little notes summoning him to advise her on some new matter that had arisen. Often he had to remove fears planted in her mind by persons who, for various reasons of their own, were endeavouring to dissuade her from leaving Paris. They told her she would never be paid; that her dressing-room would be regularly robbed; that there was no safety in the hotels, and the law gave no protection; that she would be hissed if she dared show her legs; that her private life would be ruthlessly invaded by the scurrilous newspaper press. Others, more subtly, insinuated that she could never hope to find the success she was accustomed to in a country which was still being cut out of its primeval forests, where life was often hard and where few could enjoy the luxuries of life. The taste which was essential to enjoy so refined an art as ballet was not to be found in the United States. Had Wikoff not been at hand, Fanny might well have been swayed by these arguments. But her confidence in him was daily increasing, and she was convinced when he pointed out that these ridiculous notions came from people who had never crossed the Atlantic in their lives. Far from her not being appreciated there, he added, her appearance in the States, where no other ballerina of her standing had been seen, would bring her fame and profit beyond her most sanguine expectations.

Duponchel was now regretting his moment of generosity, for he wanted her to take the leading role in the next new ballet, *Le Diable amoureux*. He offered to indemnify her and even raise her salary if she would break her contract with Price, but Fanny was not to be tempted.

Her relations with Duponchel had not been improved by what she considered to be a breach of good faith on his part. Persuaded perhaps by La Valette, she had claimed the sole right to dance the title-role in *La Sylphide*. One day, when this ballet was billed, she had fallen sick shortly before the performance, and Duponchel, instead of changing the programme, had presented Lucile Grahn in the part. Fanny was sure he had done this only in an attempt to lower her prestige, and had been so angry that she had torn up her contract in little pieces and sent it to the Director.

Affronts such as this and the campaign against her in Charles Maurice's paper were enough to give her a distaste for Paris, and she began to see the American tour not merely as a welcome escape but as a romantic adventure. But not all the difficulties had yet been removed. It was now convincingly suggested to her that the contract was weighted in Price's favour, and she became so worried about this that she sent one of her little notes to Wikoff, who arrived to find her sitting alone and very agitated in her boudoir.

"I want you to alter my contract," she said. "My friends tell me you have outwitted La Valette, and bound me hand and foot to Price."

Unable to convince her that the contract was fair, Wikoff pointed out that only Price could modify its terms. Pressed, he offered to write to Price at once, but that did not satisfy Fanny.

"No!" she exclaimed, seizing his hand, "that will not calm my fears. I shall not sleep tonight if you do not pledge me it shall be changed as I wish."

Reflecting that the changes demanded were not very significant, he gave his word that Price would vary the contract. Fanny's delight was startling, and for a moment Wikoff fancied she was going to embrace him. Instead, she went on tell him that an English friend, who was worried about the arrangements that were being made, wished to meet him.

So the two friends met, and liked one another from the outset. "I wished to know you," Mrs. Grote said to the young American, "as you have shown so much interest in the fortunes of my amiable *protégée*, and hope we shall be good friends."

It became their joint task to further Fanny's respectability by launching her into society. Wikoff found it a simple matter to present her to the leading gentlemen of the American colony in Paris, but their ladies were not so accommodating. Mrs Adeline Welles was willing to recommend her friends in the States to go to the theatre and see her dance, but baulked at the idea of asking them to make her acquaintance. Told that Mrs Grote had recommended Fanny to an American lady she

Harriet and George Grote.

Haydn Museum, Eisenstadt.

ny Elssler in practice costume.
Drawing by Mrs Harriet Grote.

British Museum.

Fanny Elssler. Miniature by
Mme. de Mirbel, 1838.

Bibl. de l'Opéra, Paris.

Fanny Elssler. Lithograph by
A. Newsam from a daguerreotype
by Cornelius of Philadelphia, 1841.

Harvard Theatre Collection.

knew, she replied tartly: "I do not know the American lady to whom it is addressed, but I know this much, that if Mrs G possesses common sense she will not undertake to make reforms among opera-dancers. Not that I do not believe Fanny Elssler to be a very interesting person, but there must be a line drawn between a woman *sold* and a woman *given*." Her husband, Samuel Welles the banker, however, took a liking to Fanny, whom he found *"très comme il faut"*, and Mrs Welles finally asked Wikoff how she could best arrange to meet her. Sensing that the moment was ripe, Wikoff argued that her social position was too firm to be affected by idle tongues and persuaded her to display her American independence of character. So Fanny received an invitation to the Welles' sumptuous mansion in the Place Saint-Georges. Adeline Welles was enchanted with her guest, who arrived dressed with great simplicity, and after dinner she offered her her arm and took her on a tour of the reception rooms. This first successful meeting was followed up with a supply of letters of introduction which were added to a growing pile, provided, thanks to the efforts of Wikoff and Harriet Grote, by General Cass, the American Minister to France, Baron Rothschild, Christopher Hughes, the United States *chargé d'affaires* in Stockholm, and others.

Harriet Grote's efforts were producing results, and before she left Paris she arranged a *soirée* for the purpose of enabling Fanny to meet some eminent people who might be useful to her. When Wikoff arrived he was astonished at the distinguished company his hostess had assembled. There was Victor Cousin, Gustave de Beaumont and his wife, who was a granddaughter of Lafayette, and Alexis de Tocqueville, author of a study of democracy in America. When Fanny entered the room the whole company turned to observe her. "She was simply attired in a robe of black velvet, and wore very little ornament," Wikoff recalled. "Her easy graceful manner, as she crossed the room to greet her hostess, charmed the company. If she had passed her whole life amid philosophers and members of the Institute, she could not have been more natural and unembarrassed, yet modest withal. Her engaging simplicity, repose, and elegance gradually won upon the sympathies of all, who found it difficult to reconcile their preconceived notions of a brilliant *danseuse* with the quiet unpretending person before them."

Now that the legal formalities were concluded, Fanny had to concern herself with a thousand and one preparations. Eventful as her career had been, she had never been so busy before. As well as performances and rehearsals at the Opéra there were dinner parties, portrait sittings, fittings at the dressmaker's, English lessons, and countless other tasks which filled nearly every moment of the day. Then she had to obtain the music and detailed scenarios of the ballets she was to dance in New York, and at her own expense order her wardrobe, both for stage and every-day use. As each box arrived from her dressmaker's, the costumes were taken out and tried on before the admiring eyes of her cousin and companion, Katti Prinster, while so many pairs of ballet slippers were delivered from Janssen's that she had to explain to the astonished Wikoff that she seldom used less than three pairs in an evening. "The slightest soil condemns them," she told him, "and that upon the dirtiest stage in the world, purposely kept so to avoid slipping."

To ensure that she should be in the best condition, she took a private class every day from Auguste Vestris, now a feeble, wrinkled old man nearing his eightieth birthday. Why she should choose to leave the Paris Opéra, which he looked upon as the very summit of earthly glory, he could not begin to comprehend. Semi-barbarous England, where he had himself gained triumphs in his youth more than half a century before, was bad enough, but the very thought of America convinced him that she had taken leave of her senses. Nevertheless he was so fond of her that he made the effort to come to the studio, telling her that playing the fiddle for her classes was his only remaining pleasure.

Then, suddenly, an unforeseen calamity struck. Henry Wikoff brought Fanny a letter sealed with black wax. It was from Edmund Simpson, Price's partner in New York, and it announced the death of Stephen Price. Fanny was very shocked by this news. Her few meetings with Price and the generous tone of his letters had done much to allay her fears. It was only a few days since she had heard from him agreeing to whatever conditions she cared to name, if only she would come. Now, realising that she would not be able to rely on the experience and ability of this trusted friend, her confidence was greatly shaken. Her contract had been with Price personally, and she was advised that she was free to abandon the project if she chose. Her first impulse was to do so, but when Simpson begged her not to disappoint the people who were look-ing forward to her appearance in New York and explained that he would suffer a serious loss if she did not come, she felt morally bound to proceed. Moreover, she had already gone to much trouble and expense in preparing for the tour, and she realised that if she cancelled her plans the Opéra would see confirmation of their belief that the American project was only a ruse to obtain better terms.

On Wikoff's suggestion, it was decided to take the opportunity to redraw the contract, incorporating some desired changes. In particular the date of her appearance in New York was put forward by a few weeks to enable her to accept an offer to dance in London in the spring. An additional clause was also inserted imposing a penalty of $2,500 on the

Park Theatre if certain conditions were not fulfilled. All this would inevitably result in delay, for Simpson's reply could not be expected until the middle of March, by which time Fanny would already be in London, but surprisingly this did not seem to concern her. "That will do," she told Wikoff, "I will take all my costumes for America with me, and if Mr Simpson's reply is unfavourable, I will bring them back to Paris, pocketing the loss. *Voilà tout.*"

Wikoff then assumed the responsibility of conducting the negotiations for the London season with Pierre Laporte, who had approached Fanny in a manner typical of that headstrong, unbusinesslike manager. Fanny had been taking a drive when, hearing her name shouted from the pavement, she perceived Laporte waving at her. She ordered her coachman to stop, and Laporte came running up through the mud and excitedly put forward the proposition which was to result in a London engagement in the spring. Although in the past their business relations had not always been satisfactory, Fanny admired Laporte not only for his talent as an actor but also for his intelligence, his good manners and his warm personality. But he was notoriously unreliable. Luxury-loving and extravagant, he often neglected business for pleasure, spending, so it was said, whole nights carousing to the detriment of his health. Behind the veneer of his charm lay a crafty mind, and Wikoff did well to impose a condition that Fanny's fee of 180 guineas was to be paid on the morning following each performance.

She was now in the throes of preparing for her benefit performance, which had been fixed to take place on January 30th, 1840. It was her responsibility to arrange the programme, and this necessitated personal approaches to the leading actors, singers and dancers whom she hoped would give their services. Much patience and tact was required, as Edouard Monnais must have realised when he received a letter from her reporting the arrangements she had made. "Mme Persiani and M. Tamburini have consented to sing with pleasure," she began, "but only M. Tamburini will sing in costume, and as I have told him that M. Duprez and Mlle Garcia will sing the last act of *Othello*, he had told me he wants to sing the duet from the second act with Duprez. We must find out whether this suits M. Duprez. Mme Persiani wants to sing two pieces, and if you can persuade Mario to sing, everything will be arranged. Although I do not see how it is possible to make Mme Persiani sing in costume, she has agreed to sing, even in the concert. Everything is going well, as you see."

To accommodate all of Fanny's friends and well-wishers, the benches of the pit had to be converted into stalls. The presence of ladies in this part of the theatre was an unusual sight, for only men were usually admitted there. The curtain rose at half past seven on the first item in the programme, Molière's *Le Bourgeois Gentilhomme*, carelessly acted (in Gautier's opinion) by the Comédie-Française and inordinately spun out by the interpolation of songs and dances, many of which were strangely out of keeping with the period of the piece. For the final scene Therese had arranged a new *pas de châle*, full of ravishing poses and floating transparent draperies, and performed with the precision which only the two sisters could achieve.

Then, after a brief pause, Fanny returned alone to perform a new *pas de caractère*, *La Smolenska*. Wearing a smart costume which Gautier described as "coquettishly bohemian", with velvet collar and cuffs and tops of her boots to match, she seemed even prettier than ever. The dance was a young girl's dream of love, beginning with a tremor of the feet which gradually spread to the whole body. Then, to a lively, bouncing rhythm, she darted, like some frightened animal, about the great stage, while the orchestra played so softly that Gautier wondered whether the musicians were invisible. In every movement there was an easy, voluptuous freedom which thrilled the audience. When she finally came to rest with a triumphant toss of her head, the whole house seemed to explode with applause, and a shower of flowers scattered on the stage at her feet. One of the bouquets, she noticed, came from the box of Dr Véron, who had first engaged her to dance in Paris. The demands for an encore were too insistent to ignore, and the public was treated to a repeat of this brilliant new dance.

The evening was still young. There followed the second act of Rossini's opera *Othello*, and the programme concluded with a revival of *Nina*. This sentimental ballet from Napoleonic times seemed sadly insipid and old-fashioned to the taste of 1840. Janin, who had found the ballet very boring, thought that Fanny seemed ill at ease. "She weeps without sorrow," he wrote, "she loses all her delicacy and grace. I would give all these great roles for just one movement from the *Smolenska*." Théophile Gautier, however, saw her with the eyes of a Romantic and, like many others that evening, was overwhelmed by her dramatic interpretation. "In her hands," he wrote, "the mad girl of the comic opera has become Shakespearean, a worthy sister to Ophelia, a white and slender vision whose eyes alone seemed alive, shining feverishly in a marble-white face that is as pallid as a Greek statue in moonlight. At the end of the ballet, when she sees that her lover is not dead, as she had believed, a phosphorescent radiance of sublime happiness bathes her face in luminous waves, forming, as it were, a halo: it is hard to give a better rendering of an unhoped for happiness and the bursting of an overflowing heart. As a mime, Mlle Elssler has no rival, and we can hardly think of anyone but Miss Smithson to compare with her." It was half-past one when the performance ended and the exhausted public went home to their beds.

So close had Fanny and Harriet Grote become that Fanny missed her friend greatly when she returned to London in January. During their walks in the Tuileries Gardens, Fanny had told the story of her life and been surprised to find how strange and romantic it seemed to her friend. Discarding her natural reserve, she had allowed herself to reveal her thoughts with a freedom she had seldom before indulged in with a friend. She found great comfort in Harriet's concern at the wounds she had suffered from scandal and calumny, and she freely told her about her friendships with Gentz, La Valette and other men who had figured in her life. Harriet restrained her reforming zeal and contented herself with the comment that one must bear the burden of one's sins and hope that one's virtues and expiatory sacrifices will outweigh them.

Harriet Grote was annoyed that Fanny did not write to her at once after she had left Paris, but she received an account of her benefit from Wikoff. In London she continued to concern herself with Fanny's interests, and made no secret of her friendship with the dancer. "I understood from my private friends," she told Wikoff, "that my intimacy with Fanny has been the subject of the greatest astonishment, and the general surmise is that I am deceived by her. No one has dared to allude to it to me, but from what I hear, I rather expect it will be tolerated in me as an odd caprice, and is not likely at all to injure me in my relations with society. I shall go on cautiously, and abstain from talking of Fanny, as I feel persuaded that no one will believe her to be what *we* know her to be. I believe Lady Blessington's jealousy of d'Orsay's admiration of Fanny Elssler to have been the fertile source of many abominable slanders against her. All my information *ends* in Lady B's circle, for each foul tongue seems to take its cue thence. Poor dear Fanny! Well, the venom shall not poison the stream of *my* kind sympathy towards this gifted woman. Long will *I* fight for her, through evil report and good report, so she be but *worthy* of my quixotic devotion, and capable of affection . . . I will stick by Fanny so long as she will love me and be discreet. If she prove insensible, I droop. Pride and temperament alike forbid a struggle of one side only." Then, after mentioning that she would be attending one of Queen Victoria's Drawing-rooms, she continued: "But, ah, no gorgeous *entourage* of Queen Victoria's proud Court will ever outvie the powerful trains of emotion with which I sat a guest at Fanny Elssler's table, and received the gentle *devoirs* of its enchanting hostess, dight with the rare gems of Nature, and beaming with conscious charms of person and mind. And the *salle de danse!* You and I, I trust, shall many a time and oft recur to that teeming glance we exchanged under the influence of a common fascination . . . Mr G feels all this sort of thing; but then he covers it over with such a thick waterproof veil that his sympathy is next to useless all the while. He is as bad as Fanny herself for reserve and external masking of emotion— which is saying much."

Scarcely a week later Wikoff received another letter from Mrs Grote, telling him that although she had still received no word from Fanny, she had reserved rooms for her in London from March 6th, "because there is a great scarcity near us, and the people would not warrant them being *disponible* in another week, or even another day. And these lodgings, I fancy, would not have been let to any theatrical person, only that I pledged myself from the respectability, &c., as round hereabout the folks are rather particular, and I shall have to lend her plate and linen as it is. However, all I said I would do shall be done, but I own I am seriously hurt at F's indifference . . . Mr G is as sore as I am . . ."

Wikoff advised Fanny to write at once to Mrs Grote, whose next letter informed him she had at last heard from the "proud hussy". "I do not marvel at your saying she is a *beau masque*," she commented.

Fanny was to leave Paris on Wednesday, March 4th, and when Wikoff went to say goodbye he found her carriage already at her door. The dancer seemed dejected and apprehensive. The thought of the great distance she was to travel and her ignorance of the English language appalled her. If only he could accompany her, she told him plaintively, she would have no fear. He explained that as much as he would like to do so, circumstances forbade it. His position would be open to mis-construction; some would suspect him of being her lover, and others would see him as a grasping manager. And furthermore, what would his friends and relatives think? At that moment Fanny's cousin, Katti Prinster, entered the room to announce that all was ready.

"Will you promise to come to London to see me off?" she begged. "It will encourage me."

"If I can manage it, I will."

"If you fail," replied Fanny, "I don't believe I shall ever go."

Therese was there too to see her off.* Their artistic partnership had ended, and the rift, begun when La Valette had entered Fanny's life, had been widened by her opposition to the American adventure. Her absence made Fanny all the more aware that a new phase in her life was beginning as her carriage rattled and splashed over the rough and muddy roads, with the rain beating against the windows and the wind

---

* Therese Elssler then went to Hamburg, where she first appeared as guest artist on March 28th, 1840, as Zoloé in *Le Dieu et la Bayadère*.

whistling outside. Boulogne was alseep when they arrived at eleven o'clock that night, just an hour before the steam packet for England was due to leave. There was barely time to stretch their weary limbs before they were summoned aboard. Fanny and Katti went down into the confined and smelly cabin, and at once realised from the rolling of the ship that boisterous weather awaited them outside the harbour. Almost at once poor Fanny was stricken with "sea-sickness and every concomitant horror."

She reached her lodgings in Belgrave Square late on Friday afternoon, and while Katti remained behind to unpack, went to pay a call on the Grotes and stayed to dinner. The next morning, still half asleep, she attended a rehearsal, and that same evening she made her appearance before the public in *La Gipsy*. The London critics noticed that she was thinner, but she betrayed no sign of fatigue in her performance, and in the *Cracovienne* she "provoked one of the noisiest encores she ever commanded".

Jean-Baptiste Barrez, the original Dr Omeopatico, had come to London to produce *La Tarentule* with all possible haste so that as many performances as possible could be given before Fanny sailed for New York. It was feared that the last scene of the original production, with its mock funeral, might cause offence to the more susceptible London public, and so it was cut, the ballet ending with the final explanations taking place in the bedroom scene. This scene too had been changed so as not to shock the London audience—by the removal of the bed!

Harriet Grote was concerned for Fanny's health. "I think I never saw her look worse—worn and haggard," she wrote in a letter to Wikoff. "She has been worked like a post-horse to 'mount' her new ballet, the *Tarentule*, daily, and even twice a day, returning after dinner to stage slavery! . . . I have a great deal to say to you about her . . . Your definition of '*un beau masque*' so far fits perfectly. Whether you or I shall ever dive deeper into that heart of hers remains to be seen."

La Tarentule was given on March 21st, just fifteen days after Fanny had arrived in London. For some reason it had been decided not to lower a drop curtain at the end of the first act, and the audience expected the ballet to be played straight through without a break. "Delusive hopes!" commented *The Times*. "First came a footman with a watering pot, and slowly and deliberately watered the whole stage before their eyes; then came two or three more with a table and looking glass, which they circumspectly and tardily arranged. *Exeunt* footmen; *manet* the stage completely empty. Thus it lasted for a long time, and John Bull had all the luxury of gazing on vacancy, without even the ceremony of a drop-scene!"

Despite this strange interlude, Fanny's performance electrified the audience and inspired *The Times* critic to write a detailed account. She, he wrote, "was herself the ballet, its centre and its circumference. It was all Fanny Elssler, and the little *pas* without her were merely to give her breathing time. Such a continued flow of animation, such a long deep draught of inspiration, is rarely seen. The manner in which she darted between two *danseuses* in the first act, and went through one of the wildest figures with almost a ferocity of spirit, was electrifying, it was a complete abandonment of self to impulse during a few moments, and when it was over, and she gave her usual arch acknowledgement to the audience, she seemed herself astonished at what she had gone through. The pause was but momentary; off she bounded to a *tarantella* to the tune well known in concert rooms as *La Danza*, and figured against her companions with all the petulance of this eccentric dance. For a few minutes she retired, and returned to describe by actions her lover's misfortunes. Here was a new field, she had to illustrate the tarantula bite, and represented the combination of trembling and dancing in a manner quite indescribable. In the second act, where she is supposed herself to be under the influence of the bite, she has an entirely new *pas*—to idealise as it were the notion of agony, and render it picturesque, becoming a Philoctetes in a ballet. The lameness gives an opportunity for some elegant movements on one foot, while the other is trembling suspended, the paroxysms, when she drags the doctor about, and drives him round the tables and chairs, are a new display of that immense spirit in which Fanny Elssler stands alone".

Meanwhile, in Paris, Henry Wikoff was finding life very lonely and dull without her. For days, knowing there was still time to yield to a growing desire, he wrestled with the problem whether to resume his former existence or to throw caution to the winds and accompany the lovely ballerina to America. A change of plan could easily be explained by the call of family business, for his guardian had died a year before and now his guardian's widow was on her deathbed. It never occurred to him until afterwards that it was April Fool's Day when he left Paris, else he might have hesitated.

A few days later he was in London, where his first concern was to call on Mrs Grote. She was delighted to hear of his decision and ridiculed his fears of public opinion. When he met Fanny again the next day at a dinner party given by the Grotes at their house in Eccleston Square, she chided him for not seeing her sooner, and then pressed him to visit Mrs Price, who was in town. After dinner Wikoff could not keep his eyes off Fanny, as she sat, dressed very simply, by Mrs Grote's side on a sofa. Her hostess seemed to be urging upon her something she was loth to undertake. Presently the two of them walked to the centre of the room, while another lady went to the piano and began to play a minuet. "I never had a greater treat," he recalled. "Mrs Grote acted as the cavalier, and Fanny's grace and elegance in the execution of this stately dance of Louis XIV's time rivetted every eye; and all applauded rapturously as she ran smiling back to her seat, throwing the blame of 'the performance' on Mrs. Grote's whimsical fancy."*

Next day, when Wikoff called on Mrs Price, she told him that she now controlled the Park Theatre. Simpson's reaction to the new contract was still not known, but they thought it likely that he would accept it.

Fanny did not conceal her pleasure at the news that Wikoff had booked a passage on the "Great Western" to accompany her to New York, and the young American had to warn her that the whole enterprise might still founder. "Mr. Simpson has not yet accepted the new engagement," he reminded her, "and you would not think of going unless he does."

"That would be a sad disappointment," replied Fanny. "I will withdraw my propositions if he objects—anything rather than give it up after all that has been said, done, and written about my trip to America."

Wikoff seemed to have sensed that Simpson was somewhat unenthusiastic about the proposed engagement. During Price's lifetime he had had to acquiesce in the project, but now that he found himself in control, as the man on the spot, he was beginning to act according to his own ideas. Shrewd and cautious by nature, he did not believe that ballet could be a success in New York, even with a star such as Fanny Elssler, and he feared that the womenfolk would disapprove and keep away from the theatre. Realising, though, that the situation required delicate handling, he entrusted one of his actors, Henry Placide, with the mission of going to London and tactfully endeavouring to dissuade Fanny from sailing to America.

In the letter which Placide handed to Wikoff on his arrival, Simpson stated clearly that he could not ratify the new agreement. He was willing to honour the contract with Price, but he could not consent to the later date suggested, nor to the penalty clause. Furthermore, presuming from Fanny's hesitation in proceeding with the Price contract that she would decline coming altogether, he had made other bookings which precluded

* Her friendship with Fanny Elssler gave Mrs Grote an urge to dance. One evening her brother called at Eccleston Street and was surprised to find the drawing room illuminated as though for a reception. When he was shown in, a strange sight met his eyes. George Grote was sitting in an arm chair as a solitary spectator while Harriet, in a short skirt and wings, was in the act of bounding forth from the back drawing-room to show him a *pas seul à la Elssler!*

the possibility of her appearing before May 18th, and he advised that she should postpone her arrival until the opening of the following season in September. That was, of course, quite impossible, because the dates had to fit into the period of leave granted by the Opéra. Wikoff's first reaction was one of relief that this adventure in which he was becoming more and more deeply involved seemed to be on the point of collapsing, but Mrs Grote soon shamed him into continuing the struggle. It was decided between them that they should draw up yet another contract with Mrs Price, who as her husband's heir was as anxious as anyone that Fanny should go, and to breathe no word to Fanny until all was settled. The following afternoon, at the Grotes' house, the document was placed before Placide. Wikoff and the two ladies were impatient to have the matter settled, but poor Placide felt cornered and ill at ease, and was reluctant to exceed his authority and "put his foot in it". Eventually, after two hours of argument, he yielded and signed the agreement. Then he took out an enormous bandana and sopped the perspiration which was streaming down his face.

Mrs Grote and Wikoff were not yet finished with the poor man, though, having been captivated by Fanny's dancing, he was more than willing to further the cause of the American visit, which he was convinced would bring profit to all concerned, including his principal, Simpson. He was a man of great charm, and he was introduced to a number of Fanny's friends who were still opposed to her going to America—Count d'Orsay, Prince Louis Napoleon and Lady Bulwer were among them—with the object of making them see the proposed visit in a more favourable light.

La Valette's absence in Persia enabled the Grotes to see more of Fanny than they would otherwise have done, but they were forced to accept that she belonged to a world that was not theirs. "She is fond of me," Harriet told her sister Frances, "but she has so much on her hands to maintain her position, that her mind is hardly free enough to respond fully to a feeling like ours of admiring sympathy, blended with compassion for the degradation to which the reputable portion of society condemns her. George is devoted to a crazy degree and she appreciates his greatness and goodness, but she is too bright a meteor to hold fast. Now and then we shall see her and commune with her, but she must belong to the art-world and not to us, or any other individual, excepting always that blessed dog La Valette."

George Grote was so taken with Fanny's charms that, as a relief from his labours on Greek history, he wrote a number of poems to her which Harriet described as "beautiful and imaginative, tinged with classical allusions and carefully written". Many years afterwards, when going through his papers after his death, she came upon them again and, deciding they were not for alien eyes to see, destroyed them.

It required some courage for Harriet Grote to sustain her friendship with Fanny, for in those days any lady in London society who befriended a ballerina was breaching the unwritten rules of propriety and risking offending her more conventional friends. "My fondness for the enchanting girl Elssler," she wrote to her sister Frances, "has been so snubbed by my friends and admirers that I have become a shade more misanthropical of late . . . My courage is equal to the occasion, and I care nought for the 'Fye for shame' hue and cry which has assailed me. If you hear ought of the hubbub . . . you will probably be assured that George is keeping up an illicit amour with Fanny and I am left in the basket. I need not say that this is altogether false, except that between us three there exists a holy and tender tie, based on a romantic attachment on our side, and a grateful affection borne us by her, on the other." To another sister Harriet Grote made it plain that she was "fully resolved upon the course I intend to pursue in relation to Mlle Elssler, and that both George and myself think our characters can *afford* to risk such dangers as may attach to the indulgence of a purely romantic and beneficent course towards one of Nature's choicest children".

The social prejudice against theatrical folk was so ingrained that many people who met Fanny were astonished to discover how refined she was. "That she was graceful and fascinating in her manners, everyone can bear witness who met her in private," wrote Chorley, the music critic. "The most prudish woman—or man—might have passed days in her society, without being recalled to any recollection of the scanty stage dress, and the attitudes, fitter for sculpture than for social life—in short, by any look, gesture, or allusion, belonging to the dancer's craft, on her part. She spoke and behaved in private with the ease, quietness and taste of a gentlewoman; but this could only be known to a few, whereas her *pirouettes* and *battemens*, and the whole artillery of her sorceries were, without stint, public property."

During her previous visits she had made many friends among the rakish young men who filled the omnibus boxes at the theatre, and her continued pleasure in their company was one factor which disappointed Mrs Grote. Another shock which this worthy friend received was the discovery that Fanny had a little daughter, Therese, who had been brought to England, perhaps by her sister-in-law Minna. But Harriet was too generous a friend to let these details interfere with their friendship, hurt though she was at this latest revelation of Fanny's irregular private life.

Harriet Grote's courage did not go unrecognised. Her friend, Anna

Jameson, felt "there is something so magnanimous in her support of Fanny Elssler, and so *truly Christian*, whatever the Pharisees might say, that I really love her", but she was reluctant to go to her house if the dancer would be there. Fanny's engagement was already nearing its close, so Harriet Grote invited Mrs Jameson to her benefit performance on April 9th. "I will keep a place for you in my box for Thursday," she wrote, "not meaning to crowd it . . . Tomorrow Fanny dines here and her sister;* no women coming except Mrs Procter, who eagerly accepted the offer to meet her here today, when she called upon me. I don't ask you, for the same reasons as before. But as this is her last week, perhaps you will cheer her with a call one morning . . . I am *unusually* depressed in consequence of Fanny's shortcomings; these two days have been days of intense mortification, and I feel the curse of having too large a soul and too soft a heart."

At her benefit Fanny not only danced in *La Tarentule*, but added the *Cachucha* and the *Cracovienne* for good measure. Two days later, on the 11th, she made her last appearance. Queen Victoria and her newly wed consort, Prince Albert, were in the Royal box; Queen Adelaide was in the theatre too; Count d'Orsay was in the omnibus box, and in another box, acting the part of an Emperor in exile, sat Prince Louis Napoleon, flanked by two aides-de-camp. The prices of the boxes had risen by several guineas during the day, and the enthusiasm of the crowded audience knew no bounds. At the end Fanny enjoyed a tumultuous ovation, with flowers falling at her feet, and Prince Albert standing up in the box to wish her *bon voyage*.

The following morning brought disturbing news. Placide heard from Simpson that the Park Theatre had closed and that there could be no question of Fanny dancing there during May and June. Acting on an impulse, Wikoff called on Mrs Price and persuaded her to place the theatre in his hands so that he could appoint a manager and open the theatre at his own risk. Then, exhilarated by the action he had taken, he went to see Fanny, explained the situation, and asked if she still wished to go to America.

"I have never moved a foot in Europe without a settled engagement," she replied, "but my confidence in you is unbounded, and a blind belief possesses me in the hearts and generous nature of your countrymen. Yes, *partons*. I have no fears. The Americans, I am sure, will not turn their backs on me."

The day of her departure was near, and it was time to make the final arrangements. Harriet Grote had agreed to look after little Therese, who was now a bright child of six. "Well, Fanny," she had said with character-

* This refers to Fanny's sister-in-law, Minna Elssler, wife of her brother Joseph.

istic brusqueness, "send the brat to me. I don't ask you whose child it is, and I don't care, so long as it isn't that fool d'Orsay's, and I'll take the best care of it I can." To provide for her maintenance, Fanny settled a trust fund on the little girl, George Grote being appointed a trustee.

The child was then in the country recovering from measles, and on the day before Fanny sailed, Harriet Grote accompanied her to say goodbye to "her angelic child". "Never shall I forget it!" she wrote. "It was worthy of a Raphaelle [sic[, and, as to the moral part of it, I was ready to burn with admiration! F was very much overcome."

Packing had been left very much to the last minute, the whole household being kept busy until three o'clock on the morning of Fanny's departure from London. It was fortunate that Mrs Grote rose early to help Fanny to start, for everyone overslept and not a soul was stirring when Charles, the coachman whom the Grotes had lent to Fanny, brought the carriage to the door at eight o'clock. As the train was due to leave Paddington Station at nine, and half an hour was needed to drive there, there was chaos and pandemonium in the house. Fanny just had time to dress and rub her eyes open before going down to the carriage, with her bonnet in one hand and a hunk of bread in the other. In a few moments she was joined by her sister-in-law Minna, who bundled herself into the carriage among a disordered heap of baskets, parcels and shawls. The Grotes followed them to the station in their own carriage. Between sobs Harriet told Wikoff that he would have a letter in the morning, and then she quietly slipped away before the train left so as to avoid an emotional leave-taking. Later in the day Harriet and Minna visited little Therese again, and it was decided to bring the child to the Grotes' house at Burnham Beeches. After nightfall George Grote accompanied Minna to the Tower steps, where she boarded the packet for France.

It had been an exhausting day. "I am perfectly *stranded* in mind," Harriet wrote to Wikoff, "and feel as if all was dead around me, and as if the sun was put out . . . I shall be some days getting my mind afloat again, for the idea of Fanny has full possession of it, and my heart has gone with her. How delightful to think I contributed to her happy residence here, and to know she fully recognises it! She is a precious gem—tend her as one. I know you will . . . Every sort of love and sorrow to Fanny."

X

Conquest of the New World

THE GREAT ADVENTURE BEGAN the moment Fanny and Katti arrived at Paddington Station and porters, wearing their new uniforms of the Great Western Railway Company, came forward to take charge of the heavy luggage, for this was to be their first journey by railway. At five minutes to nine a bell summoned them and the other passengers to take their seats and give up their tickets, and on the hour the bell rang again as the signal for the carriage doors to be shut and locked. The thrill of travelling smoothly through the countryside three times faster than was possible in a coach was lost on Fanny as she thought of all the familiar faces and surroundings she had now left behind for an unknown adventure. Suddenly overwhelmed, she burst into tears. Henry Wikoff, who had perhaps bought one of the guide books which described the landmarks along the line, tried to distract her by pointing out the beauties of the countryside that lay glowing in the April sunlight, but her heart was too heavy to take comfort. At length, emotionally and physically exhausted, she fell asleep, dreaming of "carolling birds, green hills and bleating sheep". Nearly an hour later they arrived at Reading, which was the end of the line. From there they had to continue their journey by coach, arriving in Bristol some nine or ten hours later.

The following afternoon, refreshed after a good night's sleep, Fanny and her party packed themselves and their luggage into the small steam tender which was to take them into the Bristol Channel, where the "Great Western" was lying at anchor. The liner's captain, James Hosken, at once made his way through the other passengers to greet her. Wikoff then introduced her to the Comtesse de Merlin, who was making the Atlantic crossing to collect an inheritance in Cuba, and the two ladies were still deep in conversation when they saw the "Great Western" towering above them.

Nearly two hundred and fifty feet in length and displacing over 1,300 tons, she was a mammoth among ships and one of the fastest vessels afloat. It was only two years since the ocean crossing had been dramatically shortened by the introduction of steamships, and the "Great Western", the first steamer to be specially built for the Atlantic ferry service, had taken only fifteen days to complete her maiden voyage to New York. She had opened a new era in ocean travel, not only by her increased speed but also on account of the comfort which her hundred and more passengers could enjoy—a welcome change from the cramped conditions to be endured on a sailing ship. Fanny felt a thrill of excitement as she set foot on the deck of what Katti described as "the floating palace". Their state room, however, seemed far from palatial, but after an initial protest Fanny realised that she had the best quarters on board and resigned herself to spending much of the next fortnight in this tiny closet-like room. Soon, with much creaking of machinery, the massive paddle wheels began to turn, and like a giant awakening, the ship began to move westwards towards the open sea. Dinner was served almost immediately, and the passengers assembled in the splendid saloon, where they found their needs efficiently cared for by George, the negro steward, and his band of African waiters. After Captain Hosken had explained the ship's routine, the passengers spent the rest of the evening on deck.

The first few days passed very pleasantly. Katti was an early victim of seasickness, but Fanny was able to relax and enjoy the pleasures of the cruise. Whether strolling on the deck or reclining in a comfortable chair with a book, she found the calm sunlit sea irresistibly soothing. The days ended with splendid sunsets, and before going to bed those who did not wish to play cards were lulled by strains of music from the ship's small band. Sometimes the passengers themselves took part in the entertainment: one evening the Comtesse de Merlin sang some Spanish songs so beautifully that the African servants gathered discreetly in the doorways to listen.

On the fourth day the sun disappeared and it began to rain. That night the sea became more and more violent, and the whole of the next day, which was Easter Sunday, Fanny spent in her tiny cabin, nursing a miserable Katti. After two days of pitching and rolling, the ship steamed into thick fog. Then an even more violent storm arose, which continued for many days. Captain Hosken's imperturbable calm gave everyone a sense of security. They were fortunate, he told them, to see the ocean in all its might and anger. At his invitation Fanny and Katti bravely went up on deck, and after Katti had quickly returned to the cabin, Fanny remained to gaze on the raging waters.

Captain Hosken confessed that he had never known such a bad crossing at that time of year. The storm did not abate until May 1st, nearly two weeks after they had struck it, and they would be two days late in arriving in New York. The following evening, realising that the ship's engines had stopped, Fanny, Katti and Henry Wikoff rushed up on deck to find the Captain making his soundings. Seeing them approach, Hosken held out a handful of sand. "Take this," he said to Fanny. "As you cannot yet touch American soil with your foot, you can do so with your beautiful hand."

Early next morning Katti was on deck to see the sun rise when the Captain shouted to her to look to her left. All around were sailing ships, and close by was the pilot boat which had come to guide the "Great Western" into the harbour. Fanny soon joined her, and together they watched in fascination the New World coming into view. Steaming through the Narrows between Staten and Long Islands, they admired the wooded countryside dotted with white clapboard houses, and as they approached Manhattan, Fanny delightedly pointed to a lovely tree-shaded promenade by the water's edge—the Battery.

In 1840 New York was a city of some 300,000 souls and extended as far north as 14th Street. "On landing," a guide book of that year informed its European readers, "the visitor is struck by the bustle and activity exhibited in this part of the city. If in the summer, the lightness of the dresses of the gentlemen, the straw hats, the number of Negroes, of a more jet black than those met with in London, all contribute to give the scene a foreign appearance . . . The heavy loads drawn by the light and active blood horses will also appear strange; and he may soon have occasion to remark the often noticed and universal habit of frequent expectoration. The dresses of the generality of the inhabitants indicate their easy circumstances; and the beggars and objects of pity which too often pain the sight in the cities of Europe are, happily, seldom to be met with here. Many of the stores are very handsomely built of stone, and the brick houses are neatly painted red . . . The streets are well paved and lighted."

No other theatrical celebrity—not even the great singer Malibran, who had visited New York in 1827—had been awaited with such eager excitement as Fanny. James Gordon Bennett's *New York Morning Herald*, which throve on sensational reporting of a kind not yet known in Europe, had done much to stimulate this interest, printing the puffs which Wikoff had been sending for many weeks past. So Fanny's name was well known to the public long before the "Great Western" docked. Even the customs men were filled with good will, and did not trouble to examine her luggage. Outside the Customs House the crowd was so thick that Fanny at first thought there must have been an accident. It was Sunday, and the streets in the city seemed strangely deserted as she was driven to her hotel. On the way Wikoff pointed out the Park Theatre on Park Row. Looking at the imposing City Hall, she gave a cry of delight which was cut short when she realised her mistake and saw the drab

Fanny Elssler and her son Franz Robert. Painting on porcelain by Apel, *c.* 1839.

Coll. the late Miss Lillian Moore.

Fanny Elssler in her dressing room at the Park Theatre, New York. Oil painting by Henry Inman, 1841.

Haydn Museum, Eisenstadt.

Fanny Elssler and the Baltimoreans. Caricature, 1840.

Harvard Theatre Collection.

The Fracas at Coney Island. An aggressive Philadelphian, Fanny Elssler and
Henry Wikoff.

New York Public Library.

theatre. To reassure her Wikoff explained that the interior was really very handsome. A minute or two later their carriage stopped in front of the American Hotel on Broadway, at the corner of Barclay Street— the site is today occupied by the Woolworth Building—and the manager came forward to welcome her.

Later that afternoon she received a visit from Edmund Simpson. Expecting an elegant man of the world, she was surprised to be confronted by a dour individual in black who remarked rather awkwardly as he sat down that it was a fine day. Then, after inquiring about her voyage, he gave an embarrassed cough and stood up with stiff formality, announcing he would call again. So began and ended, in five minutes, Fanny's first interview with Manager Simpson. She had been warned that he was a strange and silent man, but knowing his reputation for integrity, she felt sure she would grow to like him. That evening, before retiring to bed, she sat by her bedroom window looking out at the darkened city and the starry sky above. Happy to be on dry land at last, she felt at peace and would have stayed there dreaming all night if Katti had not firmly dragged her away.

Mrs Price had apparently come to an arrangement with Simpson, for it was with him that Wikoff had to negotiate the terms of Fanny's engagement. This was not easy since Simpson was reluctant to commit himself to paying a large fee in view of the depressed state of the New York theatre. But Wikoff's hand was considerably strengthened by the widespread interest aroused by the publicity in the *Herald*, and Simpson eventually accepted his demands for half the receipts, with a guarantee of $500 a performance.

The reality of the ordeal that faced her was Fanny's main concern in these nerve-wracking first days in New York. Owing to the restricted quarters on board ship and the bad weather, she had not practised for over a fortnight. She had much leeway to make up in all too short a time, for her debut was to take place less than two weeks ahead. Meanwhile a feverish excitement was being generated in the city. The newspapers were full of her doings. The box office was besieged from morning to night, and seats for the first few performances were soon changing hands at several times their original price. Theatre managers from Boston and Philadelphia came hot-foot to New York to tempt her with generous offers without even seeing her dance. Little wonder then that when she had time to sit and contemplate, she was filled with dread at the thought of disappointing this new public.

Nor was her apprehension lessened by the problems to be overcome in staging *La Tarentule*, in which she was to make her American debut, but happily she had a competent ballet-master to assist her in this task.

Price's suggestion to Wikoff that Lucien Petipa should be engaged as her partner had come to nought, and it was James Sylvain who had accompanied her across the Atlantic.* This pastoral surname concealed the more ordinary patronymic of Sullivan. He was admirably equipped for the dual position of partner and ballet-master, for not only had he worked in the theatre since his early boyhood, progressing from the rough and tumble of pantomime to the more refined milieu of ballet, in which he had gained successes both in London and Paris, but he possessed the most valuable advantage of speaking English as his native tongue. There was no time to lose, and he and Fanny threw themselves into the arduous task of producing *La Tarentule* with the inadequate material which Simpson could place at their disposal.

The Park Theatre was a far cry from the European opera houses when it came to providing facilities for the production of ballet. The *Herald* described its *corps de ballet* of eight men and eight women as "miserable sticks", but the greatest difficulty was experienced in distributing the parts. This was not for lack of performers, but because the actors of the establishment were nervous of the criticism they might incur. The role of Dr Omeopatico was particularly difficult to fill, but finally John Fisher, an English-born comedian who was a great favourite of the Park audiences, agreed to play it. Miss Kerr was cast as Clorinde, and Madame Arraline, who had once danced at the King's Theatre in London, took the part of Lauretta's mother.

In the intervals between rehearsals and practice Fanny found a little time for sightseeing, and in the evenings she paid several visits to the theatre, where her appearance in a box would arouse the greatest curiosity in the audience. Many leading figures in New York's society called on her to pay their compliments. The nervous strain she was undergoing seldom broke through the calm front she showed to these visitors, but Philip Hone was perceptive enough to notice a certain weariness. "She is an exceedingly fascinating person, not very handsome," he recorded in his diary. "Her face has lost its bright bloom, and her complexion appears to be somewhat faded—the result, probably, of the violent muscular exertions which are required in the profession; but her manners are ladylike. She is gay and lively, and altogether the most perfectly graceful lady I have ever seen."

Never had Fanny felt more nervous than on the day of her New

---

* Sylvain had crossed the Atlantic on the "Great Western", but Fanny seems to have preserved a social distinction between them, for Katti made no mention of his presence when describing the voyage in her letters home. Perhaps it is significant that Fanny described herself as a "Lady" in the Ship's List, while Sylvain is referred to as an "Artiste".

York debut, May 14th. Before resting in the afternoon she had a reminder of the evening's ordeal when she glimpsed through her window
the immense crowd collecting before the Park Theatre hoping to gain
admittance to the pit. Many of them were to be disappointed, for the
house was sold out within half an hour of the opening of the box office.
As he escorted her to her carriage to take her to the theatre, Wikoff,
who was doing his best to conceal his own nervousness, noticed her
pallor and the tremor in her voice.

In her dressing-room, as she was putting on her costume for the
Cracovienne, she could hear the murmur of the audience eagerly waiting
for her first appearance. When Wikoff entered he found her already
dressed and looking "very bewitching. She had rouged her cheeks, so
the paleness had disappeared". But she was still desperately nervous. "I
trembled in every limb with apprehensions I could not control," she
wrote. "I had hardly strength to walk upon the stage. The curtain rose,
and breathless silence prevailed; the music struck up, and the moment
came, and I appeared. The scene that ensued beggars description. The
whole house rose, and such a shout ascended as stunned my senses, and
made me involuntarily recoil. Men waved their hats, and women their
handkerchiefs, and all was inexplicable dumb show for several mortal
moments. I stood confounded, and tears streaming down my face."

When the ovation ceased and she began to dance, Wikoff could see
that, despite every effort, she could not summon up her usual buoyancy
and attack. "I was scarcely conscious of what I was doing," recalled
Fanny herself. "I felt only one dreadful sensation of a great weight
being attached to my limbs; or as if palsy had stricked them." The
audience seemed unaware that she had not given her best, but after the
curtain had fallen amid deafening applause, Wikoff went up to her and
said: "Very well, but you can do better than that."

"Yes," she replied, "I can and will. If they applaud such music [*sic*]
as that, I will astonish them before the night is over."

Wikoff saw she was coming to herself and felt relieved as she returned
to the stage to repeat the *Cracovienne* with much more grace and effect.

A *vaudeville* was given before *La Tarentule,* and Fanny retired to her
dressing-room to rest and change her costume. "I was not curious to
know the feeling of the house, for I feared it must be unfavourable,"
she wrote. "I began to warm to my work, and my ambition awoke. I
resolved to make some desperate efforts before I yielded the struggle.
I soon learned that such a state of feeling prevailed as had been calculated on. Great confusion of opinion and impression, perhaps some
disappointment, but just that blank state of mind that I might hope the
most from. This roused my soul to action, and I longed to be at them.

My appearance in feminine and coquettish attire seemed more in harmony with their expectations, and they evidently liked my looks. A loud murmur of surprise and intense satisfaction rose on every side, and gave me a strong impetus. It is not for me to say why I did, or how I did it, but never was I carried so resistlessly along on a buoyant tide of feeling that bore me quite away. I danced without effort, and even Katti applauded some of my feats. The most deafening exclamations of delight broke at rapid intervals from all parts of the house, till they lashed themselves into a perfect tempest of admiration. Never before did I behold so vast an assembly so completely under the sway of *one* dominant feeling, and so entirely abandoned to its inspiration. The curtain fell amid a roar that sounded like the fall of mighty waters."

All the anxieties of the past few months seemed to slip away as she received this final ovation. Though she had enjoyed countless triumphs in many great cities, this was different from them all. The applause sounded more resounding; it seemed to bubble like champagne. Carried away, Sylvain placed on her head one of the many floral crowns which lay on the stage, and still trembling with emotion, she stepped forward and crossing her arms in front of her, made a little speech in halting English: "A thousand thanks—my heart is too full for words."

Her conquest was complete, and some of her admirers, not content with the ovation they had given her, came to her hotel in the early hours of the morning and serenaded her, playing the *Cachucha* and a song of Vienna which brought tears of nostalgia to her eyes.

Most of the newspapers reported her debut with the most fulsome eulogies. Of serious criticism there was none, for ballet was still an exotic importation in New York. Since the turn of the century New Yorkers had applauded several talented dancers who had crossed the Atlantic—Francisque Hutin, the Achilles, Mme Céleste, the Ronzi-Vestrises, Augusta, Marius Petipa, and Paul and Amalia Taglioni—but none had been heralded, as Fanny was, as one of the great theatrical personalities of Europe. The few dissident voices which were raised after her debut were voicing a protest at the extravagances of the publicity given her in the columns of the *Herald* rather than denigrating her talent. Park Benjamin's *Signal*, for example, pronounced Fanny to be "a stupendous humbug", a statement which roused the ire of the *Herald*. The scathing counter-attack which the *Herald* launched in Fanny's defence only added to her publicity, and when her first New York season ended the *Signal* had joined the ranks of her admirers.

On Sundays preachers spoke disapprovingly of her from their pulpits, but not even their sermons could prevent the New Yorkers from worshipping their new goddess. "The parsons have preached, the old maids have clicked their tongues, the moralists have shaken their heads," reported the *Herald* triumphantly, "but nothing has been able to calm this excitement."

In all she gave sixteen performances during her first New York season, not counting her appearance at the benefit of the actor, Peter Richings. She and Sylvain worked hard to build up a varied repertory. At her fourth performance, on the 18th, she introduced the *Cachucha*, appearing, as the curtain rose, "standing in the centre of the stage, in an attitude which [Michelangelo] or Titian might have studied, with her magnificent throat and bosom absolutely blazing with diamonds". Four days later another ballet was ready for performance, *L'Amour, ou la Rose animée*, a *divertissement* to music by Rossini which Sylvain had originally produced when ballet-master at the St James's Theatre, London, in 1839. Later two more *pas de caractère* were added—the *Smolenska* and another classical Spanish dance, the *Jaleo de Jerez*, which she performed for the first time in New York at her second benefit on June 8th—and on June 1st *La Sylphide* appeared on the bills.

The excitement aroused at her first appearance did not wane. Whenever she was dancing the public packed into every nook and cranny of the theatre, and at the end of the performance she always had to make her way to the waiting carriage through a mass of "moustaches, imperials, whiskers and long-locks" crowding round the stage door. People came from as far afield as Baltimore and Philadelphia to see her, and one evening the actress, Fanny Kemble, was among the audience. Fanny Elssler was the rage of New York. Boats and horses were named after her. The shops were full of Fanny Elssler boots, stocking, garters, corsets, shawls, parasols, fans, even Fanny Elssler cigars, boot polish and shaving soap. More appropriately, there was Fanny Elssler champagne. "Devilish good it is," Wikoff told Gordon Bennett, who was about to be married. "It is worthy of being drunk at your wedding."

Sylvain told an amusing story that illustrated this worship of Fanny Elssler. He was approached one day by a serious-looking man who offered him a fistful of dollars if he would procure him one of Fanny's ballet slippers. Scenting the opportunity for a practical joke, he referred him to Fanny's maid, whom he told to give him one of her own worn-out shoes. The next time he saw this infatuated admirer, he was wearing the shoe round his neck like a lucky charm.

At the Olympic Theatre her fame was being stimulated by a burlesque of *La Tarentule*. William Mitchell had produced a hilarious parody called *La Mosquito*, in which he appeared as the famous ballerina—a stumpy, bandy-legged figure with a ruddy full-moon face. To simulate Fanny's leaps he sought the aid of wires, and threw the audience into gales of laughter as he kicked and floundered in mid-air, displaying a placard announcing that he could jump higher and longer than ever Fanny could. At the end of the piece he carried his imitation into the curtain calls, thanking the audience with the words, "Tousan tank, me 'art too fool". Fanny enjoyed the joke as much as anyone, and was seen more than once at the Olympic.

Now that she could relax again, she began to enjoy her stay in America. She was making new friends, and seeing more of the city. John Van Buren, son of the American President, dined with her and escorted her to the Bowery Theatre to see Edwin Forrest in *The Gladiator*. When the captain of the warship "North Carolina" showed her over his vessel, the company of so many admiring males brought out her most sparkling charm, and an onlooker at the Battery remarked that it was worth ten dollars just to see her walk.

Fanny's last appearance, on June 11th, had the aura of a gala performance. "It was a great solemnity for the City of New York," wrote a reporter. "The Park Theatre never saw so great a triumph. This narrow and dirty building bore the traces of something marvellous. Mlle Elssler has done what no other dramatic power had ever done before her; not even Malibran—this lyric giant, whose cradle was the United States. In the best days of Malibran, the feminine aristocracy of New York never became plebeian enough to sit on the last seats of the second gallery of the Park. Fanny Elssler has effected this miracle. Powerful magician! she destroyed all demarcations, humanised the most savage affectation, and, thanks to her, that part of the theatre called 'the hell' was transformed into an Eden, where sparkled the most fastidious and disdainful houris of New York. The parterre also had a new skin on it; its rags were exchanged for the most fashionable costumes."

The increased prices did not exclude the rowdier element altogether, and during the ballet the silence of the audience was broken by "some drunkard's indecent noise". Wikoff was amazed at the patience shown by the public. "Rather than interrupt the dancing," he recorded, "they endured to a degree never before equalled this insufferable disturbance for nearly five minutes without complaint or notice."

At the end Fanny made one of her little speeches which were winning the hearts of the American audiences. "Ladies and gentlemen," she said in her charming Viennese accent, "I have been so happy—along with you—that I very sorry—to go away—but—I will come back again." The simplicity of these words was so touching that the pit rose to her. Smiling through her tears, she put her hands to her lips and kissed half a dozen adieux to the audience. The effect was electric. Shouts of

"Bravo!" echoed through the theatre, and as Fanny was making her way to her dressing-room she heard the audience break into three cheers.

Meanwhile Henry Wikoff was making himself more and more indispensable. Fanny's extraordinary triumph had brought several theatre managers to New York, and it became his task to negotiate terms with them. By the close of the New York season he had laid plans for a tour of Philadelphia, Washington and Baltimore. Fanny was to travel with her own company, consisting of Sylvain and eight dancers from the Park Theatre's *corps de ballet*, and the costumes, properties and music for the ballets and dances of their repertory: three ballets, *La Sylphide*, *La Tarentule* and *L'Amour*, three of Fanny's character dances, the *Cracovienne*, the *Cachucha* and the *Jaleo de Jerez*, and an English hornpipe for Sylvain. Only the sets were to be provided from the stock of the theatres on their route.

To avoid crowds they all set out from New York in great secrecy. They crossed the Hudson by ferry and caught the train for Philadelphia at Jersey City. A railway journey was still a novelty for Katti, who looked out of the carriage window and felt a thrill as they streaked through the New Jersey countryside "with the speed of swallows".

Philadelphia charmed them with its elegant buildings and shady avenues, and the fireflies sparkling like clusters of little stars in the streets at night. The city was in a fever of excitement at their arrival. Fanny only had to enter Van Harlingen's store to be surrounded by assistants vying with each other for the honour of serving her. The sculptor Ottaviano Gori begged her to pose for him in her *Cachucha* costume, and it was possibly the resulting statuette that was cast for the girandoles of the dancer which, with other souvenirs and prints, were soon on sale in the shops. No section of the population was more excited by her presence in Philadelphia than the large German colony, and when she gave her services to dance at the Arch Street Theatre for the benefit of a German singer, their fervour knew no bounds. She was presented with a basket of flowers, decorated with red and white chenille and trimmed with pearls, which contained an ode welcoming her as a kinswoman from their Fatherland. This was not all, for that night she was called out to the balcony of her hotel room to be serenaded by the German orchestra and chorus. A few days later she had another experience of American life when she witnessed the Independence Day parade.

The demand for seats at the Chestnut Street Theatre was enormous, and on the night of her first appearance, June 17th, the surrounding streets were so packed with carriages and people that Fanny had to wait for the theatre to open before venturing across the road from her hotel. She was recalled at the end of *La Tarentule* and again after the *Cracovienne*, and at the close of the performance she stepped forward to say a few words of thanks. A final curtain speech, composed no doubt by Wikoff and learnt by heart, was now expected of her almost as part of her performance. "If this goes on," she confided to Katti, "I shall really have to learn English correctly."

She appeared fourteen times at the Chestnut Street Theatre, and many Philadelphians saw her more than once. One of her greatest admirers was the actress, Fanny Kemble, who was married to a Philadelphian. "We go every night to see Fanny Elssler," she wrote to her friend, Harriet Grote. "My admiration for her grows rather than diminishes, though she is a better actress even than dancer, which I think speaks in favour of her intellect."

Fanny was idolised by the young American dancers who had the opportunity of appearing with her and observing her at close quarters: the three Vallee girls whom she engaged in Philadelphia, and a boy called George Washington Smith. Nearly fifty years later a reporter asked Smith for his recollections of Fanny Elssler. A far-away look came into the old man's eyes. "Do I remember Fanny Elssler?" he said. "Friend, no one who ever knew Fanny Elssler could forget her. She was the queen—the matchless queen—of the ballet. The world is full of imitations, but there never was but one Elssler . . . I shall never forget the wonderful form and superb carriage of that woman . . . She was the embodiment of all that was graceful, beautiful, ravishing."

After the cool, changeable weather in Philadelphia, they arrived in Washington to be "almost suffocated by the fearful heat". It was like living in an oven. Whenever they could they escaped from their hotel to go for a drive, and at night they sat at the window trying to cool themselves with large fans.

To the politicians of Washington, which they found to be more a sprawling village than a capital city, Fanny's arrival came as a welcome diversion from affairs of state, and Congress was adjourned earlier than usual to enable them to attend her first performance at the National Theatre on July 11th. Fanny had only arrived in the capital that morning, but neither the strain of the journey, the lack of rehearsal time, nor the overpowering heat prejudiced her success. The former President, John Quincy Adams, applauded her vigorously from his seat in the second tier, and at the close Fanny was deluged with flowers and sent everyone home enchanted not only by her dancing but also by her short curtain speech.

For this one week Fanny might have been queen of Washington. At a banquet in her honour her health was drunk in champagne from her ballet slipper, and she was presented with a cross carved from the wood of George Washington's bier. Even the nation's rulers paid her homage. Henry Wikoff had arranged for her and Katti to visit the House of Representatives, where a murmur of interest arose as they entered in the middle of a debate. John Quincy Adams was just beginning an impassioned speech. Though he was an old man, and his head and hands trembled, his voice had lost none of its strength and his mind was as sharp as ever. A friend sitting near him leaned forward and remarked: "You have another auditor whose bright eye is now upon you—Miss Fanny Elssler is listening to you."

"Do you say that to rouse or to intimidate me?" thundered the venerable orator before resuming his argument. "We'll see."

When the House adjourned Fanny was surrounded by Congressmen clamouring to be presented. She was taken to the President's chair, and catching Katti's eye, smiled at the thought of the incongruity of their presence in such surroundings.

President Martin Van Buren, whose son had squired her in New York, attended the third of her five performances with the whole Cabinet, and invited Fanny to the White House the next morning. When Fanny took a last look in the mirror before leaving for the audience, she looked enchanting in her simple morning dress. "Anything for the President," she said to Katti before hurrying away so as not to be late.

Martin Van Buren, eighth President of the United States, was a cultured man whose attempts to invest his Presidential office with a modicum of elegance were not whole-heartedly welcomed. Many people disapproved strongly of the un-American taste with which he was redecorating the White House, the employment of a French chef, and the use of massive gold plate on important occasions; and it was commonly known that he scented his whiskers with Eau de Cologne. To Fanny, however, he looked every inch a nation's ruler when she found him, with his Ministers waiting to receive her. He put her at her ease at once by saying a few elegant words about her art, and then went on to express the wish that she should remain in America for some time and return to Washington in the winter. Fanny was overjoyed with excitement when she returned home. The dignity of the President had made a deep impression on her. "I observed him very close," she told Secretary Forsyth afterwards, "and think his demeanour is very easy, very frank, and very royal."

The business of the House of Representatives sometimes had to stop on her account. On one of the evenings she was dancing the

House could not muster a quorum from seven o'clock until nearly
eleven. Some of the absent members returned in high spirits after the
performance, and the proceedings ended in confusion before the
adjournment was moved. The same problem was expected the following day, when Fanny was to make her last appearance. Certainly the
speeches in the House could be of little interest when compared with
the few words which she would deliver at the end of the evening. After
she had danced in *La Sylphide* and performed the *Cachucha*, she stepped
forward to quell the vociferous cheering. "My stay among you has been
very short," she said with her hand on her heart, "but I shall carry away
with me collections that will never be effaced." The laughter which
arose at this slip of the tongue caused her momentary embarrassment,
but there was no need to forgive, for though everyone knew she had
been engaged at great expense, nobody grudged her the dollars she had
earned. "Sweet girl," commented a journalist, "may God bless her a
thousand years!"

Fanny was due to leave Washington on the following day, but when
she and Katti arrived at the station, the train was already pulling away.
Crestfallen, they returned to the "martyr's cells" of their hotel to endure
another day's heat in Washington without even a nightcap between
them, for all their luggage had been sent on to Baltimore in advance.
Wikoff suggested a drive in the country where they could enjoy the
shade of the pine forests, but this little excursion ended abruptly when
they came upon a rattlesnake. They made sure they were in good time to
catch the train the following day, and were very thankful to arrive in
Baltimore.

Though she was warmly applauded, Fanny's reception at Baltimore's
Holliday Street Theatre on July 21st was surprisingly muted. A few
days previously there had been an auction sale of tickets, but while
some had fetched more than their marked price, quite a number remained unsold. Furthermore, the manager had neglected to publish a
printed synopsis of the ballet, and a large section of the audience was
too loyal to Mme Céleste, whose husband was a citizen of Baltimore, to
judge a new ballerina uncritically.

Fanny's conquest of Baltimore, however, was not long delayed. The
frenzy broke in full force at her second performance and grew in
intensity with each appearance. On some evenings so many bouquets
were thrown that sceptical observers believed that Wikoff transported
these tributes from one city to another with all the other properties.
On the day of what was announced as her last appearance an auction
was held at the theatre for the sale of seats in the boxes. After they had
all been sold, some of them for as much as three dollars, the auctioneer

was led on to the stage by the manager and crowned with a wreath of roses, a tribute which he acknowledged with "a salaam in the Elssler style".

The Baltimore public was so notorious for its rowdiness that the management had to reassure its patrons by announcing on the advertisements that "an efficient Police is engaged, and the strictest order and decorum will be rigidly enforced". Fanny's third appearance was billed as her last in the city, and the audience clamoured so persuasively for an extension that Manager Walton, fearing that they might get out of hand, appeared before them and explained that though he had pressed Fanny to give two additional performances, she had refused because of the heat and her fatigue. But if she had resisted his request, he added wilily, he was sure she would heed the voice of the public. "Is it your wish, ladies and gentlemen," he cried, "that she dances again?" The affirmative roar that greeted this question left Fanny momentarily confused, but she concealed her annoyance at being placed in such a position, and stepped forward with a smile. The house fell silent, and her voice carried to the furthermost reaches of the theatre. Her words were to be reported in an attempt to reproduce her halting, imperfect delivery which everyone found so charming. "Ladies and gentlemen," she said, "if I could—speak well—Anglais—I should tell you how much proud I feel—I am very much happy to see so many warm hearts." She paused and then added, "For a little time I shall stay wis you!"

The audience seemed to go mad at these words, and when she emerged from the stage door she found an immense crowd waiting for her. The people parted to make a path to her carriage, but to her alarm, she had no sooner entered it than the crowd unharnessed the horses and helped down the coachman. A pack of strong young men then picked up the traces and drew her slowly through the streets. It was like a royal progress, with Fanny bowing right and left in acknowledgment of the cheering crowd who escorted her back to her hotel. It was reported that only once before, when Lafayette had been similarly honoured, had such a triumph been accorded in America. Some people were shocked that a ballerina should receive such adulation, and a caricature of the event was published in New York showing her admirers with ass's heads.

When they reached Barnum's Hotel, they found scores of startled guests leaning out of the windows in their nightcaps. The hotel manager had been so alarmed at the sight of a mob converging on his hotel that he had locked the doors. When the carriage came to a halt, Fanny skipped up the front steps, made a little speech, and then, after kissing her hands repeatedly to the delirious crowd, disappeared from their view.

The celebration was not yet over. Soon the street was lit up with countless music stands, as the German musicians assembled to give a monster concert in her honour. Fanny had only to appear at her window for everyone to start cheering and waving their hats, and when she threw some of her bouquets into the street, there was a desperate scramble for these precious souvenirs. Carousing continued in the hotel until nearly daybreak, and even distant residents were kept awake by the rounds of cheers that floated on the night air. "Well done, Baltimore," commented Wikoff. "This time her mob is no disgrace to her. Instead of pulling down houses, they are building up their reputation for chivalric courtesy to a beautiful stranger."

Fanny and Wikoff had been warned about Thomas Walton, their manager in Washington and Baltimore, and advised to insist on the salaries being paid every night before the performance. These warnings were to prove all too well founded. For the balance of the fees due to her in Baltimore Fanny had to be content with Walton's note for $1,200 instead of cash, while Sylvain, whose terms were $250 a week and a clear third of a benefit, brought proceedings to recover his final week's pay and his benefit money. Even the *corps de ballet* suffered. After agreeing to pay their travelling expenses from Philadelphia to Washington and back, Walton deducted them from their pay, even after Fanny had waived $400 of her own fee expressly to enable him to pay them in full. He made a miserly offer of $15 to Mrs Vallee, when the hotel bill for herself and her daughters amounted to $20. Fanny saw that her *corps de ballet* was paid, and would have given a performance for their benefit if they had not realised that this would only further enrich Walton, who was unlikely to hand over the receipts.

Fanny arrived back in New York to the accompaniment of a violent thunderstorm. By the following day the skies had cleared, and after a visit to the Bank of America in Wall Street, she, Katti and Wikoff left on a three-day excursion up the Hudson River. They reached West Point on the first evening, and Sylvain, who was included in the party, escorted Fanny to visit the Military Academy, where the cadets improvised a stag dance for her. Only those on guard duty were prevented from attending, but their turn came when she was walking back to her hotel in the moonlight. Suddenly a blood-curdling shout broke the stillness of the night.

"Halt! Who goes there?"

Sylvain took to his heels to seek assistance, leaving Fanny to deal with the sentry. While she was trying to explain that the Commandant could vouch for her presence, the rest of the guard arrived, all looking very sinister in their huge cloaks. Encouraged to continue the joke, the sentry embarked on a lengthy harangue about the enormity of her crime, telling her that death was the penalty prescribed.

"*Mais, monsieur,*" she cried in mock alarm, "do you not know me? *Je suis Mademoiselle Elssler, la pauvre Elssler.*"

"*Madame,*" continued the sentry, "by accepting any excuse for your crime, I render myself liable to court martial. There is only one condition whereby you may atone for your offence against the flag of my country and save your wretched life. That is, that you will here, in this solemn presence, dance the *Cracovienne.*"

"*Mon Dieu, c'est impossible,*" cried Fanny indignantly.

"Then die, proud female."

"But *messieurs,* I would dance *avec plaisir, mais* vare is de orchestra, de trombone, de flute, de feedle? I cannot dance without de *musique.*"

"Then," cried the sentry, "you know the awful penalty. Prepare for your doom."

As the guards gathered round her menacingly, Fanny decided that discretion was the better part of valour. The guns were stacked, and while the sentry tried valiantly to whistle the tune of the *Cracovienne,* she lifted her skirts and danced on the grass. At the end, when she turned to leave, they called for the *Cachucha,* but just then the corporal of the guard ordered the relief to turn out. The men instantly ran to their posts, and Fanny seized the opportunity to make her escape. On her way back to the hotel she met Sylvain coming to rescue her with a crowd of waiters, armed with brooms, mops and pokers. His gallantry, she observed tartly, might have been shown a little earlier in the evening.

The next day they continued their journey up the Hudson and disembarked at Catskill to be driven up the mountain roads to the Catskill Mountain House. The following morning they rose early to see the sun rise, and after breakfast set out for the Kaaterskill Falls, one of the beauty spots of the district. After admiring them from Inspiration Point, they carefully picked their way down the rocky slope, prudently leaving Fanny with their servant when they were half-way down for fear that she might injure herself on the roughly-hewn steps. Wikoff then helped Katti to the foot, and after Fanny had nodded her consent from above, took her behind the cascading water and brought her safely back, drenched but excited by the adventure.

Fanny's reappearance at the Park Theatre for her second New York season took place on August 12th. In spite of the stormy weather the theatre was packed to overflowing, and neither the suffocating heat of the days that followed nor the absence of many fashionable New Yorkers had any appreciable effect on the box office: the receipts averaged $1,300 and on one evening were more than $1,600. She gave nine

performances in all, enchanting the audiences again with her dancing
and her curtain speeches, and when she added *Nathalie* to her American
repertory, hundreds of people had to be turned away.

After the second performance thousands of people gathered in the
Park and around the American Hotel, drawn by the announcement that
the German colony was to serenade her. But the music had hardly begun
when a mob from the rival gangs of Soap-locks, Butt-enders and
Round-rimmers invaded the street and brought the proceedings to an
abrupt close. One of the musicians received a severe stab in the neck,
and many of the instruments were broken and burnt in the street. Fanny
was horrified by this outburst of violence, which seemed partly directed
against her. Some months before a gang leader called Armstrong had
been killed by some Germans in self-defence, and the gangs had seen an
opportunity to take their revenge. For some days past agitators had been
busy making inflammatory speeches in the Park, stirring up resentment
against the patronage of foreign artists, and the innocent German
musicians before Fanny's hotel had been marked out as the victims of a
brutal vengeance.

The gangs were in evidence on the streets for some nights afterwards,
setting off rockets and starting fires to spoil any further attempt at a
serenade. There was a danger of Fanny herself being involved in this
ugly affair, and after her third performance she was escorted back to her
hotel by a bodyguard of broad-shouldered Germans. Thus protected
Fanny and Katti walked through the menacing crowd with their hearts
pounding. They arrived to find the hotel filled with people waiting to
witness the street battle which was expected, for it was known that
another attempt at a serenade was to be made that night. Appalled at the
thought of the possible consequences, Fanny sent for the leader of the
German Musical Union to try and dissuade him from this project. He
arrived just as she was sitting down to dinner with Samuel Welles, the
banker, and the sight of an English-speaking American was enough to
fill him with indignant fury. Fanny had to exercise all her charm to
calm him down, but eventually he gave in to her pleas and agreed to call
off the serenade.

The Germans were not going to be labelled as cowards, however,
and the next night Fanny was handed a note during dinner telling her
that the Germans were going to give their serenade that evening and
that if there was any disturbance she was not to worry since they would
be adequately protected by their own compatriots. Wisely the mob
stayed away that evening, and the Germans performed no less than ten
numbers beneath her window—including the *Cachucha*, which she
accompanied with her castanets—and after each one shouted triumph-

antly: *"Vivat unserer gefeierten Künstlerin! Vivat der Fanny Elssler!"*

The calm atmosphere of Boston came as a welcome relief after the rowdiness of New York, and like many Europeans Fanny and Katti at once felt at home. The latter was struck by the tidiness and cleanliness of the city with its houses built for the most part in the English style. "Also," she added in a letter to her father, "there are none of those dreadful pigs running about the streets like dogs, as is the case in New York, Philadelphia, Baltimore and Washington, strange though it may seem. There both pleasant and unpleasant creatures seem to enjoy the same degree of freedom. In those cities one must not be surprised to meet a herd of horses or cows wandering around as they do in villages in Europe. The cows usually come home at a certain time to be milked, and then wander off again to their favourite pastures. The French Ambassador, Monsieur de Bacourt, who recently arrived in Washington, told us that when taking tea in the hotel he had asked for milk and received the reply: 'The cow did not come home today. She stayed the night in the meadow because of the fine weather.' We all had to laugh at the cow's independence."

Manager Jones of the Tremont Theatre in Boston had insisted on providing his own *corps de ballet* to support her, so Fanny had left her small company behind and brought only Sylvain with her. She therefore arrived several days in advance so as to rehearse her repertory. Curiosity was running high, and on the morning of her first performance, when some of the boxes were being auctioned in the theatre, there was a moment of excitement when a fortunate few caught a fleeting glimpse of her.

"At the close of the auction," it was reported, "Fanny herself passed through the tail of the crowd, unnoticed and unknown, to the rehearsal, attended only by her rosy faced manservant, plump as a peach. She was dressed in light pink drapery, with a white scarf and straw bonnet turned up in front, her two eyes glaring from beneath like two stars in the face of heaven. As she passed through, only one or two who had seen her in New York recognised the sylph and gave the word, 'There's Fanny, there's Fanny,' just as she disappeared into the interior of the theatre. Many of them gazed after her, as if they would pierce the wood and stone, but generally there seems to be a good deal of composure here about the whole business. Yesterday afternoon she took a walk around the Mall and Common, accompanied by her cousin, and her servant walking behind. She was dressed very simply—a sort of tartan dress, a large shawl and a straw bonnet. For all the world she looked like a sensible, unpretending New England girl, coming or going to church. So much for Fanny."

The Bostonians were too proud to be influenced by the enthusiasm which Fanny had stirred in New York and elsewhere, and furthermore, they were a little put out that Fanny had not chosen to present anything new in her repertory. Her debut in Boston on September 7th, in *La Tarentule* followed by the *Cracovienne*, would therefore be a critical test. How she fared that evening was vividly described by Wikoff in a letter to Gordon Bennett. "So, Fanny Elssler has made her debut in Boston," he wrote, "and a singular one it was. I do not know how to characterise it fully, it seemed so quiet, so genteel, so philosophical, so different in noise and nonsense, to the way we do up similar matters in New York . . .

"Everything was now ready—the bell rang and the curtain rose. Fanny does not make her appearance in Lauretta till a few seconds after the raising of the curtain. At length she issued very quietly from a side door, arrayed in white short drapery and a yellow bodice. There was a shout raised from the pit—Fanny came down very archly and made her curtsy, first to the right, then to the left, then a low one and long smile to the centre.

"The first portions of the character of Lauretta present nothing striking. It is mostly pantomime—little dancing. Towards the middle and close of the first act, Fanny begins to let out a reef occasionally. The house, during these preliminary movements, kept very quiet, with some visible signs of disappointment . . . At length she executed one of those singularly graceful movements, coming down the stage on the tips of her toes, half dance, half walk, which so electrified the Parisians. This was done with great delicacy and neatness, her face covered with an arch smile. The house could not stand this like philosophers. The shout rose from the pit, and spread like a shock of electricity all over the house. Yet there were no bravos—no huzzas—several said, capital, well done, and one enthusiast solemnly pronounced it pretty fair—pretty well. She went through the rest of the ballet, first and second acts, with pretty considerable spirit, and received pretty considerable applause. But I must in candor say, that I think I have seen her dance with inconceivably more spirit and animation in New York and London. This may have been partly occasioned by her first appearance before a new, very critical, and very calmly cold audience and partly to the wretched assistance she had from the *corps de ballet* and the other appointments of the stage, all of which were as miserable as a beautiful woman going to be executed could wish for. She was, however, encored in several of her dances, and finished the *Tarentule* amidst great applause.

"After an interval of some time, she appeared in the *Cracovienne*, which charmed the audience amazingly. She was called to repeat it,

Henry Wikoff. Lithograph by Kaeppelin from a drawing by P. C. Van Geel.

Coll. Mr Allison Delarue.

Don Francisco Martí y Torrens.

Bibl. Nac. José Marti, Havana.

The interior of the Gran Teatro de Tacón, Havana. Lithograph from a drawing by F. Mialho.

Bibl. Nac. José Marti, Havana.

Fanny Elssler. Pencil drawings by
John Hayter, 1843.

British Museum.

which she did, but unfortunately, losing one of her beautiful steel spurs, the effect was marred somewhat at the close. She was then called out with great vociferation. Sylvain led her on the stage. She came down in her usual graceful manner, first to the right, then to the left, bowing to the audience at each movement—then plump to the footlights, and spoke her speech. 'I tank you,' said she, with a smile, in a beautiful German accent, 'I tank you for this applause.' Here she made a pause, 'and I shall try to deserve it.' The rest was completely devoured in the vociferous applause . . . A wreath and two bouquets, and three-fourths of another flung at her feet, as she withdrew. One of them was prepared by a young fashionable of New York, who wears moustaches on the outside of his head, and more good sense and good temper in the inside than people give him credit for. Sylvain picked up the flowers, and the curtain fell. The fashionable company then retired from the theatre—and the philosophers of Boston have been very busy ever since, discussing the philosophy of Fanny Elssler's dancing—and are preparing an analysis of the elements which make up her powers of fascination."

At the second performance two days later the Bostonians threw off all restraint. The audience was too impatient to tolerate the preliminary items, and after ten minutes began to shout for the ballet. They paid no heed when the manager tried to explain that the dancers needed time to dress, but when the curtain rose for *La Tarentule* complete silence fell until the moment when Fanny appeared. She was the idol of the moment. She was visited by members of the leading families, and the shops were filled with Elsslerana; there were Elssler boot-jacks and Elssler bread, and the *Cracovienne* started a fashion for dresses of tartan plaid with cuffs of blue or black velvet with bright metal buttons. Fanny's engagement in Boston was extended, and in all she danced thirteen times during this visit, including two benefits for herself and another for the Bunker Hill Monument Association.*

The philosophers of Boston of whom Wikoff had written included some of its literary giants. Ralph Waldo Emerson was overwhelmed by her performance in *Nathalie*, and so was his companion, Margaret Fuller.

* According to the account books of the Tremont Theatre, preserved at the Boston Public Library, Fanny received $500 for each of her twelve performances, including her own benefits. Sylvain was paid $250 a week in addition to sums of $58, $24 and $24 respectively for the three weeks for "extra ballet services" (presumably taking rehearsals). Receipts ranged between $1,726 (her second performance) and $620.75 on the nights she appeared. The house was almost empty on the alternate evenings, on one occasion bringing in only $54.75. When Edwin Forrest followed her, he could only draw between $410.75 and $177.75, and his two benefits drew less than half those of Fanny.

"Ralph," she whispered in his ear, "this is poetry."

"No, Margaret," he answered her. "It is religion."

That evening Emerson recorded his impressions of Fanny Elssler in his journal. "She must show, I suppose," he mused, "the whole compass of her instrument and add to her softest graces of motion or 'the wisdom of her feet'—the feats of the rope dancer & tumbler: and perhaps on the whole the beauty of the exhibition is enhanced by this that is strong & strange, as when she stands erect on the extremities of her toes, or on one toe, or 'performs the impossible' in attitude. But the chief beauty is in the extreme grace of her movement, the variety & nature of her attitude, the winning fun & spirit of all her little coquetries, the beautiful erectness of her body & the freedom & determination which she can so easily assume, and what struck me much the air of perfect sympathy with the house and that mixture of deference and conscious superiority which puts her in perfect spirits & equality to her part. When she courtesies, her sweet & slow & prolonged salaam which descends and still descends whilst the curtain falls, until she seems to have invented new depths of grace and condescension, she earns well the profusion of bouquets of flowers which are hurled on to the stage . . . It is a great satisfaction to see the best in each kind, and as a good student of the world, I desire to let pass nothing that is excellent in its own kind unseen, unheard."

Another eminent admirer was Professor Henry Wadsworth Long-fellow of Harvard, who was building up a wide reputation with his poetry. Shortly after Fanny's arrival in America he had received a glowing letter from his friend Sam Ward in New York. "She is a charming dancer. The ideal of a fascinating mistress," he was told. "Her eyes charm the Pit and Boxes by a mightier spell than the boa constrictor's. He who yields to her influence must, for that moment, become a voluptuary. Her influence is sensual, her ensemble the incarnation of seductive attraction. She has been as often bought and sold as absolution from and by priests. She retains the shadow of love, the substance has long since departed." Ward was fascinated by the legend of the Duke of Reichstadt's love, but when Longfellow saw her dance in Boston, he was inspired by a very different image. In the following weeks he began work on a three-act verse drama, *The Spanish Student*, whose heroine, Preciosa, was a *cachucha* dancer of unassailable virtue who, after many blows of fortune, is eventually reunited with her student lover. Ward was puzzled and amused by the transfiguration of the dancer in Long-fellow's imagination. "You cannot imagine (even you who can imagine Fanny E virtuous) . . ." he wrote teasingly in one of his letters to the poet. But Ward appreciated the strength of the inspiration, and in the spring of 1841 Longfellow received a parcel from him with a note that read: "I send you Fanny Elssler this afternoon in a black box and I trust you will receive Preciosa safely." It contained no doubt one of the souvenir statuettes of Fanny dancing the *Cachucha*.

Another Bostonian admirer was Allyne Otis, a scion of one of the city's leading families, who took advantage of his parents' absence to throw a party in Fanny's honour in the family mansion at No. 45 Beacon Street. The bohemian company he invited consumed quantities of sherry, madeira and champagne, and Fanny may well have wondered why her host was absent at the end of the evening. A most unwelcome accident had befallen the unlucky young man who, in answer to a call of nature, had rushed to the outdoor privy and fallen in.

Fanny had found Boston in festive spirit. The Whig Party was holding a National Convention to stir up local enthusiasm for the forthcoming Presidential election, and Fanny and Katti watched the crowd streaming past their window like some fantastic masquerade on its way to Bunker Hill. At the same time the ladies of Boston had organised a fair to raise funds to complete the granite monument commemorating the Battle of Bunker Hill, one of the first engagements in the War of Independence. When she went out to watch the procession and hear the speeches, Fanny selected her costume with perfect tact. She looked ravishing in a tartan silk dress, cashmere shawl and blue silk hat, but what delighted the Bostonian ladies most of all was her diamond brooch, set in the form of an American eagle, which fastened the ribbons of her hat to her dress.

Fanny was so overwhelmed by the hospitality of the Bostonians that, not content with making many purchases at the Ladies' Fair, she offered to dance at a special benefit performance for the Bunker Hill Monument Association. The performance took place on October 1st, and ended as usual with a curtain speech. "There are two monuments which will rise together," Fanny announced from the stage, "one of granite on Bunker Hill—the other of gratitude in my heart." Some of the more proper Bostonian ladies were shocked at the idea of the earnings of a ballet dancer, and a foreigner at that, being applied to honour a glorious moment in the nation's history, but the receipts of the evening produced a substantial contribution to the funds needed for the monument.* Oliver Wendel Holmes wrote that "she had danced the capstone on to Bunker Hill Monument as Orpheus moved rocks to music", and according to a romantic legend a pair of her ballet slippers was smuggled

---

* The Bunker Hill Monument Association received $569.50. This, together with $30,000 raised by the Ladies' Fair and other contributions, enabled the monument to be completed two years later.

in among the documents and mementos deposited in the cornerstone.

It was in Boston that Fanny faced a critical decision that could be put off no longer. Her leave of absence from the Paris Opéra had originally expired on August 15th, but Léon Pillet, the new Director, had agreed that she could anticipate two months of her 1841 holidays so as to remain away a little longer. She had soon realised that the American visit was producing opportunities which she had not envisaged when making her plans in Europe. Towards the end of July she received an offer from New Oreleans of $10,000 for twenty performances. It was impossible to accept it and still honour her contract with the Opéra, for if she was to be back in Paris by October 15th, she would have to leave America shortly after the middle of September, and she was already committed to engagements in New York and Boston. She discussed the problem with Wikoff and Katti, and almost made up her mind to remain in America until the following March.

For reasons of his own Wikoff was exerting all his influence to prevent her from returning to Europe, and in September wrote a long letter to Gordon Bennett of the *Herald* beseeching his assistance. "Mark me", he told him, "she is in no way bound in *honor* or *law* to return to France, though they endeavor to prove that; for she has a contract with the Opéra till the end of April next,* with a penalty if she chooses to break it. She does not wish nor intend to break it, she entreats of the Opéra permission only to prolong her furlough for three months or so to make her fortune, and they are brutal enough to think of refusing her . . . The Opéra may, as it does, cry out against her, for their interest will suffer if she don't return. Her friends and admirers have reason to exclaim also, for they will lose her society and her dancing; but is she to sacrifice her interest, her convenience, her reasonable wishes, as she has foolishly done all her life, and as usual lost everything by it, to gratify the unjust expectations of the people on the other side of the Atlantic? . . . Bennett, I want you to help me, if necessary, in this matter which is in fact a *difficulty* . . . Give some reflection to her *position*, and to what degree you think her *compromised* before the world and the law. She makes her fortune, *between you and I*, by staying here; she *loses everything* by going back—she desires earnestly to remain. Will *you help me to detain her here*, and to save her from any *moral* cost or loss? Money she thinks less of."

Fanny had hoped that Pillet would understand her difficulty and grant her the extension she asked, but he was obdurate that she should abide by her contract. Although she was loth to dishonour her obliga-

* Wikoff was overlooking, or was unaware, that Fanny had signed an extended agreement with the Opéra for a further four years, until 1845.

tions, the opportunities she would sacrifice by leaving America were so enormous that she found it difficult to make a decision. "In Paris they are trying their best to make Fanny agree to return," wrote Katti on September 26th in a letter home. "As proof of the success which Fanny's performances in America have had, there is the fact that after paying all expenses for five months, 100,000 fr. are left to be put in the bank. Should Fanny abandon this treasure chest before it is empty, this gold-mine before it is exhausted?" Still troubled by her conscience, Fanny now decided to accept an offer to dance in Havana the following spring in the hope that Pillet would accept a *fait accompli* and relent. On October 1st the *New York Morning Herald*, informed no doubt by Wikoff himself, announced that she had made up her mind not to return to Paris until the following year. "Our Parisian friends," it added, "may rely on this intelligence. It is authentic. Fanny can make an independent fortune in this country in one year. Why should she return?"

Meanwhile Fanny's friends in Europe were not unaware of the growing influence of Henry Wikoff. A New York paper, the *Corsair*, had asked bluntly: "Why is she still called Fanny Elssler? She is no longer Fanny Elssler; she is Madame W . . ." It was reported that Wikoff and she had vanished from Philadelphia for a few days, perhaps to be married. Wikoff had countered these reports by a statement in the *New York Courier* which only drew attention to their relationship. "There is no question whatsoever of Fanny Elssler being Mrs W . . . in any way that certain miserable slanderers have suggested. For her, Mr W . . . is simply a travelling companion and a special friend to whom she entrusted herself in venturing into a foreign land. Mr W . . . is acquitting himself of the responsibilities of a host with all the honour of a gentleman and the purity of a friendship which could only be misrepresented, or whose disinterestedness could only be suspected, by perverted minds."

For very different reasons Harriet Grote and the Marquis de La Valette were very disturbed by the reports that Fanny had become Wikoff's mistress and was refusing to return to Paris. La Valette, who was afire with jealousy, used his influence to induce Pillet to extend Fanny's leave of absence until the end of the year and even threatened to go to America and bring back the errant dancer. For their part the Grotes were sadly disillusioned by Fanny's behaviour, which seemed to dash all Harriet's hopes of leading Fanny from the stage to a respectable retirement. Mrs Grote was at the centre of this drama, which she recounted at length to her friend, Mrs Jameson.

"I have been harassed about Fanny Elssler," she wrote on October 3rd. "La Valette been down to B[urnham] Beeches, & long letters

between us since. The Devil to pay about her folly in breaking engagement, but he has got the favour of a prolongation to Decr so as to allow
of his going to fetch her between this & then, should she prove still
recalcitrant. Meanwhile *I* firmly expect her by the British Queen on the
15 or 16 of Oct. I wrote so earnest a remonstrance that I am disposed to
think she will come, malgré the dictates of pecuniary interest. La
Valette wrote her the most imploring ardent letter possible, & warned
her he should go over in Nov. if she did not come by the October ship."

A fortnight later, on the 17th, Fanny's decision to remain in America
had been confirmed. "Letters from Wikoff and Sumner, from Boston,
of 1 Oct.," she wrote, "as well as from Charles our servant, (attached to
F.E. *pro tem*) inform me this day of her resolute determination to
proceed to the Havannah! Malgré all protestations of the Marquis, his
menaces of going over to fetch her, and Mr Grote's and my earnest
recommendations to her to return and keep her engagements at Paris.
I have scarcely been well enough to write since I returned hither,
which was later than I wrote you I intended, on account of my sufferings
in the beginning of this week, which were deplorable, else I shd have
communicated to you some notion of what has been transacting in
reference to Elssler's Paris affairs. La Valette returned to London last
Sunday, bringing the note from Thiers to Guizot and passed Monday
evening in Eccleston St. He signed a bond to pay 60,000 francs in case
FE does not return the end of December and either he or Therese, whose
guarantee is also given, must pay the same if pressed by M. Pillet & M.
Duponchel. This step was adopted by L to stave off the action for
damages, which the Directors were on the point of instituting against
the truant Danseuse, in conformity with the duty they owe the abonnés
and shareholders at large. There was never such a romance as this whole
affair has been, and our present relations with M. de la V are truly
remarkable! Conceive my being converted into a receipient of *his* griefs
and miseries and 'confidences,' *I* who have frankly told him from the
beginning that I would never encourage F to marry him, or even to
continue to be his '*aimée*,' because I thought him unworthy of her
esteem! He has forgiven me everything, it would seem, because he *has*
some ground for considering himself *unkindly* used, to say the least of it.
I hardly dare chalk out the probable issue of this *ravelled* history, but my
impression is that F designs to disenthrall herself from her connection
with the Marquis, and that her experience of gentlemen of high honour
and generous impulses, obtained within the last 12 months, (since she
was taken up by us) has opened her eyes to the defects of *his* character,
& lessened her affection accordingly. He must give up going over, for
she is off to Cuba, & thence to N. Orleans (Wikoff in attendance).

Therese had reckoned on going, in case L could not, but one would be as hopeless a case as the other. Sumner's letter is delightful, & full of valuable details to me, for neither F nor Wikoff are good at facts. The Br. Queen is not yet in, but I expect no letters by *her*. These came by the Boston vessel; none is come from F herself. I need not say that we are extremely vexed about all this and Mr Grote begins to become somewhat weary of such a profitless warfare as that of inspiring a sense of obligation in American bosoms. F now takes Wikoff's views of right and wrong, and those are apparently genuine American, which means 'l'argent avant tout.' I shall take no more trouble about the matter, having toiled and striven to guide her honour and credit, sans succès. She must now shift for herself, & with her £16,000 or £18,000 she will marry very well no doubt one of these days. She has sunk in my estimation by this fatal resolve, and in G's much lower, and God knows if he will ever again become much interested about her, so unseparable is his attachment to honour and good faith."

"The tiresome girl, F. Elssler", was the subject of another letter two days later. "I cannot," Mrs Grote wrote, "convey to you any *idea* of the doubts & uncomfortable presages which her recent conduct has generated in both Mr G and myself. How she *could* go on writing in the warmest strain of passion to M. de la V, & *of* him, to me, in steady terms of attachment, & *yet* refuse to listen to his counsels, his prayers, his *adjurations* to return, accompd. by his assurance that her intimacy with Wikoff was insupportable, and that if she continued to travel with him in his carriage & live in the same appartnt. etc., he wd. come over & fight him, (for all Paris is laughing at him, and *W's mistress* at Paris screaming that F has robbed her of her lover) in spite of all this, off she goes to the *Havannah, with said Wikoff;* who, writing to me date 30 Sept. does *not* tell me he is going with her) *she* writing never a word to me by this packet. I can't dive into her intentions at all, but I think it all but clear that she will lose her good name, her friends, *& her lover* by what she is doing, and in my present state of feelings towards this young man I should say a break with him is devoutly to be deprecated."

The Grotes were not to know the state of Fanny's feelings in having to resolve this conflict between duty and opportunity. It had made her very depressed, and in the hope of restoring her spirits she decided to take a short holiday and, in the company of Wikoff and Katti, to visit the Niagara Falls. It took them a week to reach their destination, travelling sometimes by railway and sometimes by stage coach. Timetables did not have to be rigorously observed, and on the last stage of their journey from Lockport the engine driver obligingly stopped the train so that Fanny could hear the distant thunder of the Falls.

When they reached Niagara, which was then a collection of a mere hundred houses, Fanny was so impatient to see the Falls that she stopped at Cataract House only long enough to deposit their luggage and send for Mr Hooker, the guide. When he arrived, she, Katti, Wikoff and another friend at once set off on a sightseeing expedition. Mr Hooker made Fanny turn her head so that she should see the Falls for the first time in all their majesty. She was so moved by the sight that she stood still for a moment in silent wonder and then wept with emotion. Determined to make the most of their stay, they set out again in the afternoon, crossing the bridge to Goat Island to see the Horseshoe Falls from the round tower on Terrapin Rock. The power of the waters, viewed from as close as they could safely venture, was quite overwhelming. Quivering with excitement, Fanny tried to express her thoughts first in one language and then in another. Finally, looking into the roaring foam, she folded her arms and remarked with a mischievous gleam, *"Quelle mousse extraordinaire!"*

The Falls, still in their unspoilt glory, had an unending supply of wonders, from the terrifying thunder of the water plunging in a curtain of white foam to the cool romantic beauty of the lunar rainbow. Courted by the local residents, Fanny was given the opportunity of seeing this wonder of the New World from many viewpoints. The owner of Goat Island received her in his mansion, and the British garrison on the Canadian bank invited her to attend a parade of the Highland regiment that was stationed there.

Crossing the river above the Falls was a frightening experience. Seeing the friendly shore receding, Fanny was overcome with panic as she felt the small boat shaking in the quickening current and imagined the awful fate that would befall them if they were to be swept over the brink. She paled at the thought and felt faint. *"J'ai peur,"* she stammered. The danger soon passed, and she had recovered her composure when they stepped ashore to be welcomed by the British commanding officer. Fanny was fascinated by the Highlanders in their kilts—"the only kind of *sans culottes* I have ever seen"—but wanted most of all to see the Falls from this other side. She insisted on going under the Falls in spite of the cold, and looked a strange sight in the protective clothing that was supplied. "It is really worth being half drowned to see Miss Fanny in such shoes and stockings," exclaimed her maid. "Whatever would they say in Vienna?" Fanny was not lacking in courage now, and the guide had to restrain her from approaching too close to the edge. Before returning to the American side, she stood for a moment on Table Rock contemplating the majestic sight. "I have seen man's finest creations," she said with emotion, "but what are Versailles and Fontainebleau compared with the overwhelming presence of God in this handiwork of His?" Mr Hooker was impatient to return, but the party had not taken many steps when they missed Fanny. Looking round they saw her kneeling on the ground, gazing in exaltation at the waters.

On the way back the old guide presented her with an eagle's feather and begged her to write a few words in his album. At first she demurred, but finally she took up a pen and, in German, expressed her feelings in two simple lines:

> Emblem of God, His power, His majesty!
> Niagara Falls, I worship thee in silence!

Resolved not to spoil her holiday, Fanny firmly refused an offer to dance in Buffalo, which they passed through on their way back to New York. It was a comparatively new settlement, surrounded by encampments of Indians who were resisting attempts to settle them further north, and one day they came upon a timid young Indian girl, brown-skinned and long-haired, who was with difficulty persuaded to remove her cloak and show Fanny her dress.

Both Fanny and Katti had caught chills from going under the Falls, and shortly after leaving Batavia Katti fell seriously ill. She was told she had rheumatic fever, and they had to spend a week in a small, friendly town called Geneva while she recovered. The rigorous New England winter was already setting in, and when they reached Albany the snow was thick on the ground and people were going their ways on sledges.

They did not stay long in New York, which was celebrating the victory of General Harrison over Martin Van Buren in the Presidential election, but moved on to Philadelphia, where Fanny was to give six performances at the Chestnut Street Theatre between November 10th and 21st. Katti told her father that Fanny would have liked to cancel this engagement but was held to it by her agent. "In North America," she added, "the strange custom prevails of washing down the stage every Saturday. Certainly it gleams like a mirror as a result of this custom, but it is also slippery and dangerous." The bitter weather deterred few people from coming to see her again, and Fanny Kemble—who was said to be writing a ballet for her: a project which never materialised—drove seven miles through a blinding snowstorm to see her a second time in the same ballet.

Fanny was now growing accustomed to the extravagant ways of the Americans, but one tribute she received in Philadelphia was quite unique. An industrialist of the city named Norris, who had manufactured a railway engine to an order from Berlin, had the happy idea of naming it after her, and it left the United States proudly bearing her name painted on the front of the boiler.

At the end of November Fanny was back in New York, where she enjoyed a short respite before setting out on the next stage of her American adventure, which was to take her to the warm south and to Cuba. At the National Theatre she saw two dancers whom she was soon to engage, a young American called Harriette Wells and the Frenchman, Jules Martin, and she spared a little time to sit for the sculptor, James Varick Stout.

Meanwhile, warnings from Paris that if she failed to return by January 1st the penalty of 60,000 fr. would be claimed fell on deaf ears. Wikoff's counsels were those she now heeded. Paris was ignored, and there was no longer any attempt to conceal the reason for this. "She has played about 65 nights since her advent here," ran an inspired report in the *Herald*, "and estimating the net proceeds at $500 per night, she will have cleared $32,500 during the past season. This amount, deducting her expenses, she has invested in American State stocks—part in New York city stocks, bearing regular interest of 5 and 6 per cent . . . She has been so engaged in negotiating with the Opéra people in Paris, and carrying on a long diplomatic correspondence, that for a month she had no time to dance at all. It seems that the Parisian managers have threatened, and scolded, and prosecuted, and received $12,000 of damages for breaking an engagement she never entered into. All this is fanfarade. If the Parisian directeurs are saucy, or insist upon the ridiculous penalty, she will never return to Paris. She will make $40,000 in her southern trip—and if she remains on this continent for the next three years, she can clear $50,000 per annum, invest it all in American stocks—leave the stage on a fortune of $200,000 and an annual income of $10,000, and travel over England, Italy, Germany, like a beautiful Marquise, in her own chariot. A fig for Paris! Who cares for Paris? Not Fanny Elssler."

XI

Havana and the Deep South

ON THE EVE OF ST NICHOLAS two feet of snow fell in New York. "A fearful blizzard, such as I have never seen in Europe, is raging in the streets of the city," Katti wrote to her father, "so that it really seems as if St Nicholas, with rod in hand, were after the New Yorkers. It is ten o'clock in the morning, but not a soul is to be seen in the streets, apart from the country folk bringing their wares to market." When the blizzard subsided, New York lay under a covering of crisp white snow, and Fanny made a spectacular appearance driving down Fifth Avenue in a sleigh drawn by four white horses.

A few days later, when she left New York with Katti, Wikoff, Sylvain and her manservant Charles, the wintry conditions played such havoc with the railway schedules that it took them seventeen hours to reach Philadelphia. They stayed there a few days to purchase clothes, flowers and other articles which had been unobtainable in New York, and then continued their journey to Baltimore. A poster announcing the appearance of Edwin Forrest in *Richard III* tempted Fanny to spend a night there, but at the last minute she discovered that the performance was on the following day. They very nearly missed the train, and it was only because it was drawn out of the city by horses to be connected to the locomotive some way out that they were able to catch up with it in a carriage. Continuing southwards they reached Washington in the early hours of the morning and took a steamer down the Potomac to a point on the Virginian shore not far from Fredericksburg, where they boarded another train which took them to Richmond, the state capital. It must have been an exhausting journey.

They arrived in Richmond very quietly, intending to stay only one night there, at the Marshall House, but the news of Fanny's presence quickly spread and a stream of callers made their appearance, each one imploring her to honour the city by dancing. After vainly trying to explain that she could not venture on the stage in anything more than a simple dance, Fanny agreed to make a single appearance at the Marshall Theatre for a fee of $600. Richmond was so appreciative that a visit to the State Capitol was organised in the form of a triumphal procession.

Behind a brass band, and reclining on a litter borne on the shoulders of
six State senators, she was escorted through the streets by the Governor
of Virginia, the Judges, the Mayor and Aldermen of Richmond, members
of the Senate and House of Delegates, soldiers and a large crowd of
citizens. When she entered the House of Delegates Fanny was invited
to sit in a chair of honour at the Speaker's right to listen to flowery
speeches of welcome. On her return after this extraordinary triumph,
she found the Marshall House besieged by a crowd eagerly waiting
to catch a glimpse of her and crying out for souvenirs.

Her *Cachucha* and *Cracovienne* inspired scenes of ecstatic enthusiasm
when she made her appearance at the theatre on December 18th.
Richmond was dazzled no less by her artistry than by the aura of her
romantic past. The myth of her love for the son of Napoleon was on
everyone's lips, and to an anonymous poet of the city it was only the
presence of Henry Wikoff that disturbed the "vision of beauty like a
bright dream sped" that was Fanny Elssler:

> As to the truth of the De Reichstadt story,
> > *N'importe*—the thought at first might move our bile
> That Sire and Son should thus divide Earth's glory,
> > But then the death in dark St. Helen's isle
> Foils all the fame the hero won in foray,
> > And even the Euthanase of thy soft smile
> Hath its alloy—how perfect!—could we strike off
> The afterthought of hated—happy W——

The following day the wintry weather dogged them all the way to
Wilmington, which they reached seven hours late to find they had
missed the steamer for Charleston. Forced to seek shelter in the small
town, they wearily trudged from house to house in the cold, dark night.
After being turned away many times they came to an open door by
which a young man was standing. "We have no room," he said, without
even waiting to be asked. This was too much for them. They were cold,
tired, hungry, and by now almost desperate. "My God!" they exclaimed,
"we cannot sleep in the street", and they marched indoors like soldiers
requisitioning billets to find many of their fellow passengers sitting
round the fireplace. Some of the men gallantly offered to sleep on the
floor so that Fanny and Katti could spend the night in a warm and
comfortable bed.

The following day they were on board ship, steaming through a
wonderfully calm sea to Charleston. In contrast to the fierce winter in
the north-east, the climate in Charleston was gently autumnal. It was a
town of wooden houses, still bearing the scars of the great fire that had

swept through its streets two years before. Mr Paige, the manager of the Charleston Hotel where they were lodged, had bought the hotel the day before the fire and seen it next day reduced to ashes. It had since been so magnificently rebuilt that Fanny exclaimed when she saw it, "Bless my soul! The Astor House has got here before us."

For the four performances which she gave at the new Charleston Theatre between December 28th and January 2nd, Fanny was supported by Sylvain, Mme Arraline and Charles Thomas Parsloe, an English pantomimist who had joined her for the trip to Cuba.

When Fanny first set eyes on the small steamship that was to take her and her party exclusively to Havana, her heart sank. It was really no more than a river steamer and had never made the journey to Cuba before. Fanny declared that nothing would induce her to venture into the ocean on such a small, frail craft. Then a two-masted schooner, the "Hayne", put into port with a cargo of oranges and began loading rice to take back to Havana. Its captain had considerable experience of the route, and agreed to take them to Havana at a fraction of the cost of chartering the steamship.

They set sail on Sunday morning, January 3rd, 1841, and made their way very slowly at first, for there was little wind. Towards evening both Fanny and Katti began to feel sea-sick, and it was two days before they felt well enough to take stock of their surroundings. It was a far cry from the luxury of the "Great Western." There were more than twenty passengers and room for less than half that number. There was a cabin on deck for the gentlemen, and a dark, doubtful-looking place somewhere below which was called the ladies' cabin. For exercise the passengers only had six feet of deck space, the rest of the deck being packed with cargo, stores, water butts, and pigs and chickens which were consumed on the voyage.

The winds were so contrary that the ship covered no more than fifty miles in the first three days. The good-humoured captain kept his passengers amused by singing sea shanties, which he interspersed with invocations to the winds to blow so that he could show the ladies the speed of his ship. As if to play a joke on him, the heavens darkened and they plunged into a furious storm. As the ship tossed and rolled in the angry waters, the passengers were ordered below. To Fanny's annoyance Katti, in a show of feigned courage, had refused an offer of an upper cabin, and the two women descended to their low, dark quarters below. There, buffeted out of bed and terrified by the battering of the waves against the sides of the ship, Katti was soon deserted by her courage. Determined to teach her a lesson, Fanny began by ignoring her whimpering pleas to go above, but when Katti could stand no more and fled in her nightdress, she had to follow. The gentleman who had earlier offered them his deck cabin relinquished it at once, and there they passed an anxious night listening to the awesome storm. Next day they left the clouds behind them and sailed into the sunshine. Hatless and wearing light clothes, Fanny and Katti sat out on the deck shaded by their parasols and reading.

Eight days after leaving Charleston they sighted the coast of Florida and anchored off the lonely outpost of Indian Key. While the captain went ashore to deliver the mail, they gazed enviously at the green grass surrounding the few shabby houses in the wild landscape. As they learnt when the captain returned, it was not an inviting place, for he brought back not only a bouquet for Fanny, picked by the lonely daughters of the local postmaster, but some blood-curdling stories of the war with the Seminole Indians which had been raging in Florida for several years. Fanny shuddered at the thought of the fierce warriors, and when darkness fell the flickering of Indian watch-fires on the coast inspired a fear which was not dispelled when someone jokingly observed that she would only have to dance the *Cachucha* to be spared. But the nightmares which disturbed her sleep were soon forgotten in the sunshine of the following morning, and she looked out across the clear blue water to the passing coastline and leisurely read Alfred Bunn's new book of theatrical reminiscences which brought back memories of far-away London.

Excited by the prospect of reaching Havana the next day, everyone went into dinner in high spirits to eat the last of the chickens. All of a sudden the ship gave a violent lurch. Fanny dropped her spoon and looked at the captain, who flushed and hurriedly left the table. As the ship continued to bump on the rocks, the passengers became alarmed and all the horrors of shipwreck and capture by Indians rose up in Fanny's imagination. In the evening a thick mist rose, and the captain decided to drop anchor. For eight hours the ship remained stationary before moving into the safety of deeper water.

The sight of Key West with its neat white buildings set in a lush landscape reminded Fanny of some exotic opera set. She and Katti were allowed to go ashore for a brief walk beneath the coconut trees, and when they returned Fanny was told that some of the rich planters had offered whatever sum she cared to ask if she would dance for them, and that if she agreed a large room could be ready in a matter of minutes and the sailing delayed. Fanny was both astonished and flattered, for it had never occurred to her that her fame would have reached such a remote spot. When she declined, the planters, thinking that perhaps she felt they did not have enough money, immediately offered security for

$1,000. In persisting in her refusal she was as disappointed as they were, but she was in no condition to dance at short notice, having found her legs strangely unsteady after more than a week at sea.

The perils of the voyage were now over, and that evening the schooner glided across the Straits of Florida beneath a clear starry sky. Early in the morning of January 14th an excited Fanny was on deck to see the coast of Cuba come into view. Soon she could distinguish the great yellow pile of the Morro fortress, with the Spanish flag flying in the breeze, and as the ship entered the harbour of Havana, it was surrounded by scores of little boats filled with men clamorously touting for business of one form or another. Fanny had been recommended to stay at Mr West's boarding-house, and Mr West himself arrived to take charge of them personally, and in half an hour had them safely ashore. Waiting to take them to their lodgings was a *volante*, the oddest carriage they had ever seen. Looking a little like a London cabriolet, it had two enormous wheels and between the shafts was a mule with a negro sitting astride it in postillion's uniform.

When she arrived at the boarding-house and saw the small, uncomfortable bedroom allotted to her, Fanny decided to remain there only long enough to find somewhere more appropriate. Charles, his ruddy English face perspiring in the tropical heat, was dispatched to fetch their luggage from the Custom House, where one of their baskets was stolen almost under his very nose. Katti was inconsolably distressed because it contained her mother's miniature, and poor Charles was so crestfallen that Fanny, wanting to show that she still had confidence in him, entrusted him with the mission of inspecting the Mansion House, a hotel of which friends had spoken highly. He soon returned with a favourable report, and two days later Fanny moved there.

No doubt on Wikoff's advice, Fanny had gambled on negotiating a contract in Havana shortly after her arrival, for in addition to her personal following—Katti, Wikoff and Charles—she had come with Sylvain, Mme Arraline and Parsloe, who were all receiving monthly salaries from her. As Wikoff had foreseen, Don Francisco Martí y Torrens, who managed Havana's two largest theatres, the Tacón and the Principal, lost no time in calling on her.

Fanny already knew enough of Pancho Martí's background not to expect the conventional type of theatre manager. Ostensibly he had made his fortune by building and exploiting the Fish Market in Havana, but stories abounded of shady profits earned in the traffic of Negro and Mexican slave labour. He had then undertaken the more reputable enterprise of constructing the Gran Teatro de Tacón, which with its capacity of about three thousand spectators was the largest theatre in the world, and he now enjoyed a virtual monopoly of the Havana theatre. But even so Fanny was hardly prepared for the extraordinary figure who entered her room. It was the oddity of his clothes which struck her first of all: the baggy white trousers and the shapeless black coat thrown over his shoulders, revealing a white cravat and an enormous pin stuck in his shirt. But even more bizarre was the man himself, with his wrinkled, colourless face and hair brushed over to one side and secured with a woman's side-comb.

As he came through the door, this extraordinary apparition raised his arms and exclaimed in a cracked voice, "*Voilà la famosa!*" Then, after staring hard at her with cunning little eyes, he explained in a quaint mixture of French and Spanish that he would like to offer her an engagement, but that it was difficult because both his theatres were occupied. With Wikoff at her side, Fanny was astute enough to see through his ruse, and to show him that she was not worried at the possibility of not appearing at all, she announced in a very demure, business-like manner that her terms would be $1,000 a night, a benefit for herself, a half-benefit for Sylvain, and allowances for the expenses of the dancers she had brought with her. Martí stared at her incredulously for some moments, then without another word put his hat firmly on his head and strode out of the room.

This was only the first of many visits in which Martí endeavoured with all his cunning to persuade her to reduce her demands. That same evening he turned up while they were taking coffee. After apologising unconvincingly for his abrupt departure that morning, he began bargaining again. When he still met with no success, he again took his hat and left, mumbling about returning with an interpreter. An hour later he was back, this time with a fat companion who sat down with great gravity, spread a yellow silk handkerchief on his knees, and declared in very fair French that he had come to explain Martí's meaning. So they began again, but the fat man's wiles were no more effective than Martí's more obvious approach.

Pancho Martí's next line was to play on the public's impatience to see her dance, and by devious means to try and work up feeling against her. Fanny countered this by writing to a number of influential people in the city telling them that she would be leaving for New Orleans if negotiations were further delayed. This move brought about the intervention of the Governor, and Martí, not with the best grace, was forced to offer her an engagement for ten performances substantially on her original terms. Her only concession had been to forgo her requirement that Sylvain should have a half-benefit, for she felt that he was well enough

Fanny Elssler. Drawing by
John Hayter, 1843.

Coll. Mr Edwin Kersley.

Fanny Elssler as Esmeralda.
Drawing by Paul Bürde.

Öst. Nationalbibliothek, Bildarchiv.

Jules Perrot and Fanny Elssler
dancing the Castilliana Bolero in
Le Délire d'un peintre.
Lithograph by J. Bouvier.

Victoria and Albert Museum.

Gustave Carey and Fanny Elss
in *La Jolie Fille de Gand*. Engra
by G. Leybold.

Coll. Mr Allison Delarue.

remunerated at $1,000 a month not to risk the negotiations collapsing on that point alone.

As soon as the contract was signed Fanny began to practise on the stage of the Tacón. To her delight she found her strength and energy returning much more quickly than she had expected. One morning as she was dancing she heard the sound of cracked laughter and clapping from the darkness of the auditorium, and peering more closely she perceived the figure of Pancho Martí sitting in the stalls. Having never seen him even smile during their negotiations, she was quite taken aback by his laughter.

"*Encora! encora!*" he shouted, and after she had continued awhile with her practice he stood up, exclaiming "*Buena! buena!*" and left the theatre puffing contentedly at his cigarito.

Meanwhile poor Sylvain was struggling against the heaviest of odds to drill a *corps de ballet*. It had proved incredibly difficult to find suitable dancers. Ballet was a totally unknown art in Cuba, and while girls could be found to perform Spanish dances, it was quite another matter to persuade them to appear in a *corps de ballet* and risk appearing ridiculous. Havana was combed from end to end, tempting rewards were offered, but all in vain. Finally Martí had to order twelve of his supernumeraries to support Fanny in *La Sylphide*. A less suitable collection of women could hardly have been found, for not only were they of all shapes and sizes, but they were dark-skinned. Furthermore, as if their appearance were not forbidding enough, these swarthy sylphides strutted about smoking cigars and discarding them only when called on to the stage, when they carefully placed them on benches and chairs with growling menaces to the stage hands not to touch them. Fanny detested the smell of cigars, but this was nothing to the apprehension she felt about the public's reception of these extraordinary ballet girls.

Fanny's series of performances was awaited with the greatest excitement, and Martí had increased the prices accordingly. On the opening night, January 23rd, the Conde de Peñalver sent one of his carriages to drive her to the theatre, which she found already surrounded by a large crowd. An hour or so later, when the curtain rose on *La Sylphide*, she looked nervously across the footlights into the huge auditorium. The absence of panelling in the lower tiers, which were protected only by a grill, gave the house a novel appearance, the white trousers of the men and the white dresses of the ladies seeming to gleam in the dim light. There was a burst of applause when she made her first entrance, but the audience then fell so silent that she began to worry. The truth was that the Habaneros, most of whom had never seen a ballet before, were puzzled by this novel form of entertainment. It was unfortunate that much of the first act consisted of mime, for they expected to see Fanny perform marvellous things. There was a little laughter at the brown-skinned Scottish peasants, but this was nothing compared with the hilarity which was to break out in the second act. Even Fanny had to smile when she saw the girls standing in the wings in their ill-made sylphide costumes. In an attempt to conceal their brown bosoms Martí had supplied them with bright yellow chemisettes, and at the last minute Sylvain had decided to complete their transformation by whitewashing their arms and legs. After Fanny had stirred some enthusiasm by a display of *pointe* work, the *corps de ballet* began to dance. For a while they observed a semblance of order, but a difficult passage threw them into confusion. From the wings Sylvain could be heard shouting, "Right! Left!" but this only made matters worse. They exchanged glances of dismay and, as the audience began to hiss, took fright and scampered into the wings. One luckless creature, heavier and more short-winded than the rest, was left alone in the middle of the stage. Horrified at find-ing herself the focus of attention, she trotted off towards the right, then changed her mind, wheeled round and broke into a wild galop of her own composition. This was too much for the audience, whose laughter became so uncontrollable that Fanny thought it would never end. Though she felt outraged at such behaviour, she could not help under-standing some of the public's amusement. After that it was quite impossible to restore the audience's gravity, and the ballet proceeded to its close to a continuous accompaniment of exhausted tittering.

The *Cracovienne* was warmly applauded, but Fanny was too distressed to accede readily to the audience's demand for an encore. Katti pleaded with her as the bell sounded imperiously from the Governor's box, signifying an order to repeat the dance. When the curtain rose, she was still refusing to go on and the stage remained empty for quite two minutes before she relented, only to be further upset by the execrable playing of the orchestra. The evening appeared to have been a disaster, and Fanny returned to her hotel in a state of utter misery, wishing she could rescind her contract and return to the United States by the next ship.

The next day a greatly alarmed Martí called at the Mansion House to see her. With brutal frankness he informed her that the coolness of the audience was due to her want of attraction, and that there must be a change of ballet at the next performance. She made it quite clear that this was out of the question. Having cast off her despondency after a good night's rest, she was facing the situation as a challenge. She at once discharged the fattest and swarthiest members of the *corps de ballet*, deciding it was better to have too few supporting dancers than incur a repetition of the hilarity that had spoilt her debut. The thought that the audience's attention would consequently be focused on her gave her added confidence at her second performance. Gradually she brought them under the spell of her dancing, until in the second act their enthusiasm erupted so violently that she was almost frightened by it. Her *Cracovienne* sealed her triumph. Time and time again she was recalled, making her *révérences* on a stage strewn with flowers.

As she was leaving the theatre, she passed Martí who was standing at the door with a broad grin on his face. She teased him by asking whether he would like to change the ballet now.

"*Non, non, famosa,*" he replied, "*jamais.*"

As the days went by the demonstrations of enthusiasm grew more and more flamboyant. The exotic flowers fell more thickly, verses printed on paper of every colour floated down from the upper boxes, and doves and humming-birds with fluttering ribbons were let loose to circle above her head. To celebrate her visit in more permanent form, a silver medallion was specially struck, bearing on one side the royal crown and the words "Havana, 1841", and on the other the inscription, "*Hommage de fidelité au mérite de F. Elssler dont l'écho étant parvenu jusqu'ici ressouvient les beaux jours de Virginie*".

Fanny had intended not to perform the *Cachucha* in Spanish Cuba, thinking that it might suffer in comparison with the more boisterous dance which went under the same name in Havana. The fame of her *Cachucha*, however, had preceded her, and requests for her to dance it soon became too pressing to ignore. So one evening she told Katti to unpack the costume and take it to the theatre. The noisy demonstration calling for the *Cachucha* came as no surprise. Stepping forward she expressed her diffidence in performing this dance and then added, to the audience's delight, that she would comply with their wishes. When she reappeared in her costume and began to dance, the public could not contain its enthusiasm. At the end the gentlemen in the pit rose to their feet cheering and waving their hats and thumping their walking sticks on the floor, while the tiers of boxes seemed to shimmer with the fluttering of white handkerchiefs. Wishing to spare her the fatigue of repeating it, the Governor, on whose orders alone an encore could be taken, withdrew from his box, but the tumult continued so uncontrollably that protocol had to be forgotten and Fanny danced it a second time.

Havana had a tradition all its own for benefit performances. The only seats sold to the public on such occasions were for the upper parts of the house, all the boxes and stalls being placed at the disposal of the artist taking the benefit. First of all she was expected to pay calls on the most distinguished patrons and invite them to the performance, retaining boxes for them unless they made their excuses. People of somewhat lesser importance were then invited but did not receive a call. The performance itself was regarded as a sort of private reception. The artist would take her seat at a table before the entrance of the theatre to receive her guests, each of whom would deposit an offering in a silver bowl. This ceremony took place before a curious crowd who noted how much each person gave and commented with all freedom on their generosity or tight-fistedness. In addition to the money which filled the bowl, many people made private offerings.

Fanny considered this custom very demeaning to an artist, but she submitted to it and paid the obligatory calls to invite her friends to her benefit. When the day came she took her seat at the table dressed in her costume for the *Jaleo de Jerez*. Since it was customary for a lady to be accompanied by a sister or a friend, Katti sat at her side watching wide-eyed as gold and silver coins poured into the bowl. As for Fanny herself, she felt humiliated and hardly dared look at the people as they passed her, and she was glad when the time came for her to escape into the theatre and receive a more traditional tribute to her dancing. The *Jaleo de Jerez*, which Havana had not seen before, was even more wildly received than her *Cachucha*. Ten times she was called before the curtain, and finally she spoke a few words in Spanish: *"Mi lengua non es Española, pero mi corazón esta noches es todo Habanero"* (My tongue is not Spanish, but tonight my heart is wholly Habanero).

She was yet to taste the full strength of the public's homage. As she came out of the theatre into the warm night air, she was met by an extraordinary sight. Across the bobbing heads of the crowd clustered around the stage door, she could see the carriage of the Conde de Peñalver surrounded by torchbearers and a band of musicians dressed as ancient Romans. The Count and his friend, Don José Urtetegui, invited Fanny, Katti and Wikoff to enter his carriage, which was then drawn slowly through the streets by a team of admirers, with a throng of laughing ragamuffins running alongside. The memory of Baltimore's tribute paled into insignificance. The procession took more than an hour to reach the Mansion House. As the band blared out its noisy homage, Fanny happily threw flowers and waved her handkerchief at the people who were cheering from their windows. At the hotel a sumptuous supper had been prepared, and the band's final task was to play a national air when she appeared on the balcony.

The receipts of the benefit amounted to some $10,000, not counting the many presents she had received in private. These included many beautiful pieces of jewellery and a costly *Cachucha* costume, but the most extravagant offering of all was that of Don José Alfaracho. At first sight it appeared to be an ordinary box of Havana cigars, but surprised by its weight, Fanny unrolled the outer leaf of one of the cigars to discover that the inside was solid gold. Her wit did not desert her in her amazement. "That would never have happened to me in Bremen," she remarked.

Their stay in Cuba was now drawing to a close. They paid a short visit to Matanzas, where Urtetegui had invited them to see the sugar and coffee plantations, and returned to Havana for the carnival. After the excitement of the previous weeks the masked ball at the Teatro de Tacón seemed a dreary affair, and on the day of their departure their spirits were damped by a torrential downpour which turned the dusty streets into rivers of mud.

On the following day, Tuesday, February 25th, they steamed out of Havana harbour expecting to arrive in New Orleans on the Friday evening. The water was choppy, but Fanny and Katti were gratified to find they were the only passengers who did not succumb to sea-sickness. Soon the sea became wonderfully calm, but they ran into a thick hot fog, which lifted momentarily to reveal an armada of ships all waiting to navigate the mouth of the Mississippi. The fog then descended thicker than ever, and it was not until Sunday afternoon that their ship docked in New Orleans.

The sun was setting in a brilliant blaze of fire as an excited crowd followed Fanny's carriage to her hotel, and a journalist wrote lyrically: "With the arrival of Fanny Elssler the sun sank in shame." After Fanny had entered the hotel, the carriage cushion on which she had been sitting was brought in and auctioned. It was bought by an admirer who had yet to see her dance for $200.

The manager of the St Charles Theatre had accepted Fanny's terms and engaged her for twelve performances from March 6th at $1,000 a night and a full benefit. To recoup some of this large outlay he offered seats for the opening performance at an auction. The demand was so great that one box was knocked down for $61 and a place in the parquet fetched $5, and similar auctions were held throughout her season. The torrential rain seemed to deter no one from going to the theatre, and it was sometimes difficult to prevent the crowd from storming the building. Many people travelled great distances to see her dance. She was boisterously applauded and showered with gifts of jewellery, and crowds gathered in the streets whenever she went out for a ride or a drive in her carriage.

Her engagement at the St Charles Theatre ended just before Easter, which she and Katti spent in their hotel, feeling very homesick and disturbed by the noisy dance music which penetrated their room until late into the night on Good Friday. It came as a welcome relief to resume her performances the following week when, on Tuesday, April 13th, she opened a season at the elegant Théâtre d'Orléans. The French and American Quarters of New Orleans were two very different worlds existing side by side in uneasy antagonism, and Fanny had shown a scrupulous fairness by signing a contract for another twelve perform-ances at the French theatre. Taking advantage of its excellent company of singers and actors, she was able to add another role to her American repertory—the Bayadère in *Le Dieu et la Bayadère*. Katti could still marvel at the enthusiasm of the public. "People no longer know what to do in order to praise her," she wrote. "There have been too many flowers, and now they are throwing her wreaths of strawberries, and a wreath was recently sent to the theatre which was so big that it would not fit into any of the boxes." Even the little Negro boys in the streets were affected by the Elsslermania and could be heard whistling the *Cachucha* and the *Cracovienne* and airs from the *Bayadère* as they went about their errands.

In the manager of the Théâtre d'Orléans, Charles Boudousquié, and his wife, the singer Julia Calvé, Fanny found two kindred souls, and she and Katti spent a few delightful days at their country house at Mande-ville, on the northern shore of Lake Pontchartrain, where they wandered under enormous pine trees and admired the magnolias.

After the twelve contracted performances Fanny was given a benefit on May 11th. At the end Julia Calvé came on to the stage bearing bouquets, and afterwards the two artists drove back together to the St Charles Hotel, where a supper party had been arranged. As they sat down to table a band of musicians began a serenade. Then, rudely, the air was shattered by the ringing of bells and the clatter of hooves, and two fire engines came hurtling down Common Street, scattering the serenaders and overturning their music stands. A few minutes later, having realised it was a false alarm, the firemen returned and angrily set about breaking up the serenade by shouting and ringing their bells. The alarmed musicians took refuge in the hotel, while Fanny watched the commotion from the window with tears in her eyes. It was an outbreak of the animosity that divided the French and American communities, and the *New Orleans Bulletin* ungallantly supported the firemen, castigat-ing Fanny's friends, and her "travelling agent" in particular, for making the people of New Orleans appear ridiculous. By organising a serenade by French musicians in the American Quarter Wikoff had been playing with fire, and this incident cast a cloud over the last days of Fanny's stay in New Orleans. Two days later, on May 13th, she appeared at Julia

Calvé's benefit, and the next day she left the city on the first stage of the long journey back to New York.

No railway connected New Orleans with New York, and Fanny was relieved to be spared a long sea voyage when it was suggested that she should travel by steamer up the Mississippi and the Ohio, and complete the journey by coach and train. They left New Orleans in the large river steamer, "Queen of the West," and their departure was celebrated by a song of the Negro labourers:

> Fanny, is you going up de ribber?
>> Grog time o' day.
> When all dese here's got Elssler fever?
>> Oh, hoist away!
> De Lor' knows what we'll do widout you,
>> Grog time o' day.
> De toe an' heel won't dance widout you,
>> Oh, hoist away!
> Dey say you dances like a fedder,
>> Grog time o' day.
> Wid t'ree t'ousand dollars all togedder,
>> Oh, hoist away!

They lived on board the river boat for a full week, halting once each day to collect wood. Fanny and Katti were glad to break the monotony of the journey by taking a walk along the river bank, even if the only object of interest was some poor Negro's wooden hut. The fast-flowing Mississippi was an unattractive river, and when they reached the junction with the Ohio the lights of a mansion at dusk was a welcome sign that they were approaching civilisation. Along the Ohio the landscape changed. Flood waters had spilled into the low lying woods near the banks, and the villages and small towns crowning the hilltops looked so secure and cosy.

They disembarked at Cincinnati, a pretty little riverside town enclosed by a crescent of hills bearing many charming villas on their slopes. Here they found letters from home, and were saddened by the news that the ship "President" was feared lost at sea with all souls, for one of them was the English actor, Tyrone Power, who had visited Fanny in Havana and seen her second performance there. They stayed at Cincinnati's Broadway Hotel for just one night before continuing their journey, so there could be no question of Fanny dancing at the theatre there: a report in the *New York Morning Herald* a few weeks later that she had demanded more than the house could take was plainly malicious. With some difficulty they found a steamer to take them further up the Ohio to

Wheeling. They did not know till later that the captain had accepted a wager that he could not overtake three other ships which had left some hours before. He won his bet in magnificent style, and Katti excitedly wrote home that they had been given an idea of what an air trip must be like!

Even in Wheeling Fanny was regarded as a celebrity, and when she left her hotel a crowd had gathered to gape at the first ballerina they had ever seen. She hired a fine comfortable carriage called "The Queen", in which they drove east through the mountainous countryside of friendly towns, picturesque villages and sparkling streams. After taking refuge from a thunderstorm in Cumberland, they continued to Frederick, where they caught a train to Baltimore. In the first week of June, some three weeks after leaving New Orleans, they were back in New York.

XII

The Second Year of the American Tour

THERE COULD BE NO DOUBT that during Fanny's absence from New York some sort of conspiracy had been hatched to drive her from the American stage. Envy had played a part in this, stirred by the high fees she was commanding in a period of difficulty for the New York theatre; and the Puritan streak in the New England character was easily irritated by reports of her growing fortune and extravagant demonstrations of enthusiasm which seemed very foreign to American eyes, coupled with sly insinuations of a wanton private life.

She and Wikoff found it specially galling to see even Gordon Bennett's *Herald* opening its columns to reports which were plainly written with malicious intent. One of these, ungallantly referring to her as "the sylphide of 34, with a son of 18", alleged that she had thumbed her nose at the New Orleans firemen during the fracas at the end of her stay in the South. Another slightingly referred to Wikoff, who had taken great care that his own name should be kept out of the press, as her "clerk". Having devoted much time and trouble to cultivating the Gordon Bennetts, he felt he was at least entitled to the protection and support of the *Herald*. At his suggestion Fanny had received the young Mrs Bennett and before sailing for Havana had given her a gold bracelet. From Cuba and New Orleans he had sent reports of Fanny's progress, which the *Herald* had not always published, even when he had offered to pay for them. Fully aware of the power of the press, he realised this was a delicate situation, and concealing his annoyance, he wrote a friendly letter of complaint to Bennett, while Fanny, no doubt on his advice, sent Mrs Bennett a silver service and a necklace with earrings to match.

The result of this approach was swift and effective. Bennett made amends in his own fashion by publishing a counterblast in the very next issue of the *Herald*. This took the form of a letter from a correspondent in London, but was in fact written by Bennett and based, with a few additional flourishes, on Wikoff's letter. Wikoff had alleged that the hostile reports had originated from Seguin, Taglioni's agent in London, and Bennett embellished this by reporting that Taglioni, "at the age of nearly forty", was contemplating a visit to America and that Seguin was preparing the ground for her by denigrating Fanny. Having emphasised Taglioni's age—she was in fact thirty-seven and Fanny thirty-one, but three years here or there mattered little to Bennett—he went on to repeat Wikoff's denial that Fanny had a son of eighteen, obviously unaware of the existence of little Franz Robert who was being brought up in Eisenstadt and was now nearly fifteen. Finally, to add a touch of authenticity, Bennett's fictitious Londoner described how he had seen Therese moved to tears when reading Fanny's descriptions of her triumphs in "the land of the big mountains and the bigger hearts".

It seemed all the more important to secure the sympathy of the *Herald* when Horace Greeley was attacking Fanny in the *Tribune* for not even having "the common excuse of necessity for a life of wantonness and shame", and was calling upon all decent females to boycott her performances at the Park. But Fanny had only to dance to silence the malicious tongues. As the opening of her fourth New York season at the Park Theatre approached, the city succumbed to another bout of Elsslermania, and her triumph seemed complete when she appeared before the first night audience on June 14th. "The house was so full that it could hold no more," wrote Philip Hone in his diary. "She was well received and much applauded, and on being called out after the performance made a very neat little speech in broken English, which every one in the audience thought was worth his dollar. I went with our lovely neighbour, Eliza Russell. Some of the newspapers—the *Commercial Advertiser, Evening Signal,* and *Tribune*—have, with a degree of insufferable arrogance, undertaken to write down this amusement, and abuse those who go to see it, calling them fools and idiots, and lying abominably about proofs of admiration bestowed upon this graceful *danseuse.* This sort of interference between men and their consciences, and dictation as to matters of taste, has become very common of late, and people seem determined not to submit to it. I have no doubt that many, like myself, went to the theatre to evince their disapprobation of this kind of impertinence."

With Sylvain, Parsloe and Harriette Wells to support her, Fanny gave thirteen performances at the Park Theatre in a space of four weeks, including her own benefit on July 7th followed by benefits for Simpson and the unfortunate manager of the National Theatre which had been burnt down a few weeks before. New York saw her for the first time in *La Bayadère,* and at her benefit she and Sylvain danced the *Menuet de la Cour* and the *Gavotte de Vestris,* and she performed a *Bolero* which she had learnt in Havana.

Few people realised how much effort it had cost her to complete this engagement. The exertions of the past year had taken their toll, and she was suffering from physical and nervous exhaustion and had lost considerable weight. But there was one bright spot on the horizon. Fanny believed that her sister Therese would soon be joining her in America, and the arrival of every big ship from Europe aroused hopes that she might be on it or that it would bring news of her imminent arrival. To recover her strength she cancelled an engagement that had been arranged in Philadelphia and went, with Wikoff and Katti, to Coney Island for a short holiday. There they were able to relax for a few days, bathing in the sea and fishing for minnows. "The childish glee with which she indulged in diversions so new was greatly diverting", Wikoff wrote to Bennett, adding that she had gained several pounds and was beginning to fear that her proportions were outrunning the sylphide standard. Katti told her family of the simple pleasures of these few days. "We went for a walk along the seashore, where there are wooden huts for bathers," she wrote. "Here we observed the play of the waves and their perpetual ebb and flow, and watched the tiny snipe digging insects out of the sand with extraordinary speed, hurrying through the foam of the moving waters as if they too wished to take a footbath. Their audacity finally gave us sufficient courage to risk a dip in the cool water. Laughingly we played in waves of ever-increasing size which rose up like hills, enveloped us in their green depths, and then broke over our heads with a roar of foam. With our backs turned towards the sea, or sitting close together, we let the mountains of water storm around us."

This little holiday was to be spoilt by the curiosity of the other guests at the hotel. In his zeal to protect Fanny from their gaze Wikoff had ordered a screen to be erected on the balcony to give her some privacy. A party from Philadelphia, who had been deprived of the rooms they had booked by Fanny's decision to stay a few days longer, considered they were at least entitled to the use of the balcony. When they went to remove the screen they found Wikoff waiting for them. A brawl ensued, and Fanny had to intervene to prevent bloodshed. On his return to New York, Wikoff told Bennett they had left Coney Island "under circumstances rather disagreeable", an understatement that the scandal sheet, *New York Polyanthos*, enlarged upon in an article entitled "The Great Kicker Kicked Out", illustrated by a crude cut showing Fanny intervening with a *grand battement à la seconde* in defence of Wikoff. "Fanny left Coney Island yesterday in high dudgeon", it reported.

Another worry which was disturbing Wikoff's equanimity was Fanny's growing friendship with the sculptor, James Varick Stout, to whom she had been giving sittings for a life-size statue of herself in *La Gipsy*. A passionate, ambitious young man, Stout saw himself as an artist working on a heroic scale. Some years previously he had returned from Europe to make a large statue of Queen Victoria, which had unluckily been destroyed when being shipped for an exhibition; then he had made a colossal bust of George Washington, and now Fanny Elssler was claiming his attention. Having been greatly flattered when his friend, L. N. Fowler, the phrenologist, compared his bumps with those of Canova, he persuaded Fanny to allow herself to be examined. The result was a privately printed pamphlet which appeared at the end of 1841, in which Fowler published his assessments of the sculptor and the dancer and added sketches of their careers, the biography of Fanny being "written by one of her most intimate friends, and under her own immediate sanction".

For some reason Wikoff took violent objection to the pamphlet and endeavoured to have it suppressed. Fowler's phrenological sketch of Fanny's character seemed harmless enough, although it did contain a passage which Wikoff might have read as a reflection upon himself. "She may be influenced by others," the phrenologist had deduced. "She . . . values her word, and does not deviate from her engagements when she has the management of her own affairs." Perhaps this touched a sensitive spot if Wikoff felt any responsibility for influencing Fanny to break her contract with the Opéra, a step which had given rise to a claim for 60,000 francs damages. Apart from that, there was little that could be seriously objected to in this far from unperceptive character study. Fowler had concluded that Fanny was not of a very passionate nature, that if she preferred male society to female, it was in order to gratify her intellect, and that she would make a more devoted friend than lover. She lacked, however, "the boldness and courage which is necessary to push along successfully without a lover". If she was acquisitive, she regarded wealth as a means rather than an end; it was not acquisitiveness but other qualities that made her "anxious to acquire and lay up". She knew how to conceal and control her feelings, she was guarded, suspicious, careful even to excess. She was mindful of appearances and very sensitive to criticism. She had a strong perception of the witty and the absurd, and enjoyed a joke.

Fanny's morale was at a low ebb at this time, and for once her art seemed to give her little satisfaction. "Her triumphs in this country," wrote the intimate friend in the biographical sketch, "have had a decided effect upon her character, whilst to the astonishment of every one, she still retains her meekness of spirit and modesty of demeanor, yet her soul may be said to have '*banqueted*' upon glory. Her ambition she feels is gone. The art which through life had been a cherished passion, an idol, is now no longer so. She cares no more for theatrical renown, the bustle and *hubbub* of her life now wearies, and she professes now only a desire to sit down in quietude and think it over. She says 'she has yet never had time to reflect, to taste leisurely of life; that she has always been so hurried along, her career so tossed about on the tempestuous waves of theatrical excitements, her ears so dinned by popular applause and uproar, that it would be a relief to fly and escape it all.' There is hardly a doubt but she would be happy in retirement, for despite her ambition, her nature is so gentle, her tastes so simple, and her feelings so disciplined, that she would find abundant resources in private life, surrounded as she would certainly be by numerous friends, to whom she would ever be the dearest object of regard. But it is not likely she will be permitted to retire, now that she has reached the meridian of her glory, and the perfection of her art."

Wikoff was probably jealous of Stout, and the appearance of this pamphlet in which the dancer and the sculptor were associated as the subjects of study was bound to upset him. When the *Sun* reported that Fanny had "for $1,000 exhibited her person entirely naked to a handsome young artist" and aroused his desire, Wikoff suggested to Bennett that the *Herald* should publish a denial from the artist. "Stout," he explained, "came to me one day last December, and told me a touching story of his reduced situation—his loss in the Victoria statue—the immense advantages he would gain in making a statue of Elssler, etc. Thinking well of him from what had often been said of his talent and worth, I spoke to Fanny; she being very ill at the time, refused, but I persisted, and worked on her feelings till she, as you recollect, at the cost of great suffering to herself, consented. As to exposing her person, she would have died first, though that may not be believed. I had the greatest difficulty, as Stout recollects, in getting her to give one leg and part of the other. Stout was most grateful, but has since behaved badly." A few days later Wikoff returned to the subject. "As to Stout, I think he will act honorably," he wrote. "But I know the *weight of your opinion*. He told you . . . that the statue was the *attitude*, and in *the dress of the Gipsey*. He intended lately to forfeit his honor and represent the thing naked. But the suffering of Elssler that he witnessed induced him to put some drapery on—but even now, it is too indecent for an individual statue. For God's sake counsel him to adhere to his honor, and not to crucify Fanny, and half ruin me, who will share the disgrace."

There was certainly nothing objectionable about the statue when it was exhibited at the Stuyvesant Institute on Broadway in October 1841. It was highly praised by the French Ambassador, and Katti wrote a glowing description of it to her father. "The statue portrays Fanny as a gypsy, waking from a dream," she told him, "and is a very fine likeness. As in the ballet, she is in a half-sitting, half-reclining position, as if she

were just about to rise from her couch. The face is finely drawn and full
of expression, and the neck and arms, indeed the whole figure, are most
natural. She is wearing a bodice, and a jacket with Greek drapery. Her
hair is dressed as she wears it every day, and is in complete harmony
with the whole conception. Her right hand is resting on a cushion, and
her left one on her breast. Her head is turned to the left, lost in contemplation of the departed dream. Her right foot is lightly curved and
pressed against the bed, while the left is artistically placed against it."

When Bennett published Wikoff's letter about the statue in the
Herald two years later, Stout was so incensed by its falsity that he wrote
a long, breathless letter promising to relate his own "history of the
Elssler statue" and "the character and real position of Wikoff . . . His
examination before Oliver Lowndes and myself, by District Attorney
Whiting, concerning his platonic affection for Elssler, and otherwise, a
rich scene—his blackmail to the *Flash* and other public prints—his offer
of blackmail to one of our reputable journals, and his withering repulse
—his opinion of yourself and Mrs. Bennett—his regrets at his misspent
life—and his attempts to reform, commencing with his curse of Elssler
—his persecution of myself, arising from jealousy, and other motives
combined—his advice to me, by letter, to stimulate the press in general
to favor me, by the payment of $25 or $50 fees—his curiosity to know
of the thousand and one stories told in the state room, of Elssler, the
Duke de Reichstadt, and himself—his belief that nothing could be said
in his favor—his interference with Fowler, the phrenologist, to suppress
his work entitled *Stout and Elssler, phrenologically, &c. &c.*—Elssler and
her cousin's opinion of Wikoff—Elssler's opinion of yourself and wife
—the opinion of many of our distinguished men, that I had conferred
too high an honor on Elssler by making a statue of her—that by so doing
I had broken the just laws of my high art, that I should have selected a
subject far more elevated and chaste—Elssler's exquisite delight at
having her statue made—her frequent dream during her journey to
Havana and the south and west—her earnest solicitations that I should
go to Europe with her, she to perform after my statue, in nearly all the
capitals of Europe—her offer to sit to me for another statue, in another
character, if I wished her so to do—Elssler's repeated avowal of the
honor and pleasure I had given to her by making the statue—my refusal
to stray from my original design, and to put more drapery on the work
—my offer to change the features of the face, and declare it an ideal work
—Elssler's remonstrance and solicitation not to have this done—my
great sacrifice to please her—the objection of some of my friends to be
seen in my room with Wikoff—my hints that his presence was odious—
his threat to destroy the statue—his boast that the most inflated Elssler

puffs in the *Herald* were written by himself—his flogging at Havana, by an eye witness—the affair of Coney Island—his opinion of Sylvain—his ideas on his marriage with Elssler—his intimations that for the future Mr Bennett would say no more in praise of my works—the gold pencil case, &c. &c."

These promised revelations never materialised, but clearly the difference that had arisen between the two men was of a nature to arouse the bitterest of feelings.

Having decided to return to Europe that autumn and even booked a passage on the "Great Western," Fanny went to Philadelphia to settle her business affairs with Wikoff's own brokers, Messrs Hendrickson & Clarkson, who had agreed to look after the investment of her American fortune. While there she received a letter from Therese announcing her decision to come to America, and the plans to return to Europe were cancelled. The weather was very hot, and after concluding her business Fanny was glad to escape from the close atmosphere of the city into the countryside of New England. Wikoff took her and Katti up the Hudson as far as Albany, and from there they went overland, through Utica, to the Trenton Falls. Then, after a visit to Saratoga, they spent two nights on the shores of Lake George, where rockets were fired to demonstrate the wonderful echo that rolled like thunder between the surrounding hills.

Fanny had signed a contract to dance at the Chestnut Street Theatre, Philadelphia, immediately after the New York season, but had been too exhausted to fulfil it. She had lent the managers $2,000 to help them recover from the financial setback they had been caused, and as soon as she had cancelled her return passage to Europe, she had given them the first call on her services. She opened her series of performances on September 1st with a supporting company that included a new member, Pauline Desjardins, who had replaced Mme Arraline, and for the *Cachucha* she wore for the first time the beautiful silver-embroidered red satin dress which she had been given at her benefit in Havana. Towards the end of the month she presented two scenes from *La Gipsy*, which brought back many nostalgic memories of Therese. For the management the season was not a financial success, resulting in a loss of about $1,000: the gross receipts for the eleven performances amounted to $10,869.25, while the expenses came to $11,826:

Received by Fanny for the nine ordinary nights	$4,550
Received by Fanny for her benefit	1,325
Received by Fanny for her half share of the management's benefit	561

Received by Sylvain	750
Received by Desjardins	150
Received by Parsloe	90
Expenses of the *corps de ballet*	1,100
Ordinary expenses of the house	3,300

While Fanny expected to be paid fully for her own services, she gave several proofs of her generosity and thoughtfulness. She made donations to charities; she gave a supper to the theatre orchestra and presented the leader with a snuff box; and she bought some warm merino dresses for the girls of the *corps de ballet* whom she had noticed shivering in thin summer clothes.

In a moment of leisure Fanny took Katti to Cornelius's photographic studio to have their portraits taken by the new daguerreotype process. When Fanny sat before the camera, it caught a serious, almost weary expression which was afterwards reproduced on a music title by a deaf and dumb lithographer, A. Newsam. He and Fanny found they could understand one another perfectly despite the difficulties of language, and he paid her a touching tribute after seeing her dance. "As I sat in the theatre," he wrote, "I saw the people around me clapping when she danced and mimed. I too was moved to applaud, for I understood every one of her movements. If everyone expressed themselves as clearly as Fanny, the world would no longer be veiled for us deaf-mutes."

Fanny's plans for the future were still uncertain. Therese had purchased costumes for the American trip and had booked her passage to Boston, but then, as a result of a letter she had received from Fanny, she cancelled her passage. There had been a misunderstanding due to a delay in the mail, and Fanny immediately wrote to her sister that she had decided to remain in America, begging her to join her as soon as she could. A tempting proposition had come from Havana, and Fanny desired nothing more than to share the delights of a return visit to Cuba with Therese. Towards the end of September Fanny accepted this offer and confidently looked forward to hearing that her sister was on her way.

Her next engagement in Boston was deferred and Edmund Simpson prevailed upon her to give five performances at the Park Theatre, New York, from October 2nd to 9th. She would rather have rested for these few days, but she yielded, partly to be able to dance for the officers of the French frigate, "Belle Poule", which had just arrived in New York. The "Belle Poule" was still basking in the glory of its romantic assignment of the previous year when it had carried Napoleon's body from St Helena back to France. When Fanny visited the ship, she was given

Fanny Elssler being drawn in triumph in Germany. Caricature, 1842.

Bakhrushin Museum, Moscow.

Fanny Elssler's ballet slippers.

Coll. Mme. Derra de Moroda.

La Esmeralda, Act I. L to R: Didier (Quasimodo), Fanny Elssler (Esmeralda),
Frédéric (Phoebus). Lithograph by V. Timm.

Bakhrushin Museum, Moscow.

La Esmeralda, Act II, Scene II. L to R: Samoilova (Aloise de Gondelaurier),
Smirnova (Fleur-de-Lys), Frédéric (Phoebus), Fanny Elssler (Esmeralda) and
Johansson, Perrot (Gringoire). Watercolour by A. Charlemagne.

Bakhrushin Museum, Moscow.

two precious mementos: a twig from the weeping willow that had shaded the grave and a splinter from the Emperor's coffin.

Fanny was welcomed in Boston as an established celebrity. She arrived with a contract to give eight performances at the Tremont Theatre from October 13th at $500 a night payable the next morning, together with a right to a clear benefit, and in order to present *The Bayadère* and a complete version of *La Gipsy*, she brought a strong supporting company: Sylvain was still her partner, and among the other dancers were Charles Parsloe, Pauline Desjardins, and some promising young Americans, Eliza Vallee and her three sisters, and George Washington Smith. On the evenings when she danced the theatre was packed with spectators, some of whom had travelled great distances—even from as far afield as Canada—to see her. Her magic was as potent as ever. Nathaniel Hawthorne was so carried away that on returning home he hung her picture on his wall between the portraits of Ignatius Loyola and Francis Xavier.

One evening Fanny invited the crew of the warship "Columbus" to see her dance. The sailors marched to the theatre with their band playing the *Cracovienne*, and at the end of the performance one of them stood up to propose a vote of thanks, but was so overcome that he forgot his words and shamefacedly had to pull a piece of paper from his pocket to aid his memory.

During her stay in America Fanny had been cultivating the art of making little speeches from the stage which one admirer considered were "certainly the most naïve and bewitching things she does". At the end of her first benefit performance in Boston she had the whole audience hanging on her words. "Ladies and gentlemen, I am much bothered," she began in her inimitable Viennese accent, "I don't like to leave you now for the last time, and I am afraid to try your patience by a longer stay. Really, I don't know what to do—I have a great mind to stay—shall I? Now remember, if you get tired of me, it is your own fault!" As Sylvain gathered up the bouquets, the men in the audience stamped and cheered and the ladies waved their handkerchiefs, and Fanny "went home", it was reported, "gay as a lark and chirruping like a wild bird". True to her promise, she delayed her departure for as long as her future plans would allow and gave six more performances, culminating with a final farewell benefit and, inevitably, another curtain speech. This time it really was a farewell, and Wikoff sent a verbatim report to the press with all the emphases carefully noted. "I have stayed too long here," she began. "I *feel* I have by the pain of this parting—gladly would I return your touching kindness to me in any way, but I *cannot* do it, not *even* with a smile. It would be a mockery to attempt it. I have been *so* happy among you that this moment of separation distresses me deeply; but I have one comfort still left me, to *remember that happiness*. I will think of Boston again and again, but never without a *swelling heart* and a *dropping* eye."*

Fanny returned to New York by way of Providence, where a delegation called on her, begging her to dance one night at their theatre. Edwin Forrest, the tragedian, who was appearing there at the time, was prepared to sacrifice his benefit performance to make way for her, and the manager offered her the whole receipts of the house if she would agree. Fanny was embarrassed at the thought of depriving Forrest of the proceeds of a benefit, but the actor was so insistent that she yielded. Forrest had the highest admiration for her, saying that she was the only theatrical celebrity he knew who was natural and not, as he put it, "artist" off the stage.

The news that Fanny was to dance in Providence spread rapidly, and on the night of November 19th scores of carriages converged on the small theatre from every corner of Rhode Island and beyond. Fanny almost regretted her boldness in agreeing to present *La Sylphide* and the *Cracovienne*, for the seven fiddlers who comprised the orchestra found the music for the ballet much too complicated for their modest capabilities. Finally her manservant Charles, who played the violin for his own amusement, came to the rescue by taking his place among them and telling them to follow him and play as fast as they could. In this manner they made enough noise to cover up their frequent mistakes and struggled through the ballet without the audience being put out of humour. Fanny took little notice of the action of the local minister, who assembled his congregation on the evening of her performance to warn them against the temptations of such earthly pleasures as the ballet, but when the City Hotel, where she had been staying, was burnt to the ground the day after she left, simple people might have been forgiven for seeing some form of divine intervention.

* A year after Fanny's departure from America, the Tremont Theatre was closed as a theatre and converted into a Baptist chapel. Dr Lyman Beecher, father of Henry Ward Beecher, delivered a merciless tirade against the theatre, offering thanks to the Almighty for having changed the place which was once the seat of Satan and his works into Christ's holy temple. "Who could describe in all their lascivious truth," he thundered, "the dress and the movements of a certain celebrated ballerina who paused on this stage during her triumphant tour of the country—her drawers, modelled so marvellously on nature that it was impossible to distinguish material from flesh, and her short skirt which lifted when she spun to the applause in attitudes that would have made the Devil blush, aroused indignation, and crushed beneath the feet of shame feminine virtue, if any was present. And people tell us the theatre is a school of virtue, a mirror of nature! Yes, the mirror of naked, shameless debauchery!"

The goddess of the dance had meanwhile returned to New York, having returned $100 of her fee to the theatre. She was in real need of rest, but the demands of her profession were inexorably pressing. There seemed just enough time to make a rapid visit to Philadelphia to transact some business before opening at the Park Theatre on December 1st, but while there she developed a heavy cold. When her doctor told her she must delay her journey to New York, her first reaction was to order Charles to prepare for the journey. She finally yielded to reason, but when she travelled to New York a few days later, she arrived in a terrible storm, feeling so weak from exhaustion that the opening night of her season had to be postponed to the 8th.

It was hardly surprising that she failed to exert her usual sway. On some evenings when *La Gipsy* was given, the house was only two-thirds full. "It has been evident to us for some time," wrote the *Herald*, "that the physical power and energy of Fanny are not equal to what they have been, and even were a year ago. Grace, elegant motion, fine attitudes and repose are elements that remain unchanged longer than the former, but it is not possible that any ordinary constitution can surmount, untouched, the severe labour she has undergone during the last two years in the midst of a hot and burning climate. Fanny Elssler has concentrated, in the last year of her life, an amount of effort that would have lasted her for five years in Europe. Here she has been dancing at the rate of three or four nights a week, in New York, New Orleans, Havana, in every climate and every range of the thermometer. Such an aggregation of effort, concentrated into one year and a half, is entirely unprecedented in Europe, and never was known in this country. The consequence of this over-exertion is now becoming visible: Fanny is pale and emaciated to what she was a few years ago, and unless she retires from the stage and recruits her strength for six months a year, she will soon become an elegant wreck—a classic ruin."

With Sylvain, Pauline Desjardins and a talented young American dancer, Julia Turnbull, heading the supporting company, Fanny danced thirteen times during her fifth season in New York, ending with a series of benefit performances: first her own, at which she introduced a new character dance, *La Polacca*, and then benefits for Placide, the firemen and Manager Simpson. The season ended unhappily with a misunderstanding. Two performances at the beginning of the engagement had had to be cancelled owing to Fanny's illness, and the artists and stage hands had not been paid for these nights. The management also claimed to have sustained a considerable loss during the engagement, the receipts on one evening being insufficient to pay Fanny and the *corps de ballet*, although she had received her contracted fee of $600. The purpose of giving a benefit for the manager was to compensate him in some measure for this loss, but he and Fanny differed over the priorities of the salaries and other management expenses. Fanny offered to indemnify the management against any loss resulting from her illness if Simpson would pay in full the salaries which had been withheld, but his agent failed to keep an appointment to discuss the matter, which remained unresolved when the time came for her to leave New York.

Fanny's nervous strain had been aggravated by uncertainty over Therese's plans. Ever since the summer she had been living for the day when her sister would join her, and when seven cases of her possessions arrived it seemed that Therese herself must soon follow. The arrival of every passenger ship from Europe filled Fanny with fresh hope. When she was in Boston she felt sure Therese would be on the "Britannia" and drove down to the harbour, only to be cruelly disappointed when her beloved sister did not appear. Then, towards the end of November, she heard that Therese was coming on the "Acadia". Unable to go and meet her herself, she sent Charles to Boston to bring her to New York. She tried in vain to restrain her mounting excitement. Hope and doubt alternated as the days went by without sign of her, and Therese's absence at the opening performance was a great disappointment. A few days later Fanny told Katti to lay out her sister's clothes in readiness and reserve a box at the theatre. "If Therese arrives tomorrow," she said, "I shall first embrace her, and then tell her to rest and go to the theatre in the evening, and not to tell me about her journey until suppertime." Then, all of a sudden, all these golden hopes collapsed when news arrived that Therese had gone no further than London, where she had cancelled her passage in fear of bad weather. In her letter home Katti referred only obliquely to Fanny's disappointment. "We are now gradually preparing for a journey to Havana," she wrote, "for at present the climate here has a bad effect on Fanny's health."

A further cause of distress was the final break with the Marquis de La Valette, who indeed had been almost forgotten in the excitement of Fanny's American triumphs. He too had had his compensations. When Fanny had refused to return to Europe at his bidding, he seemed to accept that his influence over her was at an end for he began wooing the widowed Adeline Welles. Then, in a last forlorn hope of regaining his position as Fanny's protector, he asked an American friend to break the news to her that he was thinking of marrying. Being told that Fanny had at first shown signs of distress, though she had soon collected herself and declared that she did not care, he was encouraged to write her a long, affectionate letter. In it he assured her that he loved only her, begged her to return to France, and explained that the "old lady" would be a convenience to them both since his marriage would make him wealthy again. Fanny was so revolted by his cynicism that she forwarded his letter to Mrs Welles. As a result their engagement was broken off for a time, while Fanny regarded her friendship with the Marquis as a chapter that was now finally closed.

Another partnership was also about to end. James Sylvain had been a stalwart support to her ever since her arrival in America, but to some people his position as her partner and ballet-master was beginning to turn his head. "He is by far too ambitious," wrote the *Herald*, printing no doubt an item supplied by Wikoff, "and attempts to do more than is compatible with his powers. He strives to be the Napoleon of the dance; but in his attempts he only proves the problem that there is but one step from the sublime to the ridiculous. He should be more circumspect, attempt nothing but what he knows he can do well, and should not seek to reach a fame for which he was never destined." At the end of the New York season there was some sort of disagreement, and while Fanny engaged Jules Martin to be her partner for her second visit to Havana, Sylvain made plans to reap his own harvest. He formed a company with Parsloe, Julia Turnbull and Joséphine Petit-Stéphan, and after a trial season in Philadelphia, was to follow Fanny to Cuba.

Fanny had been so unfortunate in her experiences of the sea that she must have viewed the journey to Cuba with considerable dread. She need not have worried, however, for the three-master "Louisa", in which she sailed from Philadelphia on January 15th, 1842, was large and well appointed, and her rosewood-panelled cabin was as elegant and comfortable as her quarters in the little ship which had taken her to Cuba the year before had been cramped and dark. For most of the journey the weather was kind, and in the calm of the ocean Fanny's exhaustion seemed to slip away. For a fortnight they sailed southwards in the sunshine, catching only a distant sight of the coast of Florida, and on the 29th they reached Havana.

Here Fanny was welcomed as an old friend. There was no question this time of looking for lodgings, for a lady had placed part of her house at her disposal, and when she went to a ball given in her honour, wearing a lovely white dress which Therese had sent her from Paris, Fanny felt as if she had never been away.

She had signed a contract with Pancho Martí for twenty-two performances, eight at the Teatro Principal and the remainder at the Gran Teatro de Tacón, together with two benefits. Her supporting dancers, Jules Martin and his wife Egerie, Pauline Desjardins and her brother, and the Vallee sisters, made the journey in another ship under the supervision of the indispensable Charles, and as soon as they had all found their land legs Fanny began to prepare her programmes.

For her opening performance at the Principal on February 12th she chose *La Sylphide* with Martin as James and Pauline Desjardins as Effie, and two of the Vallee girls, Emilia and Eliza, dancing a *pas de deux* in the first act. Later, at her seventh performance, she appeared in *La Somnambule* for the first time in the New World. This time she had taken care to ensure that her performances were not marred by an inept *corps de ballet*, but for some reason the response of the public was at first disappointing and when Martí failed to sell sufficient boxes in advance to guarantee him against loss, he declined to continue the engagement at the Tacón. Far from being deterred by this development—indeed, relieved perhaps to be rid of Martí—Fanny decided to become her own impresario. At her own risk she presented four performances at the Tacón between March 7th and 12th. It proved a successful venture, the final performance, which was for her benefit, culminating with an unexpected demonstration of admiration. As the last notes of the *Craco-vienne* were drowned in the roar of applause, a rain of flowers fell at her feet and a band of young men from the leading families of Havana came running on to the stage to circle round her and crown her with a laurel wreath.

Fanny had intended to leave Havana in the middle of March to sail to New Orleans, but she decided to stay longer in Cuba to give three performances at Matanzas. The success of the short season at the Tacón then prompted her to delay her departure and give seven more performances there. The people of Havana showed their appreciation in their own unforgettable way. Fruit and sweetmeats were delivered daily at her house; whenever she went driving flowers were thrown into her carriage and ladies would order their postillions to stop their *volantes* so they could converse with her; and she was invited to spend a few days on the Marquesa d'Arcos' country estate. Therese had sent over the orchestral parts of *La Fille mal gardée* and *The Fairy and the Knight*, and in a burst of activity these two ballets were produced to the wild delight of the public. Applause and bouquets were no longer enough to express their enthusiasm, and a performance never passed without white doves bearing laudatory poems fluttering on to the stage with gaily coloured ribbons streaming behind them. The feathers of one of these birds had been gilded, and the poor creature stood on the stage looking down in obvious embarrassment at the strange appearance of its breast. Another bore a little silver bell which tinkled as it flew round the auditorium.

For her last appearance in the city Fanny performed by special request a Cuban national dance, *El Zapateo* or *Buscapié del Pais*, which she had learnt in three lessons from a peasant youth. It was billed as the final item, but unbeknown to her, some of the leading ladies of Havana's society had prepared a memorable farewell tribute. As Fanny was taking her bow, a backcloth of Mount Olympus suddenly descended. Mme Martin then emerged from the wings impressively swathed in the Stars and Stripes to represent the Spirit of America, another dancer appeared as Terpsichore, and three Graces came down on a pink cloud. While a concealed choir began to sing, Fanny threw herself into Mme Martin's arms with tears streaming down her cheeks. She then knelt down to be crowned with a laurel wreath, while the Graces laid palms, flowers and golden apples at her feet. At this moment all the lights were turned on, a banner was lowered with the inscription *"A la célèbre Fanny Elssler"*, angels in clouds scattered more flowers, and a rain of golden stars fell on to the stage. Deeply moved, Fanny remained on her knees while the audience threw flowers, bouquets and poems to her and chanted, *"Adios, Fanny! Adios, Fanny!"* On this scene the curtain fell, only to rise again for Fanny to make her speech. For once her voice failed her, and she could only wave her handkerchief and express her gratitude in gestures. Finally she could restrain her emotion no longer, and when the curtain fell for the last time she was weeping on Mme Martin's shoulder.

Her plans to visit New Orleans had been upset by her decision to remain in Cuba, for the St Charles Theatre had been burnt down in February and the Théâtre d'Orléans had meanwhile closed. She was therefore free to consider a magnificent offer which had reached her from Mexico, but she hesitated to accept it because of the alarming tales she had heard about the hazards of the journey: the poor roads to Mexico City, the bands of robbers infesting the countryside, and the yellow fever that was raging in Vera Cruz. Eventually she made up her mind to go, but the English steamer bound for Vera Cruz arrived late and meanwhile news arrived from Vienna that Therese was ill and her father failing and asking to see her. There could be no more indecision, and Fanny told Katti that she would be leaving for New York to give a farewell season before returning to Europe.

Their last few weeks in Havana had been full of delights. Every evening around sunset they took a drive, receiving compliments and marks of admiration on every side. The Marquesa d'Arcos gave Fanny two tiny dogs, whose ears had been pierced so that ribbons could be threaded through them, and among other gifts was a small aviary of brilliantly coloured birds which they planned to take back to Europe. Fanny was able to accept only a small proportion of the invitations she received, but when the British warship "Illustrious" put into port, she attended a ball on board, looking lovely in a simple white dress.

At last the time came to bid farewell to Havana. Their luggage was sent aboard the "Natchez", and in the afternoon of May 21st Fanny was rowed out in the captain's boat with an escort of more than twenty small vessels packed with friends and well-wishers. Then the ship's bell sounded, the engines started up, and with shouts of farewell sounding in her ears she watched the figures of friends whom she would never see again receding into the distance.

The weather in New York was uncomfortably cold when they arrived. "Warm clothes replace the light short-sleeved dresses of Havana," wrote Katti. "Fires are burning, and there are three blankets on the bed with all the windows carefully closed. Fanny, who feels the cold, is now wearing flannel underwear, and has not set foot outside her room since she arrived." She soon had to be out and about, however, and losing little time in settling her dispute with the Park Theatre, she agreed to give a final season there, opening on June 8th, for half the receipts and a benefit. Sylvain had hoped to be re-engaged as her partner, but she had had enough of his bad temper and was well satisfied with Jules Martin, whom she considered a better dancer.

In spite of the depressed condition of the New York theatre, Fanny's performances drew large audiences. *La Somnambule* and *The Fairy and the Knight* and her character dances were received with rapturous applause, and Martin was found to be "decidedly far superior as a dancer of grace and precision to Sylvain", who had been "good, but too extravagant and too ambitious—he overheats his poker". At her benefit Fanny danced the *Buscapié del Pais* and an exquisite new dance, the *Zapateo de Cadiz*, and she made her four final appearances in America for the benefit of others: for Jules Martin, the St James Orphans Asylum, Edmund Simpson and, the last one on July 1st, for the Theatrical Fund.

Her last words from an American stage, spoken through her tears, were an expression of her gratitude for all the unforgettable experiences of the past two years. "I would fain say a word of this night's undertaking, but I have not the heart to do it," she began. "Let me conjure you to be faithful to what you have so nobly begun. The hour of parting has come at last, and it well nigh overcomes me. Must I, then, bid adieu—an eternal adieu—to a people who have poured out their gifts upon me like water—who have never wavered in their generosity or kindness from the moment of welcome to this gloomy one of separation? To my native Germany and adopted France I owe much, but how to express to thee, America, all the obligations that now overwhelm my mind and heart? Accept the humble offering of my gratitude, thus moistened by my tears. Farewell, kind friends! Farewell, America! Living, I will cherish the memory; dying, I will bless it."

Now that her American tour was at an end, she could take stock of her extaordinary triumph. In little more than two years she had made 208 appearances in the United States and Cuba.* She had earned, according to the *Herald*, nearly $140,000, out of which her expenses amounted to about $40,000, gifts to charities to over $5,000,† and losses, through the failure of managers, to $3,000; and she had made fifty-two curtain speeches in four languages, English, French, Spanish, and German.

Before leaving America there were a few final details to attend to. Messrs Hendrickson & Clarkson were entrusted with investing the proceeds of her farewell season, and were also instructed to provide Charles, who had decided to settle in Philadelphia, with the capital he required to open a livery stable there. The final leave-taking came on Saturday, July 16th, when Fanny boarded the "Caledonia" with Katti and Wikoff. James Gordon Bennett and George Washington Smith were there to see her off, and as the ship steamed out of the harbour the strains of "*My country, 'tis of thee*" and the *Cracovienne,* played by the band of the warship "Ohio", wafted across the water as a final tribute. On the Monday they reached Halifax, and just nine days later they saw the mountains of Ireland appear on the horizon. The next day, July 28th, 1842, they landed at Liverpool in the pouring rain.

---

* New York 17, Philadelphia 15, Washington 5, Baltimore 7, New York 9, Boston 13, Philadelphia 6, Richmond 1, Charleston 4, Havana 10, New Orleans 27, New York 13, Philadelphia 11, New York 5, Boston 16, Providence 1, New York 13, Havana 19, Matanzas 3, New York 13. Of these performances eighteen were for her own benefit, and nineteen for the benefit of others.

† Before leaving America Fanny set aside a small fund for the relief of distressed children of the drama. In 1849, learning of Edmund Simpson's death, she agreed that the fund, which then stood at about $300, should be paid to his widow to provide for his children.

XIII

The Breach with Wikoff

DURING THE PEACEFUL DAYS of the Atlantic crossing Fanny's thoughts had often dwelt on her family from whom she had been parted for so long. To her joy her sister-in-law Minna was in London to greet her, but most of all she wanted to see her daughter. As if oblivious of all else but the compelling desire to repossess her child, she descended without warning or ceremony on the Grotes and snatched the little girl from their care with a thoughtless, but for that no less brutal, disregard for their feelings. The English couple were bitterly hurt and disillusioned. "I suffered a cruel grief," Harriet wrote to her sister, "owing to Mlle Elssler taking away my darling little Therese, whom I loved as my own child, and had treated as such for $2\frac{1}{2}$ years. It shook me sadly, and I am much less gay and elastic than formerly."

Fanny had returned to Europe in a state of physical and mental exhaustion. A reporter who saw her in a box at Her Majesty's Theatre described her as looking "pale and *maigre*; indeed but a shadow of her former gay and sprightly self". Certainly she was in no mood to enjoy the exuberant dancing of Fanny Cerrito, who in her absence had become the darling of the London public, and the thought of struggling for supremacy against a younger rival must have filled her with despair. Giving news of her to his broker, Charles Clarkson, Henry Wikoff told him: "She will not begin dancing, I think, before the Spring, as she complains of great fatigue, and seems to desire repose."

To add to her anxieties, there now arose a misunderstanding with her *chevalier servant*. Fanny was to confide her side of the story to Gordon Bennett. Wikoff, she told him, was "dismissed from her service for certain conduct towards her, . . . wanted afterwards to be reconciled to her, but was indignantly spurned with contempt and detestation". Bennett described their relationship as a "romantic . . . philosophical and Platonic connection", and blamed "the silly and ridiculous, though harmless conduct of Chevalier Wikoff" for "their love-quarrel and final separation", in which he thought Fanny showed "gentleness, tact and good feelings". Wikoff, for his part, sought to justify himself by explaining: "Fanny, the stupid, always thought I would marry her.

I refused plump on arriving in London, and I carried it on with vigor, for I desired earnestly to be set free."

Meanwhile the unsatisfactory progress of the litigation with the Opéra was another worry. The early hearings had taken place while she was in America, and distance and her growing fortune of dollars had clouded their reality. In February 1841 the Opéra was awarded damages of 60,000 francs for breach of contract, and seven months later this judgment was upheld on appeal. Fanny's final appeal was rejected on August 23rd, 1842, by the Cour Royal de Paris.

So Fanny was beset with anxieties when she left London on the last stages of her journey to Vienna. Wishing above all to relax and spend as much time as possible with her father, she firmly declined an engagement at the Kärntnertortheater, and danced only twice: once at Court, by command of the Emperor, and then at a charity performance in aid of children's homes. Many people paid fantastic prices to attend the latter performance, but they received full value for their money, for while she was billed to dance only three numbers—a *pas de deux*, the *Jaleo de Jerez* and the *Cracovienne*—the last two were encored, and in addition she had to yield to the audience's demand to perform the *Cachucha*, which was also repeated. All Vienna seemed to have squeezed into the theatre that evening. It was a real home-coming, and to honour her a special medal was designed by Franz Gaul, with her portrait in profile on one side and on the other a dancing figure with the inscription, *Terpsichorens Liebling*, the Darling of Terpsichore.

Deciding to resume her career in Berlin, Fanny was welcomed by her brother Joseph and made her reappearance at the Opera House amid scenes of wild enthusiasm. Neither Henrietta Sontag, the great soprano, nor even Franz Liszt had created such a sensation in the Prussian capital, and the poet Friedrich Rückert was so carried away that he wrote an eulogy of her that was a parody of the *Nunc Dimittis*:

> *Nun kann ich ruhig zu Grabe gehen,*
> *Ich habe das Höchste im Leben,*
> *Der göttlichen Fanny Gebeine gesehen*
> *Sich bis zum Himmel erheben.*

While her triumphs in the New World had clothed her with a legendary sort of glamour, much of the public's curiosity was directed to the fortune which she had accumulated there. That winter a lithograph was published in Berlin, showing her astride the Atlantic in her *Cachucha* costume, holding in one hand a bag of thalers and in the other a bag of dollars, into which a kneeling cupid was shooting his arrows.

Was this a veiled allusion to the alleged insecurity of her American fortune? This was a fear that was very much in Fanny's mind at the time. When she had arrived in Vienna, her feelings deeply wounded by the circumstances of her breach with Wikoff, her family had raised the question whether her American earnings were properly invested. Katti did nothing to allay the suspicions of Fanny's father that all was not well, and Fanny wrote to Hendrickson & Clarkson to ask for the certificates. On September 30th, unaware of the storm that was about to break over his head, Wikoff himself wrote to Clarkson, explaining why she had taken this step. "She says," he told him, "her Father entertains from his distant position and ignorant anxiety great doubt of her American Securities so that she has put down all his [illegible] fears, but at his earnest prayers she promised him to send for and show him her securities to gratify his doubts and tranquillize his fears."

Not having received a satisfactory reply from Hendrickson & Clarkson, Fanny then made certain allegations which so alarmed Wikoff that he came hot-foot to Berlin. There he learnt that she had given a power of attorney to her Berlin bankers, Schickler Brothers, to withdraw from the Philadelphia brokers all the securities they held, amounting in value, according to their last statement, to $64,238 and producing an annual income of $3,533. To his dismay she would only see him in the presence of her relatives, when the allegations were repeated.

He was dumbfounded. "You could hardly believe that the infamous [illegible] about Mlle Elssler," he wrote to Clarkson on November 5th, "have been persuading her that I have made away with property *and she has believed them*. This is my recompense for all the vast labor and disgrace I have brought on myself. It is a just reward and I bear it calmly as much as possible." A fortnight later, having returned to London, he wrote again. "Like a woman," he complained, "she allows her private feelings to influence her conduct to an unjustifiable length— deeply hurt and offended with me for various reasons she allows herself to be influenced by the intriguing spirit of one of her female relatives and addressed questions to me that widened the ill feelings momentarily prevailing between us. I don't know at all, as my late intercourse with her has been so limited, whether her relatives have taken any steps with reference to her property in America."

Schickler Brothers authorised August Belmont of New York to withdraw the American securities from the hands of Hendrickson & Clarkson, and Fanny signed a power of attorney in his favour on January 7th, 1843. By then Wikoff had accepted that their relationship was at an end. "My position of *friend* and *counsellor*," he wrote sadly to Clarkson on New Year's Day, "no longer exists."

The accusations of dishonesty wounded him deeply. "Have you heard of Fanny's conduct to me?" he wrote to Gordon Bennett on February 10th. "D——d bad—nothing could be worse; and yet it is all for the best. My numerous friends here are rejoiced I am separated from her, and I don't regret it."

In this distressing incident Fanny had fallen under the influence of her family, whose opinions she was too exhausted to challenge. For them she represented financial security, and this may partly explain the acquisitive streak in her character which was noted by her detractors. Although some irregularity was in fact discovered, the original motive for suggesting that her American securities should be withdrawn from the Philadelphia brokers might have been to ensure they were more readily available should the family in Europe be in need. Fanny herself was happy to recognise her obligations, for there were strong bonds of affection uniting the family, but she felt at times, particularly when she was depressed, that she was being taken advantage of and that too little concern was being shown for herself. At this time she was finding sympathy and comfort in a friendship which developed into a deep love. Count Samuel Kostrowicki,* a rich nobleman, was pressing her to abandon her career and marry him, and she concealed his courtship from her family for weeks, fearing in her heart that their reactions might spoil the precious relationship, and wracked too by doubts whether she could ever give up dancing. As a New Year's gift her brother Joseph gave her a diary in which she confided some of the thoughts that filled her mind during this difficult period of her life.

January 1st Early to work. And once again the New Year with a will. This day last year I was in New York and gave many presents. Two years ago I was in Charleston, on the way to beautiful Havana.

January 2nd I received letters from the little one [her daughter]. She seems to be hale and hearty. May God keep her so. Have sent a copy of my Paris affair to Mrs. Grote. In the evening the second performance of *Tarentule*. Full house. I am in a bad mood. Letters from Father and Uncle in Eisenstadt.

---

* Kostrowicki may have been the author of the correspondence, extracts from which were published in Brussels in 1841, in a limited edition of 100 copies, under the title *Lettres à une artiste*. The writer of these letters reveals that he had met Fanny shortly after the death of Gentz. Ehrhard in his biography of Fanny, referring to a German translation, incorrectly states they purport to be letters from Gentz and suggests they are fraudulent. This view seems open to question: the letters read as though genuine, and surely such a small edition was published for the author's friends and not to take advantage of a wide public interest in a celebrity of the day.

January 5th (Proverb: What you have begun, carry out faithfully, diligently and joyfully.) May this proverb be fulfilled. Today I have carried out what I had begun. Yesterday I was completely downcast, and only a prayer to God raised my spirits somewhat. I wrote the letters I had already begun to Reich, to Lumley* who wants to save me from everything, according to W. Also I sent a note to Therese which will not please her. But I must act in this way, otherwise I am lost. Katti reproaches me for being unkind to my own. God knows I am doing all I can for them, not for me, otherwise I could live in peace and happiness—but their happiness comes before everything. I thank Thee, Lord, for granting me the strength to carry it through.

January 6th (Proverb: When all else fails, faith, hope and love remain.) I slept peacefully, thanks to Thee, O Giver of all good things. I had a quiet day. I could experience so much if I complied with the wishes of one person. Is it my own will, or am I still blinded by the glory of the world? I wish I could renounce this worldly glory. Yes, I believe I could, and am not afraid to admit it. In the evening I danced the *Cracovienne*; I was merry and so was the public. K seemed calmer. At the end of this day I can truly say, "My God, I have faith, I love, and I have hope. Thanks be to Thee."

January 7th I have just received a letter from Reich. I expected more of him. Everyone seems to deceive me. Proven friends are the only ones one should call friends, but it is difficult to find them. I have such a one at my feet. Why do I not accept him? Oh, Fanny, Fanny, take care, such things do not happen twice in a lifetime.

January 8th Today brought me only joy, no pain. After Church I met some friends. In the afternoon I saw K and talked about the future, How carefully he plans everything for me, like a father for his child. In the evening I was at Liszt's concert. I find him not natural, and much too calculating. This detracts greatly from his art. I did not enjoy it. I saw many people at the concert, and many people saw me. An empty evening.

January 9th I worked hard at morning rehearsal and felt very depressed. Nothing new, no letter. It only remains for me to offer thanks to Him to whom we owe everything.

January 12th I was uneasy the whole day. K wrote to me that I should not go to Strelitz. I replied that I must. Then I went to work, and

* Benjamin Lumley, who had succeeded Laporte as manager of Her Majesty's Theatre.

saw K beside himself at my decision. In the evening I was alone with Minna and talked of all that had happened. She felt insulted that I had not confided in her. K had foreseen that it would turn out like this. I was wrong not to have spoken of it immediately. But who is right in this affair? I have proofs that K means well towards me. Can I doubt it? No. Then why this weakness, this doubt? Life no longer has any value for me. Everyone says he means well towards me, but nobody ever thinks of me, but only of him. Only God knows my heart, and only He can protect me. I trust in Him.

It was on this very day, January 12th, 1843, that Fanny's father died in Vienna. Her performances in Berlin were suspended so that she and her brother could go to Vienna for the requiem in St Stephen's, and she had to decline an invitation to dance at the Court Theatre in Schwerin. She returned to Berlin for just one performance, on February 3rd, and left almost immediately for England. Her thoughts on arriving in London were full of foreboding.

February 18th My mind is uneasy, so I cannot be happy . . . I took up residence at 13 Regent Street, a fatal number. But has not God given out all numbers?

The presence of Henry Wikoff in town presented problems, for she was as determined not to meet him as he was to restore himself in her good graces. When he pressed the Gordon Bennetts to invite them both to dinner, Fanny, forewarned, excused herself on the grounds of fatigue. "He is a mean man," she said to Bennett, and Katti echoed: "He is a very mean man indeed." But Fanny's diary reveals no rancour towards him, only despair at a situation that seemed to be getting out of control.

February 22nd I hear that W would risk his life for me. Oh dear God, I am ready to die, and would be happy to fall asleep for ever if I knew that my own were taken care of. To join my parents would be a joy to me.

On the next day Wikoff signed a formal denial that he had acted in any way improperly: "I, Henry Wikoff, late of Phil[a], do hereby declare in the presence of God, and before men, that in *all* things done with reference to the investment of the property of Mlle Elssler I acted only after the fullest explanations made to her, and, of course, with her full knowledge and consent, and that Messrs Hendrickson & Clarkson in following my directions, only carried out the wishes and intentions of Mlle Elssler through me expressed."

His troubles were not yet over, for in May the New York paper, *Courrier des Etats-Unis*, published a report, apparently inspired by a source within Fanny's family, alleging that he had become vindictive after she had spurned his offer of a reconciliation. Changing his tone, this report went on, he had then asked Fanny to pay him what was owing to him. When she remonstrated that she had already paid him $40,000 for his expenses, he presented an account for a further $65,000, saying that the first sum was only on account and that if Fanny did not pay the balance, he would sell some of her stocks, of which he was the nominal holder. Fanny then took steps to recover the stocks, only to find that Wikoff had already instructed the brokers to recognise no other owner than him. Only the threat of litigation forced the brokers to recognise her title. Then two of the three partners delivered stocks worth $40,000 to her attorney, but the third admitted that he had speculated with the rest of the funds and could only account for investments of doubtful value.

Much of this report was malicious and untrue, for Wikoff was ready to swear that he had spent over $10,000 of his own money on Fanny while she was in America, but the firm of Hendrickson & Clarkson had been guilty of mismanagement. In August 1843 Wikoff gave Gordon Bennett a full explanation. "Most of her gains in the United States, above her personal expenditure and the considerable sums remitted to her family in Europe," he wrote, "were invested in the best State stocks, *in her own name*, and subject, of course, to no other control than her own. During her stay in the United States she had three different agents— Mr Belmont, then J. Duer, Esq., and lastly, Messrs Hendrickson & Clarkson, of Philadelphia. On leaving the country, she left with the latter a simple power of attorney to collect dividends, *but no powers whatever for sale or transfer*. She also left a certain sum of $10,000 or $15,000 to invest in mortgages. Some irregular conduct on the part of Mr Clarkson, one of the aforesaid agents, as to these mortgages, led to the interference of W. B. Reed, Esq., of Philadelphia, Mlle Elssler's lawyer, and a bond, with security, was given by Mr Hendrickson, the partner of Mr C, for the payment of all the balances due." In a later statement Wikoff added that Fanny had sent $10,000 to her family, and that she sold her American stocks at a considerable profit when she withdrew her capital to Europe. This was confirmed by Fanny herself in a letter to the *Bäuerles Theaterzeitung*, denying that she had lost a significant part of the money she had invested in America.

Wikoff's last act as her purported agent was to arrange a two-month engagement with Alfred Bunn, manager of Covent Garden Theatre. This caused her great embarrassment, for she herself was at the same

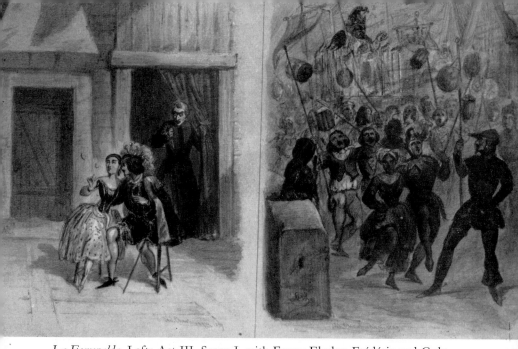

La Esmeralda, Left: Act III, Scene I, with Fanny Elssler, Frédéric and Goltz (Frollo). Right: Act III, Scene II, with Didier. Watercolour by A. Charlemagne.

Bakhrushin Museum, Moscow.

La Esmeralda, Act III, Scene II. L to R: Goltz, Fanny Elssler, Perrot. Water-colour by A. Charlemagne.

Bakhrushin Museum, Moscow.

Fanny Elssler as Esmeralda.
Lithograph by V. Timm.

Bakhrushin Museum, Moscow.

Джанни Эльслеръ
въ роли Эсмеральды.

Fanny Elssler as Esmeralda.
Statuette.

Haydn Museum, Eisenstadt.

time negotiating with Lumley of Her Majesty's Theatre and had to repudiate the Covent Garden contract. Bunn threatened to sue her, and Wikoff, smarting under the injustice of the allegations made against him, hastily took up his pen. "I see Mlle Fanny is down upon you sharply in the papers," he wrote to Bunn. "Most people believe 'she has silated [*sic*] no arrangement.' It is devillishly lucky for her you have not thought fit to reply, for your pen is an instrument that mangles a customer very roughly, even when it is not sharpened by such outrageous trifling as would give it point in this case. It is very lucky indeed for her, and the Opera, that you have not given her a *settler* at once, after your own fashion. She has, decidedly, the best of it with the public, but 'her friends and admirers' will be considerably struck, perhaps 'all of a heap,' when the truth comes out. If she and her friends were wise, they ought to take definite pains to prevent this by indemnifying you at once; but the old Roman proverb will likely apply here, 'Whom the Gods wish to destroy they first make mad,' and fancy you in like mad." Bunn's claim for £3,000 damages was amicably settled in the end on terms that Fanny would appear gratuitously at his benefit.

On this bitter note the association between Fanny and Wikoff came to an end. Only once more were their paths to cross, when, in 1844, he incurred her displeasure by publishing a collection of letters purporting to have been written by her during her American tour. When she objected that she had not written them and that they were calculated to harm her by their ridiculous tone, he contended that he had been given her "full and unqualified assent" to publish them and that this had never been withdrawn. Whether or not Wikoff ought to have published them after their breach, these letters, of which he was no doubt the author, were clearly based on conversations he had had with her and provided an authentic and amusing account of the first part of her American tour and the events leading up to it.

Wikoff possessed a flair for publicity which was in advance of his time, and he had put this to good use when acting as Fanny's business manager in the United States. It was said that he "carried the newspapers in one hand and the public in the other, and between the two he squeezed the theatrical managers". But while contributing considerably to the financial success of her American tour, his hasty and hot-headed nature had often led him into actions which had reflected unfavourably on Fanny herself. In his dealings with the press, for example, he neglected no means of pressing his demands for publicity, and Gordon Bennett had at times found him a great nuisance. "Not only did he . . . annoy us by letter," he recalled, speaking of Wikoff's barrage of requests for puffs, "but while in New York he was continually at our office boring and teasing us to such an extent that we had at last, on one occasion, to tell him we would kick him out of our office, and that was well known to all who were in at the time. Whenever he got into a row, as at Coney Island—whenever he got into difficulty, as that with Simpson, and he was eternally getting into scrapes from his impertinence, folly, ignorance and presumption—whenever he got into trouble of any kind, he always came, as he says, 'to hear what Robinson Crusoe would say.' We were his stay—his guide—his mentor—his 'Robinson Crusoe' in all difficulties."

After his breach with Fanny, the irrepressible Wikoff moved on to other adventures. He continued to seek out the great, he served for a time, not very effectively, as an agent of the British Foreign Office, and he achieved a passing notoriety when he attempted to abduct a young lady he had long wanted to marry and languished awhile for his folly in a Genoese gaol. His association with Fanny Elssler was never forgotten, and years later Bram Stoker was told a story that he made an annual pilgrimage to Paris to lay flowers "on a little grave long after the child's mother, the dancer, had died". It was a tale without foundation, for not only did Fanny survive the old *chevalier*, if only by a few months, but the schedule of the American tour allowed for no interval when she could have discreetly retired to give birth to a child.

XIV

"Giselle"

FANNY LOOKED FORWARD TO THE season at Her Majesty's Theatre with a heavy heart. She was burdened with several unsolved personal problems: the estrangement from the Grotes, the emotional conflict produced by her love for Kostrowicki, the unpleasantness of the breach with Wikoff, her litigation with the Paris Opéra. But her main anxiety was how the London public would receive her after an absence of three years, and in particular how she would fare against the competition of Fanny Cerrito. On the eve of her reappearance she confided these apprehensions to her dairy:

> *March 10th* (Proverb: Was there ever a day which did not give you cause for thanks?) Truly not, and though my soul was sore distressed I found comfort in giving thanks. Butler took me early to Covent Garden, where I stayed until 3 o'clock, then to work at the Opera. In the evening I went to rehearsal, which upset me greatly (for me). Is it blindness, or have I really nothing, no living artist, to be afraid of?

The ovation which greeted her on her reappearance in *La Tarentule* was the best possible tonic for her low spirits. During the course of the performance a nobleman was heard to cry out ecstatically, "Those are the feet that conquered America!" On stage Fanny was given added confidence by the support of her experienced partner, Sylvain, who had returned from America with a profit of £6,000. The evening's only disappointment was that Perrot, who had injured his foot in the opening *divertissement*, had to relinquish the part of Omeopatico at the last minute. Two days later Fanny enjoyed a similar triumph at Covent Garden, in Bunn's benefit performance. Her diary entries sounded a much more cheerful note:

> *March 11th.* First appearance in London. I was saving myself for the evening, and had such a violent headache that I lay down after dinner for two hours, after which I felt better. I saw nobody, but went quietly

to the Opera to await my fate. Perrot sprained his foot. I was received
with applause that left nothing to be desired. Victory was mine.

March 13th. I was at Covent Garden early for rehearsal. In the evening
I danced in *Bayadère*. What a difference from Berlin, I was often led to
think. It was unbelievably bad here. I had an extraordinary reception
and danced well. The Queen was present.

With each succeeding performance the enthusiasm grew, and she
responded by revealing new facets of her talent, particularly in the realm
of interpretation. An outstanding example of this development was her
performance of the familiar *Cracovienne*, which sent the critic of *The
Times* into raptures. "There she comes," he described, "with her little
military jacket, and her soldier's cap, and her long plaited tails which
dangle down her back, and her neat little boots, and the little brass
heels which click so prettily to the music—and her *entrée* is a triumph!
It is really a dance of character, the talents of the *danseuse* and of the
pantomimist being completely blended together. When she first bounds
on, it is as if she were springing with joy among a circle of admirers.
She stops short. She assumes a military stiffness, but it is in the happiest
spirit of irony. Now she seems only lazily beating time, and now she
rushes along as if seized by the joy of the moment, and not knowing
how to contain her delight. Then, when at the conclusion of the *pas* she
trots along the lamps in right military style, the impression she conveys
is quite unique. The dance she has been executing is one of the most
charming things imaginable—the perfection of art—and yet she
contrives to convey a notion that she has merely been playing off some
pleasant trick, and is laughing at her audience for their applause."

While Fanny had been away in America a new ballet had been produced at the Paris Opéra which had rapidly become a favourite throughout Europe and had established the reputation of the young dancer for
whom it had been created, Carlotta Grisi. *Giselle* was the brain-child of
Théophile Gautier, whose imagination had been fired by Heine's
account of the Slavonic legend of the Wilis, spirits of maidens who die
on their wedding eve. He and the dramatist Saint-Georges had produced
a scenario about a peasant girl who in the first act loses her reason and
dies after discovering that her suitor is a prince in disguise and be-
trothed to another. The second act was typically Romantic in feeling,
being set in the moonlit glade where the spirit of Giselle is admitted to
the ranks of the Wilis and, still possessing the last vestiges of her love,
saves her distraught lover from being destroyed by the malignant power
of the Wilis. To a fine score by Adophe Adam, the ballet had been
produced at the Opéra in June 1841 by the first *maître de ballet*, Jean

Coralli, but it was generally known, even though he was not given credit, that much of the choreography—and in particular the role of Giselle—had been devised by Jules Perrot. The following spring Perrot, in collaboration with Deshayes, had revived it for the opening of the 1842 season at Her Majesty's and had so impressed Benjamin Lumley, the new manager, that he was now engaged as ballet-master in succession to Deshayes, who had died during the previous winter.

Giselle was high on the list of productions for the 1843 season, and since Carlotta Grisi was not expected, it was planned to present Fanny Elssler in the title-role. It was to be Fanny's first new part in more than three years, and she found it ideally suited to her talent. During the rehearsals she had the added satisfaction of being reconciled with the Grotes, and when she first performed the part on March 30th she gave so much of herself that she was completely overwhelmed and did not comprehend the extent of the triumph she had obtained.

March 19th I went to Church. Still tired from yesterday, I went to the rehearsal of *Giselle*. I worked well and then accepted an invitation to dinner at G's. In the evening I made my peace with G. So I am once more certain of this friendship and can look to the future calmly. It gladdens my heart that I am myself again.

March 29th We had a good rehearsal and I had a great success. Everyone paid me compliments on my performance this morning.

March 30th First performance of *Giselle*. I was depressed and was scarcely able to prevent myself from bursting into tears. I never felt so exhausted.

Fanny's interpretation of the role of *Giselle* contrasted strongly with that of Carlotta Grisi, for where Grisi had brought out its "tender melancholy", excelling more in the second act where she appears as a wili, Fanny gave a performance of great dramatic power with the emphasis on the tragedy of Giselle's madness at the end of the first act. It was she who first revealed the full dramatic content of the role, and it was her rendering, rather than Carlotta's, which was to set the standard for later generations of ballerinas to follow.

"Her scene in the first act," described the *Morning Herald*, "when she becomes apprised of her lover's rank, and suspects the purity of his intentions, is a masterpiece of expression: her acting—for it amounts to acting of the highest kind—is, we believe, quite unparalleled in the annals of the pantomimic art. The guileless, trusting girl, just now so sprightly and good-humoured, changes in an instant; her vivacity gives place to the intensest anger; her frame swells with dignity and wounded pride, and the tightened lip, the lifted brow, the dilated nostril, and the erect figure, denote the scorn and indignation which consume her. Presently her countenance blanches with apprehension, and she becomes weak and tremulous with horror. A smile lightens her features—but it is the smile of a gathering insanity, the fitful and unearthly calm of an unhinged mind. She is seized with the Wili fever, and dances wildly and incoherently, mingling with her motions many little touches of feeling eminently beautiful and pathetic. She regards her lover with a glance of admiration and devotion, and caresses him with a playful tenderness—then she repulses him as a serpent; and then, with a seeming interval of consciousness, fondles him anew, and scatters imaginary flowers on his path! A moment of gloom succeeds, and she walks about lonely and dejected, as if engrossed in some horrible reverie. Her mother in wretchedness and despair embraces her fondly, but she knows her not—she is cold, insensible, and heart-stricken. Impelled by some mysterious power she attempts to dance again, but her steps falter, her eyes become fixed and lustreless, and you *feel* the chill which is creeping over her heart. The grip of death is there, and she sinks with a marble insensibility into her mother's arms."

She was no less impressive in the second act, where she is raised from her tomb to join the wilis and by seeking the sanctuary of the cross is able to resist the Queen of the Wilis' command to lure her lover to destruction. "Emerging from the shroud of death," continued the *Morning Herald*, "she assumes a new species of existence; she seems driven by an irresistible fate to work out the destruction of her lover, and yet is this influence checked by some lingering yearnings of humanity, which prompt her to save him from the fatal snare. The expression which the actress gives to the scene is distinct and awful. No smile of recognition animates the face of the poor phantom. The features are pale and immovable, wearing an air of placid resignation, yet sad, inconsolate, and deathlike. She executes the malign bidding of the Wili Queen with involuntary readiness, but the sentiment of earthly love still clings to her, although the outward manifestations of dismay and repugnance are obliterated from her countenance. The spectre maiden unconsciously binds fresh chains around the sympathies of her lover; she lures him to his doom with the bewitching phrases of her dancing, with her fanciful flittings in the pale glimmer of the moon and her erratic flights through the air—but more so by those fascinating evidences of love which she practised when living, and which even the grave cannot utterly suppress.

"In this silent pantomime Fanny Elssler is most eloquent and pathetic. The opposite characteristics of the forlorn spirit are strongly

marked, and the touches of art, which give form, substance, and elevation to the conception, are so manifold that admiration can scarcely find
terms in which to vent itself. Such a complete expression of a dramatic
sentiment has never before been evolved by the merely imitative means
of the ballet. It has been left for Fanny Elssler to show the full eloquence
of bodily gesture, and what a forcible significance and intensity may be
given to it when genius and feeling are the prime movers. The performance of *Giselle* proves the influence she can exercise at will over the
sympathies of an audience . . . It is a study worth the contemplation
of every lover of elevated and refined art."

A week later, in her benefit performance on April 6th, Fanny
appeared in a very different guise when she danced as the cavalier in the
Menuet de la Cour and the *Gavotte* with the elegant young French dancer,
Adèle Dumilâtre, in Perrot's new *divertissement, Un Bal sous Louis XIV.*
The *Morning Herald* described it as a "famous dance of pedantry and
etiquette . . . Who could ever dream," its critic asked, "that the fairy
form of Dumilâtre was encased in the bulging drapery of the seventeenth
century—and yet the expansive farthingale, the peaked stomacher, the
nipped sleeve, the stack of powdered hair, and the high-heeled shoe
became her exceedingly. Fanny Elssler, too, in the white satin coat, the
velvet smalls, and the formal peruke, was the *beau idéal* of the courtier
and refined gentleman of the period, and looked bewitchingly elegant
in her endowments of sleeve and ruffle. This pair of incomparable artists
passed through the phlegmatic minuet with profound grace. Dumilâtre
was the quintessence of prim modishness; one would never have guessed
that the curious, long-backed person, with her lower frame muffled in
those prodigious layers of rose-tinted silk, was the airy creature who
clears the stage in three bounds, and who lifts her leg as a gamekeeper
does his musket. Fanny Elssler seemed to perceive a drollery in the
antique part *she* was playing, and she mimicked the sluggish ease of bag-
wiggism with an archness and mock gravity quite irresistible. She glided
about with a diverting self-complacency, and touched the fingers of
Dumilâtre with historical indifference."

Some weeks later Fanny took a few days off to visit Bristol, where
Mrs Macready had tempted her to give a single performance at the
Theatre Royal on May 1st for a fee of £100.* By now the tension of a
few weeks earlier had vanished, and she returned to London to face the
confrontation with Cerrito with complete equanimity. On the last
performance of her engagement she even had no qualms about dancing
in the same *divertissement* as the Neapolitan ballerina, although they did

---

* Compare this with the modest £1 10s. a week which Mrs Macready paid the
principal dancer on her regular payroll.

not dance together. That was to come later. Before leaving England she earned another £100 by dancing at the Theatre Royal, Birmingham.*

Her next engagement took her to Brussels, which was perilously close to Paris, where the dispute with the Opéra was being fought as bitterly as ever. Towards the end of the previous year Therese had endeavoured to negotiate a reconciliation, and the Opéra had agreed terms for a series of performances and was beginning to rehearse the ballets in her repertory when Fanny repudiated her sister's authority. Then the Opéra had attempted to levy execution on the contents of her apartment in the Rue Laffitte. Therese, who held the lease in her name, successfully contended that the contents were her own property, but at the threat of an appeal, she settled the action by abandoning her sister's furniture, which was subsequently sold by auction. Now, learning that Fanny was appearing at the Théâtre de la Monnaie in Brussels, the Opéra tried to attach her fees, but she was too quick for them: having received her fees for the first six performances, she wisely re-negotiated her contract so as to receive her fee of 1,500 francs a performance in advance.

During the five weeks she was in Brussels she appeared in six ballets —*La Sylphide, The Swiss Milkmaid, Giselle, La Tarentule, La Gipsy* and *Le Dieu et la Bayadère*—drawing packed houses and stirring the public to an unparalleled pitch of enthusiasm. *Giselle* gave her the greatest triumph, and only *La Gipsy*, which was given without any spectacular production, met with a disappointing reception.

Her first engagement in Brussels ended on June 25th, and on the following day a company of English pantomimists from Drury Lane made their first appearance in a piece called *Arlequin chasseur*. In an attempt to introduce a topical note, Harlequin made his entrance in one of the scenes, bearing an enormous bandbox with the inscription, "Fanny Elssler". Dipping into it, he drew out a complete Cachucha costume, article by intimate article. The audience found this display of underwear to be in the worst possible taste, and when the Clown† put on the Cachucha costume and began to give a parody of the dance, uproar broke out. Amid cries of anger a volley of cushions and other missiles began flying through the air. Finally the curtain fell and the

---

* It was during this summer that continental papers reported that she had been given a Doctorate of Choreographic Art by Oxford University. There is no foundation in this. The University Registrar states that there is no record that Fanny Elssler ever came to Oxford to receive an honorary degree.

† The Clown was probably Tom Matthews, who had first parodied Fanny's *Cachucha* in the Drury Lane Christmas pantomime of 1836–7, and who later danced it in Paris when he produced the pantomime *Arlequin* at the Théâtre des Variétés in 1842.

audience streamed out of the theatre, seething with indignation at the insult offered to the ballerina who had so recently been their guest. Many of them lay in wait outside the stage door to vent their wrath on the unfortunate Englishmen who for their safety had to be spirited out of the theatre, one by one, by another door.

Fanny had witnessed this scandal concealed in the shadow of a box, sitting bolt upright in her chair and profoundly shocked. Bearing no ill will against the management, she agreed to give a few more performances, including two benefits, one for the Hospital for the Blind and Incurable and the other, her final performance, for the *corps de ballet*. The incident of the parodied *Cachucha* was quite forgotten in the warm affection which surrounded her during the final week of her visit. Count Dietrichstein, the Austrian ambassador, invited her to dinner, and what was even more heart-warming, her fellow artists gave her a banquet at which Gilbert Duprez, the tenor, sang some wittily written couplets in her honour.

After her penultimate performance Fanny was given a fright which she was afterwards to remember with amusement. Coming out of the theatre, her arms full of flowers, she was at once surrounded by a shouting mob and carried bodily to a strange carriage with a white horse between the shafts. Her first thought was that she was being kidnapped by the Paris Opera to suffer for the judgment which had been pronounced against her in the French courts. But when she saw the horse led away and a band of laughing young men take up the shafts, her alarm gave way to relief. As the carriage trundled towards her hotel with the white horse trotting contentedly behind it, she was wildly acclaimed all the way. A serenade completed the evening's homage, and Fanny stood at her window, swaying happily to the rhythm of a waltz, before wishing her admirers goodnight.

Three days later, at the end of her last performance, the bouquets fell so thickly that she had to retreat before the bombardment, and it was the *corps de ballet* who ran forward to gather them up and thrust them into her arms. Outside the theatre, despite the heavy raindrops which were beginning to fall as a prelude to a gathering storm, a large crowd had gathered to escort her to her hotel. She eventually emerged on the arm of Alderman Verhuist, and during the procession through the streets, the crowd was diverted by the spectacle of Verhuist and his fellow Aldermen quarreling over who should give her his arm. It was a happy and rewarding end to the engagement, as her diary reveals.

July 6th. I was crowned by the *corps de ballet* on the stage. It was a benefit performance in which I had appeared. During the evening I danced *Giselle* and *Cachucha* for the last time. The people were wonderful, and I had difficulty in making my way through the crowds. I reached home almost crushed to death. What enthusiasm! The serenade was enchanting, and the evening ended with thunder and lightning. I was dead tired, and like a dog dragged myself to my bed, where I gave thanks to God.

Fanny delayed her departure from Brussels to meet Maître Spinnael, the *avocat* of the Paris Opéra, with whom terms were agreed to settle the long drawn out dispute over the broken contract on payment of 50,000 francs. With this worry off her mind, she left Brussels waving happily to the group of *abonnés* who had come to the Gare du Nord to see her off. She was accompanied as far as Malines by the ballet-master of the Monnaie, Jean Petipa, whose two sons, Lucien and Marius, were at the threshold of brilliant careers in the ballet.

She arrived in London to find Cerrito in triumphant possession. In her absence the younger ballerina had gained such an extraordinary success in the new ballet *Ondine* that it was being given at every performance. Its run of ten successive performances was only broken when *Giselle* was revived on July 15th for Fanny's return. After the ovations of Brussels, London's welcome was curiously disappointing. "More than half her admirers were on the stage," reported the *Morning Post*, "the stalls were quite empty save four or five ladies and six or seven old gentlemen, left to 'keep the ground,' whilst the gay company was manoeuvring elsewhere. The stage was so crowded by bearers of congratulatory addresses, that if the scene shifters had indulged in the same eccentricites, 'with three sheets in the wind,' as on Thursday last, a hundred or two of the votaries of Terpsichore must have bitten the dust, or have gone to 'immortal smash' against the canvas clouds. There were besides some dissentient *beaux*, whose devotion to Cerrito has not yet had time to cool, and who refused their plaudits, so that we never saw Elssler so little applauded."

Meanwhile preparations were in hand for the first Command Performance of Queen Victoria's reign, and a request had been received from the Palace that Fanny Elssler and Fanny Cerrito should dance a *pas de deux* together. Possibly the idea had been suggested to Her Majesty by Lumley in the first place, for earlier in the summer Fanny had turned a deaf ear when Lumley had made a similar suggestion. A royal wish, however, could not be treated so lightly. Although they had seen each other dancing, the two ballerinas had not met personally until Perrot introduced them before discussing the proposed dance. Both were on the defensive as they gravely curtsied to one another, and the first difficulty arose almost at once. Inevitably it concerned the order of their *variations* in the *pas de deux*, since the first place would imply a certain inferiority. Fanny claimed the pride of place as the senior in age and experience, while Cerrito staked her claim by virtue of being engaged as the leading dancer of the season. For a time neither would give way. Then Cerrito suggested that they should draw lots. Accounts vary as to how the difficulty was resolved. According to one, Fanny would not agree to drawing lots and Lumley intervened firmly in Cerrito's favour. Another account, which appeared in a Viennese paper, had it that when Cerrito suggested drawing lots, Fanny gracefully conceded, seizing the hand of poor Perrot, who was beside himself with despair, and saying, "Come, let us begin."

The *pas de deux* proved to be the sensation of the season, and "worth walking bare-foot to Loretto to witness". After the Command Perform-ance it was performed ten times more before the season ended, and the unconcealed partisanship of the dancers' admirers, who were happily more or less evenly balanced, spurred them to ever greater efforts so that each performance took on the appearance of a contest. If on some nights Cerrito's supporters were the more vociferous, Fanny's took their revenge on others. Perrot's choreography was masterly, for he favoured neither at the expense of the other, displaying them both to best advantage and bringing out their individual qualities. The *pas* began with an adagio movement in which the two ballerinas danced in unison, each with an arm round the other's waist—an opening which was designed to give neither an initial advantage, but lost some of its effect because of the disparity in their heights, Cerrito being several inches smaller than Fanny. Then followed Fanny's *variation*, a masterpiece of precision and neatness in which "the tips of her toes had a busy time at the opening, preluding, however, a shower of small merry steps, so numerically profuse that her feet seemed multiplied into a dozen". "Her feet appeared as though winged, and she glided across the stage with the grace of an antelope." It was then Cerrito's turn, and for her Perrot had devised a *variation* of a very different kind. With an incredible attack, she bounded over the stage with "the most enchanting buoyancy", her feet scarcely seeming to touch the ground, and after circling the stage with wonderful speed she came suddenly to a stop as though she had performed nothing out of the ordinary. In the final coda more wonders followed. At one moment Fanny "stood in marvellous equilibrium on the point of her toe, whilst Cerrito gracefully bent her form to the ground, and then they both leapt into the air together, performing simultaneously at a tangent the quickest repeated *jetés battus*. Then Elssler glided along the stage with invisible movements of her toes in the most fascinating attitude, with the flutters of a bird, and Cerrito soon followed, flying through the air and revolving on herself with a rapidity indescribable".

Before the season closed Fanny introduced London to two more Spanish dances. At Cerrito's benefit on July 27th she performed her *Zapateo de Cadiz*, and a week later she and Perrot danced *La Castilliana Bolero* in the latter's new *divertissement, Le Délire d'un peintre*.

This was an unpretentious work, opening with a slender plot that was designed merely as an introduction to the *divertissement*. A young artist has fallen so madly in love with a dancer that he has painted her portrait and gazes at it for hours in rapt adoration. Hearing of this, the dancer decides to put his love to the test. She conceals herself in his studio and appears before him when he unveils the portrait. Thinking he is suffering from a hallucination, the painter draws aside the veil again after she has vanished. She then steps out of the frame in her everyday attire, and all is explained and ends happily with the artist cured of his melancholy obsession. In this little sketch Fanny gave a performance of compelling charm. It was impossible, wrote *The Times*, "to give an idea of the inexhaustible grace which flowed from every limb of Elssler, dazzling the eye and confounding the senses, as she flitted around the enraptured painter, mingling the most sparkling playfulness with the most deep-souled passion as she alone can do."

Fanny took her own benefit on the last night but one of the season, August 17th, and Cerrito gave her services by appearing not only in the famous *pas de deux*, but also in the *Menuet de la Reine* and *Gavotte*. In this evocation of past graces, so different from the classical *variations* and the character dances in which she was usually seen, Fanny gave a further proof of her unrivalled powers of interpretation. To the actress Fanny Kemble, her performance bore out Mrs Grote's assertion that her "genius lay full as much in her head as in her heels. I am not sure," she added, "that the finest performance of hers that I ever witnessed was not a minuet in which she danced the man's part, in full court suit . . . with the most admirable grace and nobility of demeanour."

This London season had done much to restore Fanny's confidence. Not only had she shown that she had lost none of her brilliance of technique, but in *Giselle* she had established her reputation as an interpretative artist of the first order. One of the finest tributes paid to her was published in the *Morning Herald* at the end of the season. "With those who look to dancing as a piece of artistry and desire it only as a means of expression, Elssler is the great and glorious idol. She belongs to spectators of aesthetical intelligence. Her flexibility of limb and the profuseness of her steps are the admiration and wonder of two continents. She is the Thalberg* of the ballet; but, more than that, her ability to express in pantomime tragic emotion, playful gaiety or mirthful *espiéglerie* is astonishing. She is perhaps the first dancer who has given form, character and purpose to the art. Her limbs, face and gestures are alike instinct with intelligence. But Fanny Elssler is a genius, and hence her subtle and unspeakable power over the mind."

With praises such as these ringing in her ears, Fanny sailed across the Irish Sea to Dublin, to dance at the Theatre Royal. The Irish had no pretensions to be a discerning audience for ballet, and there was no withholding of enthusiasm when she appeared before them on seven evenings between August 26th and September 6th. People fought for admittance to the pit, but once inside forgot their bruises and torn jackets to applaud her with the most vocal good humour. At one performance, during a particularly brilliant passage, a lusty shout from the gallery of "More power, Fanny!" surprised her so much that she stopped short before realising it was a compliment, and then laughingly curtsied towards the source of the cry before resuming her dance.

In Hamburg, where she went on to give six performances in October, the demonstrations of enthusiasm were more refined. Not all of them, however, turned out according to plan. When, after her last performance, a group of her admirers tried to unharness her horses to draw her carriage back to her hotel, her coachman, misconstruing their intentions, laid about them so heartily with his whip that they had to flee in disorder.

So ended an eventful and successful summer, and Fanny returned to Vienna to rest and recuperate before passing the next milestone in her career—her debut at the Scala, Milan, which was fixed for early in the New Year, 1844.

---

* A celebrated concert pianist of the time whose reputation rested on his extraordinary technical virtuosity.

XV

An Austrian in Italy

OVER THE NEXT FOUR YEARS the focus of Fanny's activities shifted to Italy, where the patriotic struggle towards nationhood was gathering momentum. Divided into a patchwork of states, the Italian peninsula fell mainly within the sphere of Austria. Lombardy and Venetia in the north were ruled directly from Vienna, several of the duchies in the centre were under Austrian control, and to maintain the status quo a large Austrian army was garrisoned at strategic points south of the Alps. The Italian people were now becoming increasingly restive. Their yearning for unification and independence, for the ejection of the Austrians, and for more liberal forms of government was already crystallising into the *Risorgimento*, the patriotic movement which was eventually to make Italy free, and the land was full of secret societies whose common aim was to expel the foreign masters.

Fanny would have been aware of these undercurrents when she arrived in Milan, but she had little reason to suspect that political passions would affect her reception at the Scala. If she had felt at all nervous on this score, the presence of white-coated Austrian officers in the audience was an added reassurance when she made her first appearance on January 13th, 1844. The Milanese public, however, was notorious for its turbulent behaviour during the Carnival season, when partisans of rival singers and dancers engaged in clamorous demonstrations to establish the supremacy of their favourites. To them Fanny was a newcomer, and her nationality apart, they expected her to prove her worth before they would admit her to the select group of divas.

Luck was not with her that evening. Not only was she received coldly when she made her first entrance, but she had a desperate struggle to win the public's sympathy in the wretched ballet, *Armida*, which Bernardo Vestris had produced for her debut. However, her brilliant technique did not go unnoticed, and the more knowledgeable spectators were delighted to observe an Italian quality in her style. The precision and intricacy of her *pointe* work also made a strong impression, reminding the critic of *La Fama* of Amalia Brugnoli. "If a comparison were asked for," wrote another critic in the *Corriere delle Dame*, "I would say that Elssler's dancing resembles the perfect execution of a musical variation rather than the mood expressed in an andante or a cantabile. The steps she performs on the *pointes* of her feet, marvellous steps for displaying their strength and agility, are like those scherzi and clusters of notes with which great instrumentalists sometimes amuse themselves."

Fanny recovered from this unfortunate start by staging *Le Délire d'un peintre*, which she danced with Hippolyte Monplaisir on January 24th. This light work came as a welcome relief after the tedious *Armida*, and was much better suited to displaying her talent. The flexible structure of its *divertissement* enabled her to introduce the *Cachucha* and later the *Castilliana*, while the opening scene gave a foretaste of her dramatic ability.

This was to be revealed to the full on February 15th, when she appeared in *Giselle*. The Italians were astounded. One critic spoke of her in the same breath as the actor Gustavo Modeno as a model of dramatic art, and she seldom had less than twenty curtain calls after a performance of this ballet.

Giselle had not become a sacrosanct classic, and the Scala, with its proclivity for multi-scene ballets, presented it for Fanny in a three-act version. This was based on an even more expanded production, in four acts, which Antonio Cortesi had staged for Cerrito the year before. The principal change was that the first act was divided into two scenes. The first of these was set by Giselle's cottage, and carried the plot to the point where the princess learns that Giselle, like her, is in love. She invites everyone—Giselle, her mother, Hilarion, and even a band of fortune-telling gypsies—to attend her wedding ball at the castle. The action then moved to the castle ballroom, where Albrecht is alarmed to recognise Giselle among the guests and hastily retires. After a *divertissement*, which included dances by the gypsies and by Giselle herself, Bathilde, who has noticed her fiancé's absence, asks her father to find him. When Albrecht appears, he is recognised by Hilarion, who accuses him of deceiving Giselle. Albrecht draws his sword. Bathilde, who is ignorant of the cause of Hilarion's anger, seeks a means of ending this embarrassing scene and leads Giselle forward to dance with Albrecht. This moment of truth, when Giselle realises her lover's duplicity, leads to the mad scene. In the last act there was little change until the end, when Albrecht dies and, in an apotheosis, is seen united with Giselle.

The Milanese critics observed that Fanny was less well suited to the last act than to the earlier scenes, which brought out the vitality of her dancing and her dramatic power. The mad scene was considered to be the highlight of her performance. Here, wrote the *Corriere delle Dame*, "the ballerina gave pride of place to the actress, or rather the one became infused with the other with such a high degree of verisimilitude that this scene produced the full effect of desolate, anguished, sombre horror. The portrayal of passion and sorrow can be taken no further. Such is Elssler's artistry that her gestures make one forget the absence of words. In the whole first part of the ballet Elssler is truly great, both in her dancing and in her acting . . . She gave life to a character which until now had only been slightly hinted at. She imbued her dancing with an ingenuousness so charming, so gay and so exhilarating as to conquer even the coldest of hearts. There were certain movements in which the free, bold sway of her body had all the fascination of the bacchantes of old . . . In the *pas de trois* . . . she showed how agile and perfect her dancing can be. The complicated sequence of foot movements, so fast, so light, so perfect, convinced even the most obdurate perfectionist, and she repeated it by unanimous demand. This did not happen in the case of the *Cracovienne*, which is out of place in this ballet." The error of including this dance in the first act—she danced it with Hippolyte Monplaisir, who was playing Albrecht—was at once recognised, and it was omitted at the second performance.

Fanny's splendid triumphs brought no comfort to the young Danish ballerina, Lucile Grahn, who had also been engaged for this season. The two dancers happened to be staying at the same hotel, and the arrival one evening of a band of Fanny's admirers to serenade her made Grahn painfully conscious of her inferiority. Smarting with envy, she complained bitterly that the noise prevented her from sleeping, and would have refused to dance the next evening had not the management taken drastic steps and sent the police to fetch her.

Before the season closed at Easter, Fanny appeared in a mediocre ballet by Bernardo Vestris, *Venere ed Adone*, which fell so flat that it was dropped after its first performance on March 21st. Appropriately, her final appearance was in *Giselle*, at the end of which, while bouquets and sonnets were falling on to the stage, a small child emerged from the wings and kneeling before her, offered Fanny a silver basket of flowers. Then the cry of "*Zapateo!*" was taken up by the whole audience, and Fanny yielded graciously and danced again on a multicoloured carpet of flowers and leaflets.

Giselle was again the highlight when she appeared for a short season in Vienna in the summer. The mad scene was acclaimed as "most shattering . . . In its realism this miming says more than words. It strikes at the heart of our feelings and lays bare a world of pain before our eyes". She followed this with *Le Délire d'un peintre*, and later with *La Fille mal gardée*, in which she danced her *variation* to the melody of "*Una tenera occhiattina*" from Donizetti's *L'Elisir d'amore* better, it was

Fanny Elssler as Catarina. Watercolour by Weingartner, 1851.

Bakhrushin Museum, Moscow.

Fanny Elssler as Lise in *La Fille mal Gardée*. Watercolour by Weingartner, 1851.

Bakhrushin Museum, Moscow.

Fanny Elssler in her Russian
dance. Watercolour by
Weingartner, 1851.

Bakhrushin Museum, Moscow.

Fanny Elssler as Georges in
Le Muet d'Ingouville. Watercolour
by Weingartner, 1851.

Bakhrushin Museum, Moscow.

said, than Tadolini had sung it two days earlier. Her engagement at the Kärntnertortheater closed with a splendid benefit, at which she repeated both the *Cachucha* and the *Zapateo de Cadiz*. "Just as we now read the myths of the Greeks," one critic prophesied, "so in a thousand years' time will there be an Elssler myth, that of a female genius who flew down to earth to delight all hearts."

A few days later Fanny boarded the steamer "Friedrich" to sail down the Danube to Pest. Hungary was a dominion of the Hapsburg empire, and its principal city, though intensely nationalistic, was, in the eyes of a Viennese, no more than a provincial centre. Having accepted an engagement to appear at the German Theatre there, Fanny had not realised the offence that might be caused in some quarters by not choosing to dance at the National Theatre, and the sarcastic and even hostile comments which were printed in some Hungarian newspapers must have seemed very undeserved. Happily this attitude had little effect on her reception. So great was the curiosity even before she appeared in the theatre that when she went for a stroll on Whit Sunday in the shaded alleys of the Horváth Garden, the worm-eaten wooden bench on which she rested was later sold for 6 florins.

Next day, May 27th, 1844, the German Theatre was filled to capacity for her first appearance. Before the performance began the excitement reached such a pitch that an English admirer and a Hungarian came to blows in the stalls, and while the opening play was being given the audience became so restive that the stage manager had to plead for patience, explaining that she was not yet dressed. That evening she was recalled sixteen times, and this enthusiasm did not diminish throughout the week of her stay in Pest. She danced at the German Theatre seven times in seven days, fortunately without mishap, for the stage there was notoriously dangerous. It was difficult, wrote an onlooker, to know who was to be more admired, the spectator who often had to sit in a very uncomfortable seat from four in the afternoon until nine in great heat, or the tireless ballerina who was obliged to repeat all her solos and who in a single week gave more than double the number of perform-ances usually expected of a dancer. The theatre was sold out at every performance, she was sometimes called before the curtain thirty times before the audience was satisfied, and every night her bouquets had to be transported to her hotel in a cart. Furthermore, her success was in no way impaired by the presence in the city of a most venerable rival. At the State Theatre in the Citadel, the oldest dancer in the world was billed—the ninety-four-year-old marionette Juno, the star of the Pratte sisters' show, who emulated the great ballerina by adding the *Cachucha* to her repertory!

Fanny did appear once at the National Theatre. She agreed to dance there at a matinée performance on June 2nd, even though her benefit was announced at the German Theatre for the same evening. At the end of the matinée, as she was acknowledging the ovation in a sea of flowers, a voice shouted, "The *Cracovienne*!" The cry was taken up by the whole audience, and when Fanny called for silence and spoke her assent in Hungarian, her conquest was complete.

Sharing in her triumph was Gustave Carey, who had partnered her well during the preceding season in Vienna. He had one anxious moment in Pest, when a serenade was being given beneath her window. The crowd perceived a man's silhouette in Fanny's room and, like jealous lovers, began to protest. They were only quietened when Fanny led Carey on to the balcony and introduced him as her partner.

There was to be no respite for her that summer, but as she hurried across Europe on her way to London, she must have reflected that the sacrifice of a period of repose was well worth the exciting prospect that awaited her. In London Jules Perrot was planning a dramatic ballet in which she was to play the character of Joan of Arc. Furthermore, since Cerrito was also engaged for the remainder of the season, the burden of maintaining the ballet performances would be shared and she would have time to learn this new role at relative leisure.

"Grown a little fuller in person", as one critic described her, she made her reappearance at Her Majesty's Theatre on June 18th in *Le Délire d'un peintre*. Soon afterwards she was seen again in *Giselle*, but apart from a new Spanish dance, the *Saragossa*, she created nothing new until the evening of her benefit on July 25th. Then, after dancing with Cerrito in the *Gavotte* and *Menuet de la reine*, she played the leading part in Perrot's new *divertissement*, *La Paysanne Grande Dame*. Like *Le Délire d'un peintre*, this was a light piece in which the plot provided no more than a framework for a selection of dances. A Count, who has taken a fancy to a country girl, invites her to his mansion, where she is dressed for a ball and is taught the graces and manners of a lady. This situation was rendered by Fanny with much wit and charm. "Running in, with her full train swelling behind her," described *The Times*, "she could not take her eyes from it, but surveyed her finery with delightful wonder. A fan is to her a new instrument, but she soon learns the art not only of fanning herself with it, but of ogling from behind it. Having acquired the art of dismissing from a room with dignity, she first puts her knowledge into practice by ordering out her preceptor. The joyousness with which, at the sight of her rustic lover (whose distress is capitally represented by Perrot), she casts aside her cumbersome headdress, and capers away in some village *pas*, while she holds up her train (now an annoyance), is absolutely charming." The final dance was a new *pas de caractère*, the *Béarnaise*, which she performed with Arthur Saint-Léon. Neither the *divertissement* as a whole, nor the new dance, was an unqualified success: only Fanny's acting relieved the ballet from tedium, while the *Béarnaise* was lacking in distinctive character.

Fanny's hopes of appearing as Joan of Arc were dashed after the first few rehearsals by a series of accidents. First Perrot badly sprained his leg, and then Henri Montessu fell and broke his arm. Time being short, the project had to be dropped, and as a measure of compensation Fanny was taught the title-role of *La Esmeralda,* which Perrot had produced for Carlotta Grisi at the opening of the season.

The part of Esmeralda, which Fanny first played on August 3rd, 1844, was to be one of her greatest interpretations, ranking with Giselle and Lise. Perrot had reduced Hugo's novel, *Notre Dame de Paris,* to five scenes for his ballet. In the opening scene Gringoire, a struggling poet, is rescued from a band of thieves when Esmeralda agrees out of pity to marry him. She is desired by a lecherous priest, Claude Frollo, who, aided by the hunchbacked bellringer Quasimodo, is about to abduct her when the patrol approaches. Esmeralda is naïvely taken with the handsome captain, Phoebus, who gallantly presents her with his scarf. Returning to her humble lodging, she daydreams of him and spells out his name in letters on the floor. After refusing to share her room with Gringoire, she is disturbed by Frollo, who unsuccessfully tries to violate her. Summoned to dance at a wedding celebration, she meets Phoebus again, for he is the prospective bridegroom. His fiancée recognises the scarf, which had been a gift from her to Phoebus, and is carried away fainting. Phoebus arranges an assignation with Esmeralda in a cabaret, but their tender exchanges are violently interrupted by Frollo, who stabs his rival and escapes through the window. Esmeralda is accused of murder and condemned to death. On the scaffold Frollo offers to save her if she will yield to his desires, but she refuses. Then Phoebus, who has only been wounded, pushes his way through the crowd and denounces the priest, who rushes madly at Esmeralda with a dagger. Quasimodo snatches the weapon from his grasp and plunges it into Frollo's heart.

Fanny's performance in this powerful drama contrasted strongly with the interpretation of Carlotta Grisi, who had given the character a certain naïve, playful and unsophisticated charm but had not fully explored its dramatic possibilities. "Carlotta Grisi," observed the *Morning Post* after seeing Fanny at rehearsal, "represented a youthful buoyant girl, full of grace and innocence. Elssler's Esmeralda is characterised by far higher intellectuality, and the shades of feeling and passion are deeper marked."

The scene of Follo's attempted rape of Esmeralda was superbly handled by Fanny. "The irruption of the ominous monk on her privacy . . . was worked up into an incident of terrific importance by the skill of the actress." wrote the *Morning Herald.* "The attitude she assumed, expressive of fear and horror, was startling; the cold shiver that seemed to pervade her frame, the fixed uplifting of her arms, and the apprehension depicted on her countenance, presented altogether a picture of mental uneasiness and womanish timidity not often realised on the stage; and it may easily be imagined that the subsequent struggle with the infuriate ravisher was elaborated strongly and effectively."

On the other hand, the assignation scene with Phoebus was less telling. "Here," the same critic continued, "the innocent confiding girl is vacillating between love and virtue—giving herself up to the tender endearments of fondness, and anon recoiling with horror under the momentary upbraidings of conscience. Carlotta Grisi gave a more affectionate and languishing cast to this interview than her successor: *her* pliancy appeared to be that of a lovesick maiden; while the latter was only grand and classical—effective, but not engaging . . . At the moment of accusation [Fanny] was again magnificent: at first she is overcome with terror, but presently she swells with pride and innocence, and indignantly confronts her denouncers; until, becoming sensible of her weak and forlorn condition, her courage forsakes her, and she droops into dejection and submissiveness."

Outside the theatre, Fanny's main need was for the company of little Therese, who was still being cared for by the Grotes. Clearly she had not realised how deeply she had wounded this generous couple when she had removed her daughter from their care without warning two years before, for now the incident was to be repeated. Suddenly deprived a second time of the child on whom they had lavished so much affection, the Grotes reflected bitterly on Fanny's total want of consideration for their feelings. Six months later the wound was still unhealed. "The charming and gifted child whom we had cherished like our own for more than four years," wrote Harriet Grote to a friend, "was torn from our arms last June, and the parting caused both George and myself cruel anguish, much augmented by our conviction that she was destined to pass from Paradise to Purgatory, or haply worse. As this was the second time that we have been cut to the soul at having our little Therese snatched from us, without even the decorous formalities of the occasion, we resolved to yield up our feelings no more during the remainder of our lives to impulses of romantic beneficence."

After the close of the London season Fanny took Therese to Liverpool, where she was to dance for three weeks at the Theatre Royal.

During the final week the public's curiosity was diverted by the arrival of two other celebrities, "General" Tom Thumb, the American midget, and his impresario, P. T. Barnum. Tom Thumb's diminutive carriage was one of the sights of the town, and large crowds packed the Liver Theatre to see him. Barnum took him one evening to see Fanny dance, and at the end of the ballet the little fellow shouted for an encore. Fanny acknowledged his outburst with a curtsy, and the house cheered Tom Thumb, who kissed his hand several times to the audience. Afterwards she went to the manager's box and embraced the midget with great warmth.

Many of her admirers must have envied Tom Thumb his good fortune, and not the least a certain German gentleman who had put up at the Adelphi Hotel, where she was staying, and spent many long hours in the coffee room with his eyes constantly fixed on the front door. After a vigil of nearly a week he was rewarded by a sight of the ballerina, who he fondly imagined would accept his hand if only he could have a few minutes to express his devotion. But his hopes were dashed when he saw her coming down the stairs accompanied by "a tall dashing and formidable gentleman, having by the hand a fine little girl".

Therese was now to leave England for good. To the distress and disapproval of the Grotes, Fanny took her back to Vienna, where she completed her education in a convent. The Grotes were never to lose touch with her, for George Grote was trustee of a fund which Fanny had settled on her in London. This trusteeship was to cause both him and his wife much heartburning, for Fanny, who did not understand the implications of the settlement and the duties imposed on a trustee, was continually levelling unjust and insulting accusations about the administration of the fund. The Grotes could do no more than reflect sorrowfully on her ingratitude, and tell their friends disapprovingly that the child's character was being "ruined by bad discipline and the total want of love and sympathy" in the Viennese convent where, as they put it, she was incarcerated.

Fanny was overjoyed to have Therese with her, and Dublin, Brussels and Munich saw her dancing at the peak of her form in the late summer and autumn of 1844. In the Irish capital, where she danced six times between August 24th and September 2nd, she introduced two new numbers: the *Redowa Polka*, which she had learnt from Cerrito, and the *Drawing Room Polka*, which she danced with Sylvain in a modern ball dress. Her triumph in Brussels was specially satisfying. Opening at the Monnaie on October 7th, just a week after Taglioni had danced there, she astonished everyone by the perfection of her technique. "Never have we seen more difficulties overcome," wrote *L'Indépendance Belge,* "never have we seen such astounding *pointe* work."

In November Fanny crossed the Alps to spend a second winter dancing in Italy. For her Turin was much more of a foreign city than Milan, for it was the capital of the independent kingdom of Piedmont and contained no garrison of Austrian troops to bring a touch of Vienna to the theatre. There was no sign of hostility, however, and the poet, Felice Romani, wrote a paean of praise in her honour. But there did seem to be a certain restraint. Though she was warmly applauded at the Teatro Carignano, there were no triumphal processions afterwards—"a noble discernment in our times," as a contemporary remarked, "approved perhaps by Elssler herself, who must feel she is a mortal, and an example to be followed wherever people still know how to give life a nobler aim than mere enjoyment."

This was the prelude to the Carnival season in Milan, where she gained further triumphs both on the stage and in society. Life smiled upon her, and when she appeared at the Countess Samailova's masked ball, she was so radiant that a journalist reporting it opened and closed his article with the words, "I saw and I marvelled". For the opening of the season at the Scala Perrot revived *La Esmeralda*. Fanny was acclaimed as "the Frezzolini of the dance", which in a stronghold of opera like Milan was an unusual tribute, inferring as it did equality with the great prima donna. After appearing in *Giselle* and *La Tarentule*, she added a new role to her repertory on March 1st, 1845, that of Beatrix in *La Jolie Fille de Gand*, produced by Antioio Cortesi. In this spectacular work she played the role of a girl who, on her wedding eve, dreams that she has succumbed to the blandishments of a nobleman and become his mistress, only to wake up at the end to profit by the moral of her nightmare. In the dances she had her greatest success in a *pas de masque*, in which she was partnered by Giovanni Pratesi, who played the part of the Marquis.

This ballet was not so successful when Bernardo Vestris restaged it at the Kärntnertortheater when she returned to Vienna in April. With Fanny in the title-role, it could not fail to have a certain success, but apart from her performance the production was truncated and weak. Fanny always enjoyed dancing in Vienna, and this summer she continued her appearances until the middle of June and at the end of her stay, on June 19th, took part in a charity performance in the Josefstadt Theater. Here she was seen in a different guise, for she played for the first time the mime role of the dumb orphan girl in Scribe's melodrama, *Yelva, ou l'Orpheline russe*.

Fanny occupied a unique position in Vienna, where she was not only admired as a theatrical celebrity but admitted to the select circles of society. Many doors were opened for her through her friendship with the Metternichs, which went back to the time when she sweetened the last years of Friedrich von Gentz. The old Chancellor appreciated "the distinction of her personality, her appearance, and her engaging, exquisite manners", and she was a frequent guest at his dinner parties. It was at one of these that Metternich's granddaughter Pauline—the future ambassadress in Paris during the Second Empire—was brought into the drawing-room to be presented. All her life the child was to retain the memory of Fanny as she saw her that evening, sitting at Metternich's side, wearing a yellow silk dress and with a rose in her hair. What impressed her most of all was the dainty way in which she kept her feet crossed. Later she was taken to the theatre to see *Giselle*, and wept copiously when Giselle sank into the grave with her arms outstretched above her head. "It was," she remembered long afterwards, "the dying of poetry itself!"

From Vienna Fanny then set off on an Italian tour which was to take her to towns and cities she had not visited before: first, Senigallia on the shores of the Adriatic; next, Brescia, where she gave six performances at the end of August at the Teatro Grande with the Monplaisirs and Pratesi; then on to Vicenza to appear at the Teatro Eritenio, and Bologna, where Ronzani staged *La Esmeralda* for her at the Teatro Comunale.

Her next engagement was in Rome, where her plan to dance in *La Esmeralda* was thwarted because the Prefect of Police forbade its performance on the ground that the plot was immoral. She therefore appeared instead in *Giselle* and *Le Délire d'un peintre* at the Teatro Argentina, and afterwards, in January 1846, in *La Jolie Fille de Gand* at the Teatro Apollo. The Romans wanted to present her with a golden crown, as they had earlier honoured Cerrito, but the Prince and Princess Doria, whose position in Roman society was immensely powerful, prevented this presentation, considering it untimely in view of Fanny's Austrian origin.

From Rome Fanny went to Foligno, where she gave a single performance, and then continued her journey to Venice. Here she arrived mourning the loss of the little goat she had trained to appear in *La Esmeralda*, and the ballet had to be produced at the Teatro La Fenice without it. "The piece lost one of its graces," wrote Paul de Musset, who had taken the precaution of buying a seat for every one of her performances, "but the ballerina had a wild success. Fanny Elssler, still a beautiful woman, revived my memories of the finest days at the Paris Opéra. Her talent for expression had developed wonderfully. I had known her to be lively, mischievous, sparkling, and I found her again with all these qualities and a tragedienne besides. Her miming, in the final scene where Esmeralda says a prayer at the foot of the scaffold, forgives her executioners and repels the tempting suggestions of Claude Frollo, attained the most moving pathos. Tears flowed, and the artist's triumph reached disturbing proportions, for when the people weep in Italy, the theatre is in danger of collapsing with the noise and the stamping of the ovation. For fifteen successive performances the tumult continued undiminished, and the impresario consoled himself for the disgrace of the King of the Huns." This was a reference to Verdi's new opera *Attila*, which at its first performance on the evening of Fanny's last appearance, had been received with comparative restraint.

That night, after the performance, she was accorded a triumph such as might have been offered to a ruling sovereign. Escorted by a fleet of torchlit gondolas, she was rowed back to her hotel on the Grand Canal through a shower of flowers scattered from the balconies of the palaces as she passed. Excited crowds swarmed through the narrow alleys to see her alight, and as the city went to sleep the melodies of her dances, played by serenaders beneath her window, filled the soft evening air.

Her triumph in Venice was made doubly sweet by her conquest of the Italian poet, Giovanni Prati, whose pen was dedicated to the nationalistic aspirations of his countrymen, to the unification of Italy and the expulsion of the Austrians. Now, after inveighing against the craze for dancers and singers because it distracted the people from their patriotic cause, he himself had been ensnared by the charms of the Austrian ballerina. His subjugation was complete, and to justify his new passion, he wrote a long lyrical poem, a *carme*, which, elegantly printed and bound in silk, was solemnly presented to Fanny on the stage of the Fenice. Most of it was taken up by an effusive and fanciful rhapsody, which was interrupted when he recalled himself to the problems of the day. He then excused himself for not writing in a more austere strain by explaining that he was impelled by a force stronger than himself, and in the final stanzas he evoked a vision of moonlit Venice slumbering in her misfortune, pointing to Fanny Elssler as a symbol of life and hope which he hoped the Venetians themselves might one day enjoy.

By the terms of her engagement with the Kärntnertortheater, Fanny was due to arrive in Vienna on March 25th. She had hoped that her performances there might begin later than planned to enable her to accept an engagement in Trieste, but this was not possible. Then her sister, who was with her, fell ill, and it was not until April 1st that Fanny was able to leave Padua. A fellow traveller came across her as she was making her way northwards, "like a Princess of Trebizond", with a great caravan of vehicles conveying her, her following and her luggage across the Alps. This traveller arrived at the Hotel della Chiara d'Oro in Chiavenna to find she had arrived a few days earlier and was resting in her room. He was told that she had insisted on leaving for the Splügen Pass against the advice of the landlord, who realised that the weather was worsening. "She imagined we were trying to detain her so as to increase her hotel bill," he said. "She drew herself up, and without listening to anybody leapt into the mail coach, with her legs looking marvellous in her velvet boots, and shouted '*Avanti!*' to the postillion. We could see from here that there must be a terrible storm at Splügen. Night fell, and we heard a cry . . . It was Fanny Elssler, frozen with cold. Her boots were wet through and stiff with ice. She herself was shivering with a temperature . . . She looked so pitiful that we dared not remind her we had advised her to put off her departure. Now she will have to spend her money here!" The traveller announced his intention to continue his own journey the next day, whatever the weather, but the landlord shook his head. That would be impossible; Fanny Elssler had engaged all the available men and horses.

Her first performance at the Kärntnertortheater a few weeks later coincided with the Viennese debut of Jenny Lind at the Theater an der Wien, but neither theatre suffered from the coincidence. During her short season Fanny introduced Vienna to *La Esmeralda*, in Ronzani's production, in which she was partnered by Francis Mérante. In June Mérante accompanied her to Pest where she gave a few performances at the German Theatre and added a spirited *czardas* to her repertory.

If she aroused less enthusiasm in Hungary than on her previous visit, her popularity in Italy proved undiminished when she returned later that summer. Leisurely making her way to Rome, she paused to dance at Senigallia and Cesena. In the Eternal City she was engaged at the Teatro Argentina, where her admirers, not content with releasing doves in the auditorium, were determined that she should not depart without the crown they had planned to present to her the year before. Since her last visit the old Pope had died, and with the election of the new pontiff, Pius IX, the influence of the Dorias had apparently waned. Some 12,000 lire had been subscribed and the crown already made when her admirers became troubled in their consciences. Would such a demonstration, they wondered, be distasteful to the Pope? An audience was requested, and they put their problem to Pio Nono, who had a reputation for liberal views.

"You do not need my consent for what you intend to do," His Holiness told them. "Give the dancer her wreath if it affords you pleasure, but allow me to remark that you do not seem to have made a very appropriate choice of a gift. I should have preferred a garland, a bouquet, or something of that sort, for until now I thought that wreaths were meant for the head, not the feet."

The presentation was duly made on the day before Fanny departed for Florence, where she was engaged for the autumn season at the Teatro La Pergola. The enthusiasm of the Florentines reached such a pitch that it was reported that only Napoleon had ever received a greater acclaim in the city. "Night after night," wrote an English visitor, "the 'Pergola' was crowded from floor to roof—from the grand-ducal box to the last inch of standing-room in the pit. Her Esmeralda charmed the Florentines so much that they would not permit it to be changed for any other ballet; and, in truth, her acting in it, as well as of course her dancing, is exquisite. And then the shouting, the roaring and throwing of flowers when she comes before the curtain at the close, in the long white robe, with her magnificent hair streaming over it, as she goes to her execution in the last scene! Florence may be called the city of flowers *par excellence*. More money is probably spent on them there in proportion to the entire expenditure of the population than in any other part of the world. And the fashion of testifying admiration for a favourite actress by throwing bouquets to her on the stage is carried to an excess there not seen elsewhere. A great cart would have been necessary to carry off all the bouquets thrown on the stage of the 'Pergola' on the night of Fanny Elssler's benefit. I saw once a '*mazzo*' . . . entirely composed of violets and at least three feet in circumference, handed to her from a stage box by a countryman of ours, while one of similar dimensions, consisting wholly of white camellias, was contributed to the beneficiata's triumph by his lady wife. '*In somma la Fanny faceva furore*'."

Fanny's stage triumphs were not obtained without physical cost, as the singer Mario was to discover. In the days of his youth, when Fanny was the star of the Paris Opéra, he had worshipped her from afar. Now he found himself in Florence with her, a handsome young tenor in the full flush of popular success and fêted by society, and his joy knew no bounds when the idol of his youth adopted him as her *chevalier servant*. He found she could still stir his passions, and his romantic ardour was aroused when she allowed him to enter her bedroom in the morning and sing to her as she lay in bed. One evening, after a triumph at the theatre, Fanny took his arm so warmly that he felt the long-desired moment of surrender was at hand. As they sat down to an intimate supper, the strains of a serenade came floating through the open window. The atmosphere seemed perfect. He took her on to the balcony, and tenderly taking her into his arms, he felt her yield, then suddenly stiffen.

"What is the matter?" he inquired.

The romantic moment was rudely shattered. "It is my haemorrhoids," she explained. "When I dance, they warm up and I feel no pain, but now . . ."

Fanny gave her last performance in Florence at the end of November, and then travelled north to Milan to take part in the Carnival season at the Scala. Jules Perrot joined her there, and before long the two of them were absorbed in the rehearsals of *Catarina*, which was to give her another strong dramatic role. Although this ballet had not been created for her—Lucile Grahn had been the first to play the title-role in London the previous spring—it was to fall to Fanny to exploit its dramatic possibilities most fully.

With its Italian setting, it had a natural appeal for the Milanese. Its hero was the artist, Salvator Rosa, who is captured by bandits under the command of Catarina, the daughter of their former chief. The interest she shows in the prisoner arouses the jealousy of her lieutenant, Diavolino. When the bandits are routed by a party of soldiers, Catarina and the two men escape. After meeting a former lover, Florida, in a tavern, Salvator recognises Catarina and Diavolino disguised as servants. When the soldiers arrive with their prisoners, Catarina dances a fiery *Saltarella* to distract them while Diavolino sets the bandits free. Catarina then makes her way to Salvator's studio, where with Florida's help she disguises herself as a model and poses before the artist as Venus. Realising that Salvator is in love with Catarina, Florida betrays her to the soldiers. Catarina is condemned to death, but helped by Salvator and Diavolino, makes her escape. It is carnival time, and Catarina and her rescuers mingle with the revellers. Consumed with jealousy, Diavolino has resolved to kill Salvator, but in the ballet's final moments Catarina sacrifices herself and receives the fatal thrust.

The first performance of *Catarina* at the Scala on January 9th, 1847, gave Fanny a memorable triumph. It was hailed as a revolutionary work in which the dance was used, not as an ornament to the mimed action, but as a means of expression in itself. As in *La Esmeralda*, Fanny "opened up . . . a new field in acting" by discarding the conventional gestures of mime in favour of a natural and realistic style of acting. Her feet seemed to charge the boards with an emotional force, animating everything around her with a heightened vitality. No other dancer, wrote the critic Lambertini, could have depicted the many varied situations of the role as she did: Catarina's heroic aloofness when first seen as the bandit leader, her passion for the artist, the beguiling fascination which she displays when dancing before the soldiers, and the heart-rending pathos of the death scene. There was great variety, too, in the dances:

the martial *pas stratégique* with the amazon bandits in the first scene, the voluptuous *Saltarella,* the *romanesca,* full of delicacy and grace, which she danced in the studio scene, and finally the *follia del carnevale* which led to the tragic finale.

The most important event of the season was the creation of a new ballet by Perrot, *Odetta, o la Demenza di Carlo VI, re di Francia,* which had its first performance on March 16th, 1847, with Fanny and the choreographer in the leading roles. It had been prepared in some haste, for Perrot only began work on it on February 11th, when plans for another ballet had to be cancelled. He was said to be suffering from jaundice which he had neglected so as not to interrupt the performances of *Catarina,* but Lambertini suspected that the real cause of the delay was some dispute with the management. *Odetta* was to be the first of the two grand ballets which Perrot composed specially for Fanny Elssler, for *Giselle, La Esmeralda* and *Catarina,* which she had seemingly made her own, had been originally produced for other ballerinas. Probably because of the limited time available for the production, three composers had been commissioned to write the music for *Odetta,* Panizza being entrusted with the action and Bajetti and Croff with the dances. The sets were designed by Carlo Fontana.

As the title indicated, the characters of the ballet were taken from the history of France in the fifteenth century: Charles VI, father of St Joan's king; Isabeau of Bavaria, his queen; Louis, Duke of Orleans, the king's brother; Simon Caboche, the popular leader who demanded reforms in the royal household; and Odette de Champdivers, the king's Burgundian mistress. The scenario did not adhere very closely to historical fact: Caboche became the father of Odette, whose relationship with the king was transformed, for propriety's sake, into a mere compassion for his condition, coupled with her desperate need to save her father from the scaffold.

In the ballet Odetta first comes to the notice of the king when he intervenes to save her from the attentions of his jester. He is mingling with the crowd in disguise in order to catch a first glimpse of his future bride. Later, when his marriage has proved unhappy, he confides his troubles in Odetta, but becoming mad, he is taken to Paris in chains on the orders of the queen. There are sinister designs afoot. While the king's brother, the Duke of Orleans, has designs on the crown for himself, the queen is treacherously plotting with the English. Odetta persuades the jester to take her to the king, and as they row across the Seine to the palace, her father believes she is being abducted by the Duke. For assaulting the Duke he is condemned to death, and Odetta desperately tries to bring the king back to reason in order to save him.

She leaves the palace in despair, thinking that her attempts have failed, and arriving at the scaffold, throws herself weeping into her father's arms. The king, however, has recovered and arrives dramatically at the last moment to assert his royal authority and pardon Odetta's father.

The role of Odetta was conceived specially to take advantage of Fanny's dramatic gifts. Her relationships with the king and his jester were developed in a series of striking scenes. There was a witty *pas d'action* in the first act in which the jester steals a bouquet she has picked for the queen and she tries to recover it, but the scenes with the king provided the mainspring for her characterisation. Most impressive of all was the passage in the fourth act when Odetta uses all her wiles to restore the king to sanity and so save her father. In this desperate struggle against time, she touched the very peak of her genius. "When she is just making gestures," wrote *Il Pirata,* "you almost imagine that she is speaking. With a movement, a glance or a sigh she expresses much more than any actress could express in an hour. She explores every avenue of the soul, she covers the full range of her emotions, she probes all the secrets of the heart, passing brilliantly from a mere request to imploring, from calm to indignation, from reason to frenzy, from frenzy to madness. Jules Perrot has discovered here a highly dramatic point, and has had the good fortune to find an interpreter who, through her extraordinary talent, can clothe his idea with the necessary proportions and splendour. To give effect to something mediocre is not difficult; to give emphasis to the sublime is something of which only an Elssler is capable."

Unpolished, or even unfinished, as it was, *Odetta* was unanimously acclaimed as a masterpiece. "It is one of the finest ballets we have seen on our stage," wrote the *Corriere delle Dame,* "and if time and the health of the choreographer had allowed him to finish it completely, it would certainly have equalled . . . *La Esmeralda.* Indeed we will say it would have surpassed [it] in its combination of historical interest and dramatic invention and the excellent correlation between dancing and action, because *Odetta,* while giving an authentically historical picture of the life of the unhappy Charles VI, presents us also with the most beautiful dance groups and *ballabili* imaginable without detracting at all from the action, which almost seems to gain a new language of expression from the dances. It is a happy invention of modern choreography—and, we believe, of Perrot himself—to use the dances not merely as an excuse for graceful movement, but to give significance to human relationships and dramatic situations."

As the season drew to a close, Fanny was acclaimed for the uniqueness of her talent. "Oh, this Elssler!" wrote the *Gazzetta di Milano.*

"How tremendous she is! She cannot be compared to anyone but herself, if we wish to discover when and where she is at her most sublime." The season's keynote, as Benedetto Bermani observed, was the confluence of the geniuses of Perrot and Elssler. "Elssler," he wrote, "is the first among ballerinas just as she is the most prodigious of mimes. Give her the smallest of parts in the most mediocre of ballets, and she will clothe it with so many treasures of taste and intelligence as to make it almost great. Give her a composer such as Perrot, and you will see what marvels result from the association of these two artists who alone can understand each other in all their greatness." On the final night of this great season, after the seventh performance of *Odetta*, Fanny was showered with flowers from all parts of the house. Her energy that evening had seemed limitless, and at the end, while Perrot was gathering up the bouquets, she endeared herself to everyone by inviting the *corps de ballet* and the children from the ballet school to help themselves.

It was now three years since Fanny had visited London, where the monopoly of Her Majesty's Theatre had been broken by the conversion of Covent Garden Theatre into an opera house. Indeed, it was at the Royal Italian Opera, Covent Garden, that Fanny was engaged to dance in the summer of 1847. Accompanied, it seems, by her friend, Count Samuel Kostrowicki, whom the knowledgeable *Satirist* referred to as "her business manager and adviser, Count ——," she lodged at the Hôtel Sablonière in Leicester Square. She made her first appearance at Covent Garden on May 1st in a new *divertissement* by Albert, *La Bouquetière de Venise*. After the furore she had been causing in Milan, she was unpleasantly surprised by the phlegmatic reception which greeted her on her first entrance. Then the sight of Perrot in one of the boxes gave her courage, and she moved leisurely to the back of the stage to take up the opening pose of her first dance. In a few moments she had conquered, and the final notes of the music were drowned in a roar of applause. Proudly Fanny stood motionless awhile, letting the ovation reverberate around her and acknowledging it with no more than the slightest inclination of her head. Then, having savoured her triumph to the full, her expression changed. "At first a pout of pretty irony—then a smile of sweet complacency—then a little frown that curled itself up in a corner of her brow like one of the good-natured devils of the German mythos—then a look that flashed the full consciousness of victory—and then she condescended to repeat the dance." The English were forgiven.

During the two months of her Covent Garden engagement she appeared in two new roles and danced the minuet with Adèle Dumilâtre in Mozart's *Don Giovanni*. The first of the new ballets was *La Salaman-*

drine, a mediocre work by Carlo Blasis, first performed on May 18th, in which she played a peasant girl who dreams she has been struck dead by a thunderbolt and turned into a fire spirit. The second ballet, in which she first appeared on June 12th, was rather more substantial. This was Giovanni Casati's *Manon Lescaut*. It was based on Aumer's ballet of the same name, but Casati had truncated the plot and used music by Pio Bellini instead of the distinguished score which Halévy had composed for the original production at the Paris Opéra in 1830. In the version given at Covent Garden Fanny was deprived of the death scene, but she had a splendid triumph nevertheless as Manon Lescaut, both as a dancer and as an actress. Her performance was described by *The Times* as "a beautiful piece of nature, as truthful in the portraiture of heedless gaiety and coquetry as in the deeper emotions of sorrow and despair. In the prison scene, when she hears that her lover is condemned to death, her anguish was portrayed with a power and vividness that were positively tragic".

After completing her engagement in London, Fanny returned to Italy. Her first triumph there was at Padua, where her dancing created a sensational impression, not only on the audience of the Teatro Nuovo, but also on the orchestra. The effect was almost catastrophic, for the musicians were so busy craning their necks to watch her dancing that they played atrociously out of tune and the ballet-master Ciocchi was at his wit's end trying to preserve some sort of order on the stage.

In Padua, too, was the irrepressible Prati, quite unabashed by the accusations that he had prostituted his art by writing his now notorious *carme*. To show his critics what he thought of them, he wrote another, no less effusive ode, and was supported by Guglielmo Stefani, who maintained his right to praise an artist who had enabled the Italians to pass "a few less unhappy moments". After forcefully denying that he had been paid for his adulation, Prati proclaimed the sincerity of his enthusiasm for Fanny Elssler.

Following a pleasantly successful engagement in Munich in the autumn Fanny packed her luggage to return to Milan, looking forward to resuming her association with Perrot and to savouring again the ardent ovations of the Scala audiences, But it was a very different city that she found on her arrival. The antipathy between the Italian populace and the Austrians had increased to a point where any spark might set off an explosion. At first the opposition to the occupation took a non-violent form in a boycott of Austrian goods, and of tobacco, which was a state monopoly, in particular. The Italians stopped smoking. Abstention bred irritation, and early in January 1848 an Austrian captain was assaulted as he walked down the Corso. The Austrian commander decided to teach the Italians a lesson. He ordered his Croatian levies to walk ostentatiously about the city smoking cigars, and the tobacco riots which followed, in which several civilians were killed and many wounded, was a foretaste of the disorders that were to follow. For the moment, however, the Austrians were masters of the situation.

The Italians were unarmed, and expressed their animosity in subtle though unmistakable ways. Not only did they refuse to smoke, they boycotted the lottery which was also a source of public revenue. Then the word went forth that the Scala was to be avoided, because it was a royal theatre. That so many people kept away showed a commendable discipline, for it could not have been easy to forgo the pleasures of the opera house, with Tadolini as its prima donna and Fanny Elssler the prima ballerina.

Fanny now found herself in the centre of a political storm. As a Viennese, and a known friend of Metternich, she was seen as an instrument of Austrian policy, a seductive siren sent to distract the Italians from their duty to their country. She was vituperated in pamphlets as "the infamous German witch, the sinister instrument (one among many) of the vilest crimes of hated Austria, the slow assassination of the son of the great Napoleon". She was featured in political caricatures, in one of which the Austrian emissary, Count Ficquelmont, was shown presenting her to the Milanese public with these words:

> FICQUELMONT Gentlemen, if you do not want to put a foot wrong, study the steps of this admirable artist.
> PUBLIC Reforms! Reforms!
> FICQUELMONT Reforms? Very well, she will reform your ballet school.

Patriots, who a year before had applauded her in the theatre, now exhorted their fellow countrymen to boycott her first appearance, threatening any ladies who dared disobey that their names would be published.

"Another sacrifice, brothers!" ran one of the many pamphlets which were circulating in the city. "It is absolutely imperative that no one should go to the theatre for the first performance of Elssler. Leave the place to the Germans, who will applaud in our name as well. Elssler was kind to the poor, and she has a claim on our gratitude, but none on the sacrifice of our honour. So that it may not be said that the Milanese were conquered by the graces of a ballerina, it is imperative to keep away. The sylphide can become a siren and bewitch you. The silence of a thousand can be ruined by the applause of a few. Many women have promised not to attend, but so that their resolution may be rewarded,

Franz Opfermann and Fanny Elssler in *Le Délire d'un peintre*. Lithograph by
Franz Seitz.

Harvard Theatre Collection.

Fanny Elssler and Gustave
Carey in the scene of the
Seven Deadly Sins in *Faust*.

*Öst. Nationalbibliothek,
Theatersammlung.*

Fanny Elssler and Katti
Prinster, *c.* 1850.

Bakhrushin Museum, Moscow.

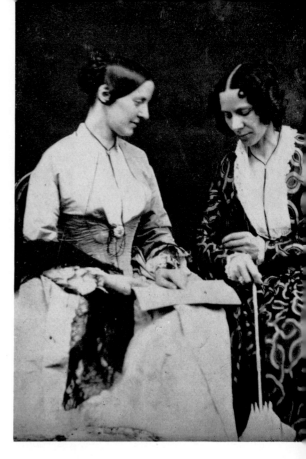

Fanny Elssler and Katti
Prinster, *c.* 1875.

Coll. Mme. Derra de Moroda.

it is necessary that the names of the few who cannot resist temptation should be made public. None of you will want to appear on the list of frivolous and curious women. Stand shoulder to shoulder, as usual, brothers! Our city has not yet shed its mourning. For Heaven's sake, do not make our enemies laugh, do not give the newspapers cause to insult you, prevent this little triumph of the Germans."

An injured foot had prevented Fanny from appearing on the opening night of the season, but as soon as her strength allowed she began to study a new ballet with Perrot. However detached she might have wished to remain from the political issues of the day, she could not help being involved. Now her nationality was a barrier between her and the Italian dancers of the company, and perhaps she felt estranged even from Perrot, who did not conceal his liberal sympathies. Indeed he took quite an active part in the struggle to eject the Austrians from Milan. A London report was to relate that he had "become a *maître de bataille* as well as a *maître de ballet*, for, calling together the waiters of the hotel in which he found himself, he reviewed them with great stage tact, and then led them forth against the Austrians, vowing he would not return until he had made these *garçons* men; which vow this old theatrical religiously performed."

Perrot's new ballet, *Faust*, was thus created under exceptional difficulties. His treatment of Goethe's story was divided into three acts and seven scenes, which took three hours to perform on the first night. The first act depicted Faust's pact with Mephistopheles, their arrival in the market place where Faust sees Marguerite with her sweetheart Valentine, Marguerite's discovery of the jewels, and a *divertissement* of the seven deadly sins. In the second act Valentine is killed by Faust and Marguerite loses her reason. In the last act Mephistopheles takes Faust into the mountains, where he finds Marguerite wandering disconsolate. He then witnesses a witches' sabbath, and the ballet ended with an imaginative *dénouement*, when Faust's pact with the devil is destroyed by the flame of Marguerite's soul and, following a massive earthquake, Marguerite is seen surrounded by a host of angels, holding out her arms to Faust.

In vain did the Scala appeal to the public to subscribe for the performances of the new ballet. The effectiveness of the boycott was revealed by the many empty seats in the house when the curtain rose on the first performance on February 12th, 1848. Not a single Italian family of distinction was present, and the few ladies who were tempted to ignore the patriots' call were hissed as they left the theatre and men were seen in the square taking down their names. With such a sparse audience it was hardly surprising that the new ballet, even with Fanny and Perrot in the leading roles, fell flat. Even so, it was much too long, its German subject was, to say the least, ill chosen considering the political climate, and the surfeit of scenic effects did not conceal the poverty of the dancing. Fanny herself was obviously ill at ease. "If Elssler could have added to the inspiration of the choreography by the powerful expression of her dancing," wrote the critic of the *Corriere delle Dame*, "the ballet would have had a much greater success, but Elssler was still unfit and had to measure her always fascinating steps to the uncertain strength of her foot."

Fanny was also keenly aware of her isolation from the Italian dancers and was very much on edge. Seeing the *corps de ballet* all wearing medals showing the Pope blessing a united Italy, she interpreted this as a personal insult. In the wings she created a violent scene, refusing to continue unless the offending medals were removed. Her demand was complied with, and when the *corps de ballet* reappeared the absence of the medals was immediately noticed. The news of the incident in the wings spread like wildfire, and when Fanny made her next entrance she was greeted with a storm of whistling, despite the presence of many Austrian officers.* From that moment on, her most strenuous efforts met with sepulchral silence from the occupants of the boxes, while the people in the gallery yawned loudly and shouted abusive and obscene remarks. At the end of the ballet Fanny was in a state of collapse.

She had no intention of submitting herself again to such behaviour, and left Milan as soon as she could. *La Sylphide* was hurriedly staged with the young American ballerina, Augusta Maywood, but the public still stayed away. The prime reason for the boycott remained even though Fanny had left, and one night only four of the two hundred and more boxes were occupied, the audience being limited to Austrian officers and government spies, who were on duty in case the youth of Milan should suddenly change its tactics and find a motive for demonstrating in the theatre. Perrot remained in Milan, and revised and shortened his *Faust*, which returned to the repertory for its second performance a few weeks later with Maywood playing the part of Marguerite.

Fanny left Milan, smarting from the injustice of politics which had painted her as a corruptor of souls, but she was not entirely forsaken by

---

* At the Teatro La Fenice in Venice the Italian dancer, Carlotta Pocchini, was the focus of another patriotic demonstration. Night after night she was presented with red flowers, which she would attach to her white ballet skirt, thus displaying the red, white and green colours of the House of Savoy. When the police intervened, yellow and black flowers—the Austrian colours—were thrown which she pointedly refused to pick up.

her admirers. To his credit, Prati remained steadfast in his admiration, and despite jeers that he had crept away to Turin and would not be tolerated in any free Italian city, he wrote another poem about the ballerina, which he entitled *La Creatura di Casa d'Austria*, the creature of the House of Austria. He saw Fanny again as the Goddess of Hope, sweetening the slumbers of Venice with her charms, and expressed the hope that "her barbarous Sire", meaning the Austrian Empire, should be foiled in his desire that the sea should remain calm.

Much of Europe was in a turmoil in those early months of 1848. In Paris at the end of February Louis-Philippe was chased from his throne, and in the middle of March, shortly after Fanny's return from the turbulent atmosphere of Milan, the people of Vienna rose and Metternich, who had been Chancellor for so long that he had seemed quite irremovable, hurriedly left the city. That summer Fanny gladly escaped to the more peaceful surroundings of Hamburg, where she made twenty-four appearances at the Stadt-Theater between July 6th and September 6th and gained a triumph which brought her the consolation and encouragement she needed before embarking on the last great adventure of her career—the conquest of Russia.

XVI

Russia: The Crowning Triumph

TO MOST WESTERNERS IN THE middle of the nineteenth century, Russia seemed as remote as the edge of the world. The vastness of the country, the strangeness of its peoples, its languages and its customs, and the rigours of its winters daunted most would-be travellers, while for theatrical artists, St Petersburg and more distant Moscow were far from the beaten track. Nevertheless many actors, singers and dancers had braved the journey, and had been well rewarded by the splendid facilities they had found in the theatres there and, in St Petersburg particularly, by enthusiastic ovations which were in no way inhibited by the cruel winter weather. Marie Taglioni's triumphs in St Petersburg, where she had discovered a splendid ballet company already established, had sown the seeds of that city's international reputation as a centre of ballet, and for some years now Fanny too had been looking to Russia as another field for conquest.

On her return from America she may have felt that no triumphs on the familiar stages of London, Paris, Berlin or Vienna could wholly satisfy her after those two pioneering years when every day held the promise of a new adventure. The idea to go to Russia first came to her in Berlin after she had refused Samuel Kostrowicki's proposal of marriage and was feeling the need to immerse herself in her art. On February 5th, 1843, she wrote to Alexandre Gedeonov, Director of the Imperial Theatres in Russia, to offer her services for a series of twenty-four performances spread over two months at a fee of 4,000 francs a night. Considering her celebrity, she must have been astonished when the days passed without bringing a reply. Being ignorant of the gossip of St Petersburg, she was not to know that Gedeonov was ruled by the whims of his prima ballerina, Elena Andreyanova, who was notoriously jealous of her position and viewed the proposed engagement of Fanny Elssler with extreme displeasure. Gedeonov deliberately took four months to inform the Tsar of Fanny's approach, and when he was officially authorised to engage her, he found, to his relief, that she had grown tired of waiting and signed a contract with the Scala, Milan.

For some time afterwards Fanny was too heavily committed to give any more thought to going to Russia, but the Tsar did not forget that the negotiations had come to nought. For all his military stiffness, Nicholas I was not blind to the beauties of the ballet, and had even bestowed his Imperial protection on one of his ballerinas, Olga Schlefogt. Curious to see Fanny Elssler, he took the opportunity to attend one of her performances during his travels outside Russia, probably in Rome in December 1845. He was charmed, and when she was brought to his box, he told her he hoped she would come to St Petersburg. Fanny was non-committal, and the Tsar, sensing that she was troubled by Andreyanova's influence, promised her his support. "I shall be your protector," he said. "You can turn to me whenever you need to, although I do not think that will arise. Nothing but triumphs and ovations will await you in Russia."

Fanny's first encounter with Gedeonov was hardly propitious. Forced to take note of his master's wishes, he set out for Vienna to make her acquaintance. Being told that she was at her country estate, he drove out to Vöslau, where he had the misfortune to arrive just as she was preparing to leave for a drive. Fanny was annoyed at the unannounced arrival of a visitor, and told her servant to say she was not at home. The falsity of this excuse was all too apparent, and Gedeonov sent back a terse message that the Director of Russia's Imperial Theatres hardly expected this sort of reception.

Negotiations were carried on in an atmosphere of mutual antipathy, and finally Fanny became so exasperated that she appealed over Gedeonov's head to the Tsar. In a letter written in the summer of 1848, she gave vent to her frustrations. "I wrote on May 23rd to His Excellency General Gedeonov," she explained, "and asked him whether my presence in Petersburg during the course of this winter would be desirable, and that is all. He deigned to answer as follows . . . [Unfortunately his reply has not survived.] You will easily understand that at any other time I would have refused to go after such a letter, but I lost no time in daring to place my feeble services at the feet of His Majesty, after which I told His Excellency General G that I had dared do this and that if I were granted the great favour of appearing before the Emperor, I would apply to His Excellency only to ask that he should invite M. Jules Perrot (who is at present in England) as choreographer to produce his own ballets for me at the Bolshoi Theatre."

If by these tactics Gedeonov had hoped to weaken Fanny's desire to visit Russia and force her to break off negotiations, he had badly miscalculated. In September, notwithstanding that no contract had been concluded, Fanny and the faithful Katti boarded the steam packet

"Vladimir" at Stettin and arrived in St Petersburg two days later, on the 20th. Fanny lost no time in calling on Gedeonov, and was greatly amused to observe his discomfiture at her unexpected arrival. After teasing him about his lack of gallantry, she boldly informed him that she wished to dance before the Tsar. In an attempt to thwart her plan, the Director pleaded poverty and offered her a derisory sum for the season, which he felt sure she would refuse. Money, however, was a minor consideration to Fanny, who to his consternation accepted the offer on the spot.

She had just three weeks to prepare for her debut at the Bolshoi Theatre, but the Tsar, who was not disposed to wait as long as his subjects, invited her to appear first at the court theatre in Tsarskoie Selo. Gedeonov was taking his defeat with ill grace, and appeared for the command performance, which it was his duty to attend, looking as miserable as a dog that had just been whipped. Fanny soon became aware of his influence. At luncheon before the performance she was seated with some French actors who, in their desire to please Gedeonov, treated her with studied coldness. Happily she soon found champions. Two Russian actors, Piotr Karatygin and Vassily Samoilov, were incensed at such ill mannered behaviour, and as soon as their glasses were filled with champagne, they stood up and loudly proposed her toast. In the performance that followed Fanny created a sensation with her *Cachucha*, and the Empress afterwards presented her with a diamond brooch.

Russia was not to be conquered at Tsarskoie Selo, as Fanny discovered a few days later, on October 13th, 1848,* when she made her first appearance at the Bolshoi Theatre in *Giselle*. The silence that greeted her as she emerged from Giselle's cottage took her aback. A less assured performer might well have been unnerved by such a glacial reception, but Fanny accepted it as a challenge which she met by giving one of her finest performances. In the *pas de trois* interpolated in the first act she gave such a brilliant display of *pointe* work that she was made to repeat her *variation*. But it was her interpretation that made the greatest impression, particularly in the mad scene and, in the second act, in the way she conveyed the overwhelming supernatural power which was impelling Giselle to lead her lover to destruction. "Fanny Elssler's miming is magnificent," wrote the critic Tan. "She has no mincing graces or stiffness. Her gestures are free and natural. They give a clear idea of what they have to express, and they are not angular, like those

---

* All dates in this chapter are given in the New Style. The Russians had not at this time adopted the Gregorian calendar, and consequently their calendar (the Old Style) was twelve days behind that which was in use elsewhere in Europe.

of Lucile Grahn, who made her debut on this stage five years ago and did not please our public."

Fanny's reception on this opening performance was decidedly reserved, but this was not the only obstacle she had to overcome. Difficulties of all sorts were put in her way: troubles with the censorship which was obstructive in passing the music for her ballets, delays in the costume department, confusion in the printing of the playbills. Finally she took a firm hand, and told Gedeonov that if these obstructions continued she would tear up her contract and complain to the Tsar. The persecutions ceased like magic.

To stress the point that no other ballerina could match her dramatic gifts, Fanny followed her debut in *Giselle* by appearing as an actress. The German actor, Franz Wallner, had invited her to take part in his benefit performance, and she agreed to appear in the melodrama, *Olga, ou l'Orpheline russe*.* Her success encouraged her to take the title-role of Olga at other benefit performances that season, and she was not thrown into the shade when Mme Volnys, who had created the part in Paris twenty years earlier, came to St Petersburg and played it with a French company. The critics were able to make an interesting comparison. If the interpretation of the French actress was generally preferred, this was no humiliation for Fanny, for the difference between them lay not in the quality of their performances but in the styles of their acting. The *Sanktpeterburgskiye Vedomosti* noted that "generally speaking, the dominant quality in Fanny Elssler's acting is a tranquillity, a quiet submissiveness to her fate—clearly a German quality such as we readily associate with the languid Gretchen and Lizchen. With her the transition from joy to despair is not too abrupt. All her changes of dramatic mood are conveyed regularly and smoothly, and with intelligence and forethought . . . But moving though her performance is, Fanny Elssler's Olga is suited only to the German stage. It is a type which harmonises with the rest of the cast, but it would hardly suit the Russian stage nor, even more, the French stage. Here a strong expression of the passions and a tangible interpretation of feelings are demanded. Seeing Mme Volnys we cannot but be convinced that her Olga is more appropriate under these conditions".

Meanwhile Fanny was tantalising St Petersburg by withholding her *Cachucha*, but at last, on October 31st, she satisfied the general curiosity. For the framework of her most famous dance, she produced *Le Délire d'un peintre*, thus gaining a double triumph, both as performer and as choreographer. The *Cachucha* itself came as a surprise to many of the

---

* This was Scribe's *Yelva*, in which she had appeared in Vienna in 1845.

audience who were expecting a display of unbridled passion. Instead, as one critic described, she performed it "very simply and modestly, and without the slightest trick or exaggerated movement", dancing it, so to speak, "more for herself than for the public".

Fanny had not expected to undertake any choreography, but the delayed arrival of Perrot had made it imperative that she should stage this ballet herself. Happily the task proved no great burden, for she found the Russian dancers to be wonderful material, and for that reason the *pas de seize* which opened the *divertissement* was specially successful. It was a joy to work with such a fine company—from Christian Johansson, the Swedish dancer who was her regular partner, and the more important soloists down to the children from the ballet school—and she did not conceal her pleasure. One evening the actor Piotr Karatygin saw her give a solemn, dark-haired child an affectionate embrace, an incident which he remembered later on when the little girl, whose name was Muravieva, had herself become a famous ballerina.

Fanny showed her satisfaction with Johansson as a partner by being unusually prodigal of her energies at his benefit performance on November 30th. Not only did she act the part of Olga, but she danced a comic polka with him and appeared in *La Fille mal gardée*. This ballet had been in the St Petersburg repertory for many years and was now regarded as a lightweight piece which was conveniently simple to stage for a benefit even if somewhat unsophisticated for the modern taste. To the amazement of the blasé Petersburg public Fanny gave this old-fashioned little ballet a vivid new meaning. In her hands the character of Lise acquired a timeless significance. Her interpretation developed logically from beginning to end. With great clarity and irresistible charm she revealed the course of Lise's relationship with Colas from bewildered shyness to the blossoming of first love. Her miming in the scene where Lise is locked in the house by her mother, while Colas, unknown to either of them, is hiding beneath the sheaves of corn, was so animated and natural that everyone understood its purport. Stamping her foot with annoyance at being left alone, she begins to daydream of her sweetheart, imagining herself married and the mother of his children. At that moment he suddenly bursts out from his hiding place. Lise is covered with confusion, and a little scared to discover herself alone with him, but gradually she melts to receive her first kiss.*

---

* This scene has become a traditional part of the ballet, surviving changes both of music and of choreography. It was retained when the ballet was given a new score by Hertel later in the century, and when Frederick Ashton produced his new version for the Royal Ballet in 1960 Tamara Karsavina recreated this scene which she herself had danced in St Petersburg in her youth.

No less delicate was the scene which brought the ballet to a close, when Lise and Colas come out of the room in which her mother has unwittingly locked them together, and Lise, her expression a mixture of happiness and embarrassment, goes down on her knees with Colas to beseech her mother's blessing. After the ballet was over Fanny remained so identified with her role that she took her curtain calls, not with the *grandes révérences* of a ballerina, but bowing artlessly like a peasant girl. For those who had seen it Fanny's performance as Lise became a golden memory. "My dear fellow," said old Ushakov to the poet Skalkovsky, "what your present-day ballerinas are to you, Fanny was once to me. At the beginning of the first act of *La Fille mal gardée* she only had to give the hens their food to move the whole audience to tears."

At long last Jules Perrot made his belated arrival in St Petersburg. He had allowed little enough time to produce two grand ballets in accordance with his contract, but Fanny had wisely begun rehearsing *La Esmeralda* in his absence to ensure that it would be ready for her benefit on January 2nd, 1849. No expense was spared for this production, and the audience, who had braved twenty degrees of frost to come to the theatre, marvelled at the sight of a fountain of real water playing on the stage. The more perceptive critics saw how skilfully Perrot had inter-woven the dance and the action, and brought into play Fanny's great dramatic genius. "We saw," wrote the *Severnaya Pchela*, "not a splendid ballerina but a supreme actress. Her dances themselves (*pas d'action*) presented a new facet of this art [of choreography]. Until today we expected only graceful poses, plastic movements, lightness, rapidity and strength. Now we saw *acting* in the dance. Every movement spoke to the mind and the heart, every moment expressed some emotion, every glance corresponded with the course of the action. This was a new and enchanting discovery in the domain of choreography." The highpoint of Fanny's performance came in the last scene when she is brought to the scaffold, wearing "a long white dress, with her dark hair flowing on her shoulders, pale, exhausted by torture and without hope for earthly succour", and after bidding a tender farewell to Gringoire, rejects the proposals of Frollo with a splendid gesture, "pointing Heavenwards where justice and reward await her". "This moment," wrote the *Severnaya Pchela*, "is one of the finest in the artistic range of Fanny Elssler. Her expressions, poses and gestures are wonderfully classical, and full of severe beauty and truth."

Perrot's second production was *Catarina*, which was given first for his own benefit on February 16th, and repeated two days later in the presence of the Tsar at Fanny's second benefit. The richness of his

choreographic invention again astounded the Russian public, and Fanny
gained another triumph in a role which displayed her remarkable
stamina.

Looking back on the season, Fanny had good cause to be pleased. It
had begun inauspiciously, but the public had warmed to her as she had
revealed her talent in a well planned sequence of roles: Giselle, the
Cachucha, Lise, Esmeralda, Catarina. She had received many gifts,
including a jewelled brooch from the Tsar; her dancing had inspired a
high-flown "critical survey" by one Nicolai Telepnev; and—a sure sign
of popularity—she had, much to her own delight, been the subject of
a farcical vaudeville by Piotr Grigoriev called *The False Fanny Elssler*, in
which Alexandre Martynov had given an uproarious imitation of the
Cachucha.

Fanny spent the summer months in Hamburg, which was still
recovering from an outburst of revolutionary fervour. To her surprise,
however, the disturbed conditions seemed to have no ill effect on the
theatres, and she successfully gave twenty-eight performances at the
Stadt-Theater and one at the Thalia Theater between June 18th and
August 26th. Now that order was being re-established in Europe, she
and Katti found the atmosphere rather exciting. "Hamburg," wrote
Katti to a friend in St Petersburg, "has a very unusual appearance at the
moment, with tents pitched and soldiers dreading every day, but guns
on the esplanade and troops billeted everywhere is not very amusing for
the Hamburgers . . . The news that Venice has finally capitulated
reached us yesterday, and it is comforting to know that there will also
soon be an end to hostilities with Hungary—many of our acquaintances
will be greatly relieved."

Katti then went on to more personal matters. "Fanny," she wrote,
"is supposed to be bent on marriage, and we hear that she will shortly
be marrying this one or that. She has often mentioned this in your
presence. In actual fact no woman was as little occupied with marriage
as she, and ever since I have known her she has always said, 'So long as
I am on the stage, I shall never marry,' and she is keeping her word."

In Hamburg Fanny made a satisfying conquest by destroying, in a
single performance, the lifelong aversion to ballet of the writer, Karl
von Holtei. He had gone to the theatre, as he later confessed, "like
Saul, to seek a mule, and found a kingdom. Anyone who has ever seen
Fanny Elssler will understand that it was not just her dancing which
enchanted me. I admired this merely as an accompaniment to her
powerful mime portrayal. I count her among the greatest performers I
have ever seen or encountered in the world of art. When I learnt that her
birthday occurred during her stay in Hamburg, I could not resist send-

ing her a poem." Another enthusiastic new admirer was the young actress, Louise Neumann, who took part in a performance of *Yelva* and remembered Fanny's portrayal as one of the great experiences of her life.

Negotiations for a second Russian season had been a foregone conclusion weeks before Fanny had left St Petersburg in the spring, and once again Gedeonov had proved difficult. For forty performances during the 1849–50 season she asked for 40,000 francs and a benefit in addition. Gedeonov considered these terms excessive, but was prepared to offer 50,000 francs and a benefit estimated to produce a further 16,000 francs for between eighty-five and ninety performances. He was very much against any increase above these figures. "Other artists would then solicit higher salaries," he warned the Minister of the Tsar's Household, "whereas now the times are better and uniquely suitable for a reduction of salaries to within reasonable limits, beyond which they have striven to rise from year to year." Fanny rejected Gedeonov's terms, and demanded a passport for her journey to Russia and threatened to appeal personally to the Tsar. Gedeonov would have preferred to engage Fanny Cerrito and her husband, Saint-Léon—"they do not ask for much money," he commented, "she is a remarkable ballerina and he the best male dancer and a very good ballet-master"—but by appealing over his head Fanny managed to obtain terms which she considered satisfactory. For a limited number of performances she was to receive 20,000 francs and have two half-benefits which would bring her about 24,000 francs more.

Disgruntled, Gedeonov looked forward to her return in September with unconcealed distaste. "I always have trouble enough, and now it is added to," he wrote to Verstovsky of the Moscow Office of the Imperial Theatres. "Tomorrow F. Elssler arrives by the mail boat."

Fanny's reception on her reappearance at the Bolshoi Theatre in St Petersburg was decidedly disappointing, and because she was at first seen only in ballets she had danced the season before, she found it doubly difficult to rekindle the public's enthusiasm. Nevertheless she was delighted to be back in St Petersburg. "It is almost impossible for me to describe to you our joy and pleasure here," Katti wrote ecstatically to a friend. "On our arrival we were overjoyed to find the same carriage with the same coachman and horses we already knew. And how pleasant to have the same lodgings, eat at the same table and sleep in the same beds, and sit again at our favourite window looking down on the beautiful Alexander Square, which seemed even more beautiful than ever. I have brought along my favourite ivy plant, my little canary and many other objects which are dear to me. My cousin had a wonderful reception from her old friends, particularly General G and Princess V, and was deluged with friendly greetings from the public just like last year . . . The winter season promises well . . . Only Perrot is needed to complete the ballet, and he will be coming. Meanwhile Fanny must manage as best she can until the middle of November . . . At the moment Fanny is dancing *Esmeralda*, but in a fortnight's time an interesting event will take place. Andreyanova is to appear with my cousin, and we can expect a great success when Fanny accompanies her in her first entrance, and perhaps all enmity will disappear which might cause unpleasantness during the season."

Some interest was aroused by her appearing with a new partner, Marius Petipa, and dancing the Minuet and Gavotte with Andreyanova, but the public generally remained indifferent and no doubt Gedeonov secretly rejoiced. "This year," commented the *Sanktpeterburgskiye Vedomosti*, "is not like last year, when flowers rained upon the stage like autumn leaves in winter so that it had to be swept with brushes and brooms." In truth Fanny was not at her best, and after her first and only appearance in *Giselle* of that season, illness forced her to suspend her performances.

By the time she was well enough to dance again, Perrot had arrived and was at work on *Catarina*. One day, suffering from a sprained foot, he asked young Petipa to take his place and rehearse the famous *pas stratégique*. In the middle of this rehearsal an official bustled in to announce that the Tsar was making one of his periodical visits to the theatre. A few minutes later the Emperor appeared with his retinue, and with a professional interest watched Fanny and the *corps de ballet* going through the dance with their property rifles. At last he could contain himself no longer.

"You are holding your rifles incorrectly, ladies," he interrupted. "I will show you how you should handle them."

The dancers obediently gathered round him as he demonstrated the correct drill. Then he turned to Fanny.

"Come closer," he said, "and do everything I do with the rifle."

The Tsar was so delighted by the skill of his new recruit that he left in the best of humour, announcing that he would be present at the first performance. The news that the Tsar had given Fanny a lesson in rifle drill stimulated the public's curiosity, and when she made her reappearance in *Catarina* on December 6th she was given a gratifying reception.

Marius Petipa's promise as a choreographer was just beginning to be recognised, and for his benefit performance on December 16th he was allowed to produce his own version of *The Swiss Milkmaid*, in which Fanny and Jules Perrot took the leading parts. *Lida*, as it was called, was his first essay in choreography for the Petersburg stage. Although the ballet itself was old, it came as a novelty to most of the audience, for few people remembered the short-lived production by Titus which had been produced in St Petersburg during a cholera epidemic in 1832. Not unnaturally the management allowed only a modest expenditure on a young choreographer's first effort, and it did not leave a strong impression. The first act was rather muddled and uninteresting, but it contained an amusing *scène dansant* in which Perrot, playing a naïve village boy, snatches a basket of fruit from Fanny's hands and demands a kiss before returning it. However, in the second act the deficiencies of the production were redeemed by Fanny's rendering of the scene where the heroine expresses her infatuation before what she thinks is her lover's statue.

It was likewise her powers of interpretation which held the attention in the next production, a revival of *La Tarentule*. Again the ballet itself made little impression, but Fanny gave one of her happiest performances. In the scene where the heroine describes in dance that her lover has been bitten by a tarantula, she was wonderfully expressive. "She is as pale as a sheet, her eyes are fixed, her hands hang limply at her side," described a Russian critic. "Like a doll she commences her tale . . . She begins with a quiver that runs through her leg. She raises it and performs a few uneven *battements*, and then, as though an unbearable pain were passing through her whole body, she begins to run from side to side." Then, in the second act, when Lauretta is avoiding the advances of the old doctor who thinks he has married her, Fanny was at her most vivacious, covering the stage with a profusion of sparkling little steps to a melody which added point to the scene—"*Buona sera*" from Rossini's *Il Barbiera di Siviglia*.

The only important novelty in which she appeared that season was Perrot's *La Filleule des fées*, which had been created for Carlotta Grisi in Paris as recently as October 8th. The St Petersburg production caused Gedeonov "continual anxiety and, one might say, displeasure". Its first performance had originally been scheduled for November, and when Perrot arrived in St Petersburg two months late, the stage designer Roller said flatly that the sets could not be ready before the end of January. Rehearsals proceeded so slowly that a further fortnight's delay was caused. Then, when it was discovered that Perrot had included in the Paris production passages from *La Esmeralda* and *Catarina*, neither of which were known in France, these parts had to be choreographed afresh. Another difficulty arose over the music. Perrot had brought with him a violin *répétiteur* of Adam's score with which he rehearsed, but the orchestral parts failed to arrive. Only a few days before the first performance the conductor, Constantin Liadov, was commissioned to make a new orchestration. Although he worked with feverish haste, the third act had to be performed to a single violin at the final dress rehearsal. On the following day, February 24th, 1850, the first performance took place in an atmosphere of confusion. The evil fairy's curse, which was a feature of the ballet's theme, seemed to hover over the production itself, for the stage hands had had only two rehearsals with the scenery and nothing worked properly.

Things went better at the second performance, but the triteness of the plot could not be concealed. It told how the black fairy lays a curse on a child when she is turned away from the christening. Whoever looks upon the girl with love, she declares, will lose his reason. In the course of the ballet the white and rose fairies temporarily strike the girl's lover blind, before finally persuading the black fairy to lift her curse when he picks out the heroine from among the naiads. The choreography contained some inspired passages, and Fanny herself gave a charming performance. In a beautiful *Valse de la coquetterie*, splendidly danced by Fanny and the choreographer, who were then joined by Johansson, Anna Prikhunova and Zina Richard in a *pas de cinq*, "whole scenes of love, coquetry, seduction and jealousy" were expressed. Then there was the *pas des fées* in which Fanny performed an incredible *tour de force* with a series of *sautés en arabesque* performed diagonally across the enormous stage on one leg and then back again on the other leg. But despite all the splendours of the production, despite the electric sun (the first use of this form of lighting on the Russian stage), despite the brilliance of Fanny's performance and all the efforts of the strong cast—Perrot himself, Andreyanova as the black fairy, and Smirnova and Yakovleva as the rose and white fairies—the ballet was not a success.

All in all, it was a disappointing season. In contrast to the year before, when Fanny had increasingly aroused enthusiasm as the weeks went by, the ballet seemed to lose momentum and there were often empty seats, while the public flocked to the Italian opera which in the previous season had been deserted. Nevertheless, if Fanny added no new role of the calibre of Esmeralda or Lise,* every performance consolidated her reputation as an incomparable dancer-actress. Feodor Koni, one of the most perceptive theatre critics of the day, observed how wonderful she was in roles from everyday life and described her talent as a mime in a passage that was echoed by the dancer Nicolai Goltz in his memoirs. "She apparently values this side of her ability far more highly than her dancing," he wrote. "Her miming is simple, playful and intelligible.

* She did perform one new mime role, that of the dumb Count Solar in Kotzebue's translation of Bouilly's historical play, *L'Abbé de l'Epée*, at Franz Wallner's benefit.

She does not use desperate poses and dreadful wavings of the hand which so often remind us of the deaf and dumb, but only has to wag her little finger, nod her head, cast a glance, or make some slight movement of the lips, and all is as clear as daylight. She is particularly charming in scenes of sweet naïvety and light coquetry. If Taglioni's example resulted in the formation of excellent dancers in our theatres, let us hope that the example of Fanny Elssler will give us good mimes."

St Petersburg was remote enough to the Europeans of the eighteen-fifties, but Moscow lay deep and distant in the Russian hinterland. But Moscow too had its ballet tradition, and if its company was treated as a poor relation by the Direction of the Imperial Theatres, it had a distinctive style of its own and its balletomanes championed their dancers—and particularly at this time their adored Sankovskaya and Irka Matias—with a fierce independent pride which irritated the official circles of St Petersburg. There were, too, obvious differences in atmosphere between the two cities: between St Petersburg with its eighteenth-century elegance, its cosmopolitan outlook and the dominance of court ritual, and the merchant city of Moscow, which was Russian to the core, much less influenced by the refinements of Western Europe, and uninhibited by demands from the palace. Fanny's engagement to dance at the Bolshoi Petrovsky Theatre in Moscow during May 1850 was concluded without formality. She was to give twelve performances for a modest fee of 2,500 silver roubles for the season plus a half-benefit; Perrot and Johansson were to accompany her, and her repertory was to consist of *Catarina, La Fille mal gardée, Le Délire d'un peintre* and *Giselle*.

Fanny arrived in Moscow in springtime and was immediately enchanted by the Byzantine, almost oriental flavour of the old city, with the onion domes of its cathedrals and the low porticoed mansions of the rich merchants. The people of Moscow were in turn charmed by the friendly interest she so obviously showed in their city and themselves. At the end of Lent she was the centre of attraction at the charity bazaar in the Hall of the Assembly of Nobles, and whenever she could escape long enough from her duties, she would drive out to visit some of the places of interest about the city: Tsaritsina, Sokolniki, Kuntsevo, the Poklonnaya hill where Napoleon had his first view of Moscow, the Vorobiev hills, Ostankino, Kuzminki, the Simonov monastery, the Neskuchny Palace. She was drawn back several times to the top of the bell tower of Ivan the Great to enjoy the vista of Moscow spread out before her, and one day she rose early to go to the Kremlin and see the rising sun touch the spires and roofs of the ancient city with its first rays.

The choice of ballet for her Moscow debut on May 14th was somewhat unfortunate, for *Le Délire d'un peintre* had already been seen in a
production by Sankovskaya. In consequence the auditorium was by no
means full, and the ovation was modest. Five days later all this was to be
forgotten in Fanny's complete triumph in *Giselle*. The critics dwelt on
details of her interpretation with an enthusiastic desire to preserve something of her performance in their descriptions. They told how clearly
she conveyed Giselle's spontaneous naïvety, recalling her childlike
deference when her mother reproaches her for being too fond of dancing, her fear at the warning of the wilis, and her blushing sincerity when
she tells the princess that she too is in love. The mad scene was magnificent. "A profound study of nature," wrote one critic, "is revealed in
the onset of madness which appears first in her features and the convul-
sive movements of her limbs. Then a gradual change came over her
lips, betraying her failing strength and grace: this was the very height
of art." The death of Giselle was acted with striking realism, and
another critic noted that her last look was not for Loys, but cast upwards
to Heaven. There were memorable moments too in the second act.
When Myrtha touches Giselle with the magic branch, the stiff motionless form which had emerged from the grave burst suddenly into
activity "like a butterfly coming out of its chrysalis", and at the end of
the act, when the sun begins to rise and the wilis' power fades, a wonderful smile came over her as she realised that Albrecht was saved, a smile
that expressed a variety of emotions at the same time: "the joy of rescue,
the pang of separation, and the suffering of mortality". "To conclude,"
wrote the critic of *Vedomosti Moskovskoi Gorodskoi Politsii*, "Elssler is the
first dancer to have made the end of *Giselle* intelligible to me. She made
it appear that this ballet has no end and that the bewitched Albrecht
would return to the glade the following night in the hope of finding the
spirit of Giselle again. He is not afraid of the evil of the wilis, nor of their
fatal dances, nor of death itself . . . But Elssler's Giselle has already
renounced her earthly love in the last scene of this ballet. She has yielded
up all earthly things. Her last look is one of prayer, and one has the
presentiment that on the following night Giselle will no longer be
among the wilis. The force which has chained her to the earth has
already been broken."*

While *La Fille mal gardée* attracted less publicity than *Giselle*, it
created a remarkable impression on those who saw it. Writing nearly
twenty years later, Vladimir Rodislavsky recalled that it gave her greater

---

* The impression that Albrecht will return to the glade could surely only have
been given if the original ending of the ballet, when Bathilde reappears to find
Albrecht, had been cut.

Fanny Elssler. Oil painting, 1852.

Historische Museum der Stadt Wien.

Fanny Elssler and her daughter Therese. Oil painting by Hermann Achten, 1854. (Formerly in the Theatermuseum, Munich, destroyed during World War II.)

Fanny Elssler, *c.* 1860.

Coll. Mme. Derra de Moroda.

Fanny Elssler in dancing costume, *c.* 1860.

Coll. Mme. Derra de Moroda.

Fanny Elssler, 1876.

Coll. Mme. Derra de Moroda.

Fanny Elssler, 1883. The last photograph. (Formerly in the possession of Princess Pauline Metternich-Sandor.)

Coll. Mme. Derra de Moroda.

scope for acting than all her other ballets, including even *Giselle*. "This was because there was life and drama, albeit very simple, in Dauberval's old ballet," he wrote. "Every lover of the art of mime who saw Fanny Elssler as Lise cherishes it as his finest memory of ballet. And indeed Fanny Elssler was brilliantly beautiful in this role. Her talent made you forget her years. In the role of Lise the forty-year-old Fanny Elssler appeared to be only sixteen. She was a young girl in love for the first time."

Catarina, the last ballet which Fanny gave in Moscow, was not so successful. Since it was already in the Moscow repertory, Verstovsky had wanted to open the season with it, but Fanny would not agree and Perrot decided to make some substantial changes which further delayed it. For his trouble the choreographer was given a half-benefit, at which Fanny appeared in *The False Fanny Elssler* to dance her *Cachucha*.

Although it was springtime and the weather was wonderfully fine, her performances had been attracting packed houses. One critic prophesied that if she were to return in the winter and give ten times as many performances, the theatre would still be full. Many of her admirers and fellow artists saw her off when she left Moscow on June 21st. She had a word for everyone, and her eyes were filled with tears as her carriage pulled away.

The parting was not to be long, for when Fanny passed through St Petersburg on her way to Germany she accepted a proposition from Gedeonov to return to Moscow for the whole of the 1850–1 season. For many anxious weeks that summer Verstovsky waited in Moscow for the contract to arrive. Although without details of her repertory or the terms of her engagement, he opened a subscription list for her performances well in advance. There was a flood of applications, and being an honourable man he was greatly relieved when the contract reached him at long last, in the middle of September.

Being also a careful man, he read this document with great care, and referred back to St Petersburg to clarify a number of points. How much was the penalty in the event of delayed arrival? When was she to take her benefits? When was the agreed fee for the season of 5,000 silver roubles to be payable? Was she to receive 1.50 roubles for each pair of ballet shoes ordered from Paris, as had been agreed in the previous season, and was she to be supplied with material for alterations and repairs to her costumes?

Verstovsky fell prey to another anxiety as the days passed without sign of Fanny, and he prudently suspended the subscription list, which had already produced nearly 5,000 roubles. Rumours that she was refusing to go to Moscow unless Johansson accompanied her were partly confirmed when Gedeonov wrote that she had been detained unavoidably in St Petersburg and that consequently the penalty clause in her contract was not to be invoked. Reluctant to deprive the capital of one of his best dancers, he had, after a long wrangle, persuaded Fanny to be content with the new ballet-master he had engaged for Moscow, Théodore Chion.

Fanny eventually had to travel to Moscow without even Théodore, who had failed to arrive from Paris. When Verstovsky met her, he found he had a disgruntled ballerina on his hands. It must have been galling to feel that Gedeonov had got the better of her, and Verstovsky reported her discontent to his superior. "It seems to me," he wrote, "that Elssler is very upset because Johansson and Didier have not accompanied her to Moscow for the production of a new ballet." Fanny was refusing to dance in *La Fille mal gardée*, and to meet her demands for a new role, preparations were put in hand to revive *Le Dieu et la Bayadère*.

The season did not open auspiciously. Fanny had decided to make her first appearance on October 23rd, 1850, in *Giselle*, and wishing to enter into the role from the outset, she acknowledged the burst of applause which greeted her on her first entrance with "the naïve curtsies and noddings of the unsophisticated Giselle". The public was noticeably cool, and enthusiasm was limited to a small number of committed admirers, led by Prince Vladimir Golitsin, who threw two bouquets to her from his seat in the front row of the stalls after the first act. "The cold reception throughout the whole ballet appeared to embitter the ballerina," Verstovsky reported to Gedeonov, adding, perhaps to please his master: "In my opinion we see no one better in this ballet than Elena Ivanovna [Andreyanova]."

Golitsin was determined that Fanny should have her triumph, and there was no one in Moscow better suited to be her champion. Immensely rich, he enjoyed too the prestige of a glorious career in the cavalry. A man of strong artistic sympathies, he had intervened to obtain a Christian burial for the poet Lermontov who had been killed in a duel, a bold gesture in defiance of the State. Now, having retired from the army, he had taken over command of the Moscow balletomanes. He was a colossus of a man with a voice that matched his bulk. From his customary seat in the stalls, he dominated the audience by the force of his personality, clapping and bellowing and imperiously encouraging everyone to join him. Pursuing his self-appointed task beyond the walls of the theatre, he was to be seen staggering along the streets of Moscow accosting friends, acquaintances and even strangers to sing the praises of his "Fannichka". In his mansion he and his friends discoursed about the ballerina long and late over the wine, and every Saturday evening he gave a dinner party at which Fanny was the guest of honour. The atmosphere was cordial and relaxed, and when dinner was over, everyone, Fanny included, danced, chatted and joked. It was here that she first met Countess Rostopchina with whom she was to strike up a close friendship, and who was to write a long and vivid description of her farewell performance at the end of the season.

But these were still early days, and the unsatisfactory reception at her first appearance had left her depressed. Probably she was feeling the onset of a cold, for her second performance was postponed on account of illness just two hours before the rise of the curtain. Verstovsky suspected at first that the real cause was her disappointment at the insignificant takings at the box office, but she was really ill. She had caught a chill in the bitterly cold weather that was gripping Moscow, and had been ordered to bed by her good friend, Dr Feh.

Fanny's illness added to Verstovsky's difficulties. She was insistent that a new production should be ready after her first six performances, and it had been agreed that this would be *La Esmeralda*. However, the problem remained of who was to be responsible for the production. Clearly this could not be Théodore, for not only had he not arrived, but he had never seen the ballet. Verstovsky then suggested that as she had conducted the early rehearsals in Petersburg, she might produce it herself, but she firmly refused, explaining that she was expected to dance much more frequently in Moscow. Persistently, Verstovsky changed his tactics. His discussions with Fanny during her illness necessarily took place at her hotel, and there he gained a valuable insight into the domestic relationship between the ballerina and Katti Prinster. Over the many years which she had devoted to Fanny's service, Katti had become quite indispensable. She was both companion and confidant; her advice carried great weight, there were few of Fanny's secrets which she did not share, and she undertook a multiplicity of responsibilities, from distributing old ballet shoes to important admirers to watching over Fanny's welfare and health with the stern authority of a governess. When Fanny was recovering, Katti would accompany her to rehearsal and, if she noticed the ballerina flagging, she would at once intervene to order her to stop. Realising that in Fanny's present condition he was unlikely to gain his end by using direct persuasion, Verstovsky directed his efforts and charm to making an ally of Katti. When he succeeded in convincing her that it was in Fanny's interests that she should produce *La Esmeralda*, it was only a matter of time before the matter was arranged to his satisfaction.

It proved a happy outcome all round, for as soon as she was better,

Fanny began rehearsing *La Esmeralda* with great energy and diligence, while finding time to appear in *Olga* and *Le Dieu et la Bayadère*. If the role of Fatma in *Le Dieu et la Bayadère* was not particularly well suited to her style, her generous gesture in allowing Irka Matias to take the first performance for her benefit gained her much popularity.

La Esmeralda was presented for Fanny's benefit on December 4th, and was a complete success. Only a few empty stalls in the second and third rows prevented it from being a full house. Fanny insisted that Théodore, who was making his debut, received a full share of the applause, but both the public and the dancers saw to it that the evening was hers. At Golitsin's instigation the English Club had subscribed towards a pair of emerald earrings which were presented to her in an enormous bouquet, but the gift that touched Fanny most of all came from the dancers themselves, who appreciated her not only as an artist but also as a thoughtful colleague. Only a few days before, at the end of an exhausting rehearsal which had lasted very late, Fanny had called the dancers around her to praise and thank them, and later she had entertained them and the orchestra to a splendid breakfast. The compliment was returned before the first performance of *La Esmeralda*, when a delegation of *coryphées*, headed by Evgenia Milova, went to Fanny's dressing-room and presented her with a sheaf of flowers on behalf of the *corps de ballet* with the name of each dancer inscribed on the ribbon.

One of the pupils taking part in that performance was a boy called Piotr Medvedev, who retained an indelible impression of Fanny's performance. "Neither at rehearsal nor in performance," he was to write years later, "did I miss the scene in the tavern where she meets Phoebus. She sat down with him on the bench, every muscle of her face quivering with love. She gazes at him, unable to see enough of him, and when Phoebus tells her his feelings, she indicates: 'Can you love as I love? Is your love the same?' Then she takes a piece of fluff and looks at it. She blows it, and it vanishes into the air. 'That is how quickly your love will pass.' And then her horror when Claude stabs Phoebus! Oh, she was a great artist! The public wept in the last act to see her brought to the scaffold. And indeed those on the stage wept most naturally at every performance."

There was still the question of her second benefit, which was the subject of long wrangling discussions with Verstovsky. Realising that there was no time to produce *La Filleule des fées*, she thought of *Stella*, a ballet which had been produced by Saint-Léon in Paris earlier in the year and was well known to Théodore. To her annoyance this idea had to be dropped because Pugni had not brought the music to Russia. The Direction then suggested *L'Elève d'Amour*, an old ballet by Filippo

Taglioni, which she rejected. Fearing that the public was cooling towards her, she wanted to appear in something that would make a striking impression. When *La Paysanne Grande Dame* was suggested, she objected on the ground that it was too slight, but finally, accepting that funds would not be forthcoming for a large-scale production, she began to yield, though not with the best of grace. After complaining that Perrot would not spare time to refresh her memory about certain production details of *La Paysanne Grande Dame*, she returned to the charge and Verstovsky again had to make it clear that the production of another grand ballet was out of the question. A proposal to stage *La Jolie Fille de Gand* within a budget of 1,000 roubles was found wildly impracticable, and convinced of the futility of continuing the struggle, Fanny at last gave in.

If she could not have her grand ballet, she was at least determined to give a cachet of originality to *La Paysanne Grande Dame*. To this end she made the bold decision to perform a Russian dance. Remembering Taglioni's failure when attempting such a dance in St Petersburg, she rejected any thought of the *Smolenska* she had performed in Paris, London and America, and took the trouble to make a serious study of the authentic folk dancing of the country. Her teacher was Nikita Peshkov, who may have taken her to see the peasants dancing in the surrounding countryside. Her appearance, at her benefit performance on January 24th, 1851, wearing the simple *sarafan* and *kokoshnik* of a Russian peasant woman, was greeted with cries of delight. The *Moskovskiye Vedomosti* called her dance "a remarkable novelty . . . To understand even the slightest nuances of the national character which are expressed in our dance, and to master them, can be done only by an artist of genius such as Fanny Elssler. Her shoulders spoke, she glided like a white swan, she looked with languishing eyes, and in every way she resembled a real Russian maiden".

Her next new role was not so successful. Verstovsky had allowed her to produce a *divertissement* of her own composition, *The Butterfly and the Flowers*, which proved to be of little interest. "*The Butterfly,*" Verstovsky reported to Gedeonov after the first performance on February 11th, "although very old-fashioned, has attracted a fair public . . . Elssler was not shown to very great advantage. Nowhere did her years show more clearly than when she was surrounded by all the youth and freshness of our *coryphées* and excellent *corps de ballet*, each of whom represented a flower. Fanny chose such an unflattering hair-style that the invariably passionate butterflies found her quite uninteresting. Although her antennae were decorated with brilliants, they did not suit her." Two days later, at Frédéric's benefit, Fanny appeared for the first and only time in a ballet called *La Paysanne lunatique*,* which Frédéric had produced for the occasion.

During the final week of her engagement Fanny accomplished what no other visiting celebrity had dared undertake before. She danced at every performance, sometimes appearing in two ballets, and as if spurred on by some extraordinary will power, seemed to gain each day in strength and energy. Her announcement that she planned to retire and that except for a few farewell performances in Vienna, this would be her final season, moved the Moscovites to fill her last days in their city with experiences which had no equal even in her extraordinary career.

On the day before her farewell benefit, as she was preparing for a performance of *Catarina*, the Russian and French actors in whose benefits she had danced, gathered outside her dressing-room and charged Irka Matias to invite her to come with them on to the stage. There, a few minutes later, the actress Agrafena Saburova presented her with a bracelet bearing the names of the fifteen artists who had subscribed to it and the inscription, "*Au talent le plus beau, au coeur le plus noble*". Irka Matias made a little speech, and the actor Dmitri Lensky then read a short poem which he had composed for the occasion and which one of the French actors translated. Fanny was so moved that some of the actors feared that she might be unable to go on stage. But all was well, and she wore the bracelet throughout the performance and again at her farewell performance the following day.

Neither Fanny herself, nor anyone who was present, whether as a performer or as a spectator, would ever forget the fantastic enthusiasm at her farewell performance in *La Esmeralda* on March 2nd. Long before the curtain rose it was clear this would be no ordinary occasion. The crowd was so determined to gain admittance that they broke down the theatre's heavy wooden doors, while touts in the street outside were offering up to 100 roubles for a stall. Every seat was quickly occupied, and many of the boxes, even in the upper tiers, were crammed with two and three times the number they were supposed to hold. Few people paid any attention to the opening piece, but when the orchestra struck up the opening bars of *La Esmeralda* a sudden silence fell. The curtain rose, and after a few minutes Fanny made her entrance brandishing her tambourine. At once the whole audience rose to their feet, waving hats and handkerchiefs and cheering. Flowers flew through the air until the whole stage seemed to be covered with a multicoloured carpet. Many of the bouquets were tied with gaily coloured ribbons, one of the finest

---

* This was a revival of *Edmond and Teresa*, ballet in three scenes by Théodore Guérinot, first produced at the Bolshoi Petrovsky Theatre, Moscow, on December 19th, 1839, for Sankovskaya.

being wrapped in *point de Bruxelles* lace lined with flame-coloured velvet
and knotted with a superb ribbon of the same colour. A bouquet of
hyacinths had a tail of coloured ribbons on which the various qualities
of Fanny's dancing were printed. From two facing proscenium boxes
flowers, ribbons, crowns and escutcheons bearing Fanny's initials flew
out like a shower of fireworks, and the Countess Rostopchina threw a
bouquet containing a poem she had written. But the climax of this
unforgettable demonstration was still to come. From his seat in the front
row of the stalls the enormous figure of Prince Golitsin rose up to hand
across the orchestra pit the largest and most splendid bouquet of all,
presented in the name of the city of Moscow, whose name was con-
spicuously spelled out in red camellias against a background of white
camellias. Accompanying the bouquet, on a silver plate, was a cardboard
kalatch, the symbolic bread of Moscow's hospitality. Théodore, who
was in the secret, took it and broke it, drawing out a bracelet set with
semi-precious stones whose initials made up the name, Moscow:

Malachite
Opal
Sapphire
Kalcedon (Chalcedony)
Venisa (Garnet)
Amethyst

After he had fastened it on Fanny's arm, she dropped to her knees,
kissed it and then pressed it to her heart.

No less than three hundred bouquets had been thrown, and in the
second scene these were all heaped on Esmeralda's couch. This scene
opened with Esmeralda alone on the stage dreaming of Phoebus, whose
name she writes on the wall, and on this occasion Fanny, on a sudden
impulse, chalked the word Moscow in Russian characters large enough
for everyone to see. This gesture gave rise to renewed cheering and
clapping, and it was some minutes before the ballet could be resumed.
By now the audience was in a fever of excitement, and applause broke
out anew when Fanny began her lively dance with the tambourine. Soon
the applause resolved itself into a rhythmical clapping in time to the
music which was so loud that the musicians, realising that they could no
longer be heard, laid down their instruments and joined in. It was a
demonstration the like of which had never been known in Moscow
before, and years afterwards old theatregoers were still talking of it as a
unique and unforgettable experience.

This display of enthusiasm had inspired Fanny to dance with an
ardour and strength which were remarkable even for her, but she

generously remembered her partner, Théodore, who was playing
Gringoire. Before hustling him out of her room as the scenario demanded, she dragged him to the front of the stage and presented him
with a bouquet which had been thrown to her from the auditorium.
When the ballet continued there was no room for her on the flower-
decked couch and she had to lie down on the floor in front of it.

After the ballet had ended, she was given forty-two curtain calls and
was weeping unashamedly when the Russian dancers came to bid her
farewell. When she had dressed, she hardly recognised the staircase
leading to the stage door, for a rich carpet had been laid down and
flowers strewn everywhere. Outside a good-humoured crowd was waiting. They had already enjoyed some fun by seizing an officious function-
ary who had tried to make them disperse and holding him under the
legs of the carriage horses. The terrified little man was only released
when Fanny emerged. As she walked to the carriage, the crowd pressed
round her. A fortunate few were able to arrange the fur rug around her
legs, while others threw bouquets into the carriage. Meanwhile, in spite
of attempts by the police to prevent it, the horses were unhitched and
the carriage was drawn through the streets by a team of young men,
escorted by an excited shouting crowd. Sitting importantly on the
coachbox, carrying Golitsin's enormous bouquet, was the editor of
the *Moskovskiye Vedomosti*, Vladimir Khlopov. Arriving at last at the
Dresden Hotel, where a carpet had been laid on the pavement, Fanny
found more friends waiting to toast her health in champagne. Outside
the hotel the cheering continued, and Fanny ordered the great bouquet
of camellias to be dismembered and the flowers thrown from the
window to the crowd below.

This unprecedented triumph was celebrated in a number of satirical
verses. Typical was one which told of a citizen who was puzzled by the
sight of a great crowd rushing along the streets. Surely, he thought, the
Tsar himself was paying a visit to the city, but no—the object of the people's curiosity was merely a ballerina. Official quarters in St Petersburg were horrified at such excessive adulation, and when the poems
were published in the press, the Censorship Committee passed a minute
censuring the people of Moscow for their lapse from decorum in confusing "the transitory praise of a few enthusiasts with the holy and
universal sentiment of love and devotion" for the person of the Tsar.
Nicholas I shared their disapproval, and in fact had personally authorised
the publication of the poems "as a salutory lesson for the buffoonery of
some of the Moscow idlers". The sensitive government in St Petersburg
even saw revolutionary allusions in Countess Rostopchina's poem,
which had included the lines: "For us you are a sun in a time of snow-

storms, a rose on an inclement winter's day." On instructions from St Petersburg a list was compiled of everyone who was considered to have disgraced himself on the day of Fanny's farewell. Prominent among these names was that of the unfortunate Khlopov, who had been so carried away as to sit on the coachbox of Fanny's carriage with the bouquet on his knees. He was to suffer cruelly for his enthusiasm, being summarily dismissed from his post as editor.

Fanny's official farewell was not in fact her last appearance in Moscow, for characteristically she agreed to take part in some *tableaux vivants* in the benefit performance of the machinist Pinaud on March 11th. Her unfailing readiness to give her services on such occasions gained her great popularity, for her participation inevitably brought increased takings at the box office. In these performances she often appeared in one of those mime roles in which she was so charming—Olga, or Georges in F. Genée's *Le Muet d'Ingouville**—and sometimes she danced her Russian dance, which was taken as a delicate compliment. No wonder that the artists of the Moscow theatre vied with the balletomanes in presenting her with a valuable farewell gift. For her part, she forgot no one on her departure, generously distributing gifts which included a splendid gold-handled cane for Peshkov, who had initiated her into the dances of old Russia.

It was a sad day when Fanny took her departure, for no one doubted her resolve to retire. For Fanny herself it must have been an occasion for tears, for she knew she would never return to this ancient and hospitable city, nor hear again the full-throated acclamations of its public. Katti and the manservant, Leonide Giacciangeli, saw that she was spared the tiresome details that attended their departure, and Fanny left Moscow like a queen. Her admirers, the humbler ones on foot and the aristocracy and gentry in their carriages, turned up in force to see her coach move off from the Imperial General Post Office on Miasnitsky Street. Many people followed her as far as the city limits to speed her on her way, and the last recorded scene of her progress out of the heart of Russia showed her at Klin, the first station outside Moscow, taking tea in her coach while the horses were being changed.

She left behind her a legend that was to endure, not only in the memories of those who had applauded her, but more lastingly, in the minds of those artists who recalled her genius as a model of dramatic interpretation. Perhaps the most important evaluation of this aspect of her talent came from the pen of Apollon Grigoriev, who wrote:

"There are two kinds of artistic nature. There is one kind of artist who can create types which are complete and all of one piece, and which

* She first acted the part of Georges on December 14th, 1850.

stem almost perfectly from their own personality. A character created by such an artist has only to appear on the stage and you know him, his habits, his way of life, and you can justifiably guess at the psychological motivations of his existence. Out of the most insignificant data such artists create for you a full, rounded form, they instinctively divine all the most delicate lines from which the personality of a well-known creature is made up. The creation of roles by such artists can really be compared only with the portraits of Briullov, who in the judgment of connoisseurs catches everything that is indispensable in his sitter, subordinating everything that is accidental to the whole and yet neglecting no nuance. Such artists are very rare: they include, for example, Fanny Elssler, Sadovsky, Samoilov, and in former times Garrick.

"The other type of artist impresses the stamp of his own personality on every work, and draws, so to speak, the outlines but not the integral whole. You cannot resist the strength, humour and charm of his personality, and you are amazed by him no less than by the first kind. Such are Kean, Mochalov, Shchepkin, Martynov, Repina, Samoilova."

Russia had seen Fanny at the end of her career, when her strength as a dancer may have been declining, but when her dramatic gifts had so developed as to place her on a pinnacle to which eye-witnesses of her performances would admit no other dancer of her own or any later generation. Writing many years afterwards, an old admirer tried to equate her talent with those of other ballerinas he had seen. "I have seen many celebrities in my lifetime, from Grisi to Vazem," he wrote, "but I can place not one of them on a level with Fanny Elssler. Some of them, however, approach her in one or another aspect of their talent more than others: Ferraris, Muravieva, Grantzow and Vazem in technique, M. S. Petipa and Dor in plasticity, and Lebedeva in miming. In this last side of her talent Fanny Elssler was immeasurably superior to all the celebrities. Watching her acting one involuntarily began to regret that she was not a dramatic actress. She would have been a Rachel or a Ristori."

Now only a short farewell season in Vienna remained before her retirement. After visiting her sister Therese in Berlin, she arrived in the city of her birth. Her career had come full circle, and in this final season she gave twelve performances at the Kärntnertortheater in three ballets by Perrot: *La Esmeralda, Catarina,* and finally *Faust,* in which she had made that one unhappy appearance in Milan three years before. In addition to these performances she took part in a number of benefits, appearing in *Yelva* and *Le Muet d'Ingouville.* All Vienna, from the Emperor Franz Josef down to the humblest citizen, wanted to bid her farewell, and the performances ran their course amid an enthusiasm that only Jenny Lind had aroused previously. At last the sad occasion arrived when, on June 21st, 1851—a third of a century after her first performance on that same stage as a child—Fanny danced her last steps in public in the role of Marguerite.

Franz Grillparzer, aghast at the thought of the theatre existing without her, wrote her an impassioned appeal not to abandon her "sacred art", but she was not to be shaken from her resolve. Two days after taking her final curtain call, she celebrated her forty-first birthday with the tranquillity of one whose task is accomplished.

XVII

The Years of Retirement

HAVING PUT HER CAREER BEHIND HER, Fanny slipped quietly out
of Vienna to savour the joys of family life. She had found a pleasant
house near the Dammthor in Hamburg, where she was to spend an
idyllic few years watching her daughter grow up into a young woman.
This, at last, was her compensation for the long separations which she
had had to endure for the sake of her career, and something of the
happiness of these years was caught by Joseph Achten in his pastel
portrait of mother and daughter standing side by side in the garden on a
fine summer's day: Fanny, serenely beautiful, with a parasol resting on
her shoulder, and Therese, trim and delicate of figure, with a wistful,
far-away look which has a gravity surprising in one so young.

When Therese came of age in the autumn of 1854, Fanny took her to
England to visit the Grotes. The main object of this visit was to attend
to the winding up of the settlement which Fanny had made on her child,
and of which George Grote was trustee, but the reunion had a pleasanter
consequence. The breach which had separated the two friends was
healed. Harriet Grote could never resist Fanny's charm. "Elssler's
connection revived 'willy nilly,'" the Englishwoman breathlessly wrote
to her sister on October 24th, 1854. "Therese's coming of age, and my
husband her trustee—over Fanny came, and I forgave her again." The
following summer they met again. "Then on to Cologne, where G.G.
met me," Harriet reported on July 5th, 1855, "Elssler and Therese also:
G to resign his trust to Therese, now twenty-one, and pay her half a
year's dividend, informing her of the fact that she had a little fortune of
her own."

That same year, 1855, Fanny returned to Vienna and took an apartment at No. 14 Kärntnerstrasse. She had not been forgotten in the city
of her birth, and there were many friends who were delighted to welcome her back. Before long a new face was seen among the many visitors,
that of a handsome young army officer, Captain Viktor von Webenau.
Unlike the others he had come not to pay homage to the former
ballerina, but to court Therese. The two young people were in love, and
in 1859 a cheerful family wedding took place in the church at Eisenstadt.

Shortly after the wedding Fanny moved again, to a smaller apartment in Seilerstätte, a street which had associations with her father, who had lived for a short time with Haydn in No. 15 and had died in No. 21. Fanny's new apartment was on the fourth floor of No. 19, and was just large enough for Katti and herself. There was a salon, two main bedrooms, a maid's room, kitchen and water-closet. A long glass-covered verandah stretched the full width of the apartment at the back, and from here Fanny had a fine outlook over the Coburg bastion and across the Glacis towards the suburb of Landstrasse, where Therese and her husband were living in their first home and their baby, who was called Fanny after its grandmother, was born. Fanny indulged herself to the full in being a grandmother, and spoilt the child outrageously.

It seemed sometimes that she gave little thought to her theatrical renown. Both in conversation and correspondence she showed a modest reluctance to refer to her triumphs, and she would often refuse to be drawn when Katti could no longer resist her own urge to raise the subject. The apartment was of course filled with souvenirs of her career, but as the years passed these diminished in number. Fanny was not sentimental, and if an object faded or was broken, she would consign it to the dustbin with only a passing regret. But much remained. She could never part with the coverlet which she used when resting on her ottoman and which was made from ribbons that had once adorned bouquets presented to her on the stage, and there were innumerable portraits, prints and other objects which her dancing had inspired.

Fanny could not, nor wished to, divorce herself completely from the theatre. The stage was too much part of her life for that, and many of her friends were in the profession. But it was the drama which absorbed her more than the dance, for it grieved her to see the ballet slipping into a decline. Sometimes tears would come to her eyes as she deplored the neglect of traditions, the disappearance of the noble style, and the lack of true technique and taste in the lascivious displays which were debasing her art as she had known it. To her sorrow the great ballets in which she had danced were being forgotten, and her advice was sought less and less by later generations of dancers. One of the few ballerinas who were wise enough to benefit from her experience was Hedwig Schläger, whom Fanny coached in the role of Fenella in *La Muette de Portici*, and again for the ballet *Flik and Flok*.

Pained though she was by these decadent trends, she did not hold herself entirely aloof from the dance. From time to time she would visit the classes which her brother-in-law, Franz Opfermann, gave at the Theater an der Wien. One of his pupils was Julius Werther, the future theatre manager, who recalled how she appeared one day and "watched him for a while with a gracious smile, then took off her jacket, lifted her skirt and gave a proof of her art which astonished me". This incident was to have an interesting sequel. Many years later Werther met Isadora Duncan and told her of his link with the great ballerina. Isadora went into raptures at the very mention of her name, and revealed that one of her most precious possessions was a picture of Fanny Elssler.

Ironically Fanny felt a much greater affinity with the actors and actresses of the Burgtheater than with the dancers at the Opera. They appreciated what her experience and genius had to offer, and frequently and eagerly sought her advice. Gratefully the tragedienne Charlotte Wolter, who had studied ballet as a child and recognised the importance of controlled movement, learnt from her the art of falling down a flight of stairs for Messalina's death scene in Wilbrandt's *Arria und Messalina*. Her fellow actor, Josef Lewinsky, was given a revelation when she showed him what a wealth of expression there can be in the movements of the back.

Another actress who benefited from her advice was Auguste Baudius, who studied the role of Marie in Goethe's *Clavigo* under her guidance. "It always gives me a start when I read of Fanny being a dancer," she wrote in her memoirs, "for it seems to suggest that she was no more than a dancer. But what of her magic, of her power over people? I prefer to say that she was a dancer, and that because she was so completely mistress of her art and devoted her gifts of beauty and charm to the highest purpose, she was a perfectly balanced human being who served God and man in the truest sense of the term." Auguste Baudius feared that because she was a comedy actress, she might not be able to give the role the tragic overtones it demanded, but Fanny's counsels enabled her to present a rounded and impressive interpretation. To portray pain, Fanny advised, she should force the mouth into a smile while retaining a sad expression in the eyes. Let her practice weeping before a mirror, remembering that tears only appear natural when they derive from deeply felt emotion. And only a discreet indication of a cough was needed in the death scene, for the audience is aware that Marie is ill and is more interested in her heart than in her lungs. "To [Fanny]," she concluded, "I owe one of my finest triumphs, when I first played a Goethe role. Someone once wrote that Fanny Elssler danced Goethe, but I know that Fanny Elssler *felt* Goethe."

There was still the very rare occasion when she could be prevailed upon to perform in the intimacy of a friend's house. One evening, at a party given by the actor, Ludwig Gabillon, she wrapped a tablecloth around herself and gave an impressive sketch of a peasant girl appeasing an irate lover. On another occasion, at the request of Adolf Wilbrandt, she acted the Seven Deadly Sins, recollecting no doubt the scene in Perrot's ballet, *Faust*. "We could scarcely believe our eyes," recalled Wilbrandt's wife, Auguste Baudius. "I only know that each one filled us with admiration. When she played Avarice, her beautiful fine hands became long and pointed, her face, arms and whole body exuded greed and covetousness, and at the end she just sat down again in her russet-coloured woollen dress as if nothing had happened, happy to have given us pleasure."

Eduard Hanslick, the music critic, recalled another such occasion. He had been invited to a *soirée* at the home of the great actress of the Burg-theater, Julie Rettich, when Fanny was among the guests. "The illustrious dancer who had been idolised by all Europe," he wrote, "was then a woman of about sixty, but she still conveyed an impression of great charm, almost of youthfulness. Her face was perfectly oval and unwrinkled, and her full white shoulders and arms were admired whenever she appeared *en décolleté*. I had never seen Fanny Elssler dance, for she had left the stage long before. This admission earned me looks of the most profound compassion from Frau Rettich's older guests. The two oldest in particular, Minister Schmerling and Dessauer, could not find words enough to describe the grace with which Fanny had danced the *Cachucha*, performing it more with her arms, bust and head than with her feet. From this lively description it was but a step to entreat her to give us young men an idea of her art.

"'What, here? In a black silk dress? An old lady like me?'

"For a moment she declined with the most charming modesty. But it was to no avail. The hostess added her plea to that of her friends, and Fanny Elssler rose from her chair. She asked me to go to the piano and indicated to me the tempo of the *Cachucha*, much slower than one usually hears it. It was lucky for me that this simple music was so easy to play, for I was obliged to play with my head turned away from the piano so that I should not miss one of Fanny's movements. It was an unforgettable sight. Fanny Elssler lifted up her dress a little and danced, or rather drifted, two or three times up and down the vast room with such graceful and expressive inclinations of the head and body and such rounded and undulating movements of the arms that for the first time I understood the meaning of the ideal dance. All our ballerinas dance only with their legs."

Invitations to her dinner parties and her weekly receptions were eagerly accepted, for she was an amusing hostess and retained her power of fascination to the very end. In her entertaining she showed taste and imagination, but there was never any show of ostentation. Her guests were made to feel at home, and at the same time to regard the

evenings they spent under her roof as special occasions. The food and
wine were always excellent: among the delicacies to which her guests
looked forward were the tasty dish of plover's eggs, which was reserved
traditionally for her New Year's dinner, and the inimitable salad dressing which she prepared herself. And if her older friends had to rest
content with their memories of her dancing, she could still arouse their
admiration by the grace with which she carved the meat.

Her Thursday evenings were attended by a number of faithful old
admirers who had known her from the early days of her career, many
of them bearing illustrious names and the honours of a lifetime's service
to their Emperor. They arrived punctually, some to fall asleep immediately in armchairs which had become theirs by a sort of prescriptive
right until their manservants came to wake them and take them home.
A few had become so frail that they were collected like children,
obediently accepting their servant's refusal to let them stay longer and
allowing their mouths and noses to be wiped before tottering away to
be put to bed. While these venerable relics slept on, the younger and
livelier guests enjoyed themselves, for Fanny gathered round her many
of the celebrated writers and actors of the time.

She was adored by old and young alike. "All who knew her," wrote
her friend, Auguste Baudius, "and indeed anyone who was seeing her
for the first time, must have had the feeling that she was quite an
exceptional creature, a noble, beautiful and charming woman. Modest,
kindness itself, a woman of the world with the smile of a child. But how
could one know that she was a dancer, or had been one? She might
just as well have come from an old Viennese patrician family or the
aristocracy. Indeed, it was noticeable that she had no kind of accent.
She was simply a pleasure to both ear and eye. I often noticed the effect
she had on people when she entered a room, the expression on people's
faces when they heard her name and saw her for the first time. You
never heard her laugh loudly, but rather noted that she was amused
. . . She simply became one of the guests as soon as she had made her
modest, old-fashioned curtsy. Thanks to her tact and gaiety she put
everyone at their ease. She would come into a room with a mixture of
modesty and self-possession. One day, I forget where, she arrived when
her hostess was momentarily absent, and an over-zealous person stepped
in. Having pronounced her name, he added: 'The famous—should I say
Frau or Fräulein Elssler? I shall simply say Fanny Elssler.' Whereupon
Fanny said with a smile: 'Well, that is certainly my name.'"

This little incident was revealing of the modesty of Fanny's character.
Modesty, indeed, was her favourite virtue, as she admitted when once
she was asked to write in one of the Confession Books which were so

popular in her day. Some of her other answers revealed not only her sharp Viennese wit, but her serene and tolerant philosophy which must have endeared her to her friends:

The dominant trait of your character? To live and let live.

Your idea of greatest happiness? To please both God and men.

Your idea of greatest sorrow? To be misunderstood.

What would you have liked to be? My double.

Your favourite authors? Victor Hugo, the creator of *Esmeralda*.

Your favourite painters and composers? Guido Reni (Dance of the Hours),* Haydn (People's Hymn).

Your favourite dishes? Soufflé, and Champagne drunk to the health of my friends.

Your favourite pastime? Satisfaction at having endured so many rehearsals.

To what faults are you most indulgent? Mistakes in accountancy in my favour.

Your favourite motto? Always to dance through life with a light heart.

While those who had applauded her in her prime were growing old, she, it seemed, had discovered the secret of eternal youth. "She possesses something of Ninon de Lenclos," wrote the dramatist, Friedrich Hebbel, when she was nearing her sixtieth birthday. "She is a grandmother already, but she is still elegant and graceful. Added to which she understands the secrets of dress, the innocent secrets, if I may say so, those which combine simplicity with the work of nature."

Ten years later her beauty could still arouse admiration. In 1875, when the son of her Moscow friend, Dr Feh, came to Vienna, he immediately fell under her spell and found it doubly difficult to leave the city the following year. A few years later, an article appeared in a German magazine which flattered her so much that she sent it to her old friend in Moscow. "During the summer," she wrote to him, "when Katti and I were at Lützenhaus, I was sent a German weekly magazine in which I had the pleasure of reading an article, 'Fanny Elssler, A Picture of Life,' by C. Schreiber. It seems to me that the author of this biography *cannot* be unknown to you. He knows too much. Shall I send it to you?"

The article in fact appeared above the signature of a woman, Clara Schreiber, but Fanny's remark to Dr Feh suggests that it was a *nom de*

---

* Reni's fresco, *Aurora*, showing Apollo in his chariot attended by the dancing Hours, is in the Palazzo Rospigliosi, Rome.

plume and that she guessed the true identity of the writer. It was an affectionate portrait, which read like a friend's tribute. "On her face shone eternal youth," it began. "It was high summer. She wore light pale grey silk, closely fitting her still beautiful figure. At her waist was a La France rose. Her smoothly parted hair, still without any threads of silver, hung in a Grecian knot at the nape of her neck. On her head were pale pink ribbons tied in the manner of a Greek fillet. Any other woman of advancing years would have looked ridiculous, but Fanny made a charming picture and nothing disturbed the harmony of her appearance."

Affectionately, the Viennese excused the little eccentricity of keeping to the fashions of her youth, and they would often recognise her by the white burnous which she wore elegantly about her shoulders, fastened at the neck by pink ribbon. At first nights at the Burgtheater, which she attended with unfailing regularity, at the great balls of the season, in the town, and in the intimate surroundings of her home, her youthfulness and elegance were a continuous source of wonder. While Katti became more and more matronly, time seemed to stand still for her. Another word portrait from these years pictured her at the ball. "She always wore her favourite colour, pink, and her fine features, sparkling eyes and humourous mouth would not have been at all suited to the dark colours which matrons usually wear. Although she was known to be approaching seventy, no one minded that she behaved like a young woman, so magnificently did it suit her."

Fanny was not to be spared her share of sorrow, and the first blow was the heaviest of all. In the spring of 1870 news reached her from Merano that her daughter was suffering from inflammation of the lungs. Her son-in-law did not conceal the seriousness of her condition, for the doctor had prepared him for the worst. Fanny and Katti went to take the waters at Carlsbad, where Viktor von Webenau telegraphed them to say that the patient was better. Fanny began making plans to have her daughter stay with her during the summer instead of visiting her in Merano. But these hopes were all too premature, for in July the news arrived that Therese was dead.

In London Harriet Grote spent several hours shut up alone in her room, reading the manuscript she had written about her friendship with Fanny. She had thought to send it to the bereaved widower, but as memories of heartbreak rose to the surface of her mind, she decided to destroy the pages which described the romantic attachment which she and her husband had conceived for Fanny after first seeing her dance the *Cachucha* in 1838. "The revival of circumstances so revolting and fraught with such painful incidents which occurred on her departure for New

York in 1840 has positively given me the spleen," she wrote in her diary, "and I am thoroughly out of all patience with myself for ever having descended into such a foul stratum of immorality—lucky indeed to have preserved my own quality of mind intact." So she consigned her intimate confessions to the flames and instead wrote a letter of condolence to Fanny, sending her some press cuttings she had found among her papers. Viktor von Webenau found comfort in the wise, eccentric old Englishwoman who had taken such care of his beloved Therese when her mother had been dancing in America, and Harriet Grote's warm heart was touched by the love which the father lavished on his little daughter. They last met in 1876, not long before Mrs Grote died. "I go to R on the 15th to receive Captain von Webenau and his daughter," she wrote to her sister. "You remember my little Therese Elssler. He is her inconsolable husband, the girl now fourteen. They live in the Tyrol."

Three years after Therese's death, another blow fell, but this time without warning. On a summer's day in 1873 her son Franz Robert threw himself into the waters of the Mürz after a calamitous speculation on the stock market. He had never made a success of his life. He had spent four years as a junior officer in the Infantry, and then resigned to return to Eisenstadt, where he married and had a family. Fanny frequently sent him money, and once, when he was out of work, used her influence with Prince Esterhazy's administrators to obtain a post for him as a forestry clerk. Now all his failings were forgotten in her grief. "What I have suffered during these last days," she wrote to her friend, Betty Paoli, "you cannot imagine, my dear friend, for my heart has now lost everything . . . May God give me strength to bear this grief and allow me once more to do His will. My heart has now lost everything."

Her two brothers and her sister Anna were also dead. Johann, who had entered the Franciscan order and had taken the name of Brother Pacificus, had passed away at the convent of Maria-Lanzendorf in 1856, and Joseph had died in 1872 in Berlin, where he had long been chorus master at the Opera. Now only her sister Therese was left.

Life had seemed to smile on Therese when, in 1850, she became the morganatic wife of Prince Adalbert of Prussia with the title of Freifrau von Barnim, but the marriage, though a happy one, was not without its frustrations. She had entered a strange new world, hidebound by the rigid etiquette of the Prussian court. Her father-in-law, Prince Wilhelm, carried protocol to such a ridiculous extreme that he required a space to be left at the dinner table separating princes of the blood from those of common stock. The atmosphere of the palace, with its constant reminders that she was an outsider, must have been irksome in the extreme, and Therese sought comfort in her love for her husband and their son. But the boy was frail. The doctors advised that he should be sent to Egypt in the hope that the dry atmosphere might cure his consumption. He did not return, and the actress Agnes Wallner found the mother overwhelmed with despair. Not long afterwards Prince Adalbert died of a similar complaint. Therese went to live at the Villa Fanny in Merano, where on November 19th, 1878, she was released from a life which held no further pleasure for her.

The resilience with which Fanny bore these cruel blows which had struck down first her children and now her beloved sister, owed much to her staunch faith in God. She had always derived great support from religion. When dancing in Paris she attended Mass regularly at the church of Notre Dame de Lorette, where she had her own satin-covered *prie-dieu*, and now, in her bedroom, there was a *prie-dieu* by her bedside.

Another source of joy and comfort was the company of her grand-children—Therese's daughter, Fanny, and her son's children, Franz and Rosa. She watched over their education, and fussed about their ailments. When Franz caught a cough, the dread spectre of tuberculosis rose in her imagination, but the doctors reassured her that he was suffering from nothing more than overwork and the normal strains to which a growing boy was prone. She looked forward to their visits with doting anticipation. "At last all is well," she once wrote to Auguste Baudius, "and we are expecting the Webenaus on the 16th. Then things will liven up, and Grandmama will have to hold on to her purse-strings so as not to fall victim to consumption too quickly! But what joy also to have my granddaughter here—my granddaughter who, believe it or not, dared to appear in her husband's delightful comedy, *Youthful Love*, for charity. Can you imagine anyone daring to do such a thing after Baudius ? It could only happen in Merano. Katti and I embrace you."

As the years went by Katti became more and more indispensable, for Fanny could hardly remember a time when she had not been at her side. The two old ladies, who had spent nearly sixty years of their lives to-gether, fussed over one another's health, but now it was Fanny, who till then had seldom been ill, who was ailing. The doctors attributed her trouble to a violent blow which she had received in the chest when coming out of St Stephen's Church one Sunday. In the summer of 1881 they decided to go to Vöslau to take the waters. On the way there they spent a few days at Lockenhaus, where Katti's brother lived with his family, and the peace and simplicity which reigned in the little home made Fanny yearn for just such a small estate where she could spend the summers, but she realised, with a pang of regret, that it was too late to change the pattern of her life. Katti benefited from the waters, but Fanny was unable to complete the cure, and on her return to Vienna the doctors advised that an operation was necessary.

By Christmas she seemed to have made an excellent recovery. She began to receive friends and pay calls. She resumed coaching Charlotte Wolter, and was seen again at the theatre, though less frequently than before. The following summer she and Katti returned to Vöslau, where they were joined by the latter's niece, Caroline Eltz from Lockenhaus. But their plans for a restful visit collapsed when Caroline had a heart attack and they found themselves taking turns to act as her night nurse. For two elderly women who were seeking rest themselves this was a heavy trial, and although they were able to spend a few pleasant days at Reichenau, they were worn out when they returned to Vienna.

Fanny was worrying about Katti's health, and tried her best to conceal her own weakness. This was not always easy. "A very bad leg prevents me from visiting you," she wrote to Betty Paoli in August 1883. "It is very painful and I am not able to take a bath." In November she attended the first performance at the Opera of a new ballet, *Die Assassinen*. It was her last visit to the theatre. A few days later she was lying seriously ill. The doctors were worried, and she was forbidden to receive any visitors. Warned of the seriousness of her condition, her son-in-law and his daughter left their home in Merano to be with her in Vienna. To their relief the danger passed, and the following summer she was able to go to Baden bei Wien to take the sulphur baths. The expected improvement did not materialise. The baths did not agree with her, and she returned to Vienna desperately ill. She never left her apartment again. Soon her disease spread to her neck and the left side of her face, and she spent the days on the verandah, lying listlessly on the ottoman. By November she had become so weak that she could hardly speak, and on the 17th she asked for the Last Sacrament to be administered. Gradually she slipped into a coma, regaining consciousness only once, when she called Katti to her side to thank her for her devotion. Early in the morning of November 27th, 1884, she passed peacefully away.

It had been her wish to be buried with her parents at Hundstummer, but the cemetery there was full and so her body was interred at Heitzing, next to the grave of her devoted friend, Count Samuel Kostrowicki. Many years before, after she had declined his proposal of marriage, he had purchased two adjoining plots at Heitzing and made her a gift of one of them in the hope, as he expressed it, that they might at least be united in death. He had died in 1863, and the other plot had remained vacant and almost forgotten for twenty-one years until the elaborate procession that escorted Fanny's mortal remains entered the cemetery gates.

Custom and her renown required that her funeral should be a memorable occasion. There was a service in St Stephen's, and afterwards the imposing procession made its way to Heitzing. Preceded by a mounted herald and lantern bearers, the massive hearse bearing the coffin was drawn by eight black horses and flanked by eight mourners in Spanish costume, carrying burning torches. Following it was an open carriage filled with flowers which were afterwards laid on the grave. Many of these tributes were from her friends in the theatre, who mourned her as one they had loved and revered. There was a sheaf from Pauline Lucca, the soprano, and from the prima ballerina of the Vienna Opera, Camilla Pagliero, an enormous bouquet with the inscription, "To the immortal memory of the great and celebrated artist, a token of gratitude".

For Katti Prinster this was the end not only of a companionship that had lasted for more than sixty years, but of her life's work. When she had come from Eisenstadt in September 1823 to join the Elssler household in Vienna, Fanny was an infant prodigy of thirteen at the threshold of her brilliant career. At first Katti had watched the young ballerina's progress from a distance, but when the ways of Fanny and her sister parted, she became the dancer's intimate companion, accompanying her on her travels, basking in reflected glory, sharing fears, discomfort and all the varied experiences which came their way, and undertaking a multitude of tasks to relieve her cousin of unnecessary cares.

Alone now with her memories, Katti lived on in Vienna until 1888. It was during these last years that a journalist made a pilgrimage to hear her speak of her famous cousin. He found it a strange experience. The air in her apartment seemed so cool and pure that he felt no living being could have breathed it. Then Katti had darted into the room like a jack-in-the-box and looked at him with her "clever old eyes which had seen more of the world than the mouth could tell". The visitor was somewhat disappointed, for while the old lady spoke to him freely about Fanny Elssler, she would answer his questions with excited generalities instead of the precise indications he wanted. When he asked her whether she remembered Gentz, she became lost in reflection and merely murmured, "Gentz? Oh yes, the kind old man!" But then she had gone to a cupboard and brought out an alabaster carving of Fanny's leg which seemed to bring the ballerina to life much more vividly than her reminiscences. It had been taken, she explained, from a plaster cast made by Félicie de Fauveau in Florence in 1847.

Discovering where the original plaster cast was to be found, the journalist was able, to his joy, to examine it a few days later. As he handled it, he imagined himself transported back in time to the day when the plaster had shaped itself round the strong leg of the great dancer. He could even observe the "traces of use and misuse" which revealed that it had belonged not to the young dancer whom Gentz had known but to the mature ballerina almost at the end of an exhausting career. "The foot," he noted, "is placed with the toes widely spread, except that the big toe is somewhat turned in, rather long, longer than the second toe—the exact opposite of the feet of antiquity—and the third and fourth toes are somewhat pressed together, with the little toe, the stepchild of the feminine foot, completely free. There is a distinct hardening over the second joint of the big toe, and a somewhat smaller one on the little toe, and the veins of the foot stand out strongly. The knee is plumper and the skin looser than the requirements of beauty demand, and the bones are strongly delineated. It is a mature foot . . . but what a powerful impression it makes when seen as a whole! From this foot one learns that strength is the root of charm. The foot, which is not small and is rather fleshy, is firmly vaulted, or rather arched. The instep is high, the ankle is slim, the slightly curved line of the shin bone is charming and combines well with the curve of the calf, showing no trace of the three muscles brought sharply into play by dancing. In the two places where there is the greatest possibility of movement, the ankle and the knee, one senses a great energy, an energy suggestive of grace. The line, the surface and the plastic form of the leg are incomparable."

It may have appeared a poignant reminder of the ephemeral nature of a dancer's art, but it was not only in the memories of her mortal contemporaries that Fanny Elssler lived on. The work of great performers endures by merging into the developing tradition of their art, for true genius oversteps the bounds of individuality to become, by its power of example and inspiration, a beacon of artistic endeavour. So it was with Fanny Elssler, whom posterity recalls as one of those rare phenomena in the theatre who personify the achievements of their age. Now, in historical perspective, she represents one of the twin facets of Romantic ballet, that brilliant flowering of the theatrical dance which raised the art to a level never before achieved and exerted an influence that has endured with undiminishing strength to the present day. Hers was a two-fold legacy. In the field of style she provided the necessary counterbalance to Taglioni's ethereal vision of the Sylphide, by revealing the earthly and human roots of Romantic dance. She was a dancer who was moved by human emotions and passions, and herein lay her other gift to posterity. As an interpreter she was a true innovator, for no other dancer before her, or even in her own time, displayed such a wide and deeply etched range of feeling in her portrayals. She more than anyone else formed the ideal of the dancer-actress, uniting the arts of drama and dance in a single genius, the ideal of the complete artist of the dance.

Bibliography

Alheim, Pierre d' *Sur les Pointes* (Paris, 1897)
Anon. *Lettres a une artiste* (Brussels, 1842)
Barbiera, Raffaello *Figure e Figurine del secolo che muore* (Milan, 1899)
Bauer, Otto *150 Jahre Theater an der Wien* (Vienna, 1952)
Baxa, Jakob *Friedrich von Gentz* (Vienna, 1965)
Beaumont, Cyril W. *Complete Book of Ballets* (London, 1937)
Beaumont, Cyril W. *Fanny Elssler* (London, 1931)
Beaumont, Cyril W. and Sitwell, Sacheverell *The Romantic Ballet in Lithographs of the Time* (London, 1938)
Bermani, Benedetto *Pleiade Artistica* (Milan, 1847)
Bignami, Luigi *Cronologia di tutti gli spettacoli rappresentati nel Gran Teatro Comunale di Bologna* (Bologna, 1880)
Binney, Edwin, 3rd. *Les Ballets de Théophile Gautier* (Paris, 1965)
Bournonville, August *Mit Theaterliv* (Copenhagen, 1848–77)
Bournonville, August *Reiseminder, Reflexioner og biographiske Skizzer* (Copenhagen, 1878)
Brown, Thomas Allston *History of the American Stage* (New York, 1870)
Brunelli, Bruno *I Teatri di Padova dalle origini alla fine del secolo XIX* (Padua, 1921)
Bunn, Alfred *The Stage* (London, 1840)
Cambiasi, Pompeo *La Scala, 1778–1906* (Milan, 1906)
Cametti, Alberto *Il Teatro di Tordinona, poi di Apollo* (Rome, 1938)
Carrieri, Raffaele *La Danza in Italia, 1500–1900* (Milan, 1946)
Cesana, Giuseppe A. *Ricordi di un giornalista* (Milan, 1890–2)
Chorley, H. F. *Thirty Years' Musical Recollections* (London, 1862)
Clapp, William W., jun. *A Record of the Boston Stage* (Boston, 1853)
Crow, Duncan *Henry Wikoff, the American Chevalier* (London, 1963)
Dayton, Abram C. *Last Days of Knickerbocker Life in New York* (New York, 1897)
Delarue, Allison *The Chevalier Henry Wikoff* (Princeton, 1968)
Dieke, Gertraude *Die Blütezeit des Kindertheaters* (Emsdetten, 1934)
Eastlake, Lady *Mrs. Grote. A Sketch* (London, 1880)

Ehrhard, Auguste *Une Vie de danseuse. Fanny Elssler* (Paris, 1909)

Elliott, Maud Howe *Uncle Sam Ward and his Circle* (New York, 1938)

Emerson, Ralph Waldo *The Heart of Emerson's Journals,* edited by Bliss Perry (Boston, 1926)

Farga, Franz *Die Wiener Oper von ihren Anfängen bis* 1938 (Vienna, 1947)

Fiorentino, P. A. *Les Grands Guignols.* 1ᵉ *série* (Paris, 1870)

Fleischmann, Hector *Le Roi de Rome et les femmes* (Paris, 1910)

Fowler, L. N. *The Phrenological Developments and Characters of J. V. Stout, the Sculptor, and Fanny Elssler, the Actress* (New York, 1841)

Gabillon, Ludwig *Tagebuchblätter—Briefe—Erinnerungen* (Vienna, 1900)

Gatti, Carlo *Il Teatro alla Scala* (Milan, 1964)

Gauitier, Théophile *Histoire de l'art dramatique en France depuis vingt-cinq ans* (Paris, 1858–9)

Gautier, Théophile *Portraits contemporains* (Paris, 1874)

Gentz, Friedrich von *Staatsschriften und Briefe* (Munich, 1921)

Gentz, Friedrich von *Tagebücher* (1829–1831) (Vienna, 1920)

Ghislanzoni, Antonio *Storia di Milano dal* 1836 *al* 1848 (Milan, 1869)

Giordano, Carlo *Giovanni Prati* (Turin, 1907)

Glossy, Karl *Zur Geschichte der Theater Wiens* (Vienna, 1915)

Goncourt, Edmond and Jules de *Journal* (Paris, 1956)

Guest, Ivor *Fanny Cerrito. The Life of a Romantic Ballerina* (London, 1956)

Guest, Ivor (editor) *La Fille mal gardée* (London, 1960)

Guest, Ivor *A Gallery of Romantic Ballet* (London, 1965)

Guest, Ivor *The Romantic Ballet in England* (London, 1954)

Guest, Ivor *The Romantic Ballet in Paris* (London, 1966)

Hebbel, Friedrich *Hebbels ausgewählte Werke* (Stuttgart and Berlin, 1904)

Hevesi, Ludwig *Wiener Totentanz* (Stuttgart, 1899)

Holstein, Hippolyte *Historiettes et souvenirs d'un homme de théâtre* (Paris, 1878)

Holtei, Karl von *Vierzig Jahre* (Berlin, 1843–50)

Hone, Philip *The Diary of Philip Hone* (New York, 1889)

Hoole, W. Stanley *The Ante-bellum Charleston Theatre* (Tuscaloosa, 1946)

Hutton, Laurence *Curiosities of the American Stage* (New York, 1891)

Isnardon, Jacques *Le Théâtre de la Monnaie* (Brussels, 1890)

Jameson, Anna *Letters and Friendships,* 1812–1860 (London, 1915)

Kemble, Frances Anne *Records of Later Life* (London, 1882)

Kisch, Wilhelm *Die alten Strassen und Plätze von Wiens Vorstädten und ihre historisch interessanten Häuser* (Vienna, 1895)

Landau, Paul *Mimen. Historische Miniaturen* (Berlin, 1912)

Leitich, Ann Tizia *Die Wienerin* (Stuttgart, 1939)
Levinson, André *Ballet romantique* (Paris, 1929)
Levinson, André *Marie Taglioni* (Paris, 1929)
Levinson, André *Meister des Balletts* (Berlin, 1923)
Lewin, T. H. (editor) *The Lewin Letters* (London, 1909)
Linden, Irma *Fanny Elssler. Die Tänzerin des Biedermeier* (Berlin, 1921)
Löhle, Franz *Theater-Catechismus* (Munich, n.d.)
Lumley, Benjamin *Reminiscences of the Opera* (London, 1864)
Mann, Golo *Secretary of Europe* (New Haven, 1946)
Maurice, Charles *Histoire anecdoctique du théâtre, de la littérature et de diverses impressions contemporaines* (Paris, 1856)
Menzel, Wolfgang *Reise nach Oesterreich im Sommer* 1831 (Stuttgart, 1832)
Metternich-Sandor, Pauline *Geschehenes, gesehenes, erlebtes* (Vienna, 1920)
[Mills, John] *D'Horsay, or The Follies of the Day* (London, 1844)
Mocenigo, Mario Nani *Il Teatro La Fenice* (Venice, 1926)
Monaldi, Gino *Le Regine della Danza nel secolo XIX* (Turin, 1910)
Moore, Lillian *Artists of the Dance* (New York, 1938)
Moore, Lillian *George Washington Smith* (*Dance Index*, New York, June/August 1945)
Morini, Ugo *La R. Accademia degli Immobili ed il suo teatro "La Pergola,"* 1649–1925 (Pisa, 1926)
Morison, Samuel Eliot *Harrison Gray Otis* (Boston, 1969)
Moses, Montrose J. *The Fabulous Forrest* (Boston, 1929)
Musset, Paul de *Voyage pittoresque en Italie* (Paris, 1855)
Odell, George C. D. *Annals of the New York Stage* (New York, 1927)
Pallerotti, A. *Spettacoli melodrammatici e coreografici rappresentati in Padova . . . dal 1751 al 1892* (Padua, 1892)
Paoli, Betty *Betty Paolis Gesammelte Auflätze* (Vienna, 1908)
Pirchan, Emil *Fanny Elssler. Eine Wienerin tanzt um die Welt* (Vienna, 1940)
Priddin, Deirdre *The Art of the Dance in French Literature* (London, 1952)
Prokesch von Osten, Count Anton *Aus den Tagebüchern des Grafen Prokesch von Osten, 1830–34* (Vienna, 1909)
Prokesch von Osten, Count Anton *Mes Rélations avec le duc de Reichstadt* (Paris, 1878)
Raab, Riki *Fanny Elssler. Eine Weltfaszination* (Vienna, 1962)
Rosain, Domingo *Necropolis de la Habana* (Havana, 1875)
Roséri, Margitta *Erinnerungen einer Künstlerin* (Hanover, 1891)
Royer, Alphonse *Histoire de l'Opéra* (Paris, 1875)
Sadleir, Michael *Blessington-D'Orsay. A Masquerade* (London, 1933)

Schönherr, Max and Reinöhl, Karl *Johann Strauss Vater* (Vienna, 1954)

Séchan, Charles *Souvenirs d'un homme de théâtre,* 1831–1855 (Paris, 1883)

Seyfried, Ferdinand Ritter von *Rückschau in das Theaterleben Wiens seit den letzten fünfzig Jahren* (Vienna, 1864)

Smith, Sol *Theatrical Management in the West and South* (New York, 1868)

Sweet, Paul R. *Friedrich von Gentz, Defender of the Old Order* (Madison, 1941)

Tiersot, Julien *Lettres de musiciens écrites en français du XVe au XXe siècle* (Paris, 1934)

Vaillat, Léandre *La Taglioni, ou la Vie d'une danseuse* (Paris, 1942)

Vályi, Rózsi (editor) *A Magyar Balett Történetéböl* (Budapest, 1956)

Véron, Louis *Mémoires d'un bourgeois de Paris* (Paris, 1853–5)

Viel-Castel, Comte Horace de *Mémoires sur le règne de Napoléon III* (Paris, 1884)

Wagenknecht, Edward *Longfellow* (London, 1955)

Wallaschek, Richard *Das k. k. Hofoperntheater* (Volume IV of *Die Theater Wiens*) (Vienna, 1909)

Wallner, Agnes *Lebenserinnerungen* (Berlin, 1900)

Werther, Julius von *Erinnerungen und Erfahrungen eines alten Hoftheater Intendanten* (Stuttgart, 1911)

Wikoff, Henry *The Reminiscences of an Idler* (London, 1880)

Wilbrandt-Baudius, Auguste *Aus Kunst und Leben* (Zürich, 1919)

Wollrabe, Ludwig *Chronologie sämmtlicher Hamburger Bühnen* (Hamburg, 1847)

Wood, William B. *Personal Recollections of the Stage* (Philadelphia, 1855)

Zorn, Friedrich Albert *Grammatik der Tanzkunst* (Leipzig, 1887)

Бахрушин, Ю. А.   Балет Большого Театра. (Гос. Орд. Академический Большой Театр. М, 1947.)

——— История Русского Балета. М, 1965

Берг, Н.   Фанни Элсьлер перед ее От'ездом из Москвы. М, 1851

Борисоглебский, М.   Материалы по Истории Русского Балета. Л, 1938–39

Вольф, А.   Хроника Петербургских Театров с конца 1826 года по начала 1855 года. СПБ, 1877

Всеволодский-Гернгросс, В. Н.   Краткий Курс Истории Русского Театра. М, 1936

Глушковский, А. П.   Воспоминания Балетмейстера. Л, 1940

Гольц, Н. О.   В Память Пятидесятилетия Сценической Деятельности Артиста Балетной Труппы. СПБ, 1872

Каратыгин, П. А.   Записки. Л, 1929

Красовская, В. М.   Русский Балетный Театр от возникновения до середины XIX века. Л, 1958

Лифарь, С.   Исторія Русского Балета. Парижъ, 1945

Петипа, М.   Мемуары. СПБ, 1906

Плещеев, А.   Наш Балет, 1673—1899. СПБ, 1899

Ростопчина, гр.   Воспоминания о Фанни Эльслер. М, 1851

Скальковский, К.   В Театральном Мире. СПБ, 1899

Телепнев, Н.   Критический Взгляд на госпожу Эльслер. СПБ, 1848

Худеков, С.   История Танцев. том. 3, 4. СПБ, 1915, 1918

ARTICLES AND MONOGRAPHS

Chujoy, Anatole   *Elssler in America* (*Dance Encyclopedia*, New York, 1949)

Delarue, Allison   *America's First Impresario* (*Dance News*, December 1954 and January 1955)

Ehrhard, Auguste   *La Dernière Passion de Gentz* (*Revue Germanique*, Paris, November–December 1907)

Fisher, Sidney George   *The Diaries of Sidney George Fisher*, 1839–1840 (*Pennsylvania Magazine*, January 1953)

Guest, Ivor   *The Cachucha Reborn* (*Dancing Times*, London, October 1967)

Guest, Ivor   *Fanny Elssler and Her Friends I: Henry Wikoff, II: Mrs. Grote, III: Friedrich von Gentz* (*Ballet*, London, November 1947, June 1948, October 1948)

Hanslick, Eduard   *Aus meinem Leben* (*Deutsche Rundschau*, November, 1893)

Mansfeld, Herbert A.   *Theaterleute in den Akten der k. k. Obersten Hoftheaterverwaltung von 1792 bis 1867* (*Jahrbuch der Gesellschaft für Wiener Theater-Forschung*, vol. XIII, Vienna, 1961)

Mansfeld, Herbert A.   *Wiener Theaterleute auf Wanderschaft, Passanweisungen des Wiener Magistrates, Konskriptionsamtes in den Jahren 1792–1850* (*Jahrbuch der Gesellschaft für Wiener Theater-Forschung*, vol. XI, Vienna, 1959)

Moore, Lillian   *Ballet Slippers and Bunker Hill* (*Dance*, New York, September 1937)

Moore, Lillian   *Elssler and the Cachucha* (*Dancing Times*, London, August 1936)

Moore, Lillian   *Fanny's Farewell to Italy* (*Dance Magazine*, April 1944)

Moore, Lillian   *Like Cinderella, Giselle once went to a ball* (*Dance News*, New York, April 1954)

Newald-Grasse, Anny von   *Fanny Elsslers Gastpiele in Mailand vor 70 Jahren (1848)* (*Die Merker*, March 1st, 1918)

Prinster, Katti   *Fanny Elsslers amerikanische Kunstreise im Jahre 1840* (*Österreichische Rundschau*, Vienna, May–October 1905)

Raab, Riki   *Fanny Elsslers Testament* (*Wiener Geschichtsblätter*, 1960, No. 2)

Saretzki, N.   *Fanny Elssler in Russland* (*Der Tanz*, Berlin, 1927)

Schönfeld-Neumann, Louise Gräfin   *Erinnerungen* (*Österreichische Rundschau*, Vienna, November–December 1906)

Spiegel, Ludwig   *Fanny Elssler's Fuss* (*Neue Freie Presse*, June 5th, 1892)

MANUSCRIPT SOURCES

Les Cancans de l'Opéra (1836–38, Bibliothèque de l'Opéra, Paris; 1839–40, Lillian Moore Collection)

Delarue, Allison   *Impresario 1840*

Бахрушин, Ю.   Фанни Эльслер в России

Мухин, Д.   История Московского Балета

(Bakhrushin Theatre Museum, Moscow)

NEWSPAPERS

BERLIN: *Berlinische Zeitung*

BIRMINGHAM: *Birmingham and General Advertiser*

BOLOGNA: *Teatri Arti e Letteratura*

BOSTON: *Boston Daily Times, Boston Evening Transcript, Boston Folio, Boston Sunday Herald*

BRISTOL: *Bristol Mirror*

BRUSSELS: *L'Indépendant* (*L'Indépendance Belge*)

DUBLIN: *The Freeman's Journal*

HAMBURG: *Staats- und Gelehrte Zeitung des hamburgischen unpartheyischen Correspondenten*

HAVANA: *Diario de la Habana*

LIVERPOOL: *The Albion, Liverpool Chronicle, Liverpool Journal, Liverpool Mail*

LONDON: *The Age, Court Journal, The Era, The Examiner, Morning Herald, Morning Post, The Satirist, Sunday Times, The Times*

MATANZAS: *La Aurora*

MILAN: *Corriere delle Dame, La Fama, Gazzetta Musicale di Milano, Gazzetta Privilegiata di Milano, Il Pirata*

NEW YORK: *Courrier des Etats-Unis, New York Clipper, New York Evening Signal, New York Mirror, New York Morning Herald, New York Polyanthos, New York Sun, Spirit of the Times*

PARIS: *Le Constitutionnel, Courrier des Théâtres, Le Figaro, Gazette des Théâtres, Gazette des Tribunaux, Journal des Débats, Le Moniteur Universel, La Presse, Le Siècle*

VIENNA: *Allgemeine Musikalische Zeitung, Allgemeine Theater Zeitung, Der Humorist, Der Österreichische Beobachter, Die Presse, Der Sammler, Der Telegraph, Wiener Zeitschrift fuer Kunst, Literatur, Theater und Mode*

MOSCOW: Москвитянин, Русская Старина, Русский Архив

ST. PETERSBURG: Библиотека для Чтения, Вестник Общественно Политической Жизни и т. д., Исторический Вестник, Отечественные Записки, Пантеон и Репертуар Русской Сцены, Репертуар Русского Театра, Северная Пчела, Современник, Сын Отечества, Театральный Мирок.

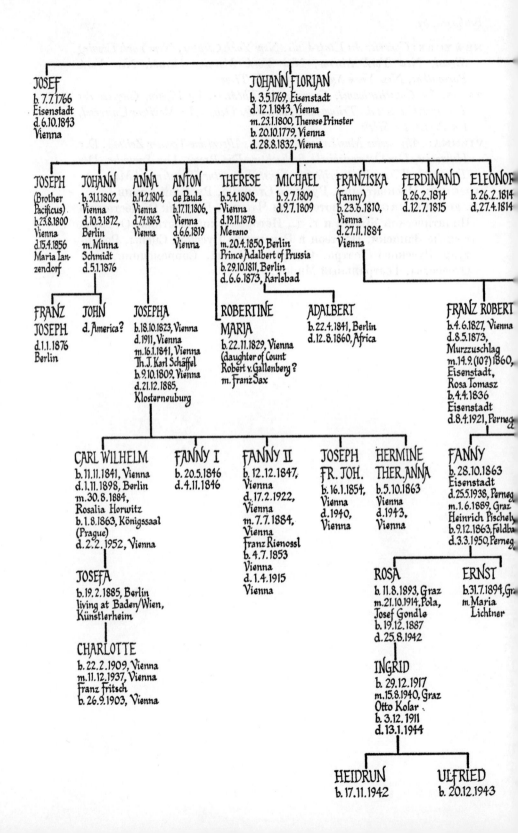

JOSEF
b. 7.7.1766
Eisenstadt
d. 6.10.1843
Vienna

JOHANN FLORIAN
b. 3.5.1769, Eisenstadt
d. 12.1.1843, Vienna
m. 23.1.1800, Therese Prinster
b. 20.10.1779, Vienna
d. 28.8.1832, Vienna

JOSEPH
(Brother
Pacificus)
b. 23.8.1800
Vienna
d. 15.4.1856
Maria Lan-
zendorf

JOHANN
b. 31.1.1802,
Vienna
d. 10.3.1872,
Berlin
m. Minna
Schmidt
d. 5.1.1876

ANNA
b. 14.2.1804,
Vienna
d. 7.4.1863
Vienna

ANTON
de Paula
b. 17.11.1806,
Vienna
d. 6.6.1819
Vienna

THERESE
b. 5.4.1808,
Vienna
d. 19.11.1878
Merano
m. 20.4.1850, Berlin
Prince Adalbert of Prussia
b. 29.10.1811, Berlin
d. 6.6.1873, Karlsbad

MICHAEL
b. 9.7.1809
d. 9.7.1809

FRANZISKA
(Fanny)
b. 23.6.1810,
Vienna
d. 27.11.1884
Vienna

FERDINAND
b. 26.2.1814
d. 12.7.1815

ELEONOR
b. 26.2.1814
d. 27.4.1814

FRANZ
JOSEPH
d. 1.1.1876
Berlin

JOHN
d. America?

JOSEPHA
b. 18.10.1823, Vienna
d. 1911, Vienna
m. 16.1.1841, Vienna
Th. J. Karl Schäffel
b. 9.10.1809, Vienna
d. 21.12.1885,
Klosterneuburg

ROBERTINE
MARIA
b. 22.11.1829, Vienna
(daughter of Count
Robert v. Gallenberg?
m. Franz Sax

ADALBERT
b. 22.4.1841, Berlin
d. 12.8.1860, Africa

FRANZ ROBERT
b. 4.6.1827, Vienna
d. 8.5.1873,
Murzzuschlag
m. 14.9. (10?) 1860,
Eisenstadt,
Rosa Tomasz
b. 4.4.1836
Eisenstadt
d. 8.4.1921, Perneg

CARL WILHELM
b. 11.11.1841, Vienna
d. 1.11.1898, Berlin
m. 30.8.1884,
Rosalia Horwitz
b. 1.8.1863, Königssaal
(Prague)
d. 2.2.1952, Vienna

FANNY I
b. 20.5.1846
d. 4.11.1846

FANNY II
b. 12.12.1847,
Vienna
d. 17.2.1922,
Vienna
m. 7.7.1884,
Vienna
Franz Rienossl
b. 4.7.1853
Vienna
d. 1.4.1915
Vienna

JOSEPH
FR. JOH.
b. 16.1.1854,
Vienna
d. 1940,
Vienna

HERMINE
THER. ANNA
b. 5.10.1863
Vienna
d. 1943,
Vienna

FANNY
b. 28.10.1863
Eisenstadt
d. 25.5.1938, Perneg
m. 1.6.1889, Graz
Heinrich Pischely
b. 9.12.1863, Feldba
d. 3.3.1950, Perneg

JOSEFA
b. 19.2.1885, Berlin
living at Baden/Wien,
Künstlerheim

ROSA
b. 11.8.1893, Graz
m. 21.10.1914, Pola,
Josef Gondle
b. 19.12.1887
d. 25.8.1942

ERNST
b. 31.7.1894, Gra
m. Maria
Lichtner

CHARLOTTE
b. 22.2.1909, Vienna
m. 11.12.1937, Vienna
Franz Fritsch
b. 26.9.1903, Vienna

INGRID
b. 29.12.1917
m. 15.8.1940, Graz
Otto Kolar
b. 3.12.1911
d. 13.1.1944

HEIDRUN
b. 17.11.1942

ULFRIED
b. 20.12.1943

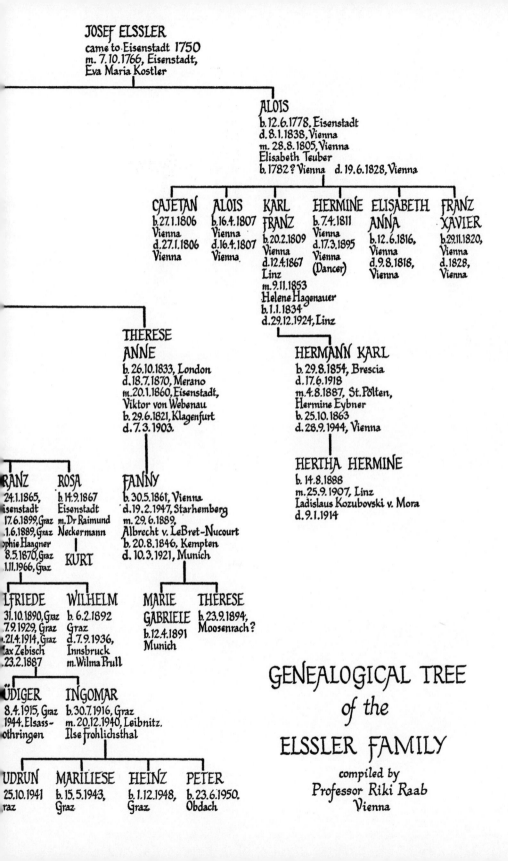

JOSEF ELSSLER
came to Eisenstadt 1750
m. 7.10.1766, Eisenstadt,
Eva Maria Kostler

ALOIS
b. 12.6.1778, Eisenstadt
d. 8.1.1838, Vienna
m. 28.8.1805, Vienna
Elisabeth Teuber
b. 1782? Vienna   d. 19.6.1828, Vienna

CAJETAN
b. 27.1.1806
Vienna
d. 27.1.1806
Vienna

ALOIS
b. 16.4.1807
Vienna
d. 16.4.1807
Vienna

KARL FRANZ
b. 20.2.1809
Vienna
d. 12.4.1867
Linz
m. 9.11.1853
Helene Hagenauer
b. 1.1.1834
d. 29.12.1924, Linz

HERMINE
b. 7.4.1811
Vienna
d. 17.3.1895
Vienna
(Dancer)

ELISABETH ANNA
b. 12.6.1816,
Vienna
d. 9.8.1818,
Vienna

FRANZ XAVIER
b. 29.11.1820,
Vienna
d. 1828,
Vienna

THERESE ANNE
b. 26.10.1833, London
d. 18.7.1870, Merano
m. 20.1.1860, Eisenstadt,
Viktor von Webenau
b. 29.6.1821, Klagenfurt
d. 7.3.1903.

HERMANN KARL
b. 29.8.1854, Brescia
d. 17.6.1918
m. 4.8.1887, St. Pölten,
Hermine Eybner
b. 25.10.1863
d. 28.9.1944, Vienna

HERTHA HERMINE
b. 14.8.1888
m. 25.9.1907, Linz
Ladislaus Kozubovski v. Mora
d. 9.1.1914

[F]RANZ
24.1.1865,
[E]isenstadt
17.6.1899, Graz
1.6.1889, Graz
[So]phie Haagner
8.5.1870, Graz
1.11.1966, Graz

ROSA
b. 14.9.1867
Eisenstadt
m. Dr Raimund
Neckermann

KURT

FANNY
b. 30.5.1861, Vienna
d. 19.2.1947, Starhemberg
m. 29.6.1889,
Albrecht v. LeBret-Nucourt
b. 20.8.1846, Kempten
d. 10.3.1921, Munich

[E]LFRIEDE
31.10.1890, Graz
7.9.1929, Graz
21.4.1914, Graz
[M]ax Zebisch
23.2.1887

WILHELM
b. 6.2.1892
Graz
d. 7.9.1936,
Innsbruck
m. Wilma Prull

MARIE GABRIELE
b. 12.4.1891
Munich

THERESE
b. 23.9.1894,
Moosenrach?

[R]ÜDIGER
8.4.1915, Graz
1944. Elsass-
[l]othringen

INGOMAR
b. 30.7.1916, Graz
m. 20.12.1940, Leibnitz.
Ilse Frohlichsthal

[G]UDRUN
25.10.1941
[G]raz

MARILIESE
b. 15.5.1943,
Graz

HEINZ
b. 1.12.1948,
Graz

PETER
b. 23.6.1950.
Obdach

GENEALOGICAL TREE
of the
ELSSLER FAMILY
compiled by
Professor Riki Raab
Vienna

Index